# T·H·E
## Authoritative
# CALVIN
## AND
# HOBBES

## Also in Sphere Books:

CALVIN AND HOBBES

SOMETHING UNDER THE BED
IS DROOLING

YUKON HO!

WEIRDOS FROM ANOTHER PLANET

LAZY SUNDAY BOOK

THE REVENGE OF THE BABY-SAT

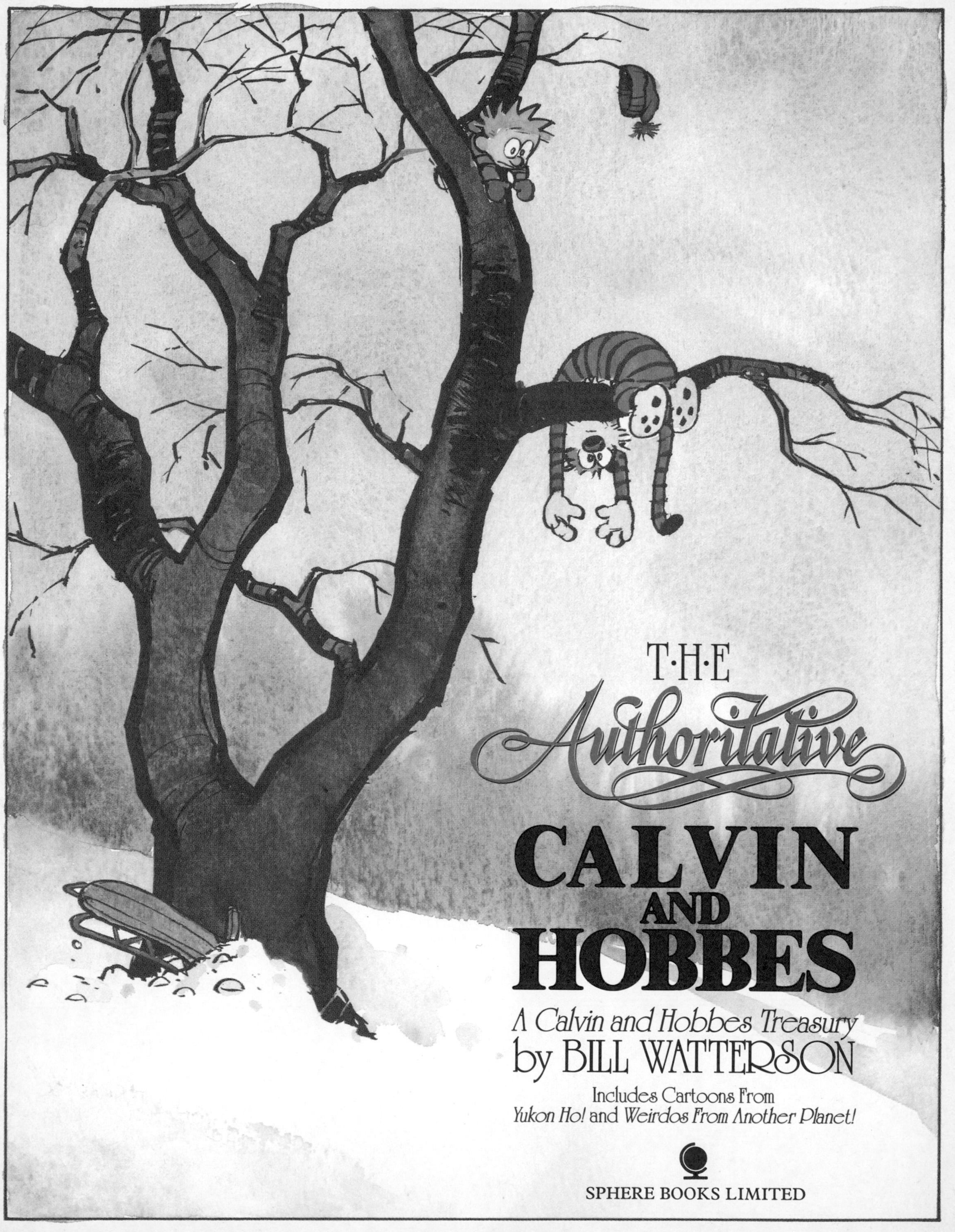

THE

# The Authoritative CALVIN AND HOBBES

*A Calvin and Hobbes Treasury*

by BILL WATTERSON

Includes Cartoons From
*Yukon Ho!* and *Weirdos From Another Planet!*

SPHERE BOOKS LIMITED

A *Sphere* Book

First published in Great Britain by Sphere Books Ltd 1990

Printed and bound in Great Britain by
BPCC Hazell Books
Aylesbury, Bucks, England
Member of BPCC Ltd.

ISBN 0 7474 0938 2

Sphere Books Ltd
A Division of
Macdonald & Co (Publishers) Ltd
165 Great Dover Street
London SE1 4YA

A member of Maxwell Macmillan Publishing Corporation

To Doctor Dave and
Fellow Moosers John, Brad, and The Frey

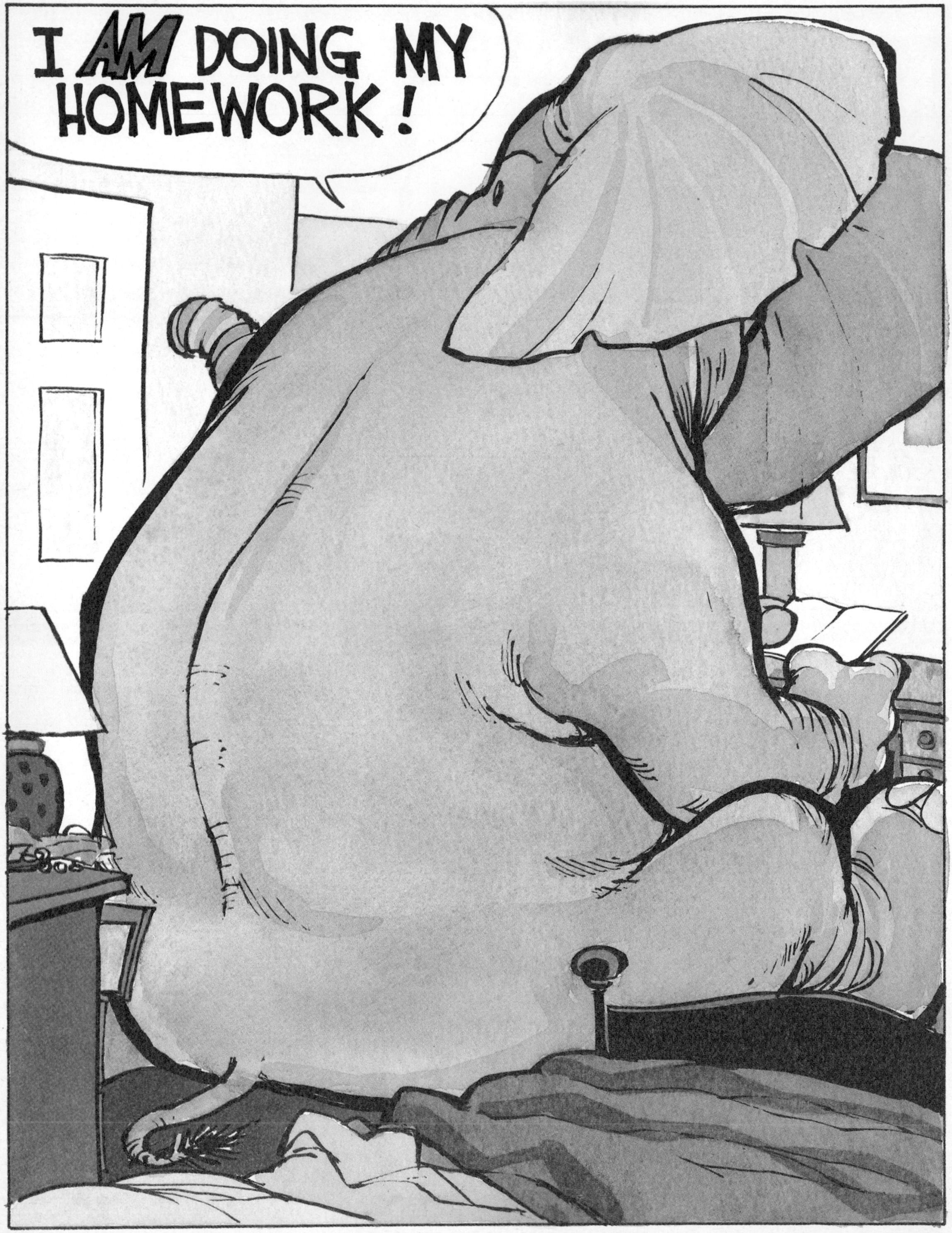
I AM DOING MY HOMEWORK!

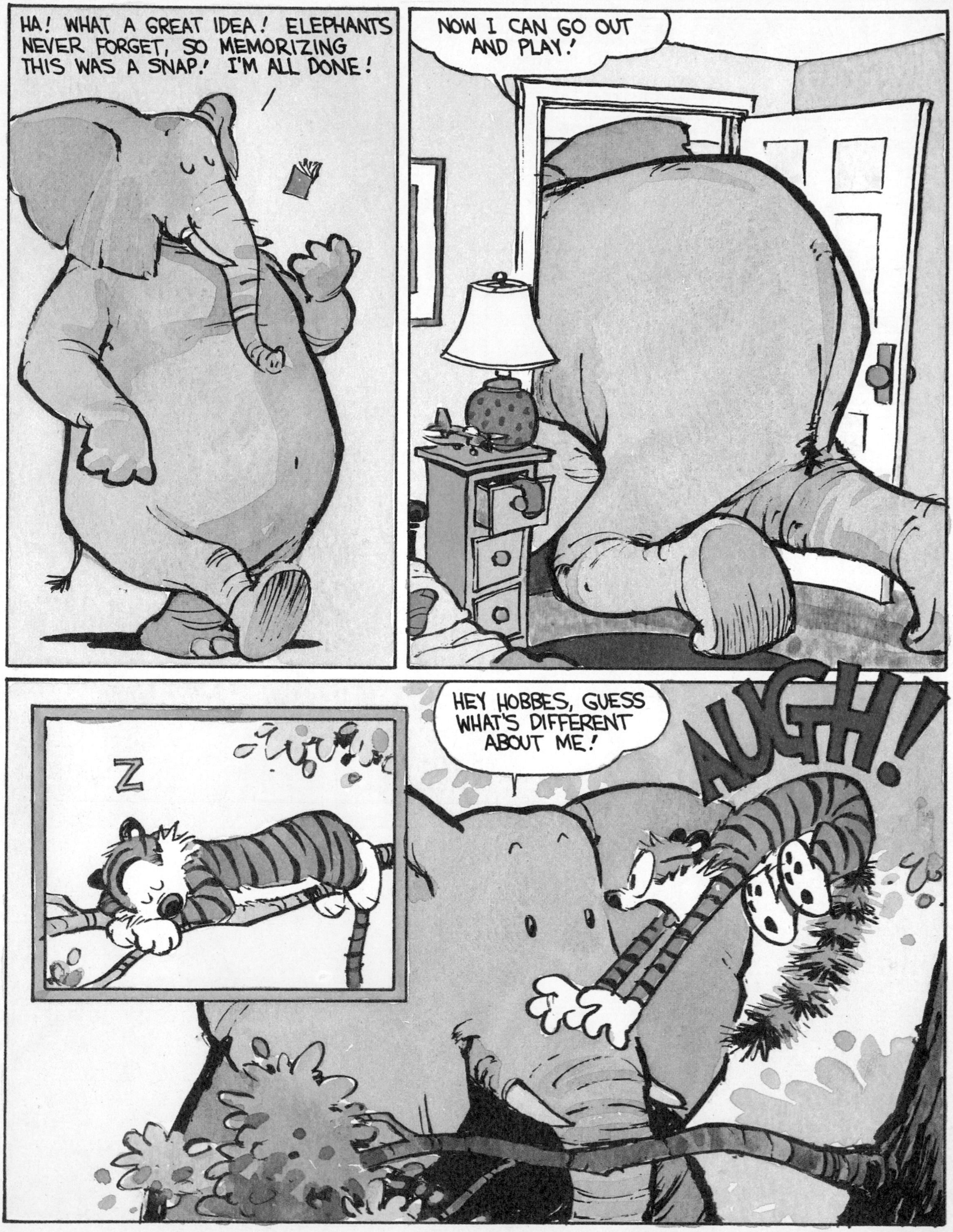
HA! WHAT A GREAT IDEA! ELEPHANTS NEVER FORGET, SO MEMORIZING THIS WAS A SNAP! I'M ALL DONE!
NOW I CAN GO OUT AND PLAY!
Z
HEY HOBBES, GUESS WHAT'S DIFFERENT ABOUT ME!
AUGH!

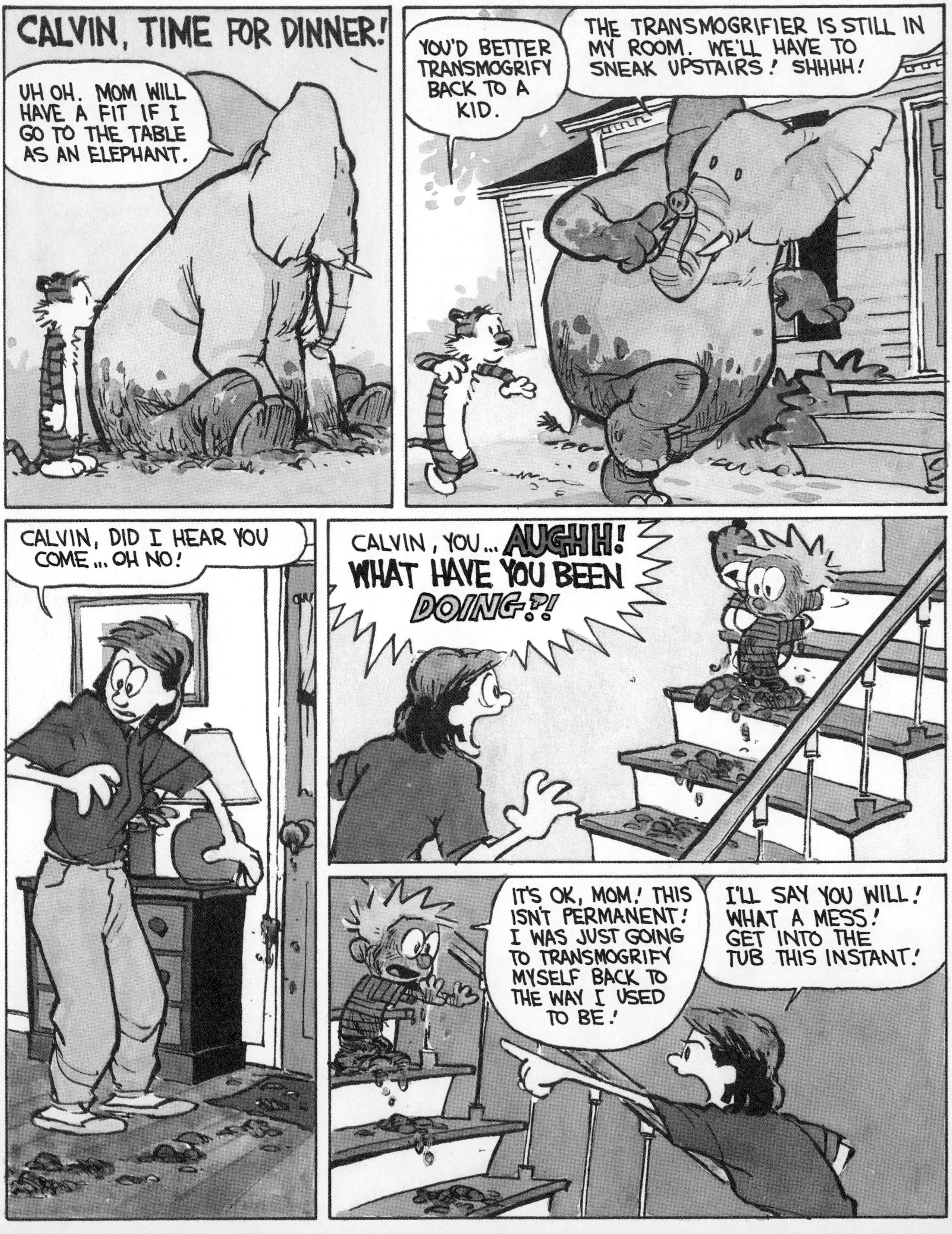
CALVIN, TIME FOR DINNER!
UH OH. MOM WILL HAVE A FIT IF I GO TO THE TABLE AS AN ELEPHANT.
YOU'D BETTER TRANSMOGRIFY BACK TO A KID.
THE TRANSMOGRIFIER IS STILL IN MY ROOM. WE'LL HAVE TO SNEAK UPSTAIRS! SHHHH!
CALVIN, DID I HEAR YOU COME... OH NO!
CALVIN, YOU... AUGHHH! WHAT HAVE YOU BEEN DOING?!
IT'S OK, MOM! THIS ISN'T PERMANENT! I WAS JUST GOING TO TRANSMOGRIFY MYSELF BACK TO THE WAY I USED TO BE!
I'LL SAY YOU WILL! WHAT A MESS! GET INTO THE TUB THIS INSTANT!

The End.

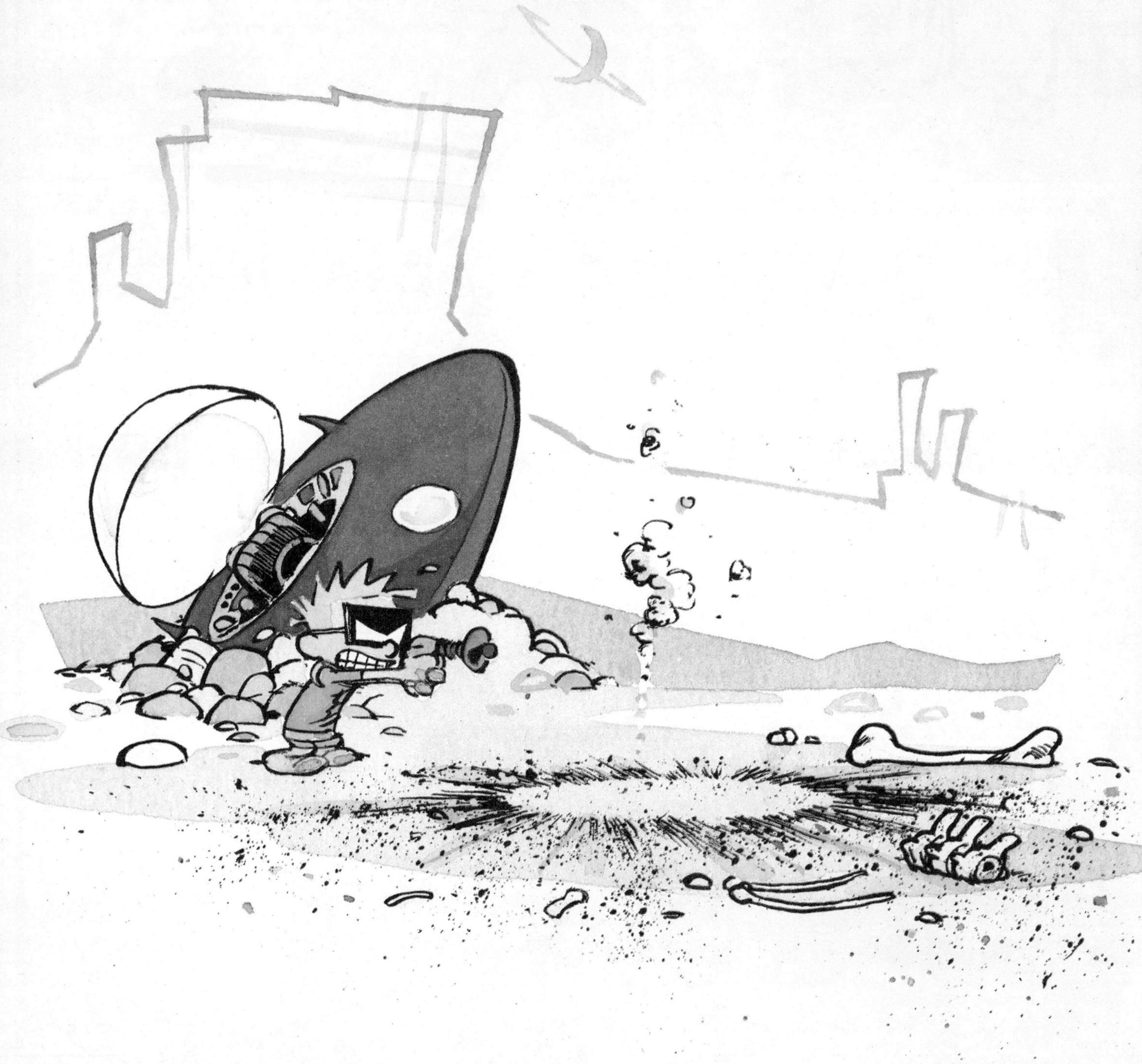

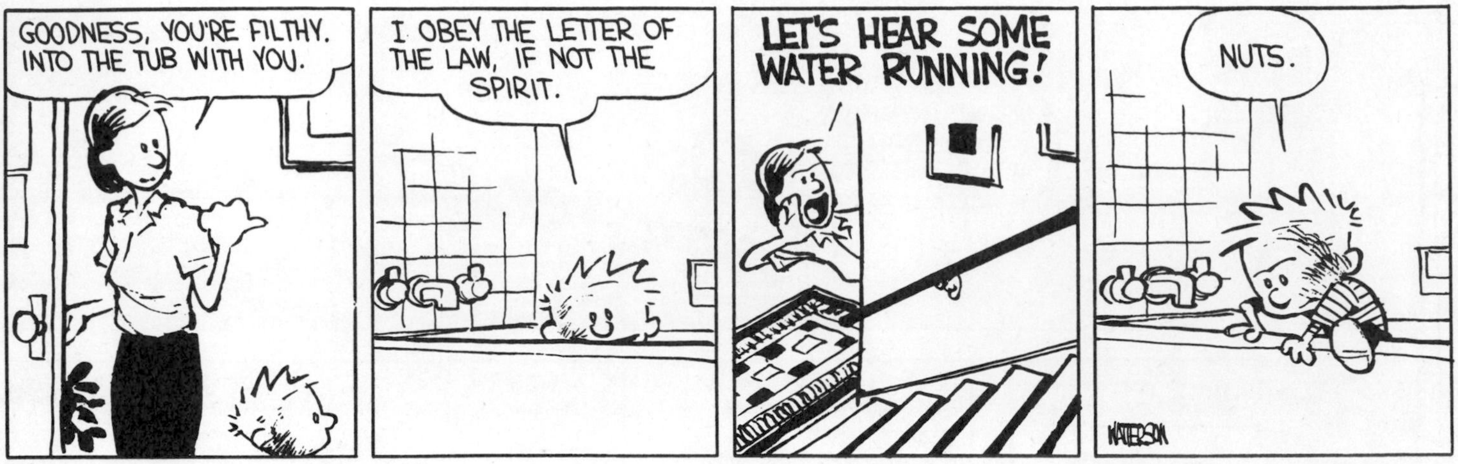
GOODNESS, YOU'RE FILTHY. INTO THE TUB WITH YOU.
I OBEY THE LETTER OF THE LAW, IF NOT THE SPIRIT.
LET'S HEAR SOME WATER RUNNING!
NUTS.

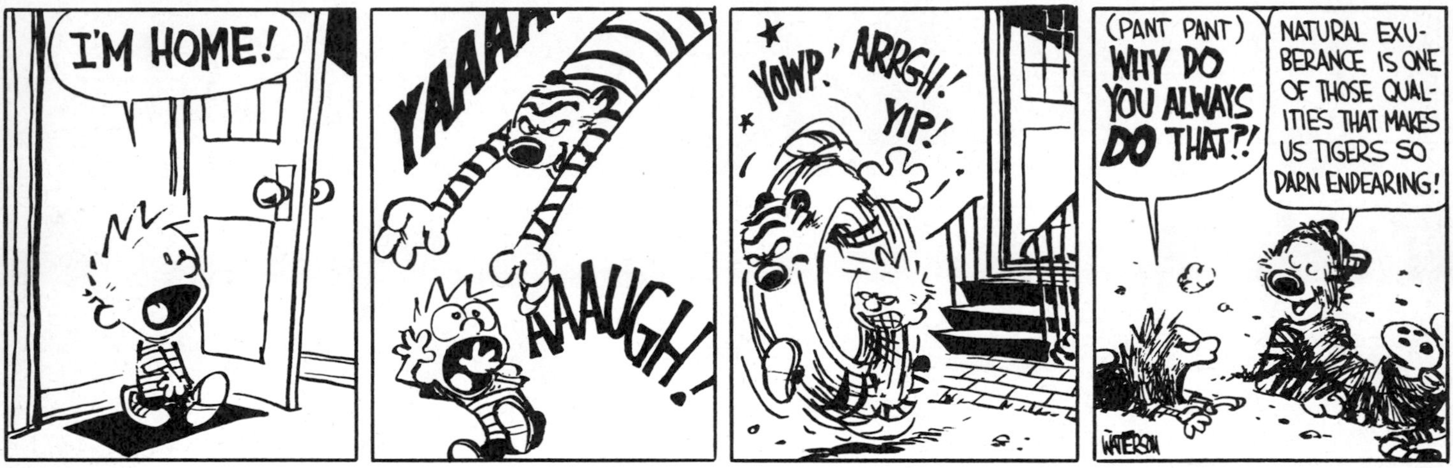
I'M HOME!
AAAUGH!
YOWP! ARRGH!
YIP!
(PANT PANT) WHY DO YOU ALWAYS DO THAT?!
NATURAL EXUBERANCE IS ONE OF THOSE QUALITIES THAT MAKES US TIGERS SO DARN ENDEARING!

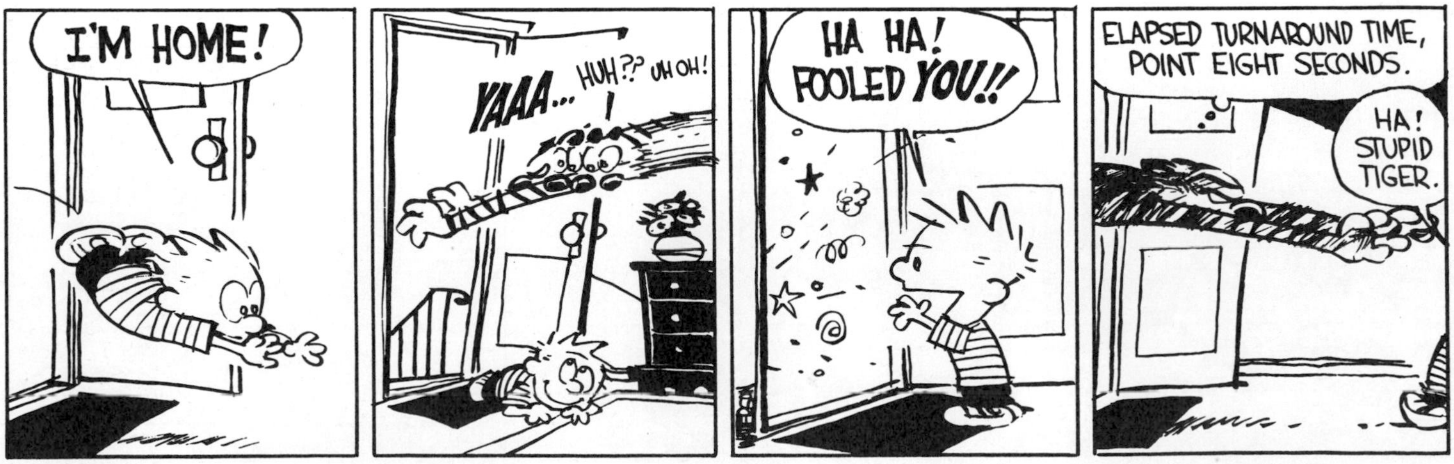
I'M HOME!
YAAA... HUH?? UH OH!
HA HA! FOOLED YOU!!
ELAPSED TURNAROUND TIME, POINT EIGHT SECONDS.
HA! STUPID TIGER.

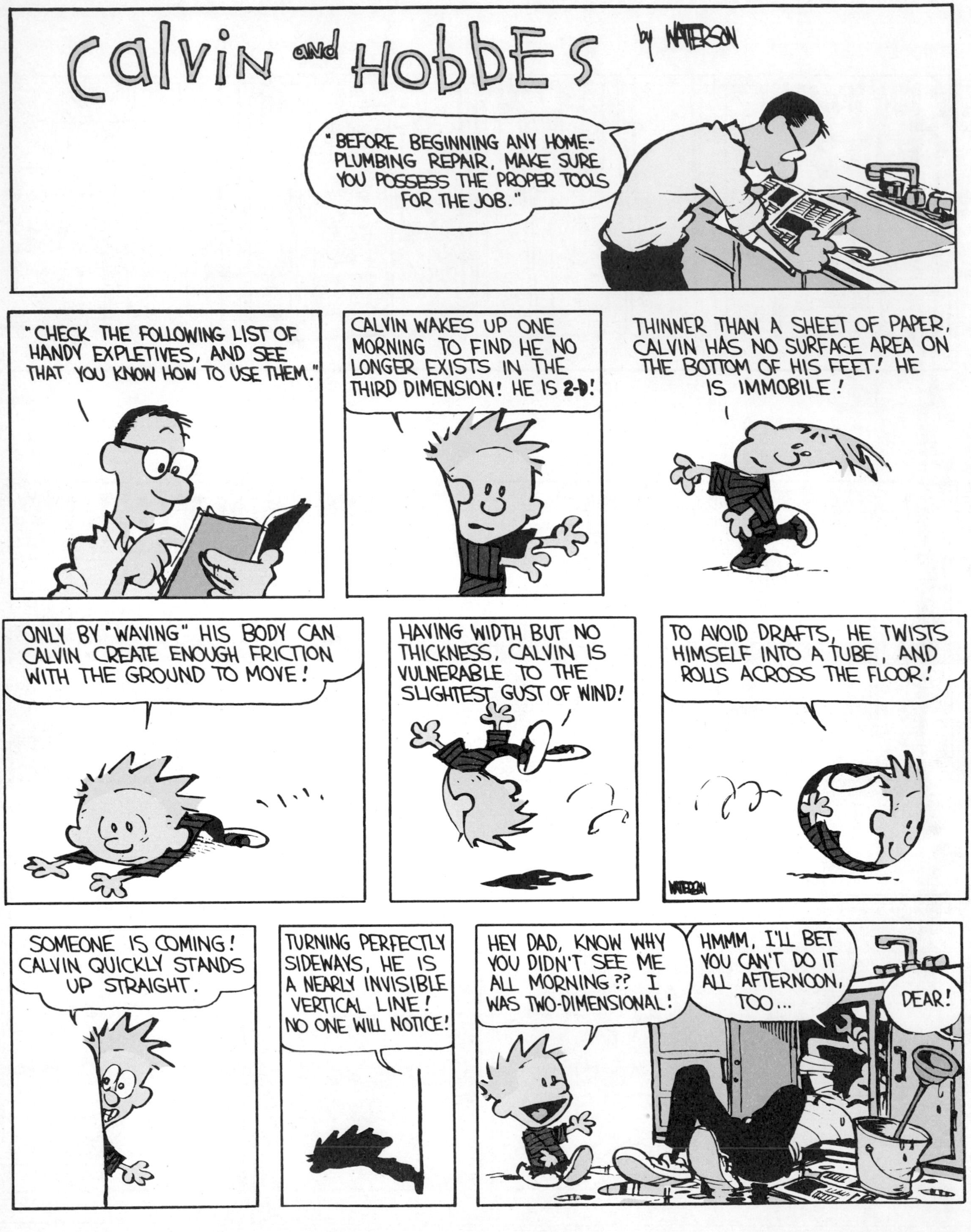
Calvin and HOBBES
by WATTERSON
"BEFORE BEGINNING ANY HOME-PLUMBING REPAIR, MAKE SURE YOU POSSESS THE PROPER TOOLS FOR THE JOB."
"CHECK THE FOLLOWING LIST OF HANDY EXPLETIVES, AND SEE THAT YOU KNOW HOW TO USE THEM."
CALVIN WAKES UP ONE MORNING TO FIND HE NO LONGER EXISTS IN THE THIRD DIMENSION! HE IS 2-D!
THINNER THAN A SHEET OF PAPER, CALVIN HAS NO SURFACE AREA ON THE BOTTOM OF HIS FEET! HE IS IMMOBILE!
ONLY BY "WAVING" HIS BODY CAN CALVIN CREATE ENOUGH FRICTION WITH THE GROUND TO MOVE!
HAVING WIDTH BUT NO THICKNESS, CALVIN IS VULNERABLE TO THE SLIGHTEST GUST OF WIND!
TO AVOID DRAFTS, HE TWISTS HIMSELF INTO A TUBE, AND ROLLS ACROSS THE FLOOR!
WATTERSON
SOMEONE IS COMING! CALVIN QUICKLY STANDS UP STRAIGHT.
TURNING PERFECTLY SIDEWAYS, HE IS A NEARLY INVISIBLE VERTICAL LINE! NO ONE WILL NOTICE!
HEY DAD, KNOW WHY YOU DIDN'T SEE ME ALL MORNING?? I WAS TWO-DIMENSIONAL!
HMMM, I'LL BET YOU CAN'T DO IT ALL AFTERNOON, TOO...
DEAR!

I COULDN'T READ IT BECAUSE MY PARENTS FORGOT TO PAY THE GRAVITY BILL.

MAKE A PREDICTION, HOBBES.
WHAT FOR?
SO WE CAN SEE IF YOU HAVE ESP.
OK, I PREDICT YOU'LL FIND AN IRRESISTIBLE ATTRACTION TO A MUD HOLE.
!
HA HA. YOU STAY AWAY FROM ME.
IT'S GOING TO COME TRUE! I CAN FEEL IT!

HEY DAD, HOW DOES A CARBURETOR WORK?
I CAN'T TELL YOU.
WHY NOT?
IT'S A SECRET.
NO IT ISN'T! YOU JUST DON'T KNOW!

BOMBARDED BY HIGH-ENERGY PHOTONS, CALVIN IS TRANSFORMED INTO A LIVING X-RAY!

ALTHOUGH THIS CONDITION WILL FACILITATE FUTURE MEDICAL DIAGNOSES, IT DOES MAKE CALVIN'S PRESENCE AT THE DINNER TABLE A DISGUSTING ORDEAL!

EVERYONE CAN SEE CALVIN'S FOOD BEING GROUND INTO MUSHY PULP AND SWALLOWED! AT THIS MOMENT, CALVIN CHEWS UP A LARGE SPOONFUL OF CREAMED CORN!

FOR GOSH SAKES, CLOSE YOUR MOUTH WHEN YOU CHEW!! YOU THINK WE WANT TO *SEE* THAT?!

MKGHH! SMACK! BLAGHKH!

HERE'S A LITTLE TOWN.

HERE'S A STEAMSHOVEL SCOOPING OUT A GIANT HOLE.

HERE COMES THE BULLDOZER, PUSHING THOUSANDS OF BARRELS OF TOXIC NUCLEAR WASTE INTO THE GIANT HOLE.

OVER THE YEARS, THESE DANGEROUS POISONS SEEP INTO UNDERGROUND WATERWAYS.

THE CANCER RATE OF THE NEARBY LITTLE TOWN TRIPLES.

IF YOU WANT ME, I'LL BE UNDER THE BED.

A STRIKE?? THAT PITCH WAS FOUR FEET ABOVE MY HEAD!

HA! IT WAS A *PERFECT* PITCH! YOU'RE JUST TOO SHORT!

YEAH? WELL, *YOU'RE* JUST TOO STUPID!

WELL, YOU'RE JUST TOO *UGLY!*

KICK KICK KICK

KICK KICK KICK KICK

KICKING DUST IS THE ONLY PART OF THIS GAME WE REALLY LIKE.

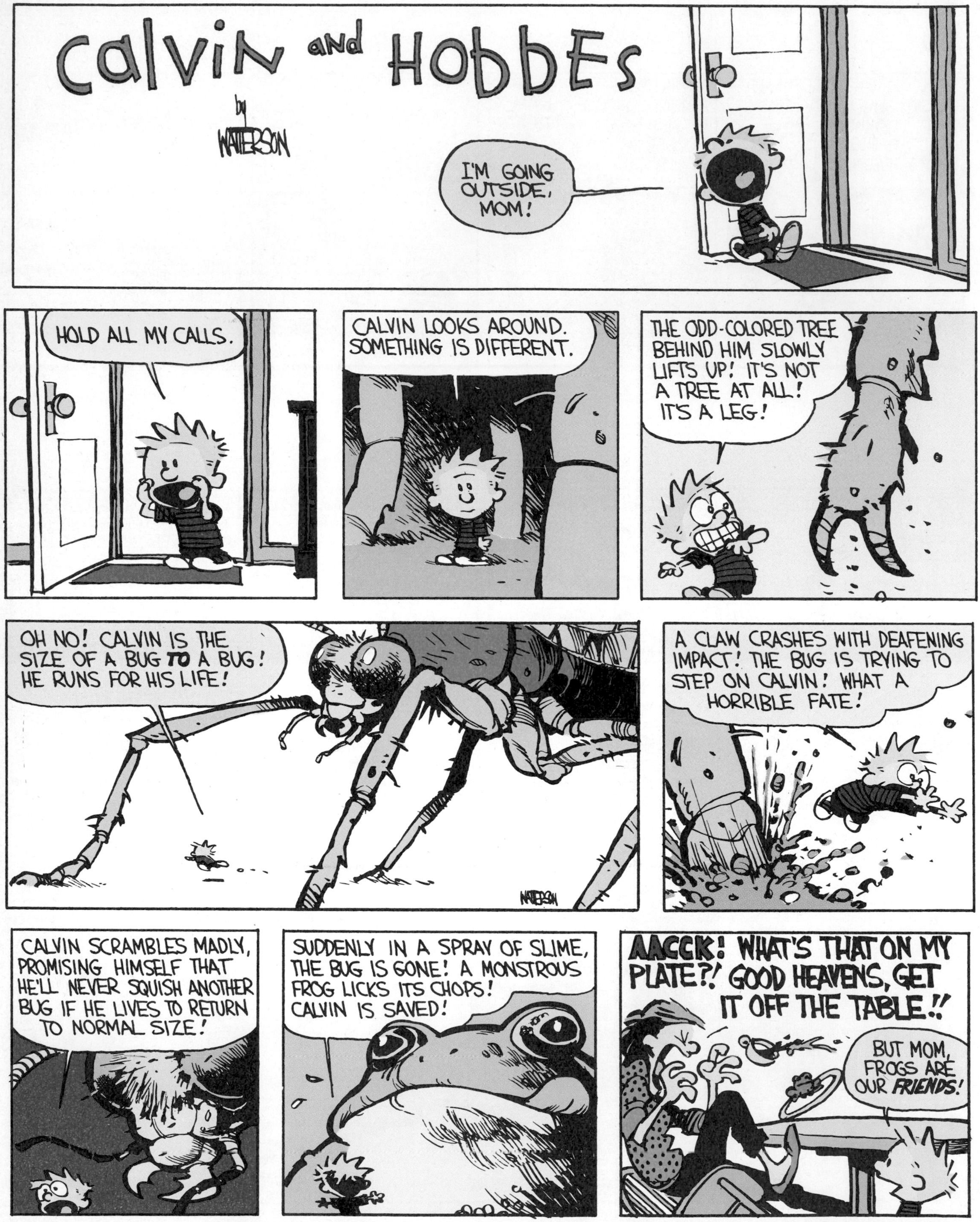
Calvin and HOBBES
by WATTERSON
I'M GOING OUTSIDE, MOM!
HOLD ALL MY CALLS.
CALVIN LOOKS AROUND. SOMETHING IS DIFFERENT.
THE ODD-COLORED TREE BEHIND HIM SLOWLY LIFTS UP! IT'S NOT A TREE AT ALL! IT'S A LEG!
OH NO! CALVIN IS THE SIZE OF A BUG TO A BUG! HE RUNS FOR HIS LIFE!
WATTERSON
A CLAW CRASHES WITH DEAFENING IMPACT! THE BUG IS TRYING TO STEP ON CALVIN! WHAT A HORRIBLE FATE!
CALVIN SCRAMBLES MADLY, PROMISING HIMSELF THAT HE'LL NEVER SQUISH ANOTHER BUG IF HE LIVES TO RETURN TO NORMAL SIZE!
SUDDENLY IN A SPRAY OF SLIME, THE BUG IS GONE! A MONSTROUS FROG LICKS ITS CHOPS! CALVIN IS SAVED!
AACCK! WHAT'S THAT ON MY PLATE?! GOOD HEAVENS, GET IT OFF THE TABLE!!
BUT MOM, FROGS ARE OUR FRIENDS!

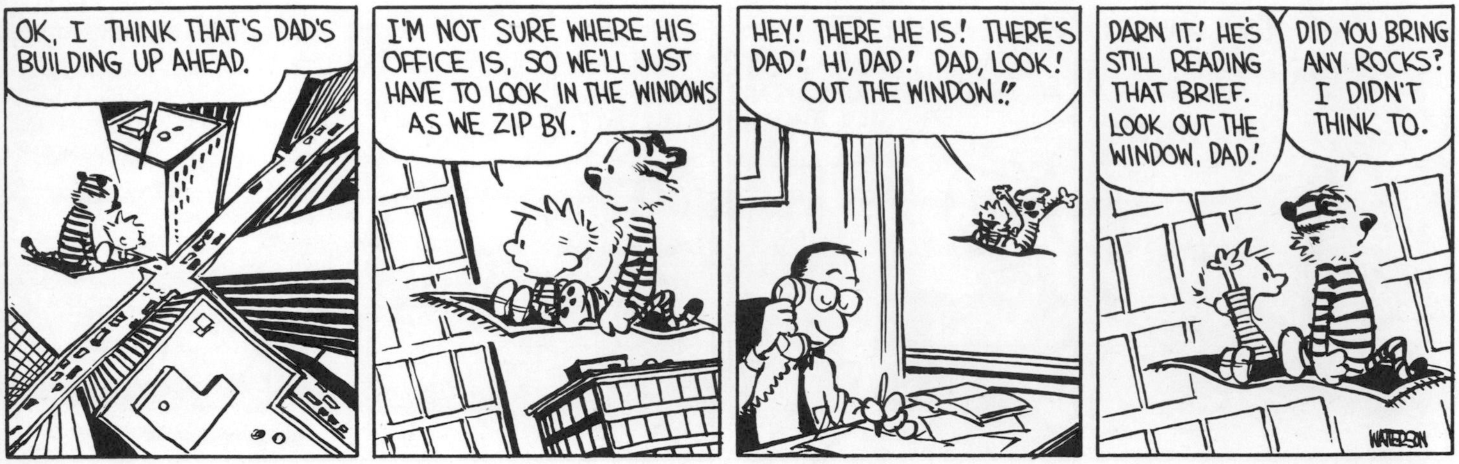
OK, I THINK THAT'S DAD'S BUILDING UP AHEAD.
I'M NOT SURE WHERE HIS OFFICE IS, SO WE'LL JUST HAVE TO LOOK IN THE WINDOWS AS WE ZIP BY.
HEY! THERE HE IS! THERE'S DAD! HI, DAD! DAD, LOOK! OUT THE WINDOW!!
DARN IT! HE'S STILL READING THAT BRIEF. LOOK OUT THE WINDOW, DAD!
DID YOU BRING ANY ROCKS? I DIDN'T THINK TO.
WATTERSON

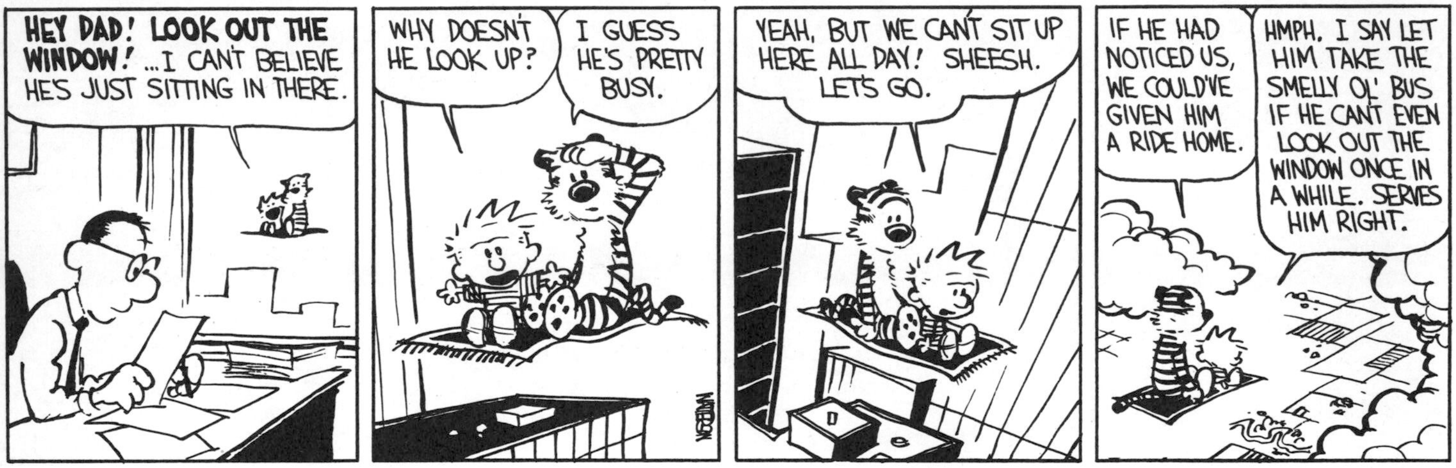
**HEY DAD! LOOK OUT THE WINDOW!** ...I CAN'T BELIEVE HE'S JUST SITTING IN THERE.
WHY DOESN'T HE LOOK UP?
I GUESS HE'S PRETTY BUSY.
YEAH, BUT WE CAN'T SIT UP HERE ALL DAY! SHEESH. LET'S GO.
IF HE HAD NOTICED US, WE COULD'VE GIVEN HIM A RIDE HOME.
HMPH. I SAY LET HIM TAKE THE SMELLY OL' BUS IF HE CAN'T EVEN LOOK OUT THE WINDOW ONCE IN A WHILE. SERVES HIM RIGHT.

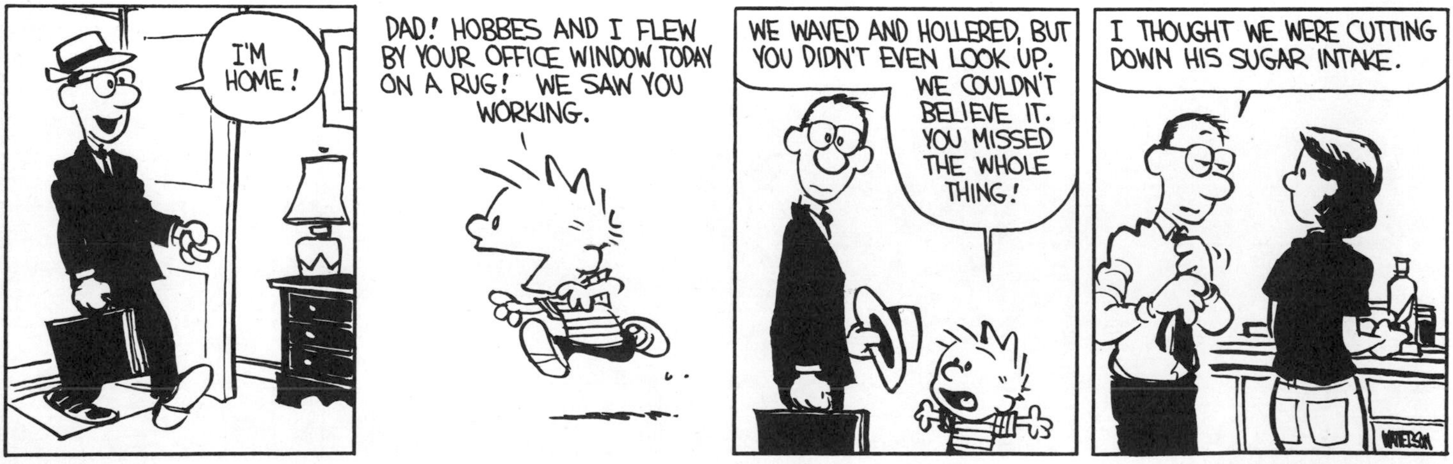
I'M HOME!
DAD! HOBBES AND I FLEW BY YOUR OFFICE WINDOW TODAY ON A RUG! WE SAW YOU WORKING.
WE WAVED AND HOLLERED, BUT YOU DIDN'T EVEN LOOK UP.
WE COULDN'T BELIEVE IT. YOU MISSED THE WHOLE THING!
I THOUGHT WE WERE CUTTING DOWN HIS SUGAR INTAKE.
WATTERSON

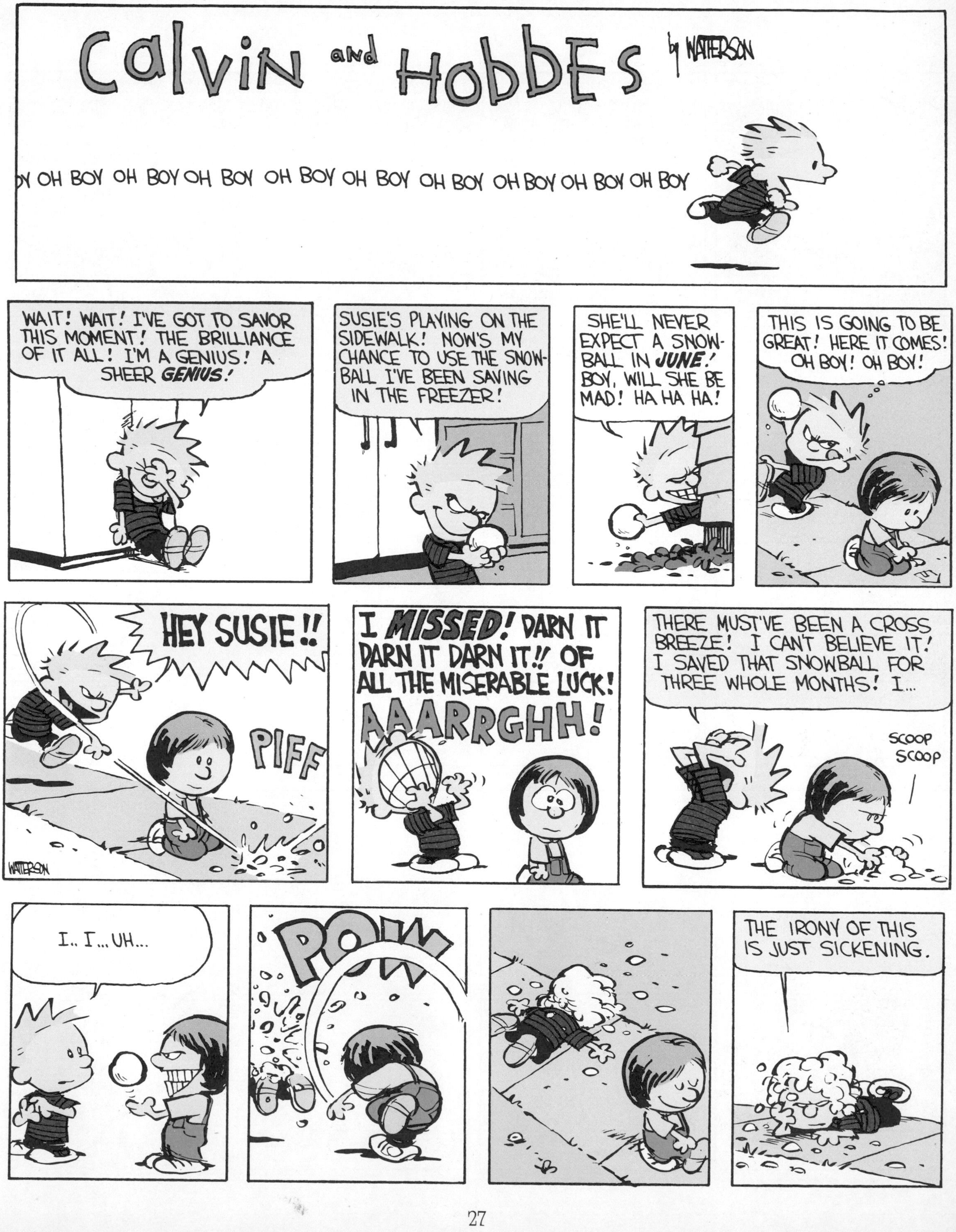
Calvin and Hobbes
by WATTERSON
OY OH BOY OH BOY OH BOY OH BOY OH BOY OH BOY OH BOY OH BOY OH BOY
WAIT! WAIT! I'VE GOT TO SAVOR THIS MOMENT! THE BRILLIANCE OF IT ALL! I'M A GENIUS! A SHEER GENIUS!
SUSIE'S PLAYING ON THE SIDEWALK! NOW'S MY CHANCE TO USE THE SNOWBALL I'VE BEEN SAVING IN THE FREEZER!
SHE'LL NEVER EXPECT A SNOWBALL IN JUNE! BOY, WILL SHE BE MAD! HA HA HA!
THIS IS GOING TO BE GREAT! HERE IT COMES! OH BOY! OH BOY!
HEY SUSIE!!
PIFF
WATTERSON
I MISSED! DARN IT DARN IT DARN IT!! OF ALL THE MISERABLE LUCK!
AAARRGHH!
THERE MUST'VE BEEN A CROSS BREEZE! I CAN'T BELIEVE IT! I SAVED THAT SNOWBALL FOR THREE WHOLE MONTHS! I...
SCOOP SCOOP
I.. I... UH...
POW
THE IRONY OF THIS IS JUST SICKENING.

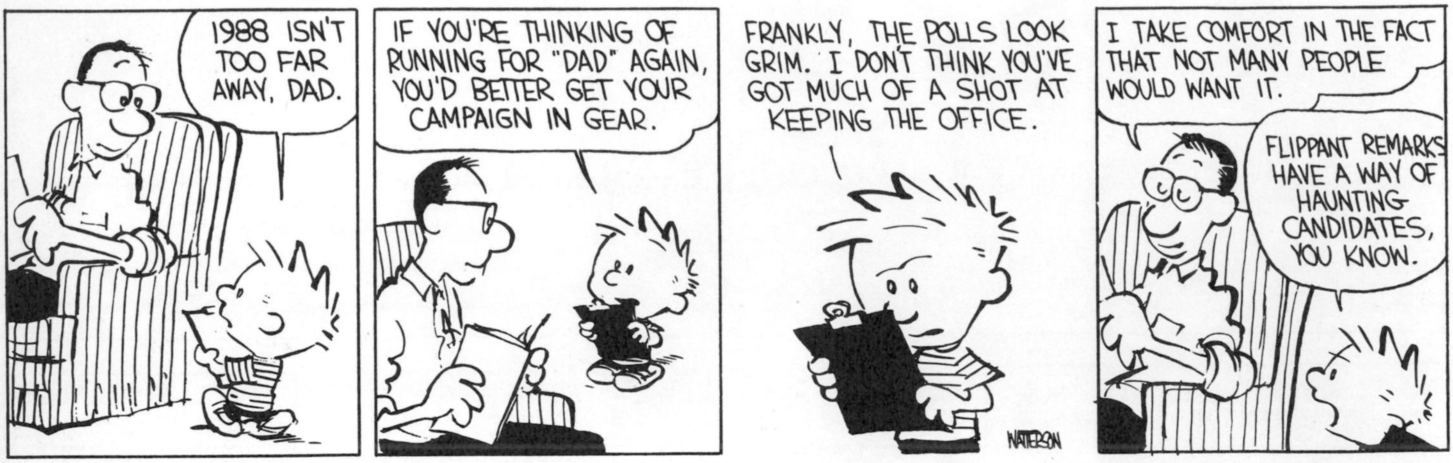
1988 ISN'T TOO FAR AWAY, DAD.
IF YOU'RE THINKING OF RUNNING FOR "DAD" AGAIN, YOU'D BETTER GET YOUR CAMPAIGN IN GEAR.
FRANKLY, THE POLLS LOOK GRIM. I DON'T THINK YOU'VE GOT MUCH OF A SHOT AT KEEPING THE OFFICE.
I TAKE COMFORT IN THE FACT THAT NOT MANY PEOPLE WOULD WANT IT.
FLIPPANT REMARKS HAVE A WAY OF HAUNTING CANDIDATES, YOU KNOW.
WATTERSON

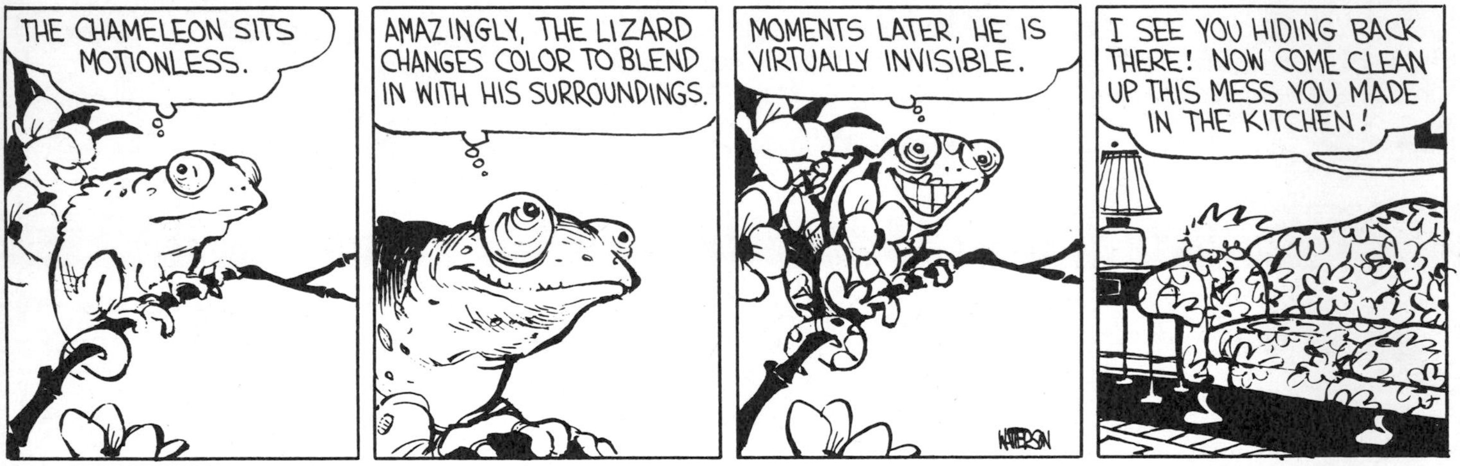
THE CHAMELEON SITS MOTIONLESS.
AMAZINGLY, THE LIZARD CHANGES COLOR TO BLEND IN WITH HIS SURROUNDINGS.
MOMENTS LATER, HE IS VIRTUALLY INVISIBLE.
WATTERSON
I SEE YOU HIDING BACK THERE! NOW COME CLEAN UP THIS MESS YOU MADE IN THE KITCHEN!

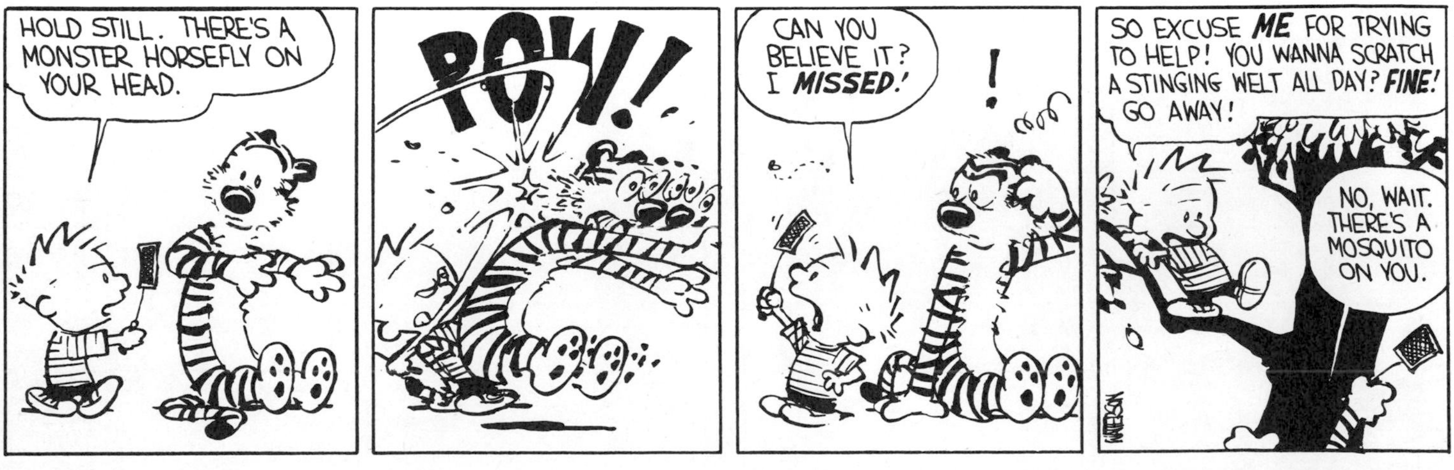
HOLD STILL. THERE'S A MONSTER HORSEFLY ON YOUR HEAD.
POW!
CAN YOU BELIEVE IT? I MISSED!
!
SO EXCUSE ME FOR TRYING TO HELP! YOU WANNA SCRATCH A STINGING WELT ALL DAY? FINE! GO AWAY!
NO, WAIT. THERE'S A MOSQUITO ON YOU.
WATTERSON

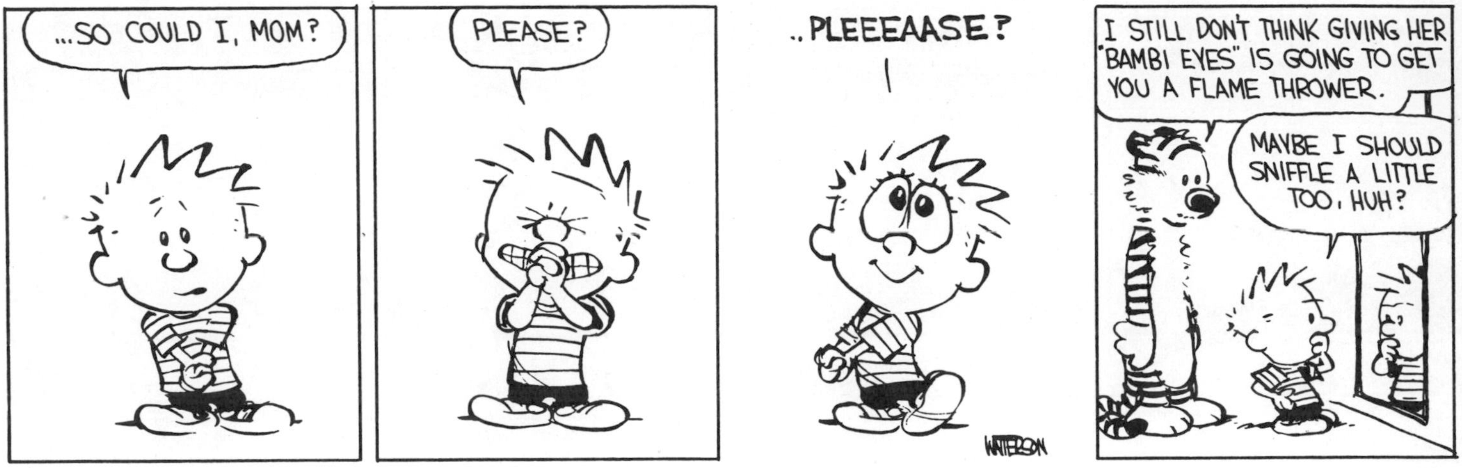
...SO COULD I, MOM?
PLEASE?
..PLEEEAASE?
I STILL DON'T THINK GIVING HER "BAMBI EYES" IS GOING TO GET YOU A FLAME THROWER.
MAYBE I SHOULD SNIFFLE A LITTLE TOO, HUH?
WATTERSON

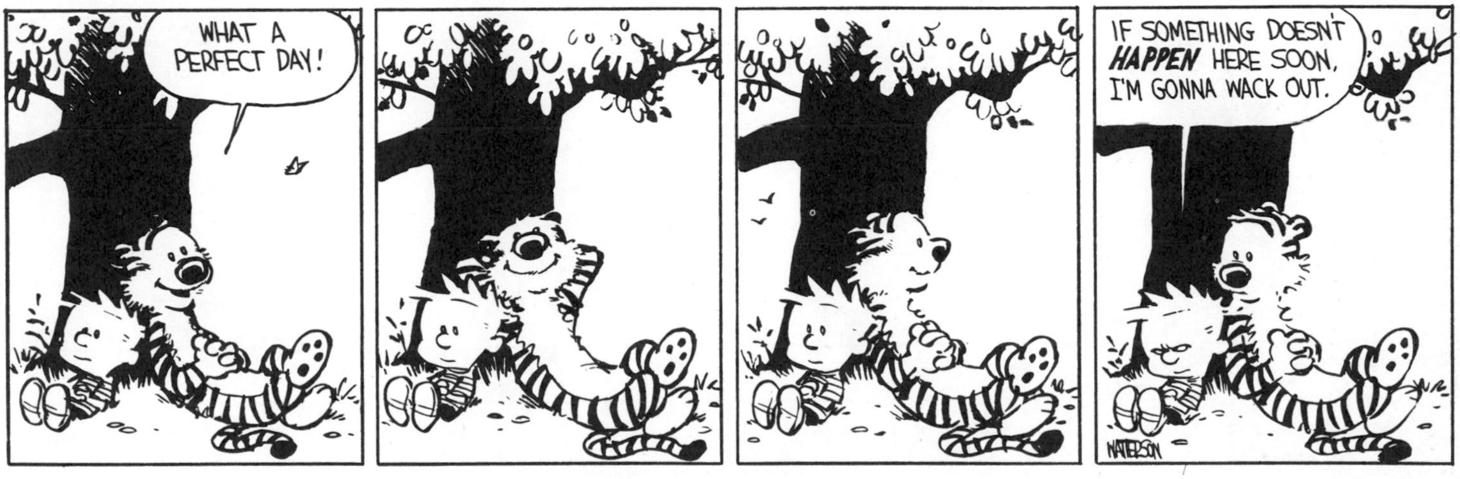
WHAT A PERFECT DAY!
IF SOMETHING DOESN'T HAPPEN HERE SOON, I'M GONNA WACK OUT.
WATTERSON

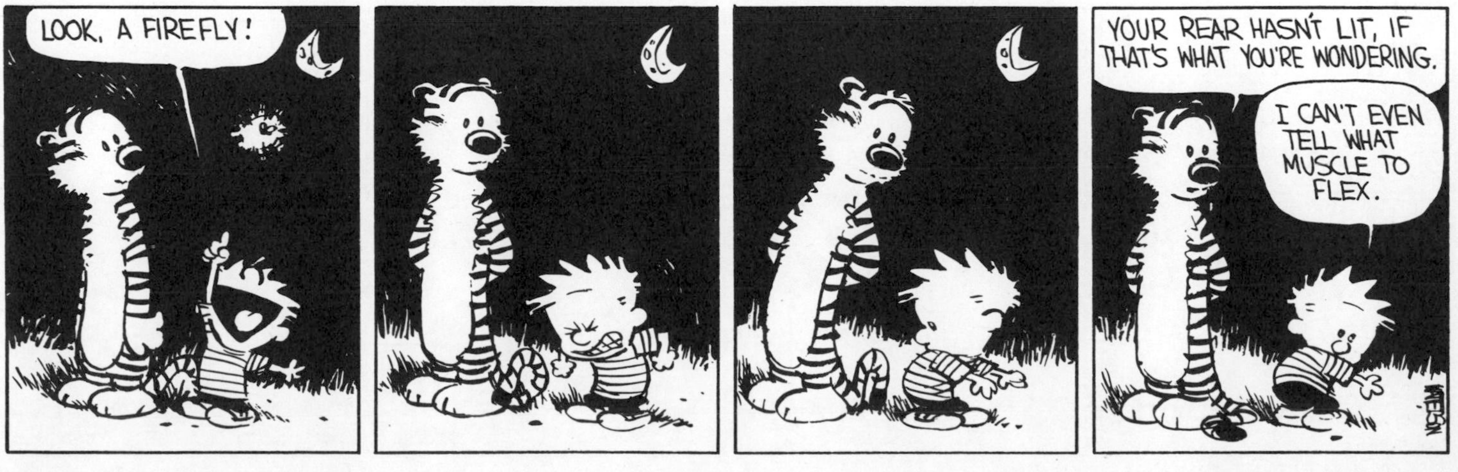
LOOK, A FIREFLY!
YOUR REAR HASN'T LIT, IF THAT'S WHAT YOU'RE WONDERING.
I CAN'T EVEN TELL WHAT MUSCLE TO FLEX.
WATTERSON

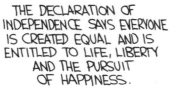

32

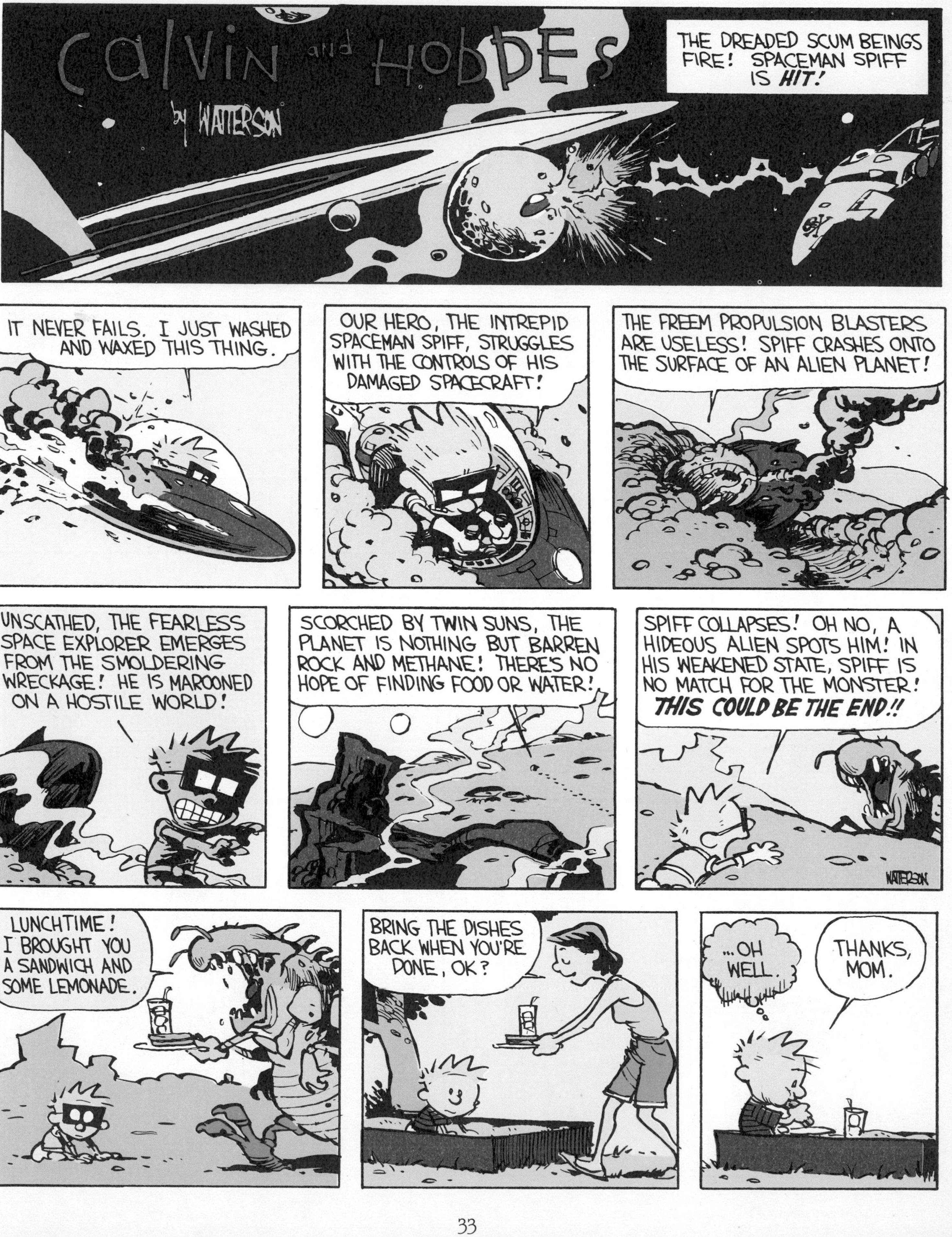
Calvin and Hobbes
by WATTERSON
THE DREADED SCUM BEINGS FIRE! SPACEMAN SPIFF IS HIT!
IT NEVER FAILS. I JUST WASHED AND WAXED THIS THING.
OUR HERO, THE INTREPID SPACEMAN SPIFF, STRUGGLES WITH THE CONTROLS OF HIS DAMAGED SPACECRAFT!
THE FREEM PROPULSION BLASTERS ARE USELESS! SPIFF CRASHES ONTO THE SURFACE OF AN ALIEN PLANET!
UNSCATHED, THE FEARLESS SPACE EXPLORER EMERGES FROM THE SMOLDERING WRECKAGE! HE IS MAROONED ON A HOSTILE WORLD!
SCORCHED BY TWIN SUNS, THE PLANET IS NOTHING BUT BARREN ROCK AND METHANE! THERE'S NO HOPE OF FINDING FOOD OR WATER!
SPIFF COLLAPSES! OH NO, A HIDEOUS ALIEN SPOTS HIM! IN HIS WEAKENED STATE, SPIFF IS NO MATCH FOR THE MONSTER! THIS COULD BE THE END!!
WATTERSON
LUNCHTIME! I BROUGHT YOU A SANDWICH AND SOME LEMONADE.
BRING THE DISHES BACK WHEN YOU'RE DONE, OK?
...OH WELL.
THANKS, MOM.

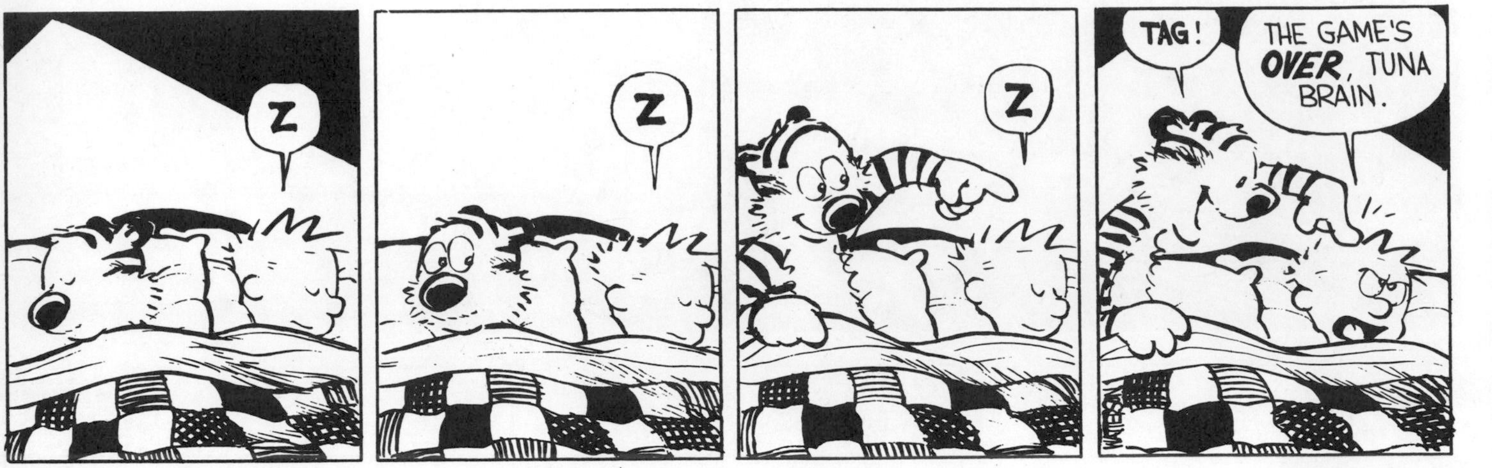
Z
Z
Z
TAG!
THE GAME'S OVER, TUNA BRAIN.

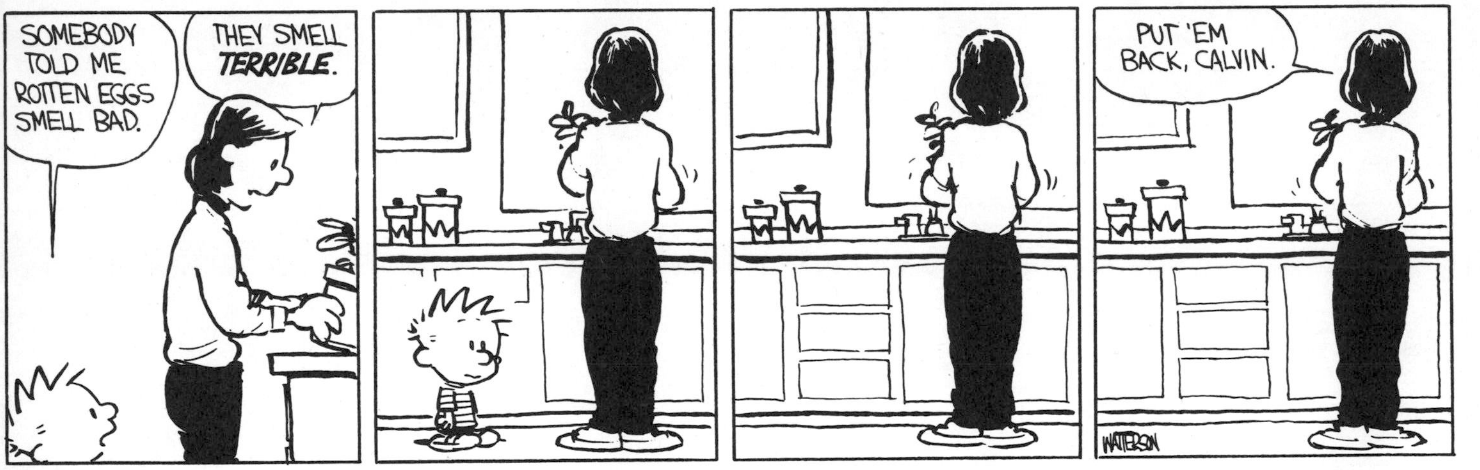
SOMEBODY TOLD ME ROTTEN EGGS SMELL BAD.
THEY SMELL TERRIBLE.
PUT 'EM BACK, CALVIN.
WATTERSON

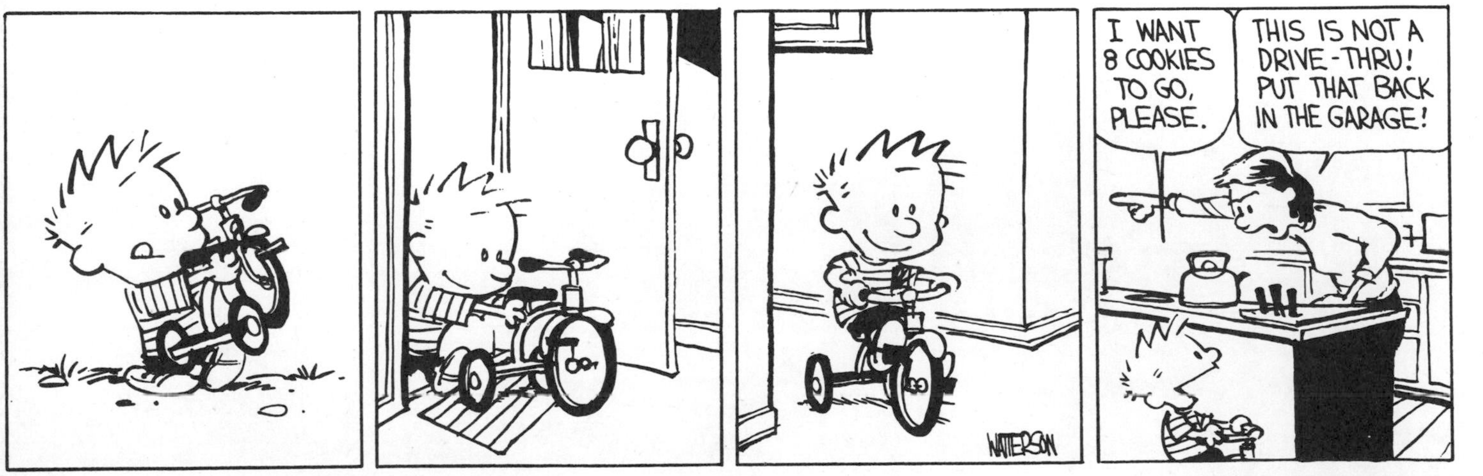
WATTERSON
I WANT 8 COOKIES TO GO, PLEASE.
THIS IS NOT A DRIVE-THRU! PUT THAT BACK IN THE GARAGE!

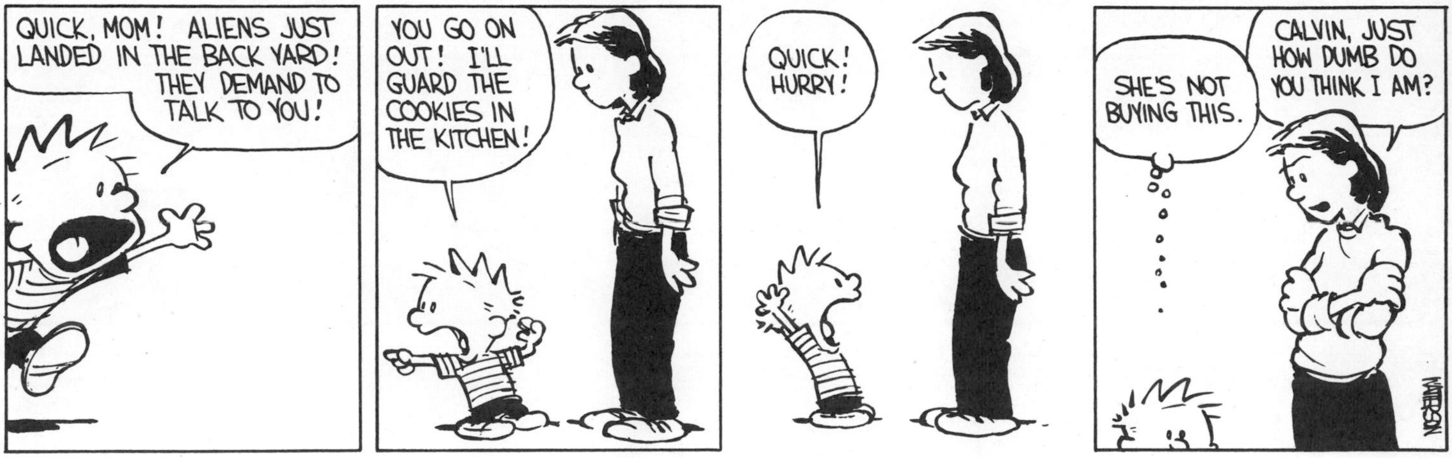
QUICK, MOM! ALIENS JUST LANDED IN THE BACK YARD! THEY DEMAND TO TALK TO YOU!
YOU GO ON OUT! I'LL GUARD THE COOKIES IN THE KITCHEN!
QUICK! HURRY!
SHE'S NOT BUYING THIS.
CALVIN, JUST HOW DUMB DO YOU THINK I AM?

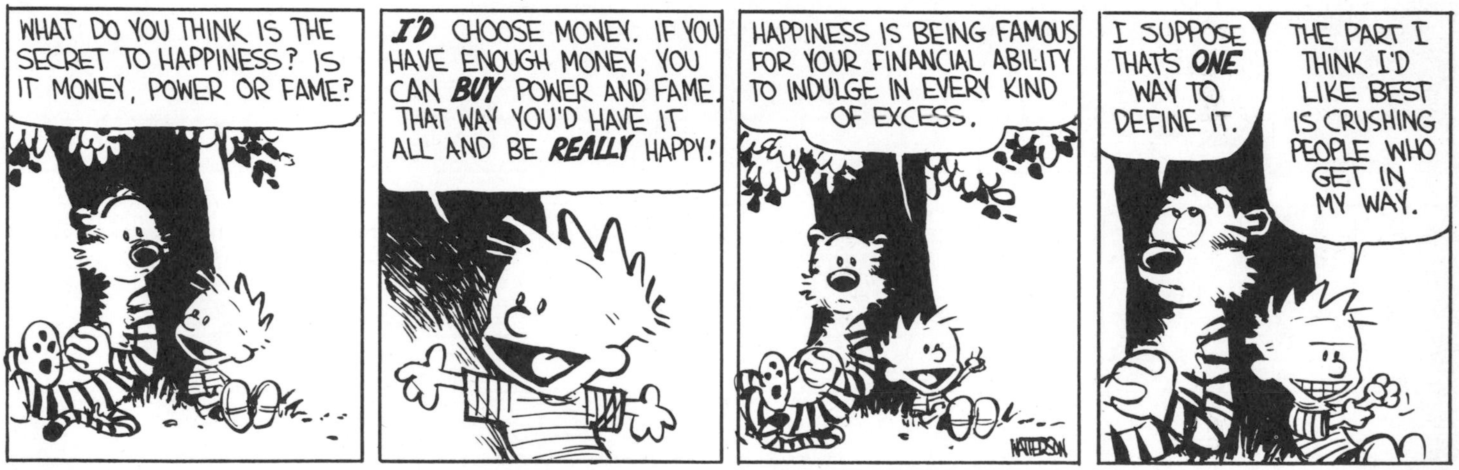
WHAT DO YOU THINK IS THE SECRET TO HAPPINESS? IS IT MONEY, POWER OR FAME?
I'D CHOOSE MONEY. IF YOU HAVE ENOUGH MONEY, YOU CAN BUY POWER AND FAME. THAT WAY YOU'D HAVE IT ALL AND BE REALLY HAPPY!
HAPPINESS IS BEING FAMOUS FOR YOUR FINANCIAL ABILITY TO INDULGE IN EVERY KIND OF EXCESS.
I SUPPOSE THAT'S ONE WAY TO DEFINE IT.
THE PART I THINK I'D LIKE BEST IS CRUSHING PEOPLE WHO GET IN MY WAY.

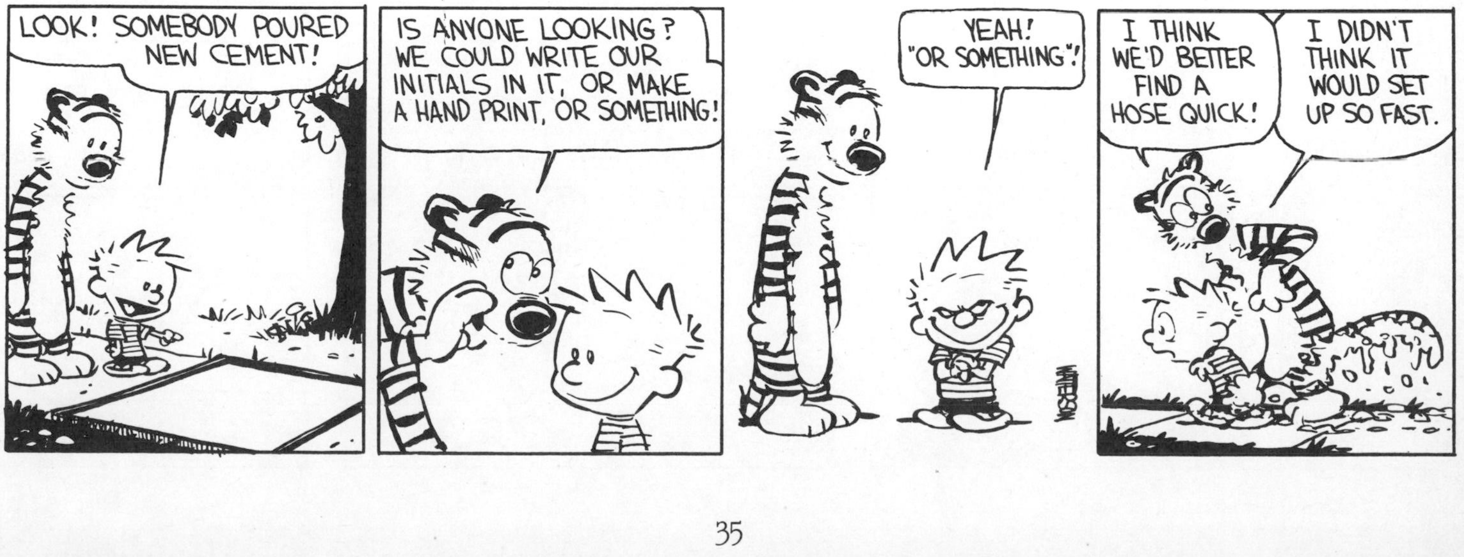
LOOK! SOMEBODY POURED NEW CEMENT!
IS ANYONE LOOKING? WE COULD WRITE OUR INITIALS IN IT, OR MAKE A HAND PRINT, OR SOMETHING!
YEAH! "OR SOMETHING"!
I THINK WE'D BETTER FIND A HOSE QUICK!
I DIDN'T THINK IT WOULD SET UP SO FAST.

# Calvin and Hobbes
by WATTERSON

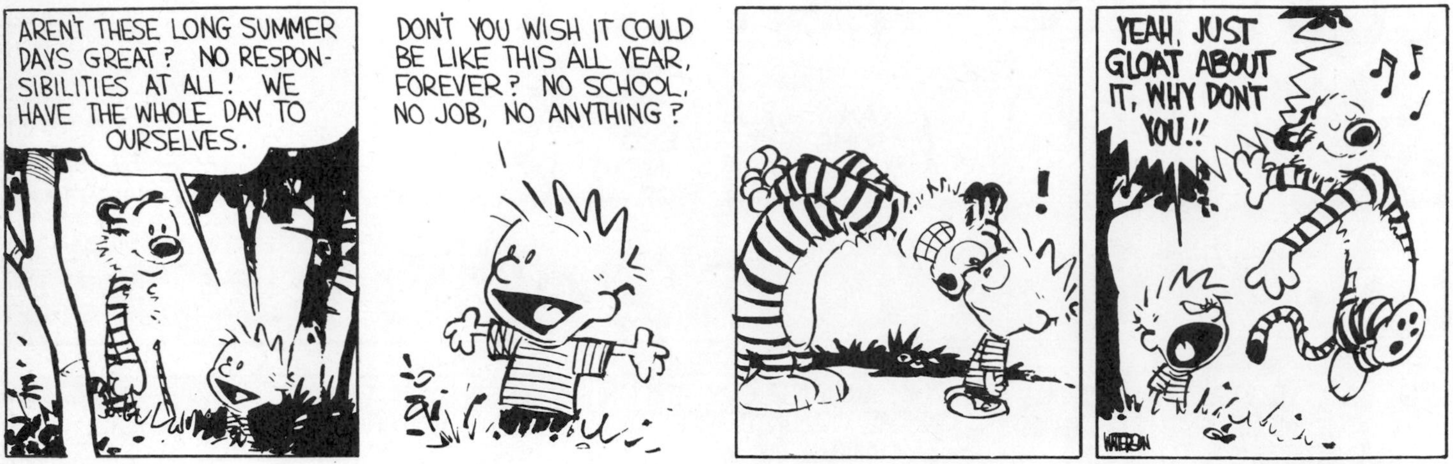
AREN'T THESE LONG SUMMER DAYS GREAT? NO RESPONSIBILITIES AT ALL! WE HAVE THE WHOLE DAY TO OURSELVES.
DON'T YOU WISH IT COULD BE LIKE THIS ALL YEAR, FOREVER? NO SCHOOL, NO JOB, NO ANYTHING?
!
YEAH, JUST GLOAT ABOUT IT, WHY DON'T YOU!!
WATTERSON

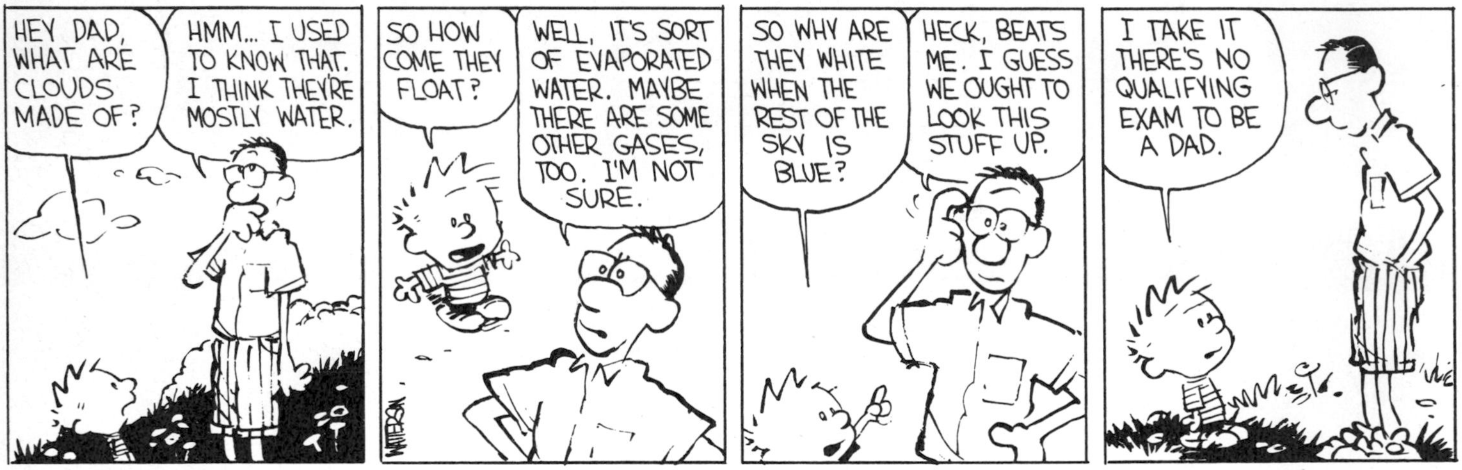
HEY DAD, WHAT ARE CLOUDS MADE OF?
HMM... I USED TO KNOW THAT. I THINK THEY'RE MOSTLY WATER.
WATTERSON
SO HOW COME THEY FLOAT?
WELL, IT'S SORT OF EVAPORATED WATER. MAYBE THERE ARE SOME OTHER GASES, TOO. I'M NOT SURE.
SO WHY ARE THEY WHITE WHEN THE REST OF THE SKY IS BLUE?
HECK, BEATS ME. I GUESS WE OUGHT TO LOOK THIS STUFF UP.
I TAKE IT THERE'S NO QUALIFYING EXAM TO BE A DAD.

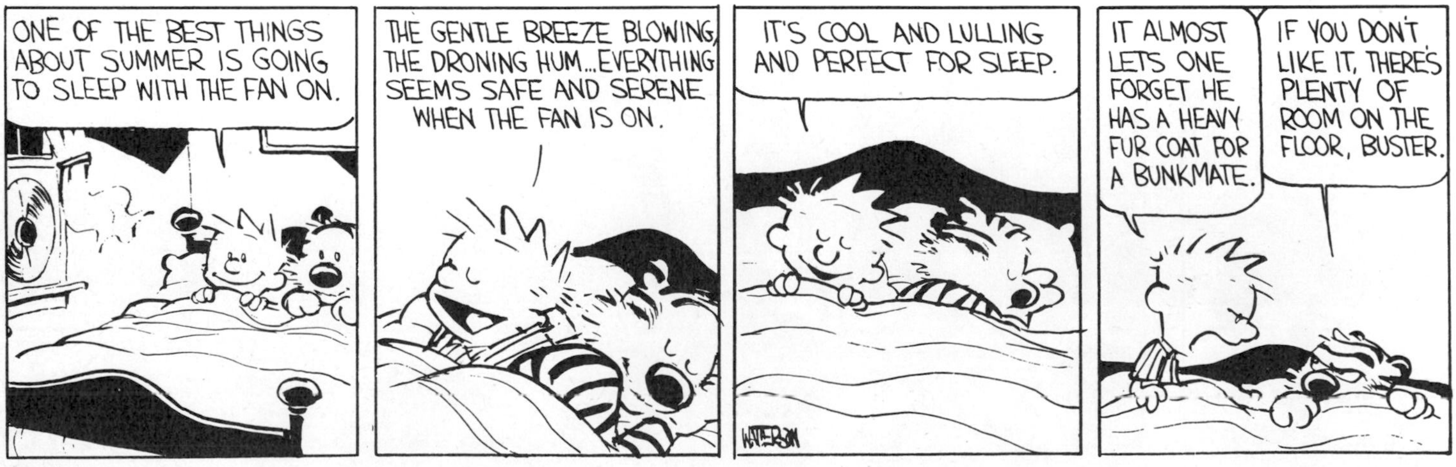
ONE OF THE BEST THINGS ABOUT SUMMER IS GOING TO SLEEP WITH THE FAN ON.
THE GENTLE BREEZE BLOWING, THE DRONING HUM... EVERYTHING SEEMS SAFE AND SERENE WHEN THE FAN IS ON.
IT'S COOL AND LULLING AND PERFECT FOR SLEEP.
WATTERSON
IT ALMOST LETS ONE FORGET HE HAS A HEAVY FUR COAT FOR A BUNKMATE.
IF YOU DON'T LIKE IT, THERE'S PLENTY OF ROOM ON THE FLOOR, BUSTER.

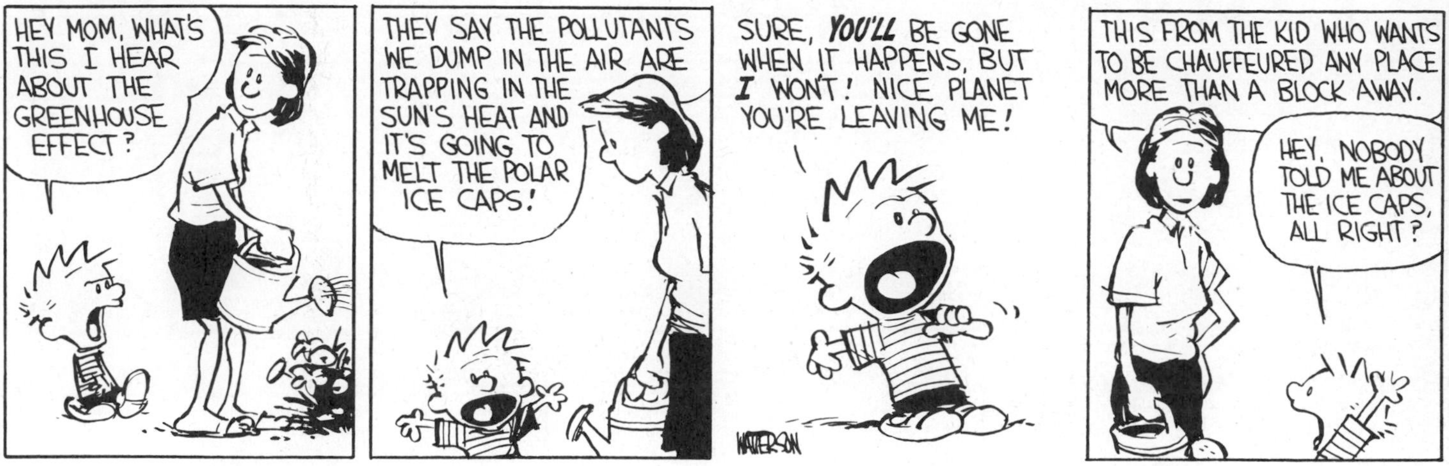
HEY MOM, WHAT'S THIS I HEAR ABOUT THE GREENHOUSE EFFECT?
THEY SAY THE POLLUTANTS WE DUMP IN THE AIR ARE TRAPPING IN THE SUN'S HEAT AND IT'S GOING TO MELT THE POLAR ICE CAPS!
SURE, **YOU'LL** BE GONE WHEN IT HAPPENS, BUT **I** WON'T! NICE PLANET YOU'RE LEAVING ME!
THIS FROM THE KID WHO WANTS TO BE CHAUFFEURED ANY PLACE MORE THAN A BLOCK AWAY.
HEY, NOBODY TOLD ME ABOUT THE ICE CAPS, ALL RIGHT?

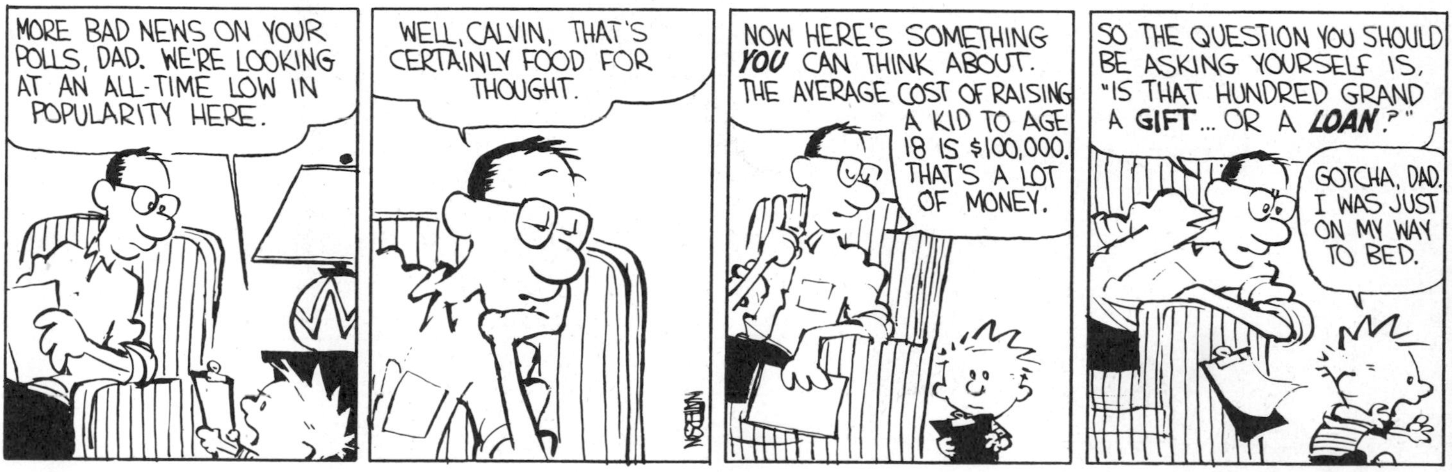
MORE BAD NEWS ON YOUR POLLS, DAD. WE'RE LOOKING AT AN ALL-TIME LOW IN POPULARITY HERE.
WELL, CALVIN, THAT'S CERTAINLY FOOD FOR THOUGHT.
NOW HERE'S SOMETHING **YOU** CAN THINK ABOUT. THE AVERAGE COST OF RAISING A KID TO AGE 18 IS $100,000. THAT'S A LOT OF MONEY.
SO THE QUESTION YOU SHOULD BE ASKING YOURSELF IS, "IS THAT HUNDRED GRAND A **GIFT**... OR A **LOAN**?"
GOTCHA, DAD. I WAS JUST ON MY WAY TO BED.

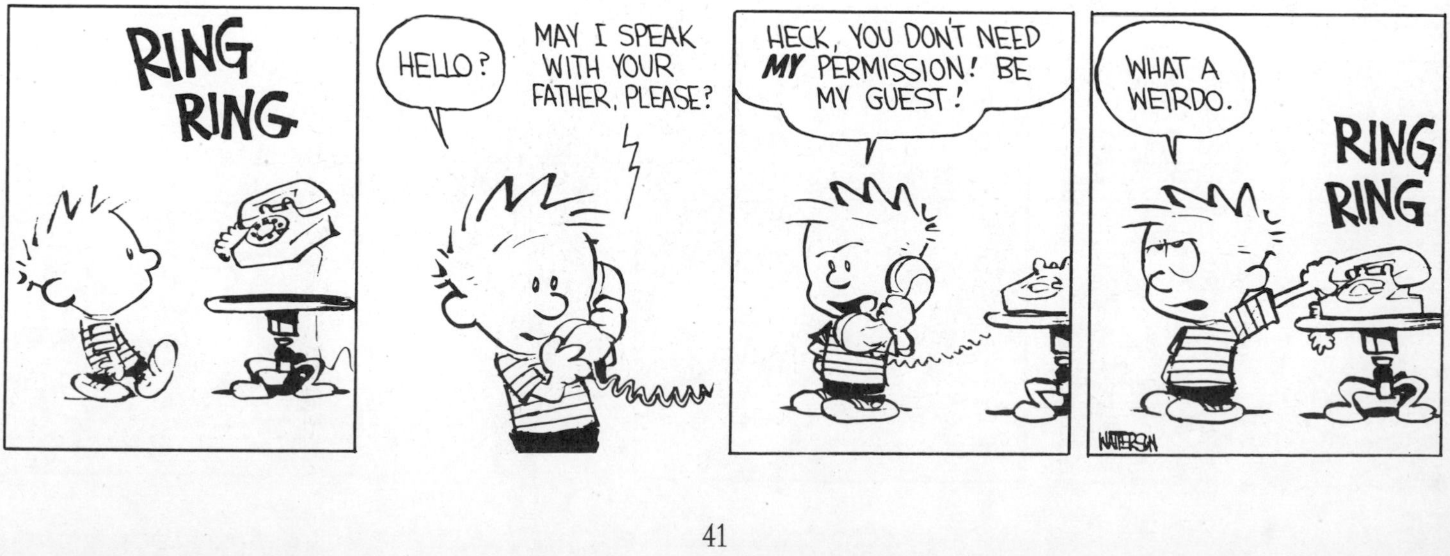
RING RING
HELLO?
MAY I SPEAK WITH YOUR FATHER, PLEASE?
HECK, YOU DON'T NEED **MY** PERMISSION! BE MY GUEST!
WHAT A WEIRDO.
RING RING

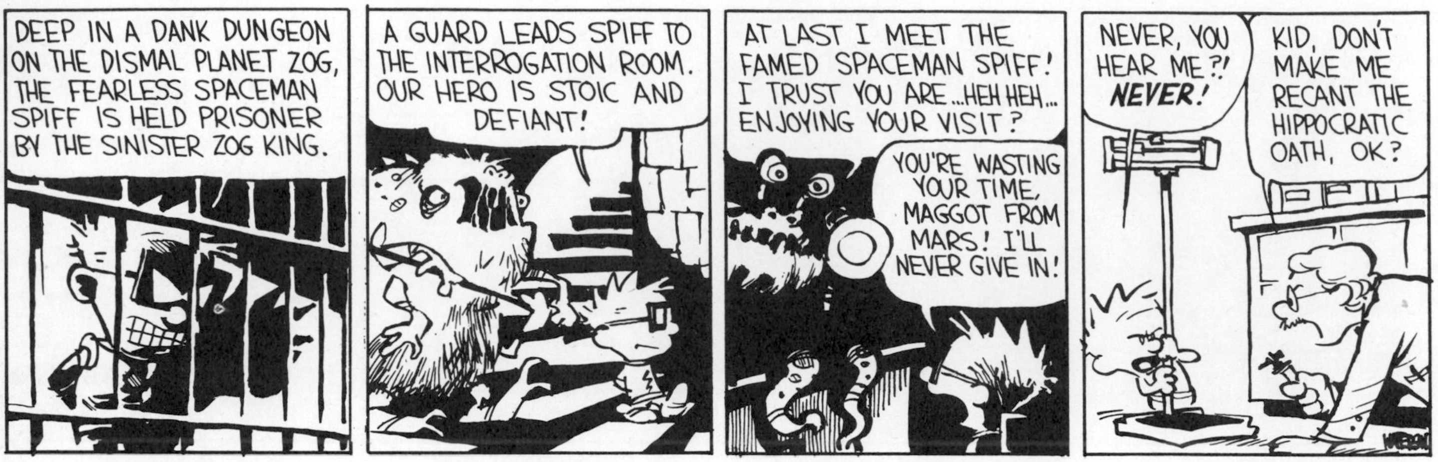
DEEP IN A DANK DUNGEON ON THE DISMAL PLANET ZOG, THE FEARLESS SPACEMAN SPIFF IS HELD PRISONER BY THE SINISTER ZOG KING.
A GUARD LEADS SPIFF TO THE INTERROGATION ROOM. OUR HERO IS STOIC AND DEFIANT!
AT LAST I MEET THE FAMED SPACEMAN SPIFF! I TRUST YOU ARE...HEH HEH... ENJOYING YOUR VISIT?
YOU'RE WASTING YOUR TIME, MAGGOT FROM MARS! I'LL NEVER GIVE IN!
NEVER, YOU HEAR ME?! **NEVER!**
KID, DON'T MAKE ME RECANT THE HIPPOCRATIC OATH, OK?

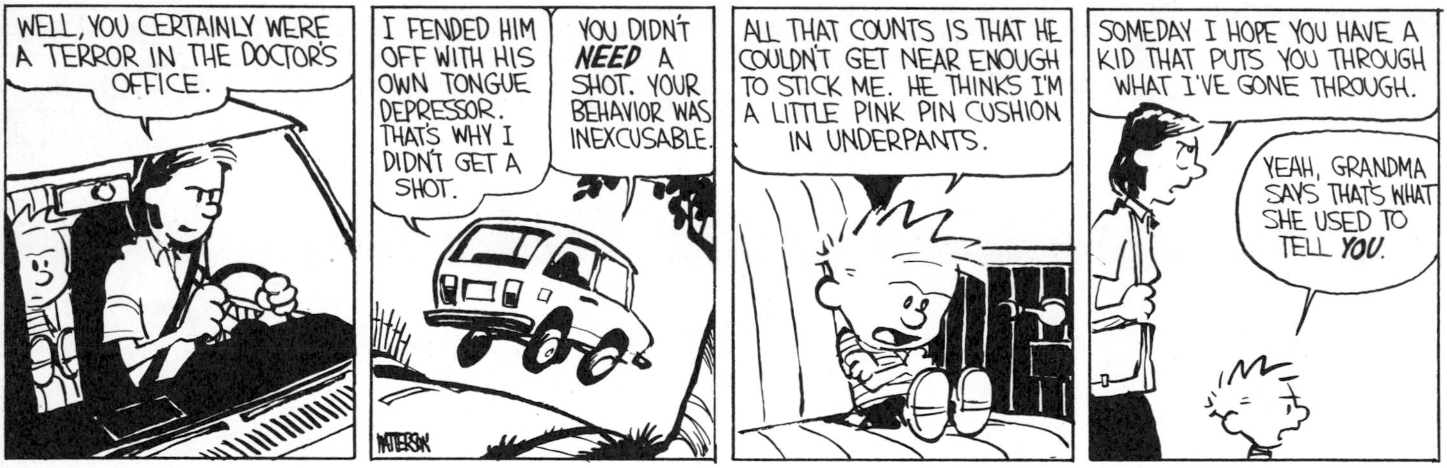
WELL, YOU CERTAINLY WERE A TERROR IN THE DOCTOR'S OFFICE.
I FENDED HIM OFF WITH HIS OWN TONGUE DEPRESSOR. THAT'S WHY I DIDN'T GET A SHOT.
YOU DIDN'T ***NEED*** A SHOT. YOUR BEHAVIOR WAS INEXCUSABLE.
WATTERSON
ALL THAT COUNTS IS THAT HE COULDN'T GET NEAR ENOUGH TO STICK ME. HE THINKS I'M A LITTLE PINK PIN CUSHION IN UNDERPANTS.
SOMEDAY I HOPE YOU HAVE A KID THAT PUTS YOU THROUGH WHAT I'VE GONE THROUGH.
YEAH, GRANDMA SAYS THAT'S WHAT SHE USED TO TELL ***YOU***.

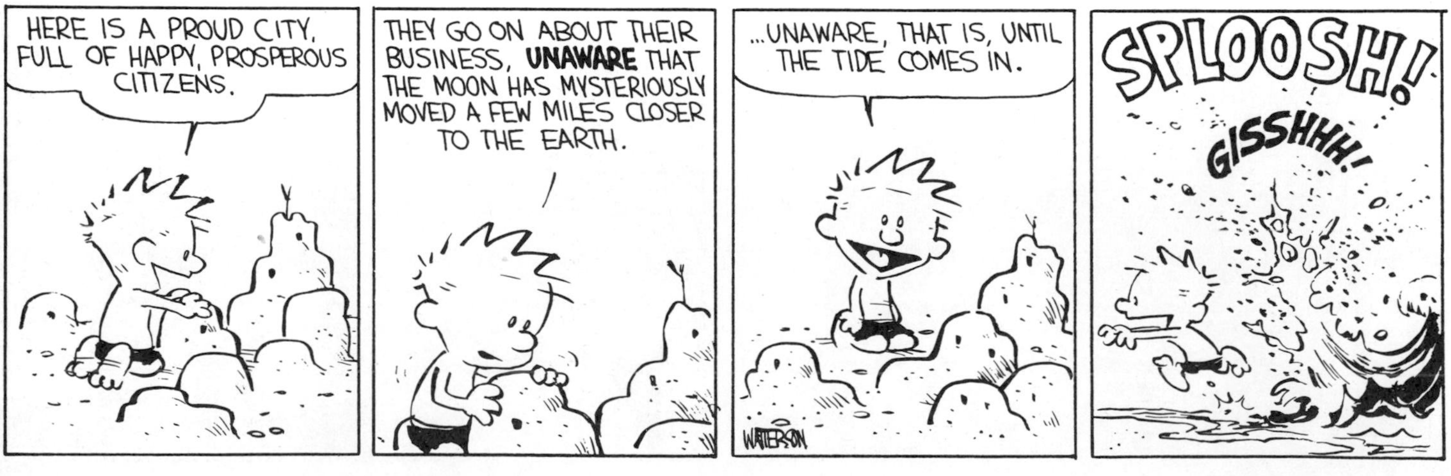
HERE IS A PROUD CITY, FULL OF HAPPY, PROSPEROUS CITIZENS.
THEY GO ON ABOUT THEIR BUSINESS, **UNAWARE** THAT THE MOON HAS MYSTERIOUSLY MOVED A FEW MILES CLOSER TO THE EARTH.
...UNAWARE, THAT IS, UNTIL THE TIDE COMES IN.
WATTERSON
SPLOOSH!
GISSHHH!

# Calvin and Hobbes
by WATTERSON

THE FIRE'S NOT LIGHTING, HUH? CAN I MAKE A SUGGESTION?

GIVE UP ON THAT SISSY LIGHTER FLUID.

CAN'T WE COOK THE HAMBURGERS YET?

THE COALS AREN'T HOT ENOUGH.

BUT I'M HUNGRY! I WANT TO EAT *NOW!*

WELL, YOU'LL JUST HAVE TO WAIT.

YOU KNOW, CALVIN, SOMETIMES THE ANTICIPATION OF SOMETHING IS MORE FUN THAN THE THING ITSELF ONCE YOU GET IT.

HERE WE ARE, IT'S A BEAUTIFUL EVENING. IT'S NICE TO JUST SIT HERE AND LOOK AT THE TREES WHILE WE WAIT FOR THE COALS TO GET HOT, DON'T YOU THINK?

DINNER WILL BE OVER SOON, AND AFTERWARD WE'LL BE DISTRACTED WITH OTHER THINGS TO DO. BUT NOW WE HAVE A FEW MINUTES TO OURSELVES TO ENJOY THE EVENING.

THESE SUMMER DAYS GO BY SO QUICKLY. IT'S GOOD THAT EVERY NOW AND THEN WE HAVE TO WAIT FOR SOMETHING.

SO SHOULD I GO TO McDONALD'S THEN, OR WHAT?

YEAH, I KNOW. YOU THINK YOU'RE GOING TO BE SIX ALL YOUR LIFE.

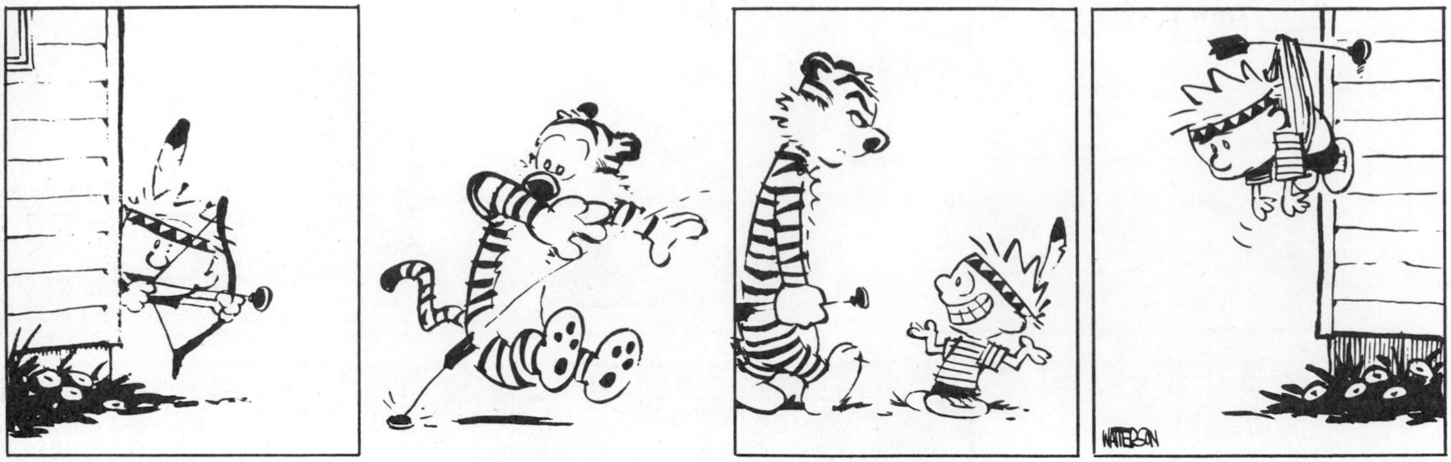
WATTERSON

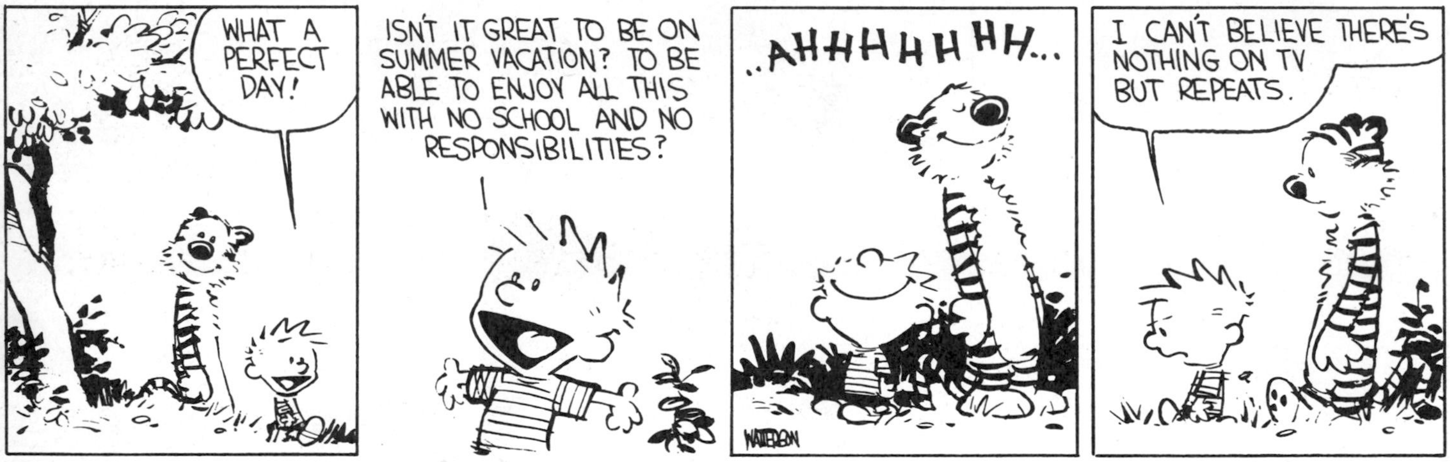
WHAT A PERFECT DAY!
ISN'T IT GREAT TO BE ON SUMMER VACATION? TO BE ABLE TO ENJOY ALL THIS WITH NO SCHOOL AND NO RESPONSIBILITIES?
..AHHHHHHH...
WATTERSON
I CAN'T BELIEVE THERE'S NOTHING ON TV BUT REPEATS.

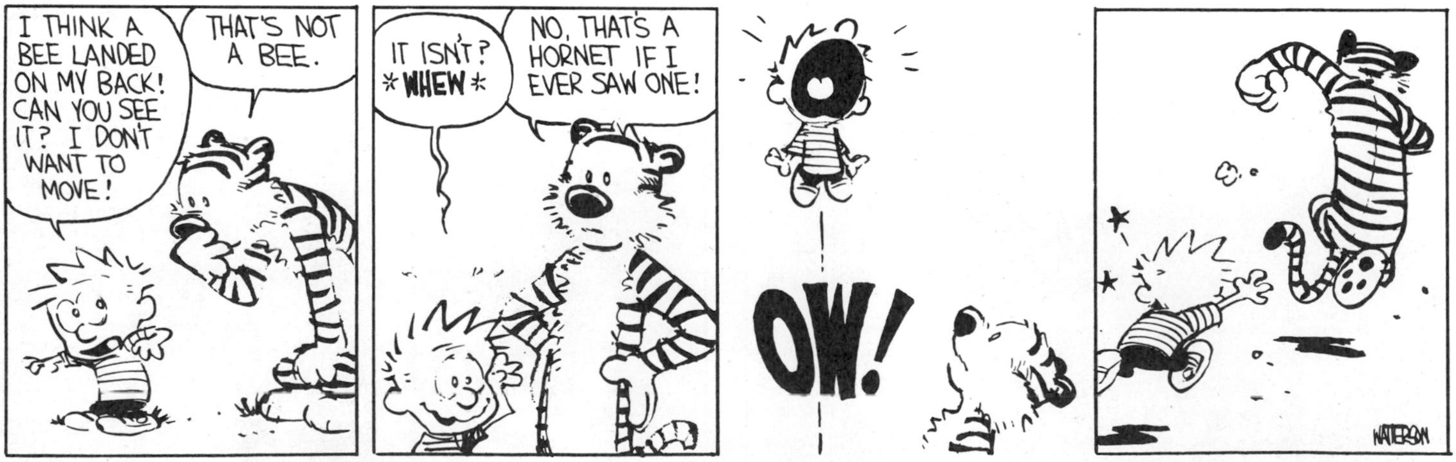
I THINK A BEE LANDED ON MY BACK! CAN YOU SEE IT? I DON'T WANT TO MOVE!
THAT'S NOT A BEE.
IT ISN'T? *WHEW*
NO, THAT'S A HORNET IF I EVER SAW ONE!
OW!
WATTERSON

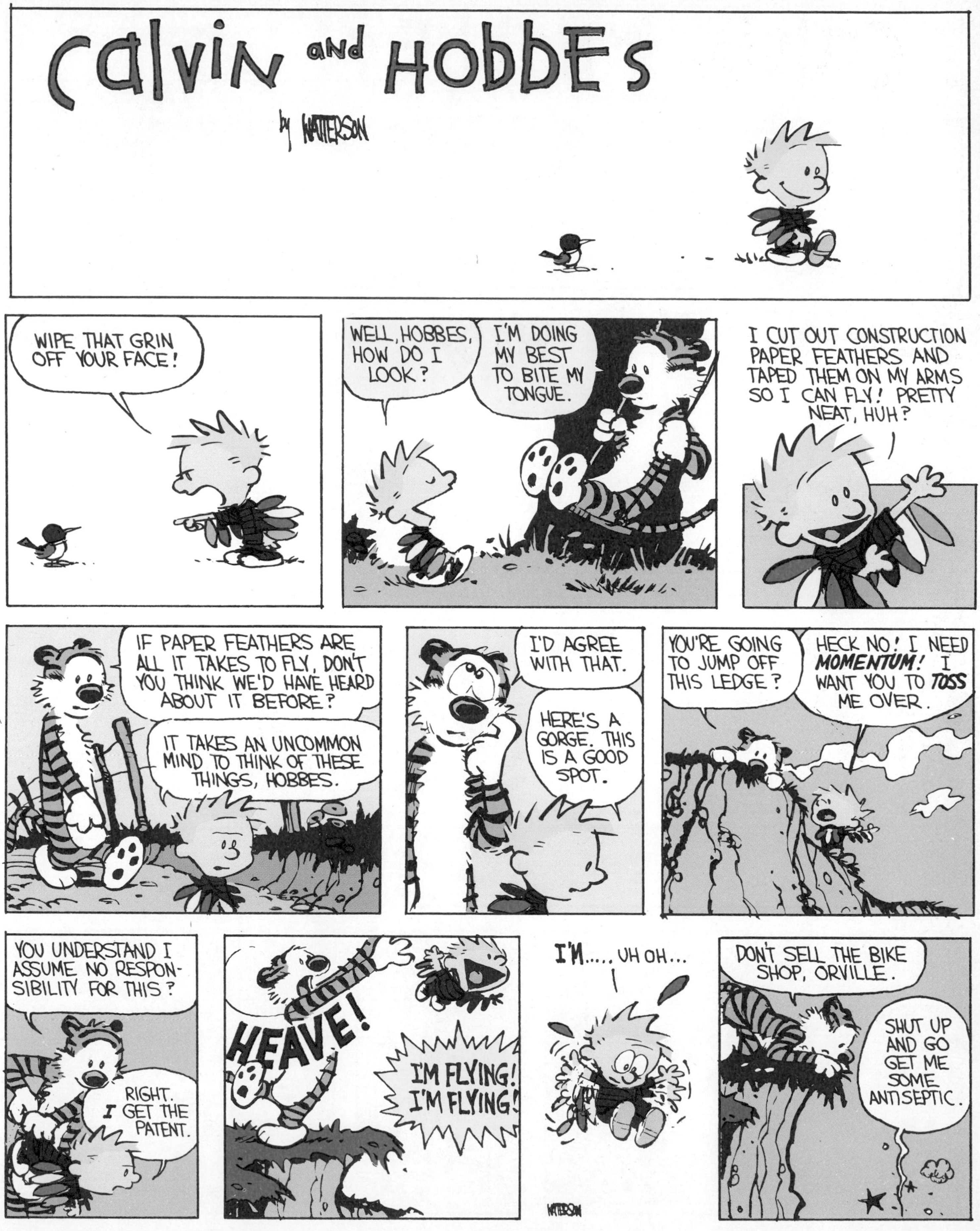
Calvin and HOBBES
by WATTERSON
WIPE THAT GRIN OFF YOUR FACE!
WELL, HOBBES, HOW DO I LOOK?
I'M DOING MY BEST TO BITE MY TONGUE.
I CUT OUT CONSTRUCTION PAPER FEATHERS AND TAPED THEM ON MY ARMS SO I CAN FLY! PRETTY NEAT, HUH?
IF PAPER FEATHERS ARE ALL IT TAKES TO FLY, DON'T YOU THINK WE'D HAVE HEARD ABOUT IT BEFORE?
IT TAKES AN UNCOMMON MIND TO THINK OF THESE THINGS, HOBBES.
I'D AGREE WITH THAT.
HERE'S A GORGE. THIS IS A GOOD SPOT.
YOU'RE GOING TO JUMP OFF THIS LEDGE?
HECK NO! I NEED MOMENTUM! I WANT YOU TO TOSS ME OVER.
YOU UNDERSTAND I ASSUME NO RESPONSIBILITY FOR THIS?
RIGHT. I GET THE PATENT.
HEAVE!
I'M FLYING! I'M FLYING!
I'M...., UH OH...
DON'T SELL THE BIKE SHOP, ORVILLE.
SHUT UP AND GO GET ME SOME ANTISEPTIC.
WATTERSON

49

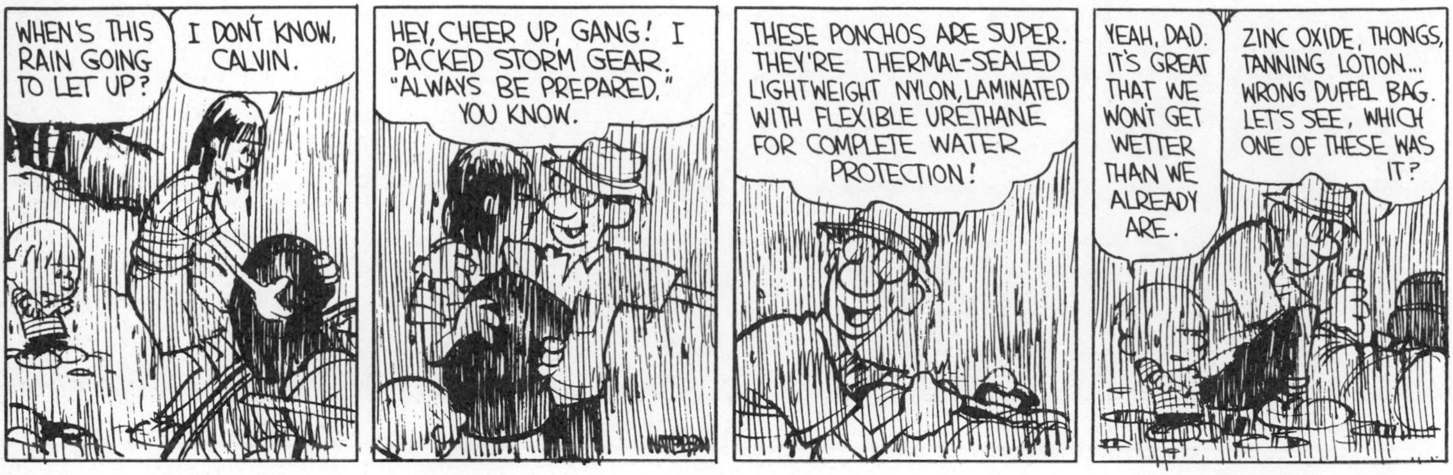
WHEN'S THIS RAIN GOING TO LET UP?
I DON'T KNOW, CALVIN.
HEY, CHEER UP, GANG! I PACKED STORM GEAR. "ALWAYS BE PREPARED," YOU KNOW.
THESE PONCHOS ARE SUPER. THEY'RE THERMAL-SEALED LIGHTWEIGHT NYLON, LAMINATED WITH FLEXIBLE URETHANE FOR COMPLETE WATER PROTECTION!
YEAH, DAD. IT'S GREAT THAT WE WON'T GET WETTER THAN WE ALREADY ARE.
ZINC OXIDE, THONGS, TANNING LOTION... WRONG DUFFEL BAG. LET'S SEE, WHICH ONE OF THESE WAS IT?

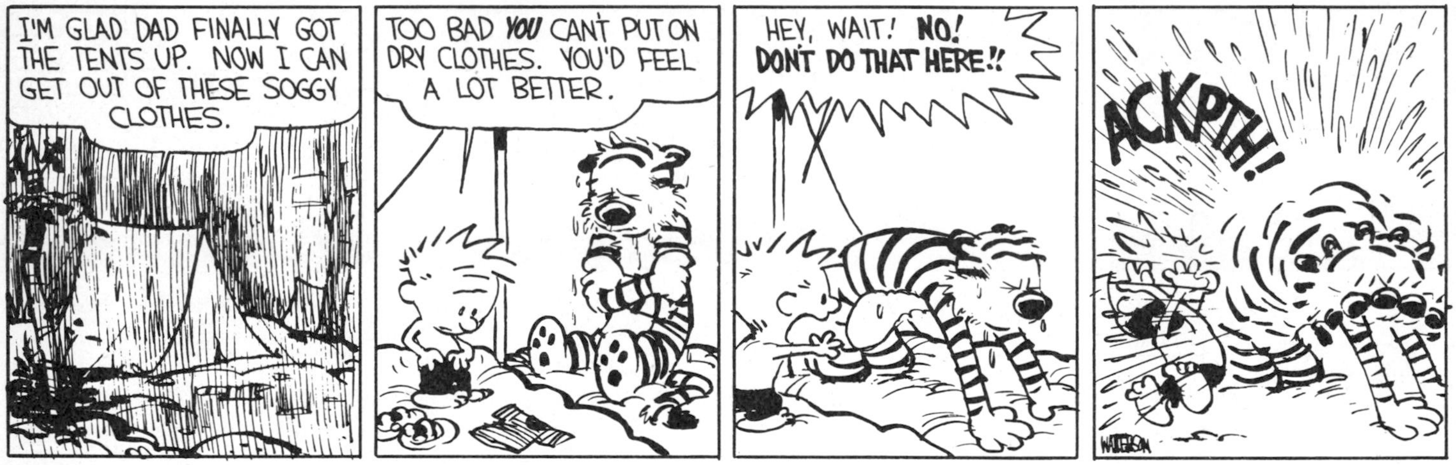
I'M GLAD DAD FINALLY GOT THE TENTS UP. NOW I CAN GET OUT OF THESE SOGGY CLOTHES.
TOO BAD YOU CAN'T PUT ON DRY CLOTHES. YOU'D FEEL A LOT BETTER.
HEY, WAIT! NO! DON'T DO THAT HERE!!
ACKPTH!

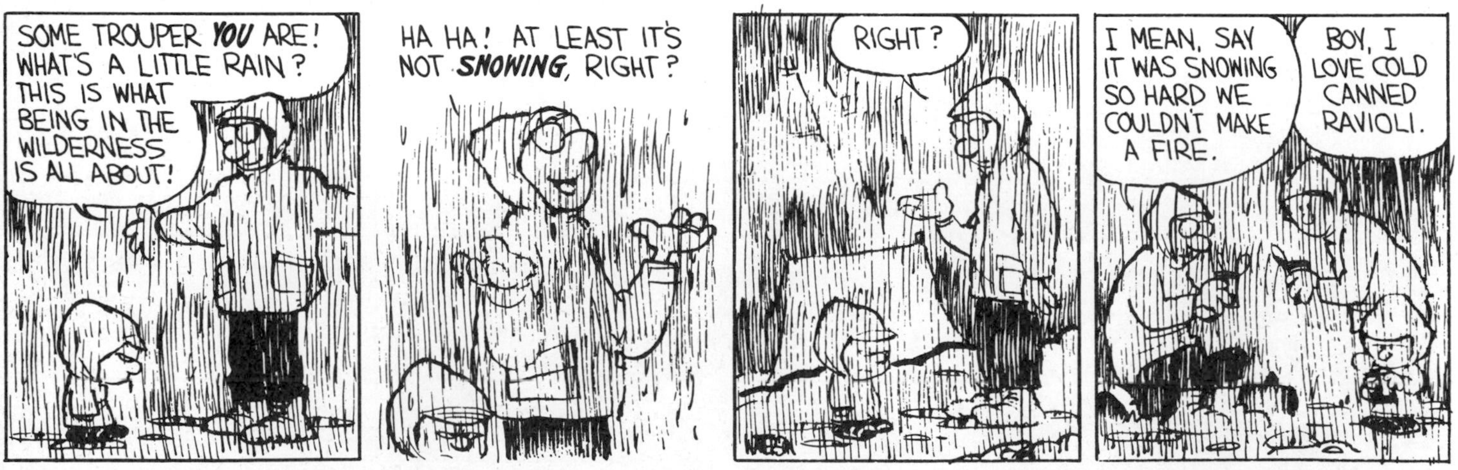
SOME TROUPER YOU ARE! WHAT'S A LITTLE RAIN? THIS IS WHAT BEING IN THE WILDERNESS IS ALL ABOUT!
HA HA! AT LEAST IT'S NOT SNOWING, RIGHT?
RIGHT?
I MEAN, SAY IT WAS SNOWING SO HARD WE COULDN'T MAKE A FIRE.
BOY, I LOVE COLD CANNED RAVIOLI.

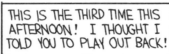

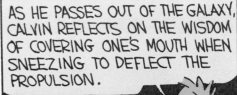

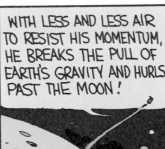

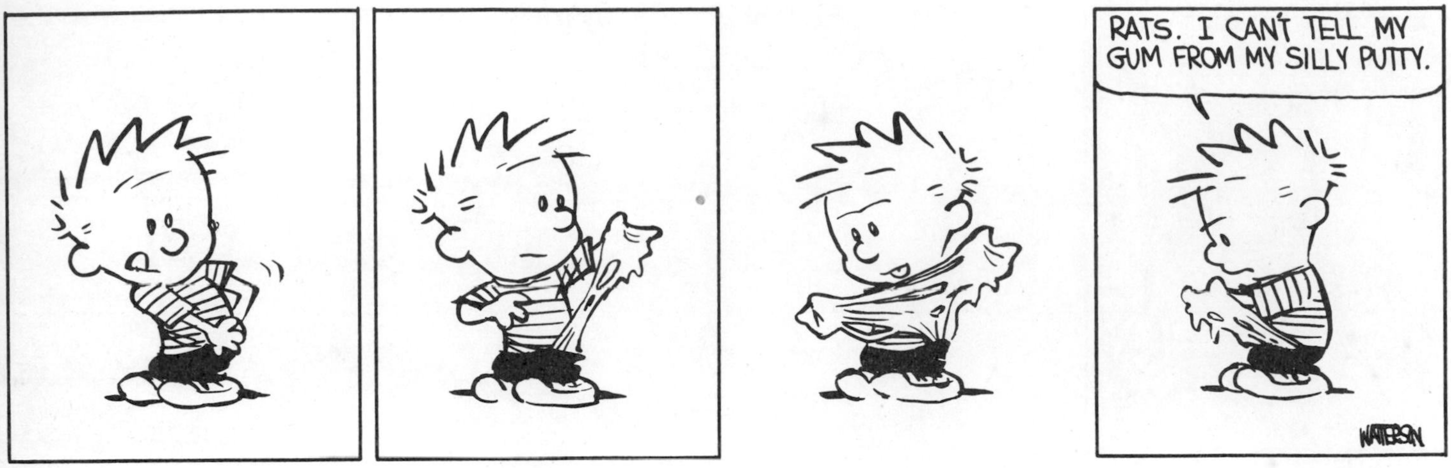
RATS. I CAN'T TELL MY GUM FROM MY SILLY PUTTY.
WATERSON

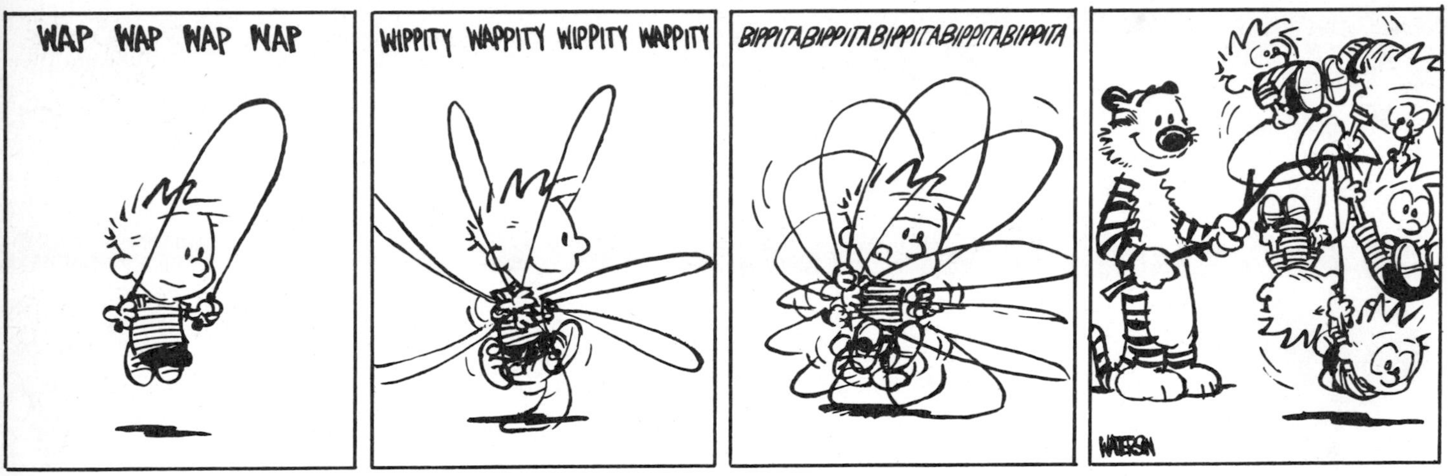
WAP WAP WAP WAP
WIPPITY WAPPITY WIPPITY WAPPITY
BIPPITABIPPITABIPPITABIPPITABIPPITA
WATERSON

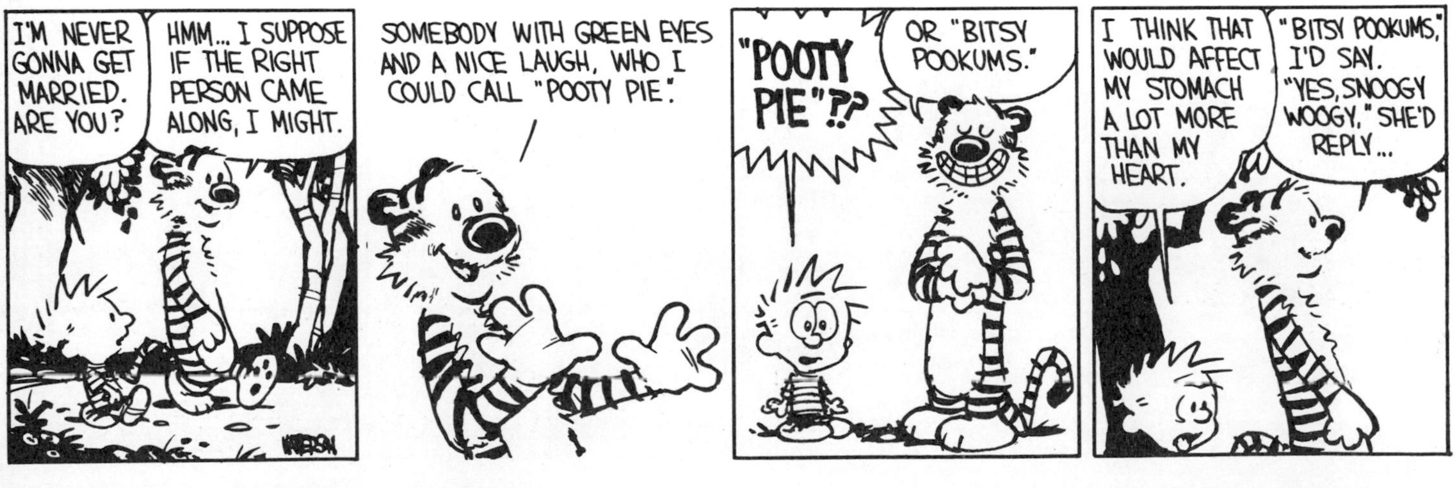
I'M NEVER GONNA GET MARRIED. ARE YOU?
HMM... I SUPPOSE IF THE RIGHT PERSON CAME ALONG, I MIGHT.
WATERSON
SOMEBODY WITH GREEN EYES AND A NICE LAUGH, WHO I COULD CALL "POOTY PIE."
"POOTY PIE"?!?
OR "BITSY POOKUMS."
I THINK THAT WOULD AFFECT MY STOMACH A LOT MORE THAN MY HEART.
"BITSY POOKUMS," I'D SAY. "YES, SNOOGY WOOGY," SHE'D REPLY...

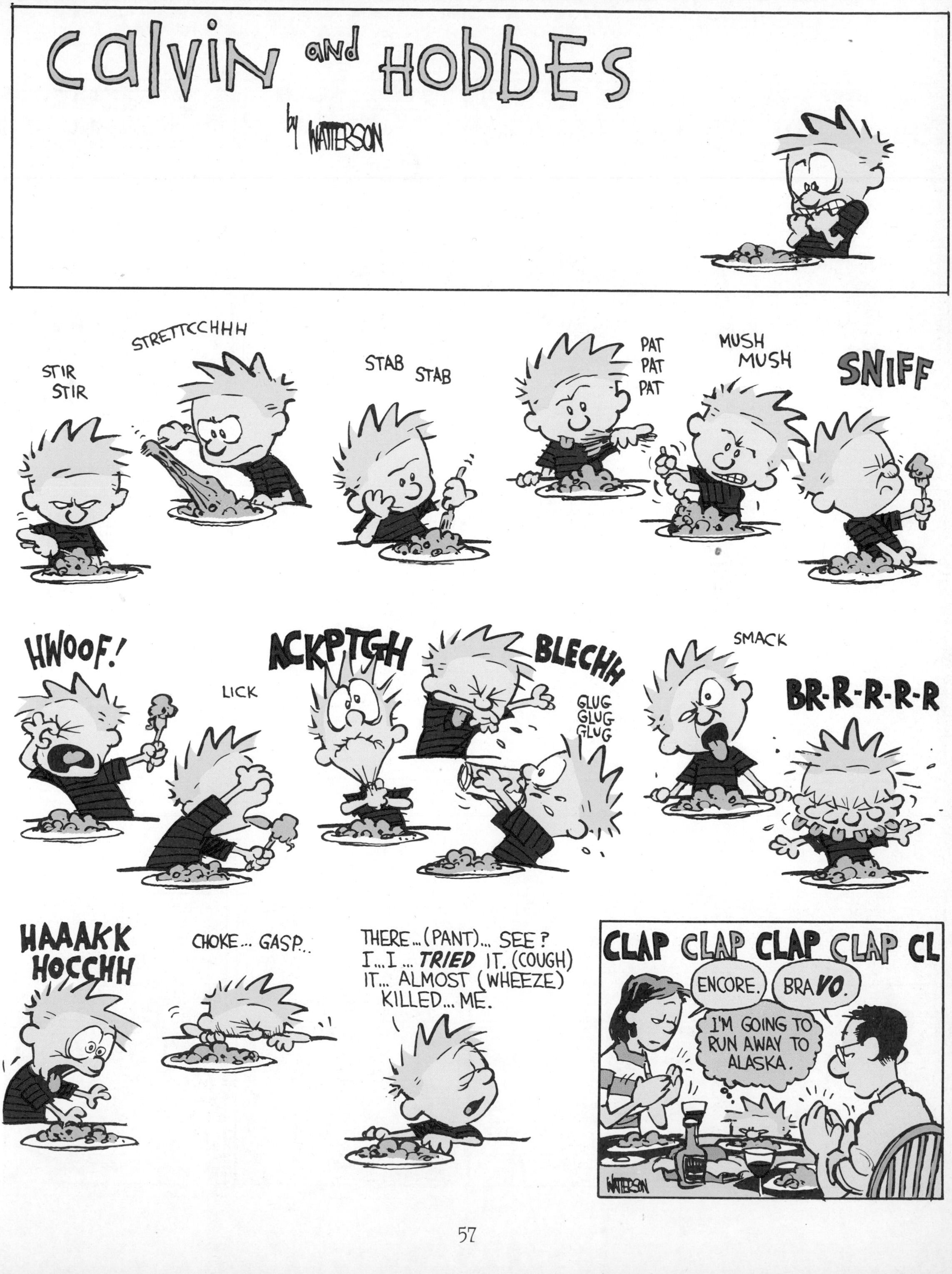
Calvin and HOBBES
by WATTERSON
STIR STIR
STRETTCCHHH
STAB STAB
PAT PAT PAT
MUSH MUSH
SNIFF
HWOOF!
LICK
ACKPTGH
BLECHH
GLUG GLUG GLUG
SMACK
BR-R-R-R-R
HAAAKK HOCCHH
CHOKE... GASP...
THERE... (PANT)... SEE? I...I ... TRIED IT. (COUGH) IT... ALMOST (WHEEZE) KILLED... ME.
CLAP CLAP CLAP CLAP CL
ENCORE.
BRAVO.
I'M GOING TO RUN AWAY TO ALASKA.
WATTERSON

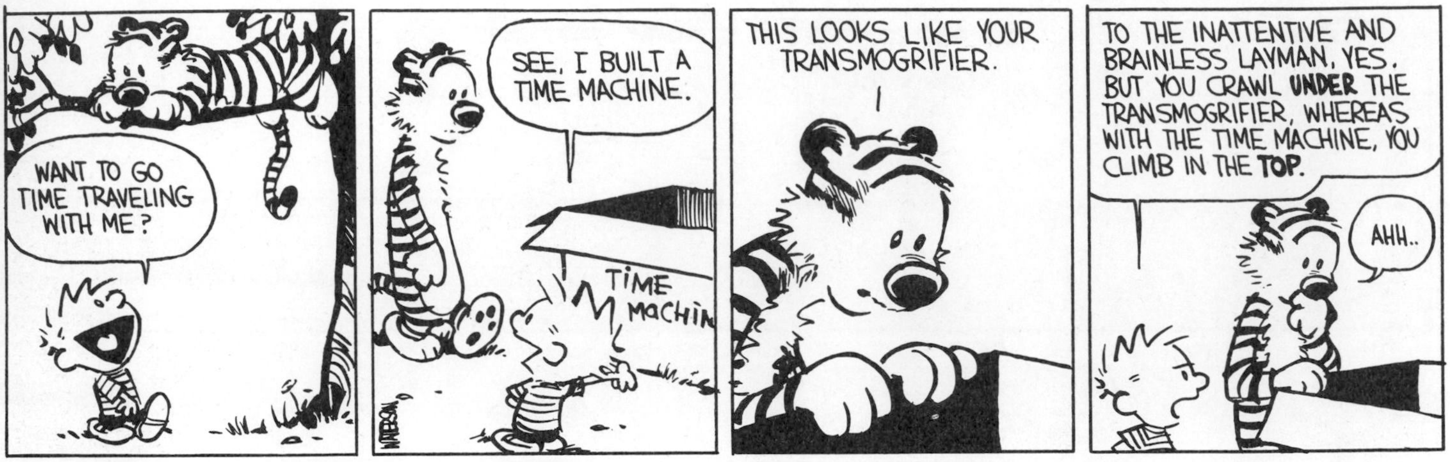
WANT TO GO TIME TRAVELING WITH ME?
SEE, I BUILT A TIME MACHINE.
TIME MACHIN
THIS LOOKS LIKE YOUR TRANSMOGRIFIER.
TO THE INATTENTIVE AND BRAINLESS LAYMAN, YES. BUT YOU CRAWL **UNDER** THE TRANSMOGRIFIER, WHEREAS WITH THE TIME MACHINE, YOU CLIMB IN THE **TOP**.
AHH..

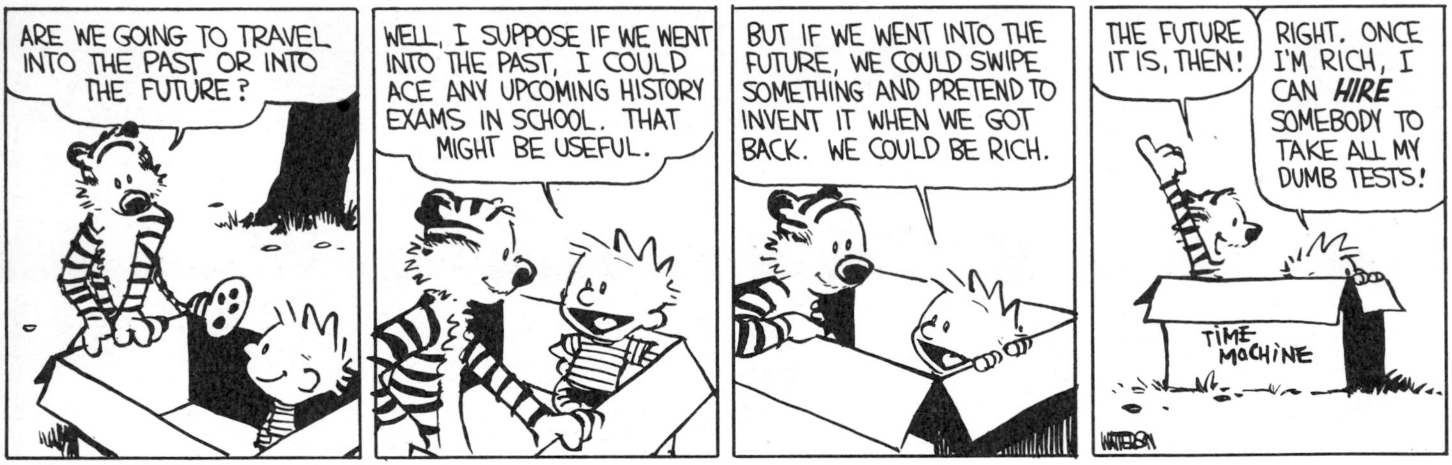
ARE WE GOING TO TRAVEL INTO THE PAST OR INTO THE FUTURE?
WELL, I SUPPOSE IF WE WENT INTO THE PAST, I COULD ACE ANY UPCOMING HISTORY EXAMS IN SCHOOL. THAT MIGHT BE USEFUL.
BUT IF WE WENT INTO THE FUTURE, WE COULD SWIPE SOMETHING AND PRETEND TO INVENT IT WHEN WE GOT BACK. WE COULD BE RICH.
THE FUTURE IT IS, THEN!
RIGHT. ONCE I'M RICH, I CAN ***HIRE*** SOMEBODY TO TAKE ALL MY DUMB TESTS!
TIME MACHINE

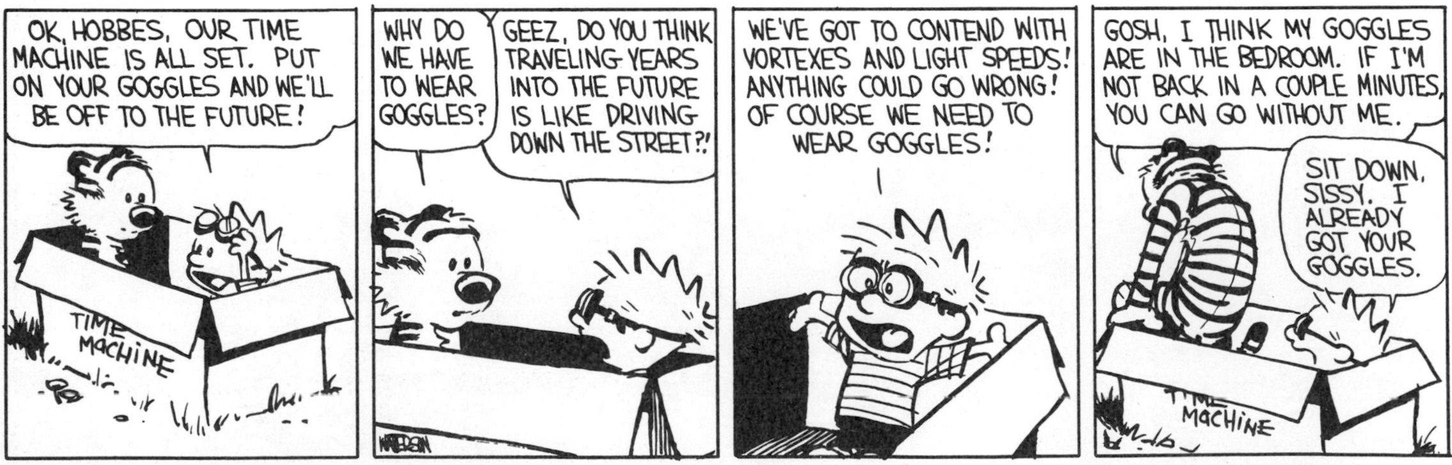
OK, HOBBES, OUR TIME MACHINE IS ALL SET. PUT ON YOUR GOGGLES AND WE'LL BE OFF TO THE FUTURE!
TIME MACHINE
WHY DO WE HAVE TO WEAR GOGGLES?
GEEZ, DO YOU THINK TRAVELING YEARS INTO THE FUTURE IS LIKE DRIVING DOWN THE STREET?!
WE'VE GOT TO CONTEND WITH VORTEXES AND LIGHT SPEEDS! ANYTHING COULD GO WRONG! OF COURSE WE NEED TO WEAR GOGGLES!
GOSH, I THINK MY GOGGLES ARE IN THE BEDROOM. IF I'M NOT BACK IN A COUPLE MINUTES, YOU CAN GO WITHOUT ME.
SIT DOWN, SISSY. I ALREADY GOT YOUR GOGGLES.
MACHINE

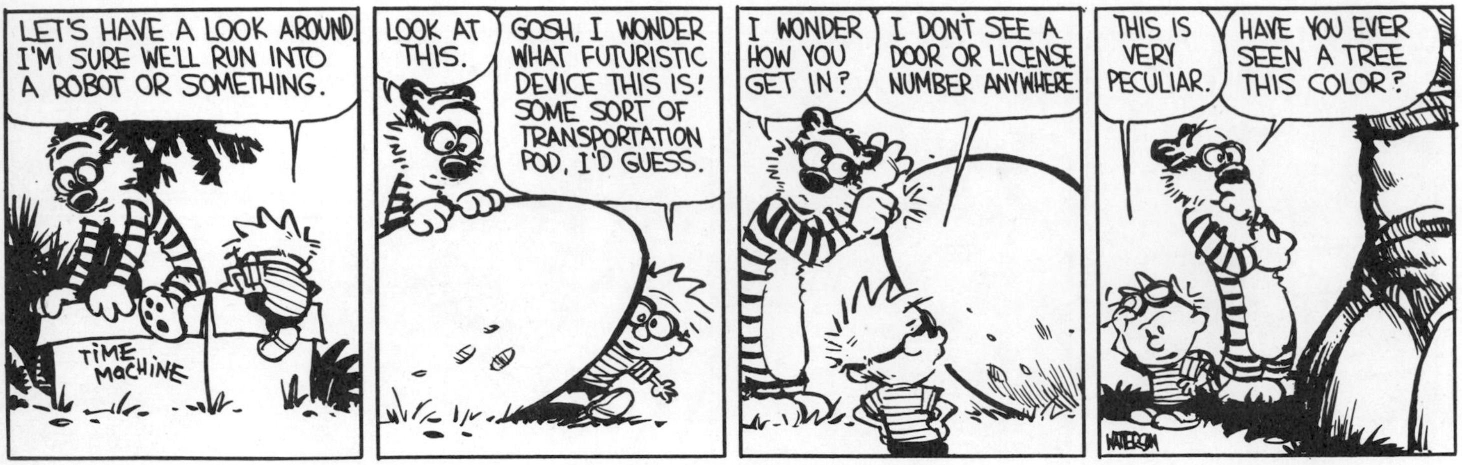
LET'S HAVE A LOOK AROUND. I'M SURE WE'LL RUN INTO A ROBOT OR SOMETHING.
TIME MACHINE
LOOK AT THIS.
GOSH, I WONDER WHAT FUTURISTIC DEVICE THIS IS! SOME SORT OF TRANSPORTATION POD, I'D GUESS.
I WONDER HOW YOU GET IN?
I DON'T SEE A DOOR OR LICENSE NUMBER ANYWHERE.
THIS IS VERY PECULIAR.
HAVE YOU EVER SEEN A TREE THIS COLOR?
WATTERSON

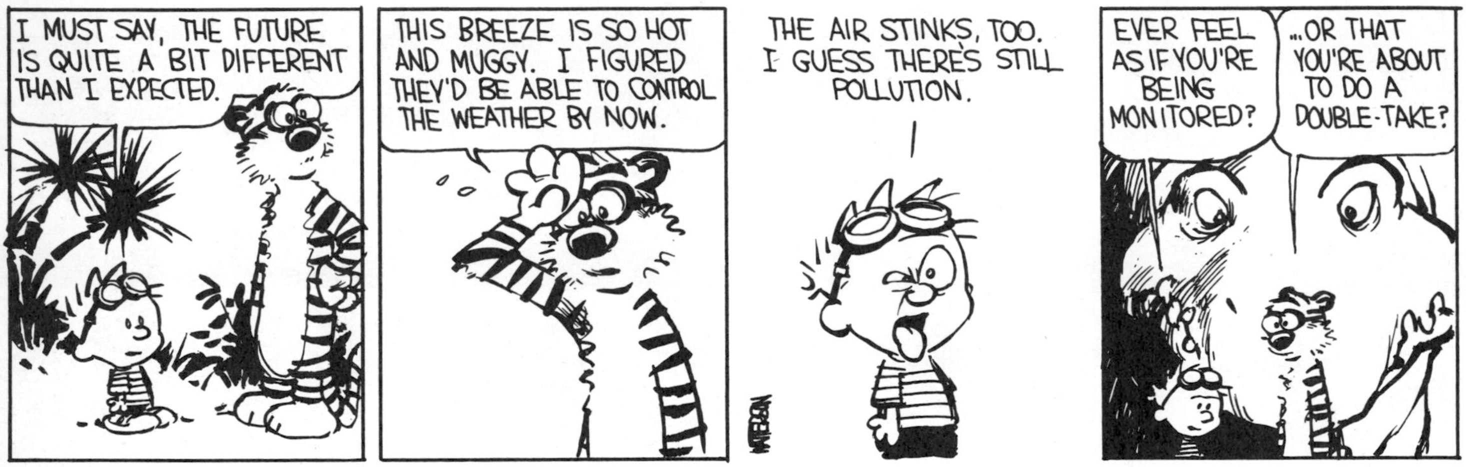
I MUST SAY, THE FUTURE IS QUITE A BIT DIFFERENT THAN I EXPECTED.
THIS BREEZE IS SO HOT AND MUGGY. I FIGURED THEY'D BE ABLE TO CONTROL THE WEATHER BY NOW.
THE AIR STINKS, TOO. I GUESS THERE'S STILL POLLUTION.
WATTERSON
EVER FEEL AS IF YOU'RE BEING MONITORED?
...OR THAT YOU'RE ABOUT TO DO A DOUBLE-TAKE?

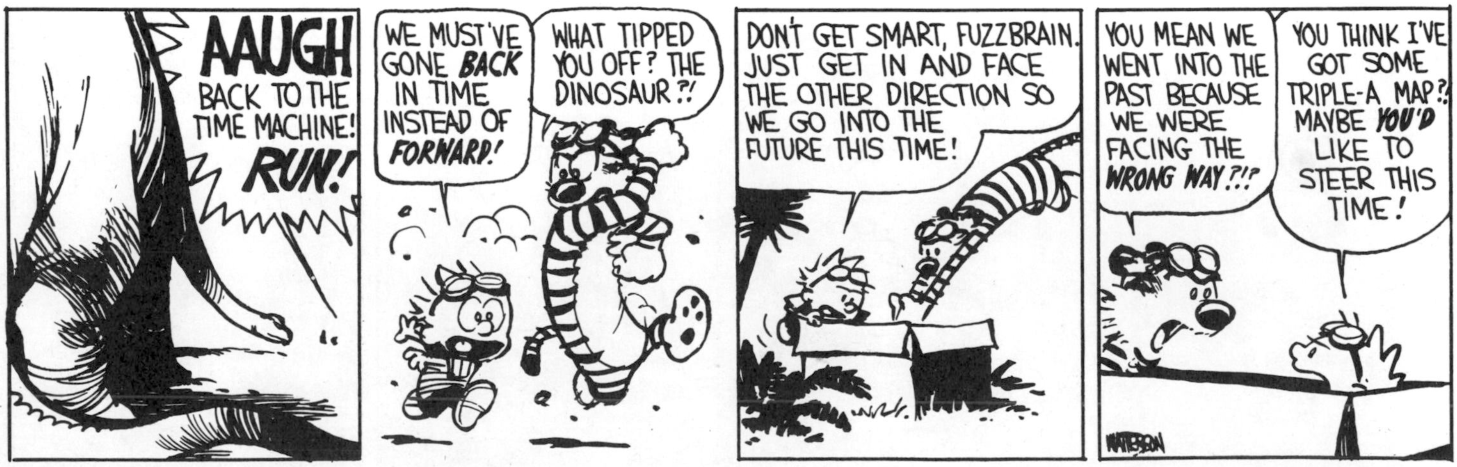
AAUGH
BACK TO THE TIME MACHINE! RUN!
WE MUST'VE GONE BACK IN TIME INSTEAD OF FORWARD!
WHAT TIPPED YOU OFF? THE DINOSAUR?!
DON'T GET SMART, FUZZBRAIN. JUST GET IN AND FACE THE OTHER DIRECTION SO WE GO INTO THE FUTURE THIS TIME!
YOU MEAN WE WENT INTO THE PAST BECAUSE WE WERE FACING THE WRONG WAY?!?
YOU THINK I'VE GOT SOME TRIPLE-A MAP?! MAYBE YOU'D LIKE TO STEER THIS TIME!
WATTERSON

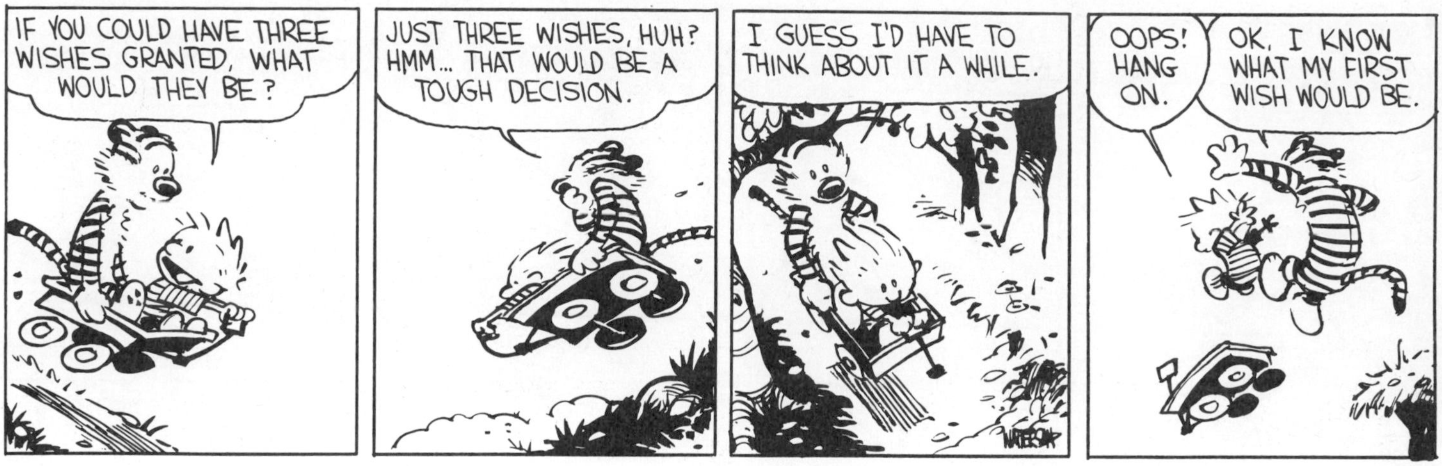
IF YOU COULD HAVE THREE WISHES GRANTED, WHAT WOULD THEY BE?
JUST THREE WISHES, HUH? HMM... THAT WOULD BE A TOUGH DECISION.
I GUESS I'D HAVE TO THINK ABOUT IT A WHILE.
OOPS! HANG ON.
OK, I KNOW WHAT MY FIRST WISH WOULD BE.

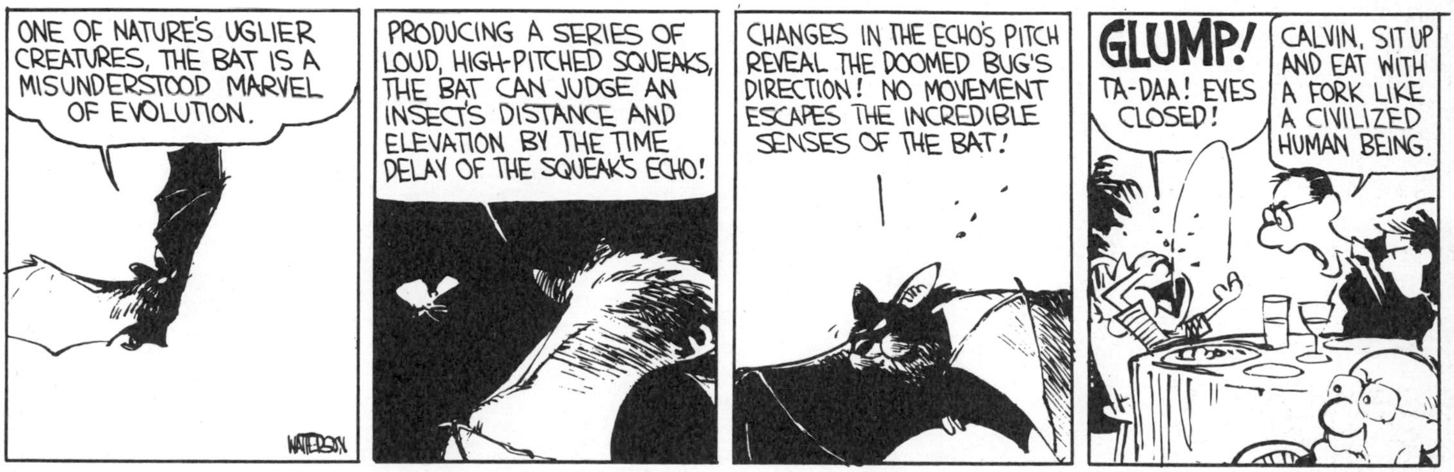
ONE OF NATURE'S UGLIER CREATURES, THE BAT IS A MISUNDERSTOOD MARVEL OF EVOLUTION.
PRODUCING A SERIES OF LOUD, HIGH-PITCHED SQUEAKS, THE BAT CAN JUDGE AN INSECT'S DISTANCE AND ELEVATION BY THE TIME DELAY OF THE SQUEAK'S ECHO!
CHANGES IN THE ECHO'S PITCH REVEAL THE DOOMED BUG'S DIRECTION! NO MOVEMENT ESCAPES THE INCREDIBLE SENSES OF THE BAT!
GLUMP!
TA-DAA! EYES CLOSED!
CALVIN, SIT UP AND EAT WITH A FORK LIKE A CIVILIZED HUMAN BEING.

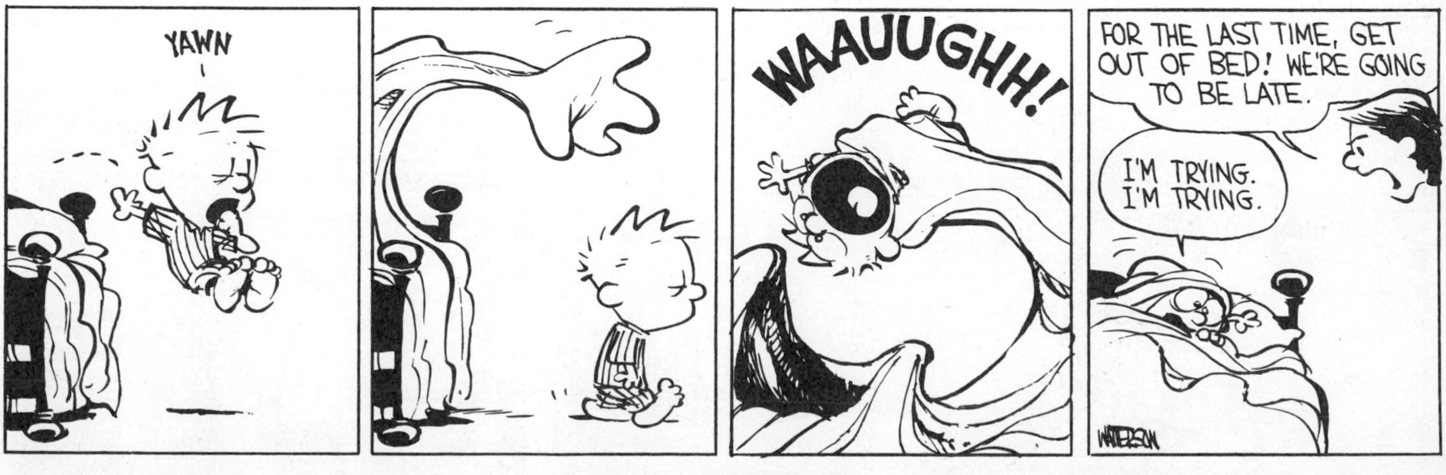
YAWN
WAAUUGHH!
FOR THE LAST TIME, GET OUT OF BED! WE'RE GOING TO BE LATE.
I'M TRYING. I'M TRYING.

MOM WANTS ME TO CLEAN MY ROOM. THIS IS THE LAST STRAW!

I DON'T HAVE TO PUT UP WITH THIS TOTALITARIANISM! I'M SECEDING!

GEE, CAN YOU SECEDE FROM YOUR OWN FAMILY?

WHY NOT?! I NEVER SIGNED UP FOR THIS GROUP! I WASN'T EVEN CONSULTED!

THE ONLY REASON MOM AND DAD ARE MY PARENTS IS BECAUSE I WAS *BORN* TO THEM!

A BIOLOGICAL CONSPIRACY, HUH?

WE CAN LIVE ANYWHERE WE WANT TO NOW THAT WE'RE SECEDING FROM THE FAMILY!

WHERE DO YOU WANT TO GO? THE SAHARA? ANTARCTICA?

HOW ARE WE GOING TO GET TO ANY OF *THOSE* PLACES? WE DON'T EVEN HAVE A CAR!

OK DAD, FOR *THIS* AMAZING TRICK I'LL NEED AN ORDINARY AMERICAN EXPRESS CARD. NOW CLOSE YOUR EYES...

HOBBES AND I ARE SECEDING FROM THIS FAMILY, MOM.

OH REALLY?

YEP. WE'RE TAKING MY SLED AND MOVING TO THE YUKON.

WELL, *THAT'S* A LONG WAY AWAY.

I KNOW. HERE'S A LIST OF SANDWICHES AND SUPPLIES WE'LL NEED.

WHY SHOULD I DO ALL THIS IF YOU'RE SECEDING FROM THE FAMILY?

WE HAVEN'T SECEDED *YET!* GEEZ, WHAT KIND OF MOM *ARE* YOU?

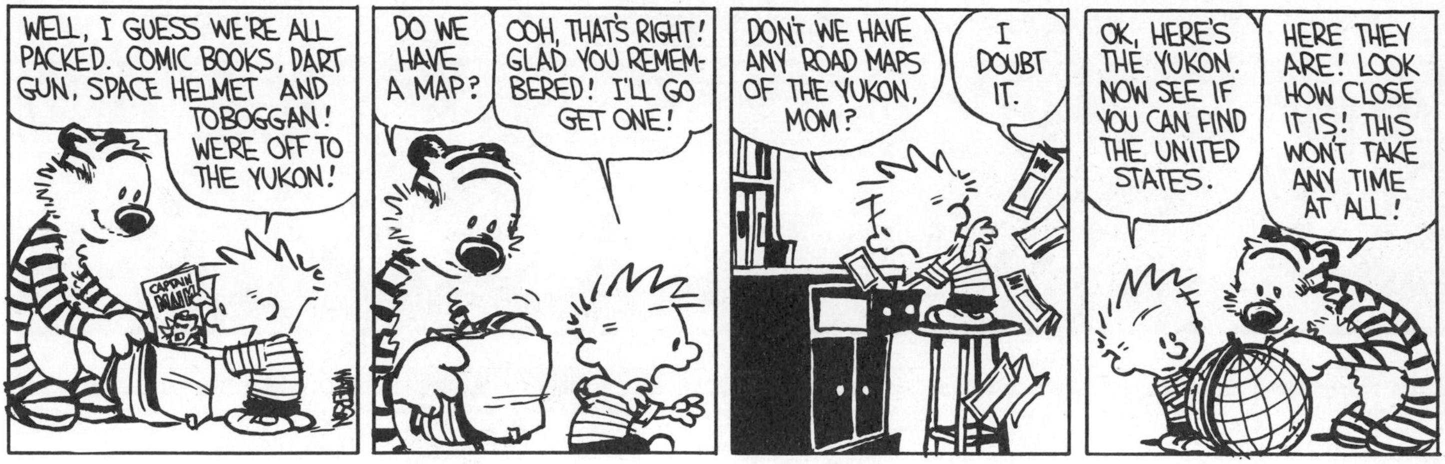
WELL, I GUESS WE'RE ALL PACKED. COMIC BOOKS, DART GUN, SPACE HELMET AND TOBOGGAN! WE'RE OFF TO THE YUKON!
DO WE HAVE A MAP?
OOH, THAT'S RIGHT! GLAD YOU REMEMBERED! I'LL GO GET ONE!
DON'T WE HAVE ANY ROAD MAPS OF THE YUKON, MOM?
I DOUBT IT.
OK, HERE'S THE YUKON. NOW SEE IF YOU CAN FIND THE UNITED STATES.
HERE THEY ARE! LOOK HOW CLOSE IT IS! THIS WON'T TAKE ANY TIME AT ALL!

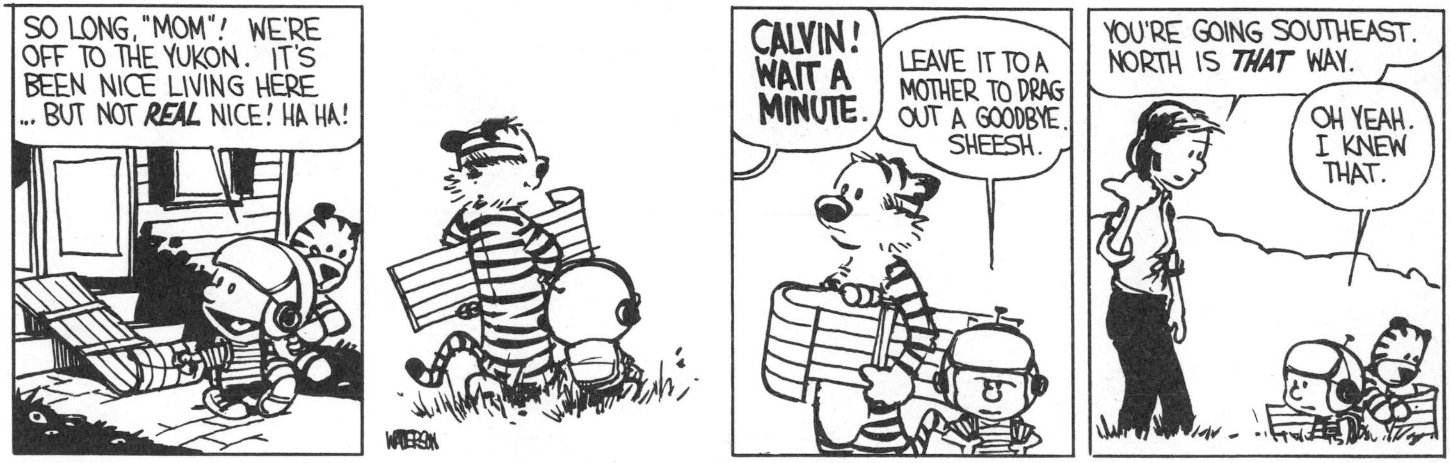
SO LONG, "MOM"! WE'RE OFF TO THE YUKON. IT'S BEEN NICE LIVING HERE ... BUT NOT *REAL* NICE! HA HA!
**CALVIN! WAIT A MINUTE.**
LEAVE IT TO A MOTHER TO DRAG OUT A GOODBYE. SHEESH.
YOU'RE GOING SOUTHEAST. NORTH IS *THAT* WAY.
OH YEAH. I KNEW THAT.

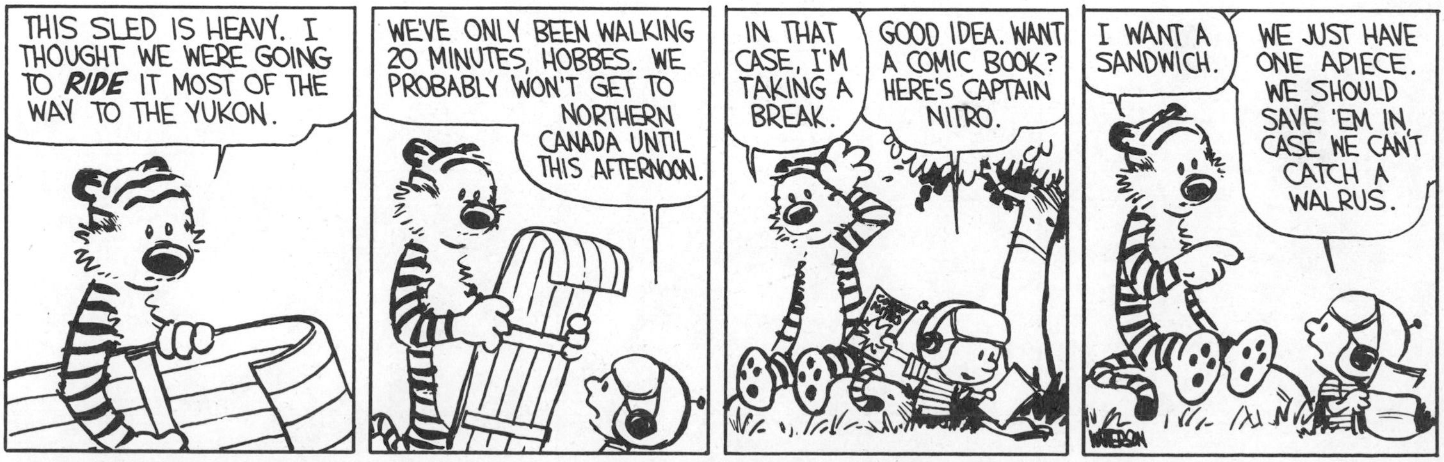
THIS SLED IS HEAVY. I THOUGHT WE WERE GOING TO *RIDE* IT MOST OF THE WAY TO THE YUKON.
WE'VE ONLY BEEN WALKING 20 MINUTES, HOBBES. WE PROBABLY WON'T GET TO NORTHERN CANADA UNTIL THIS AFTERNOON.
IN THAT CASE, I'M TAKING A BREAK.
GOOD IDEA. WANT A COMIC BOOK? HERE'S CAPTAIN NITRO.
I WANT A SANDWICH.
WE JUST HAVE ONE APIECE. WE SHOULD SAVE 'EM IN CASE WE CAN'T CATCH A WALRUS.

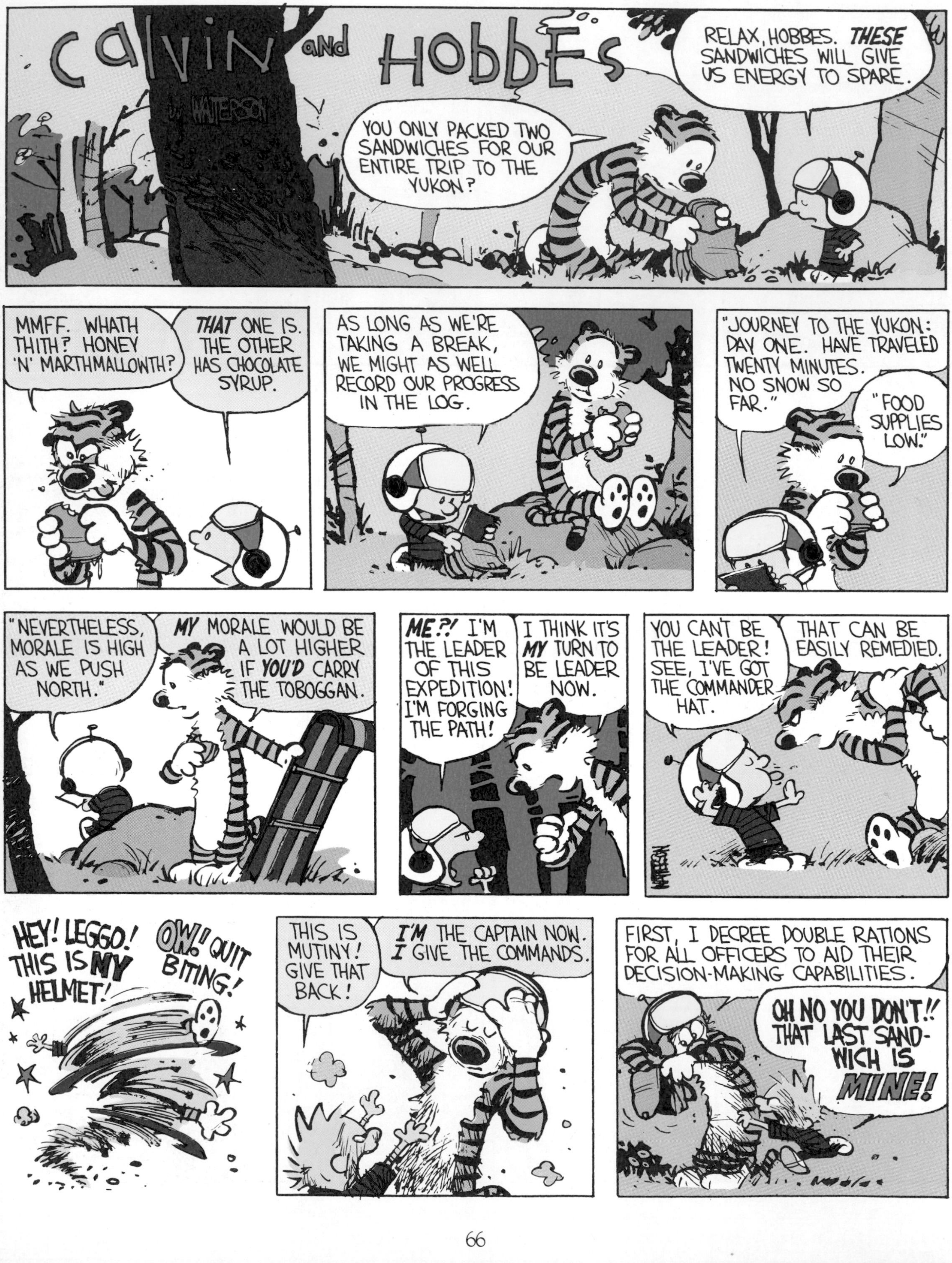
Calvin and HOBBES
by WATTERSON
YOU ONLY PACKED TWO SANDWICHES FOR OUR ENTIRE TRIP TO THE YUKON?
RELAX, HOBBES. THESE SANDWICHES WILL GIVE US ENERGY TO SPARE.
MMFF. WHATH THITH? HONEY 'N' MARTHMALLOWTH?
THAT ONE IS. THE OTHER HAS CHOCOLATE SYRUP.
AS LONG AS WE'RE TAKING A BREAK, WE MIGHT AS WELL RECORD OUR PROGRESS IN THE LOG.
"JOURNEY TO THE YUKON: DAY ONE. HAVE TRAVELED TWENTY MINUTES. NO SNOW SO FAR."
"FOOD SUPPLIES LOW."
"NEVERTHELESS, MORALE IS HIGH AS WE PUSH NORTH."
MY MORALE WOULD BE A LOT HIGHER IF YOU'D CARRY THE TOBOGGAN.
ME?! I'M THE LEADER OF THIS EXPEDITION! I'M FORGING THE PATH!
I THINK IT'S MY TURN TO BE LEADER NOW.
YOU CAN'T BE THE LEADER! SEE, I'VE GOT THE COMMANDER HAT.
THAT CAN BE EASILY REMEDIED.
WATTERSON
HEY! LEGGO! THIS IS MY HELMET!
OW! QUIT BITING!
THIS IS MUTINY! GIVE THAT BACK!
I'M THE CAPTAIN NOW. I GIVE THE COMMANDS.
FIRST, I DECREE DOUBLE RATIONS FOR ALL OFFICERS TO AID THEIR DECISION-MAKING CAPABILITIES.
OH NO YOU DON'T!! THAT LAST SANDWICH IS MINE!

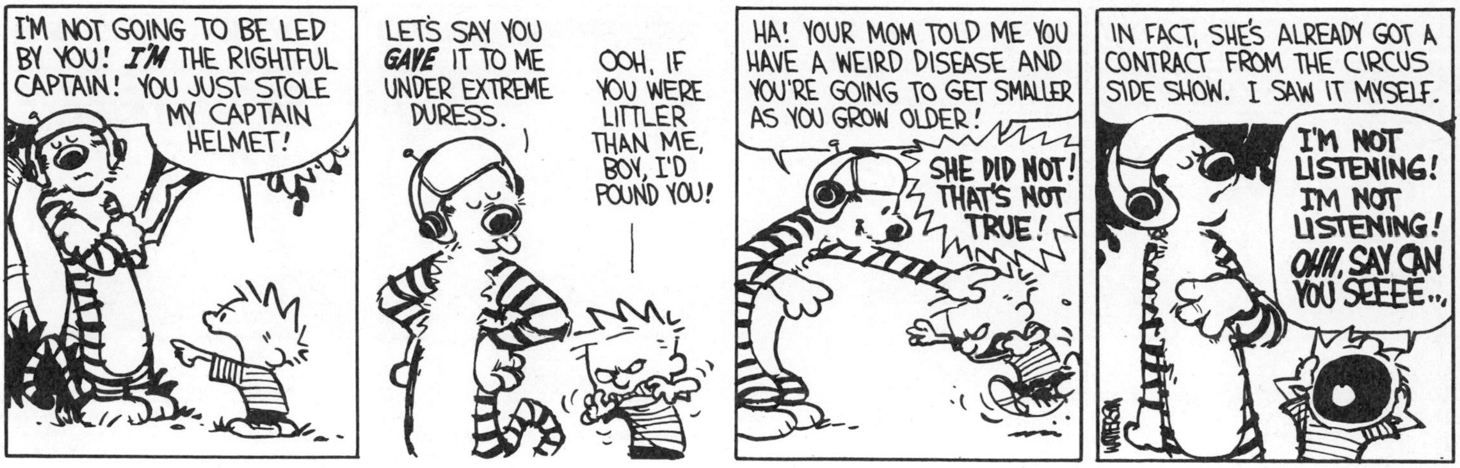
I'M NOT GOING TO BE LED BY YOU! I'M THE RIGHTFUL CAPTAIN! YOU JUST STOLE MY CAPTAIN HELMET!
LET'S SAY YOU GAVE IT TO ME UNDER EXTREME DURESS.
OOH, IF YOU WERE LITTLER THAN ME, BOY, I'D POUND YOU!
HA! YOUR MOM TOLD ME YOU HAVE A WEIRD DISEASE AND YOU'RE GOING TO GET SMALLER AS YOU GROW OLDER!
SHE DID NOT! THAT'S NOT TRUE!
IN FACT, SHE'S ALREADY GOT A CONTRACT FROM THE CIRCUS SIDE SHOW. I SAW IT MYSELF.
I'M NOT LISTENING! I'M NOT LISTENING! OHH, SAY CAN YOU SEEEE...

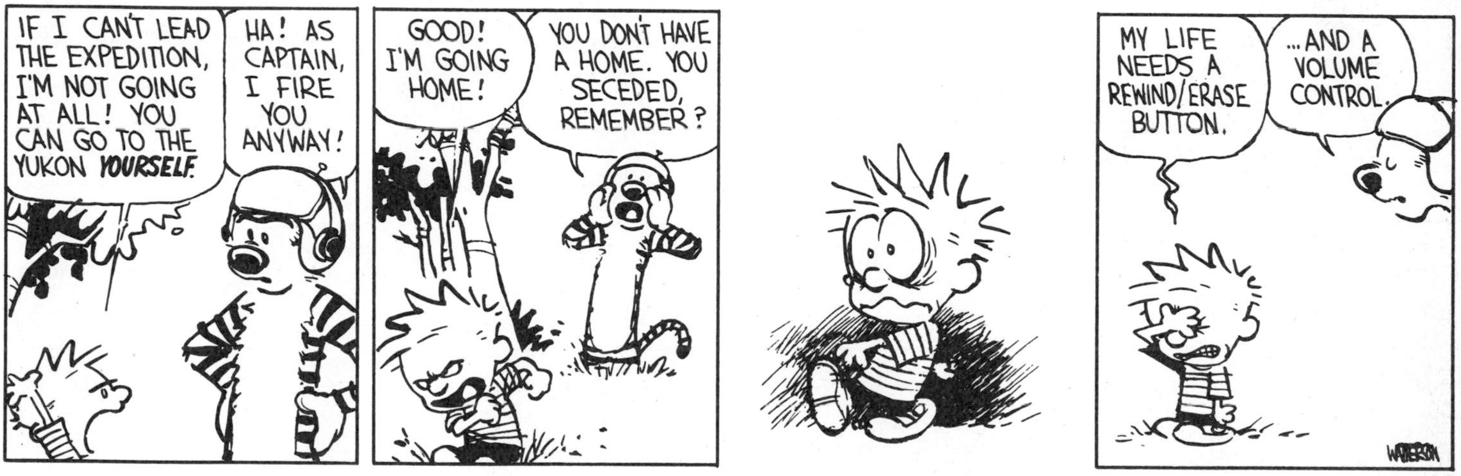
IF I CAN'T LEAD THE EXPEDITION, I'M NOT GOING AT ALL! YOU CAN GO TO THE YUKON YOURSELF.
HA! AS CAPTAIN, I FIRE YOU ANYWAY!
GOOD! I'M GOING HOME!
YOU DON'T HAVE A HOME. YOU SECEDED, REMEMBER?
MY LIFE NEEDS A REWIND/ERASE BUTTON.
...AND A VOLUME CONTROL.

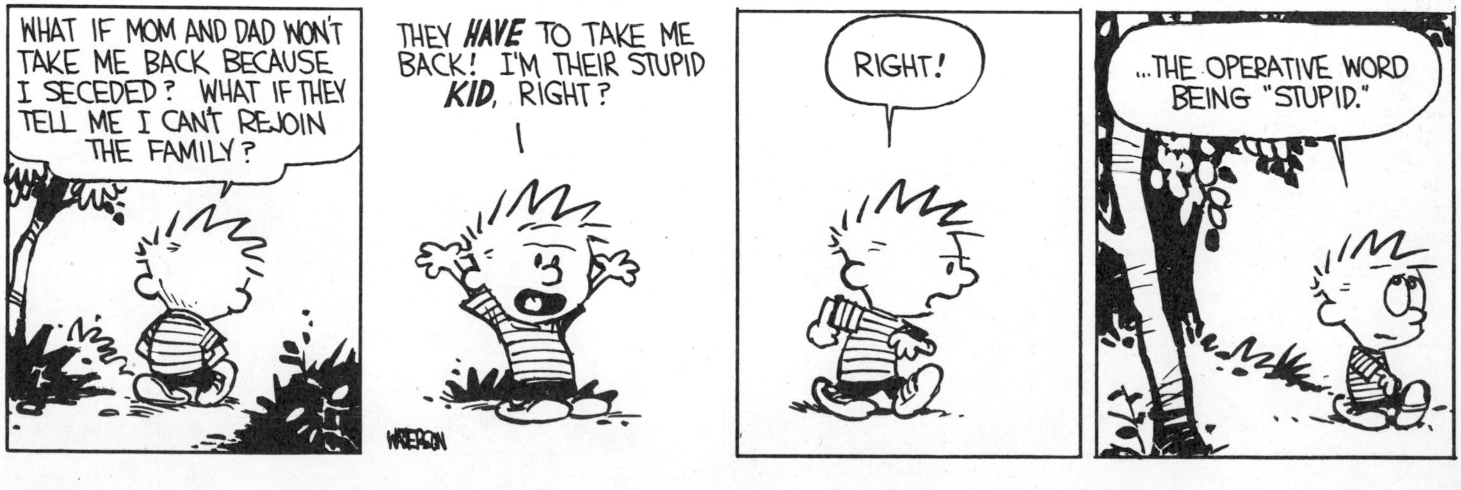
WHAT IF MOM AND DAD WON'T TAKE ME BACK BECAUSE I SECEDED? WHAT IF THEY TELL ME I CAN'T REJOIN THE FAMILY?
THEY HAVE TO TAKE ME BACK! I'M THEIR STUPID KID, RIGHT?
RIGHT!
...THE OPERATIVE WORD BEING "STUPID."

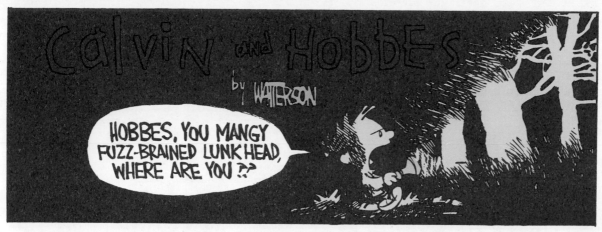

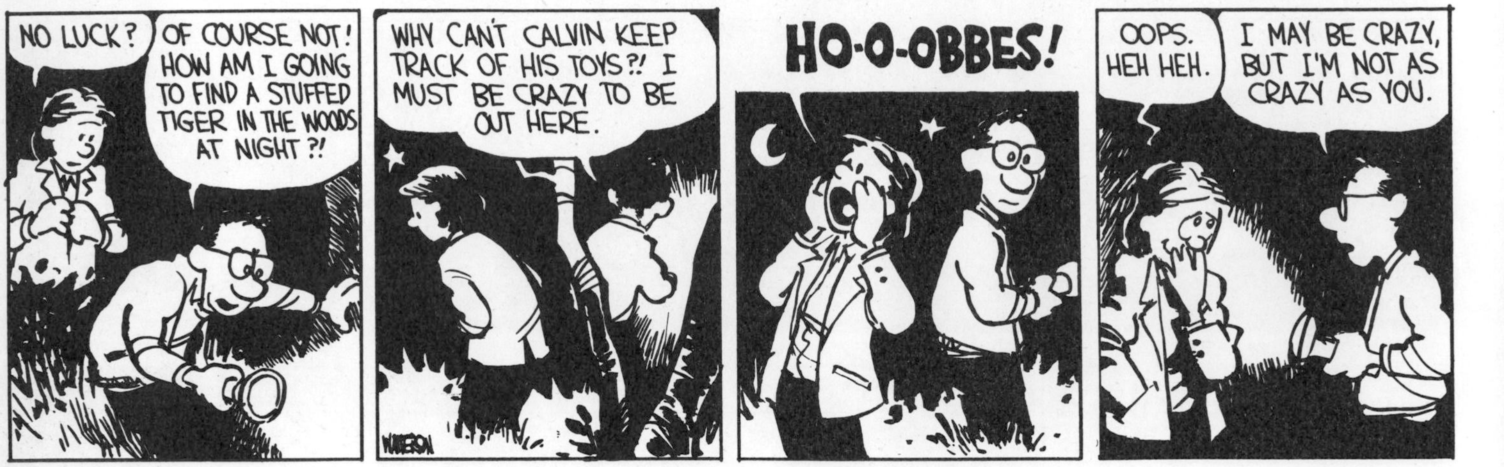
NO LUCK?
OF COURSE NOT! HOW AM I GOING TO FIND A STUFFED TIGER IN THE WOODS AT NIGHT?!
WHY CAN'T CALVIN KEEP TRACK OF HIS TOYS?! I MUST BE CRAZY TO BE OUT HERE.
HO-O-OBBES!
OOPS. HEH HEH.
I MAY BE CRAZY, BUT I'M NOT AS CRAZY AS YOU.

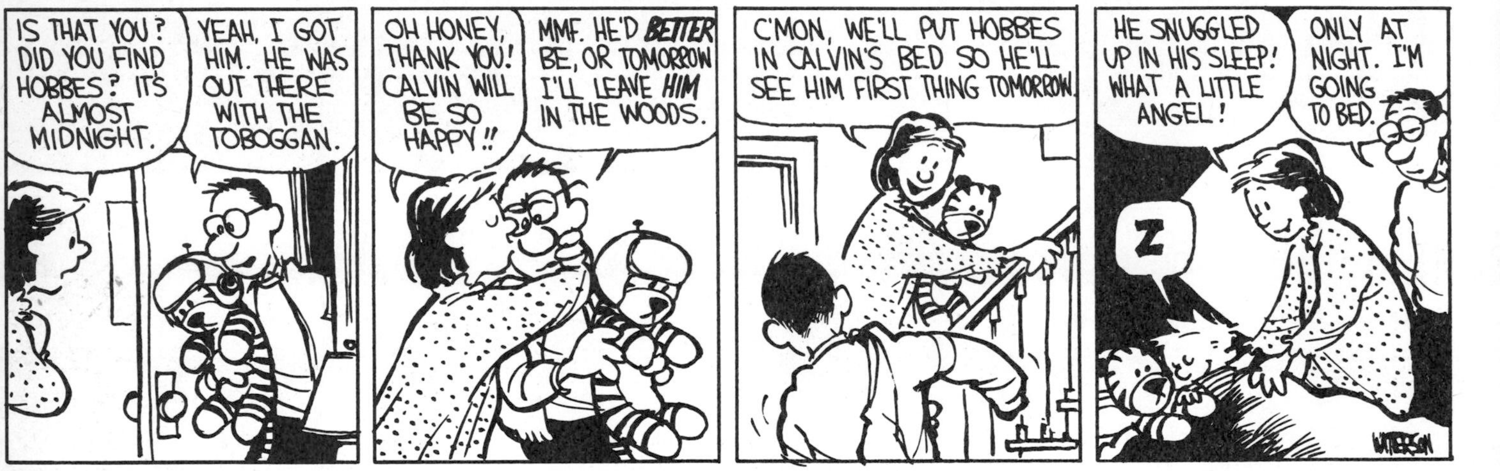
IS THAT YOU? DID YOU FIND HOBBES? IT'S ALMOST MIDNIGHT.
YEAH, I GOT HIM. HE WAS OUT THERE WITH THE TOBOGGAN.
OH HONEY, THANK YOU! CALVIN WILL BE SO HAPPY!!
MMF. HE'D BETTER BE, OR TOMORROW I'LL LEAVE HIM IN THE WOODS.
C'MON, WE'LL PUT HOBBES IN CALVIN'S BED SO HE'LL SEE HIM FIRST THING TOMORROW.
HE SNUGGLED UP IN HIS SLEEP! WHAT A LITTLE ANGEL!
ONLY AT NIGHT. I'M GOING TO BED.
Z

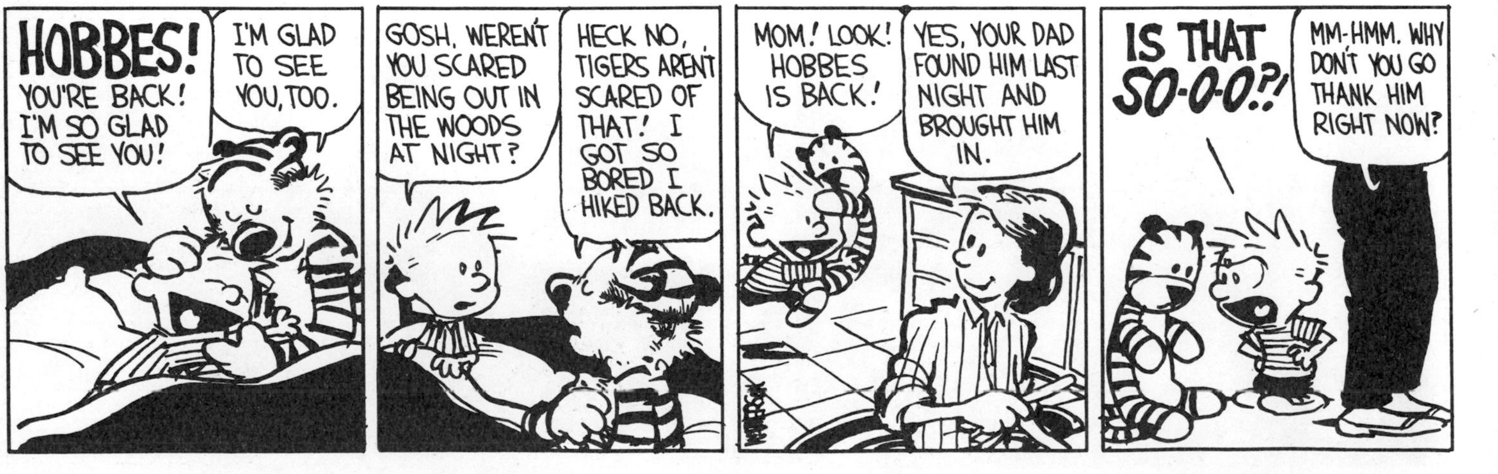
HOBBES! YOU'RE BACK! I'M SO GLAD TO SEE YOU!
I'M GLAD TO SEE YOU, TOO.
GOSH, WEREN'T YOU SCARED BEING OUT IN THE WOODS AT NIGHT?
HECK NO, TIGERS AREN'T SCARED OF THAT! I GOT SO BORED I HIKED BACK.
MOM! LOOK! HOBBES IS BACK!
YES, YOUR DAD FOUND HIM LAST NIGHT AND BROUGHT HIM IN.
IS THAT SO-O-O?!
MM-HMM. WHY DON'T YOU GO THANK HIM RIGHT NOW?

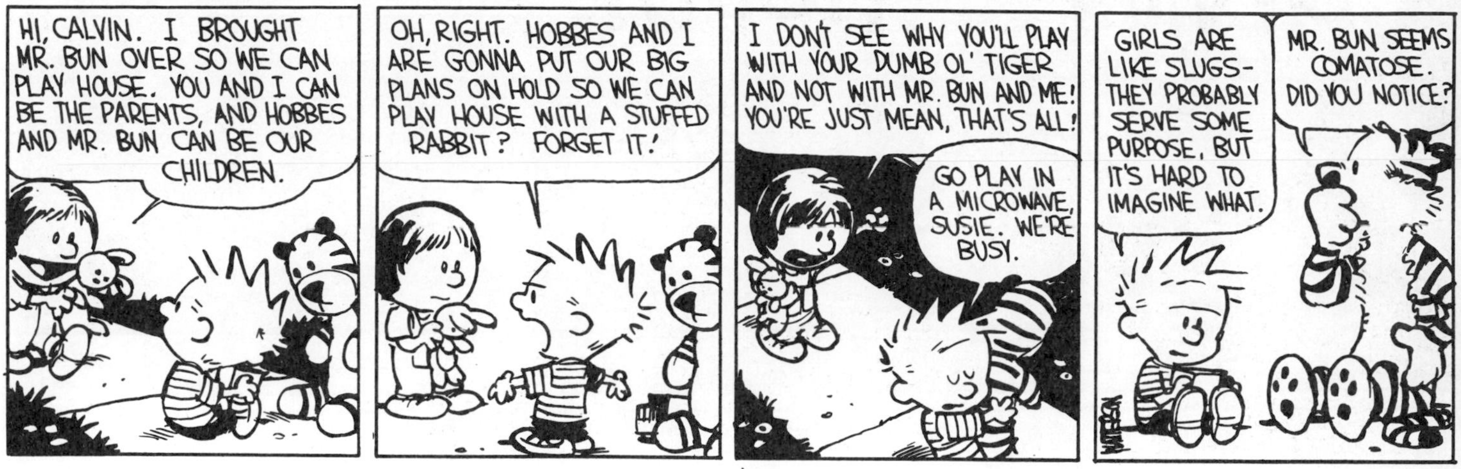
HI, CALVIN. I BROUGHT MR. BUN OVER SO WE CAN PLAY HOUSE. YOU AND I CAN BE THE PARENTS, AND HOBBES AND MR. BUN CAN BE OUR CHILDREN.
OH, RIGHT. HOBBES AND I ARE GONNA PUT OUR BIG PLANS ON HOLD SO WE CAN PLAY HOUSE WITH A STUFFED RABBIT? FORGET IT!
I DON'T SEE WHY YOU'LL PLAY WITH YOUR DUMB OL' TIGER AND NOT WITH MR. BUN AND ME! YOU'RE JUST MEAN, THAT'S ALL!
GO PLAY IN A MICROWAVE, SUSIE. WE'RE BUSY.
GIRLS ARE LIKE SLUGS- THEY PROBABLY SERVE SOME PURPOSE, BUT IT'S HARD TO IMAGINE WHAT.
MR. BUN SEEMS COMATOSE. DID YOU NOTICE?
WATTERSON

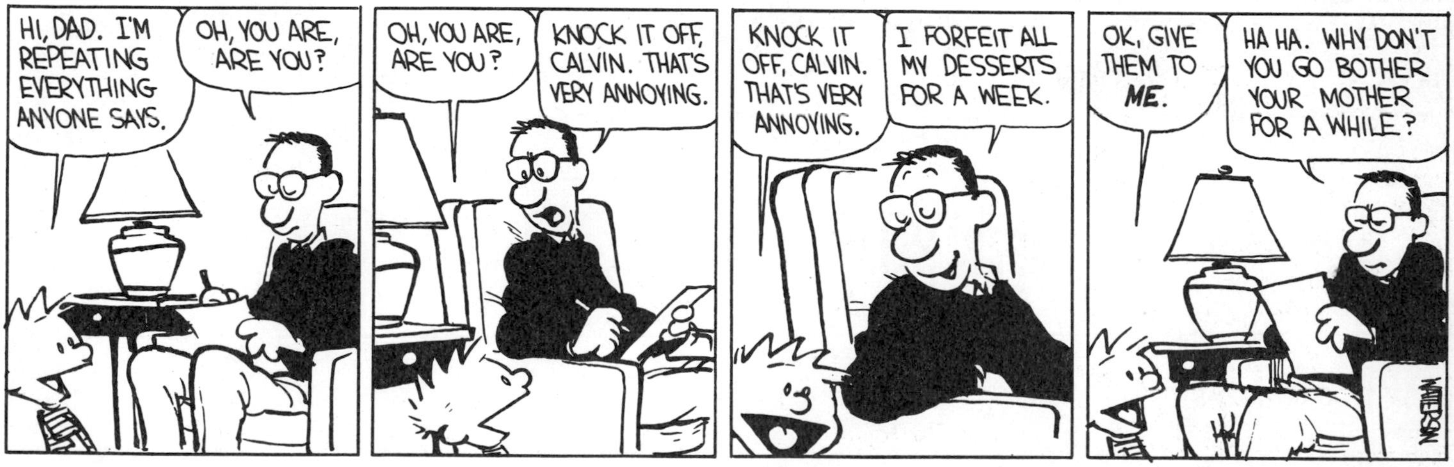
HI, DAD. I'M REPEATING EVERYTHING ANYONE SAYS.
OH, YOU ARE, ARE YOU?
OH, YOU ARE, ARE YOU?
KNOCK IT OFF, CALVIN. THAT'S VERY ANNOYING.
KNOCK IT OFF, CALVIN. THAT'S VERY ANNOYING.
I FORFEIT ALL MY DESSERTS FOR A WEEK.
OK, GIVE THEM TO ME.
HA HA. WHY DON'T YOU GO BOTHER YOUR MOTHER FOR A WHILE?
WATTERSON

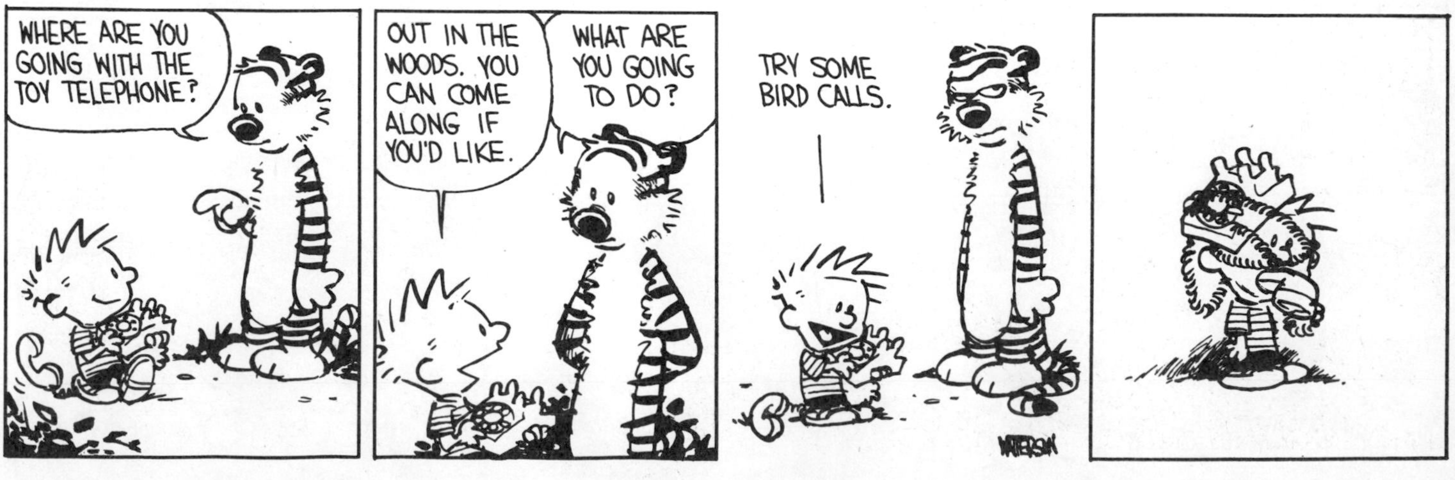
WHERE ARE YOU GOING WITH THE TOY TELEPHONE?
OUT IN THE WOODS. YOU CAN COME ALONG IF YOU'D LIKE.
WHAT ARE YOU GOING TO DO?
TRY SOME BIRD CALLS.
WATTERSON

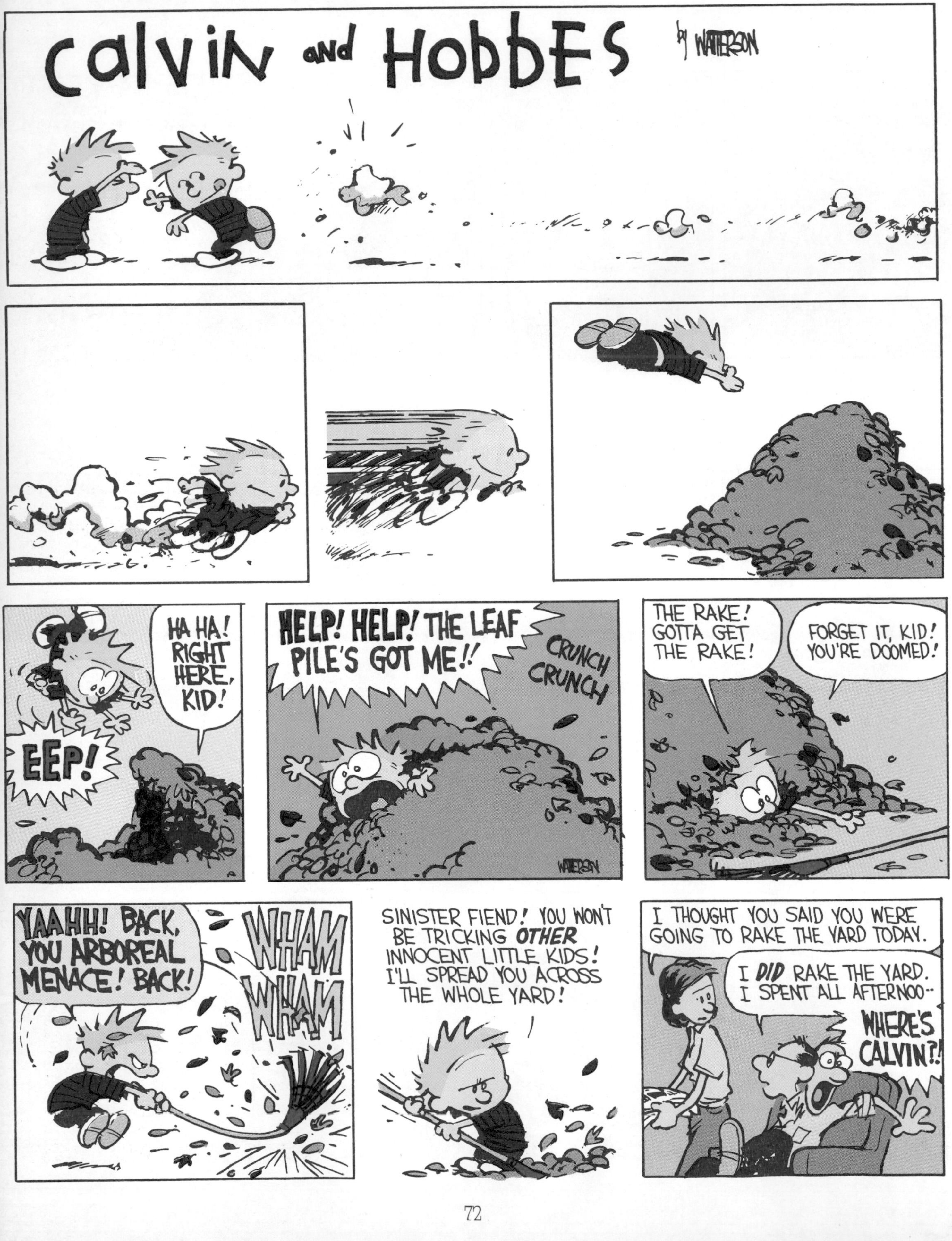
Calvin and Hobbes
by WATTERSON
HA HA! RIGHT HERE, KID!
EEP!
HELP! HELP! THE LEAF PILE'S GOT ME!!
CRUNCH CRUNCH
WATTERSON
THE RAKE! GOTTA GET THE RAKE!
FORGET IT, KID! YOU'RE DOOMED!
YAAHH! BACK, YOU ARBOREAL MENACE! BACK!
WHAM WHAM
SINISTER FIEND! YOU WON'T BE TRICKING OTHER INNOCENT LITTLE KIDS! I'LL SPREAD YOU ACROSS THE WHOLE YARD!
I THOUGHT YOU SAID YOU WERE GOING TO RAKE THE YARD TODAY.
I DID RAKE THE YARD. I SPENT ALL AFTERNOO--
WHERE'S CALVIN?!

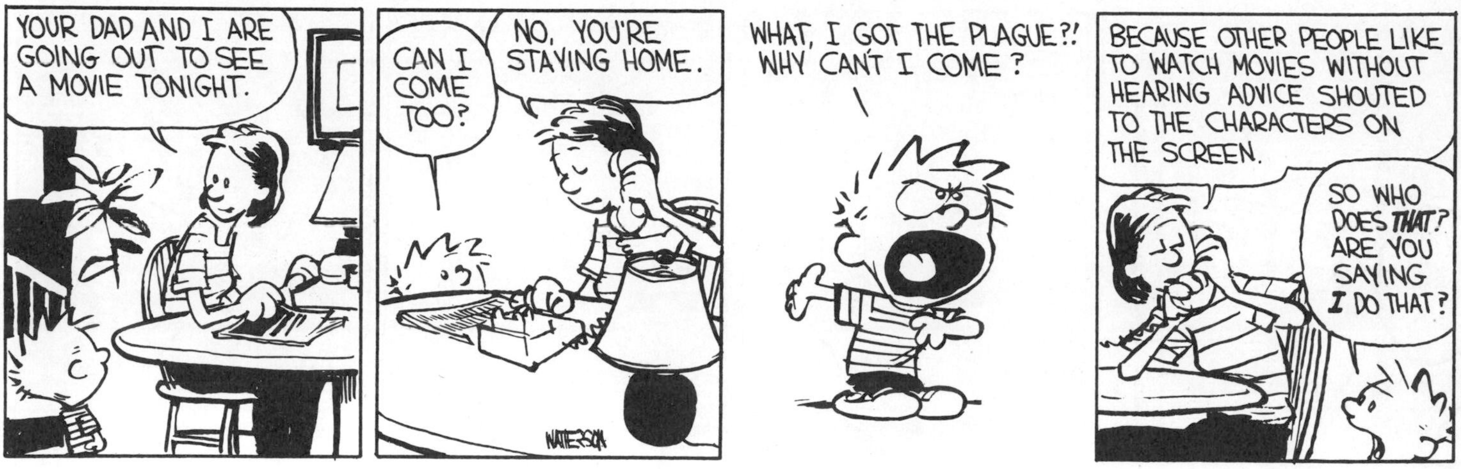
YOUR DAD AND I ARE GOING OUT TO SEE A MOVIE TONIGHT.
CAN I COME TOO?
NO, YOU'RE STAYING HOME.
WHAT, I GOT THE PLAGUE?! WHY CAN'T I COME?
BECAUSE OTHER PEOPLE LIKE TO WATCH MOVIES WITHOUT HEARING ADVICE SHOUTED TO THE CHARACTERS ON THE SCREEN.
SO WHO DOES THAT? ARE YOU SAYING I DO THAT?

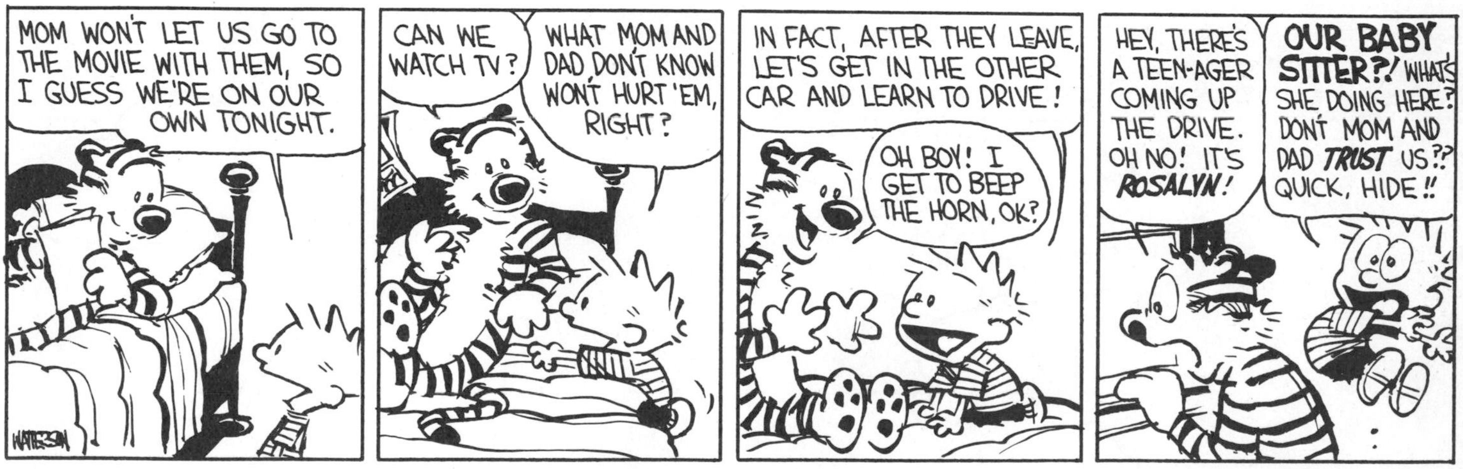
MOM WON'T LET US GO TO THE MOVIE WITH THEM, SO I GUESS WE'RE ON OUR OWN TONIGHT.
CAN WE WATCH TV?
WHAT MOM AND DAD DON'T KNOW WON'T HURT 'EM, RIGHT?
IN FACT, AFTER THEY LEAVE, LET'S GET IN THE OTHER CAR AND LEARN TO DRIVE!
OH BOY! I GET TO BEEP THE HORN, OK?
HEY, THERE'S A TEEN-AGER COMING UP THE DRIVE. OH NO! IT'S ROSALYN!
OUR BABY SITTER?! WHAT'S SHE DOING HERE? DON'T MOM AND DAD TRUST US?? QUICK, HIDE!!

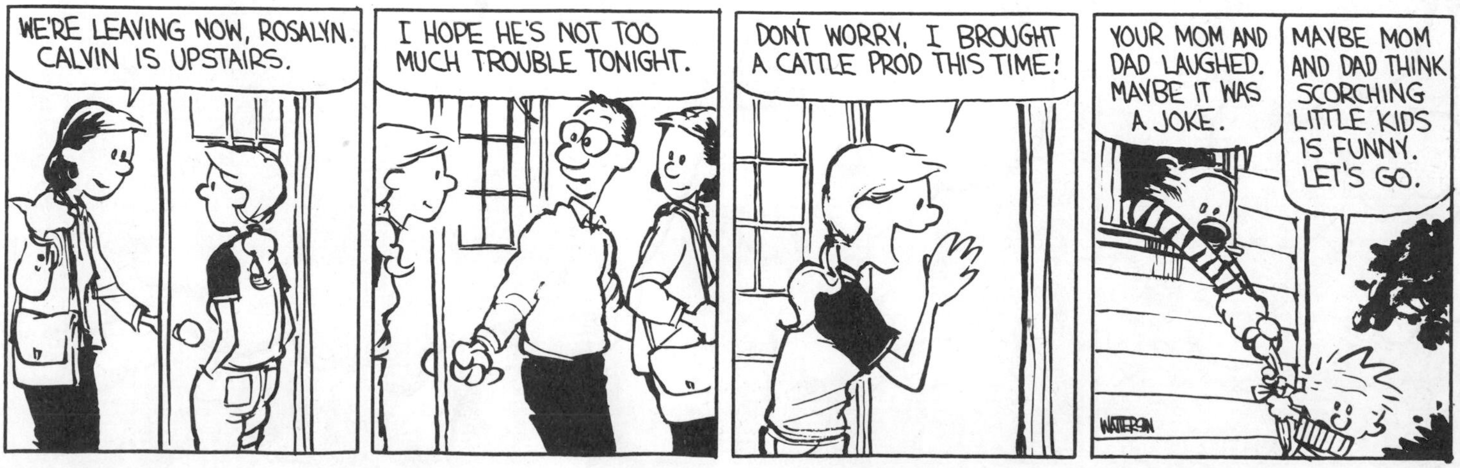
WE'RE LEAVING NOW, ROSALYN. CALVIN IS UPSTAIRS.
I HOPE HE'S NOT TOO MUCH TROUBLE TONIGHT.
DON'T WORRY, I BROUGHT A CATTLE PROD THIS TIME!
YOUR MOM AND DAD LAUGHED. MAYBE IT WAS A JOKE.
MAYBE MOM AND DAD THINK SCORCHING LITTLE KIDS IS FUNNY. LET'S GO.

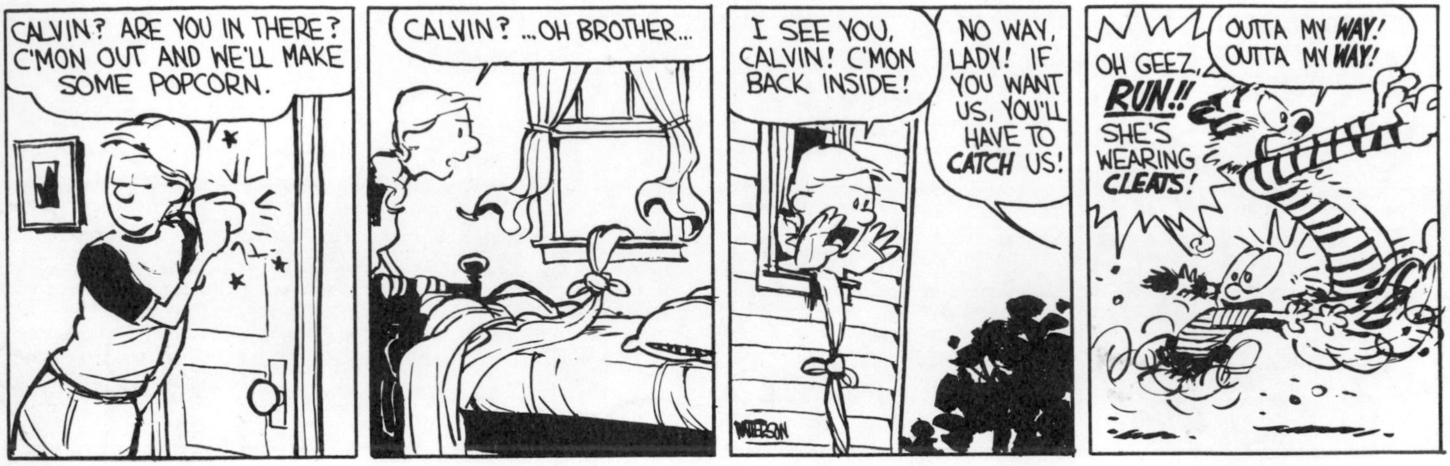
CALVIN? ARE YOU IN THERE? C'MON OUT AND WE'LL MAKE SOME POPCORN.
CALVIN? ...OH BROTHER...
I SEE YOU, CALVIN! C'MON BACK INSIDE!
NO WAY, LADY! IF YOU WANT US, YOU'LL HAVE TO CATCH US!
OUTTA MY WAY! OUTTA MY WAY!
OH GEEZ, RUN!! SHE'S WEARING CLEATS!

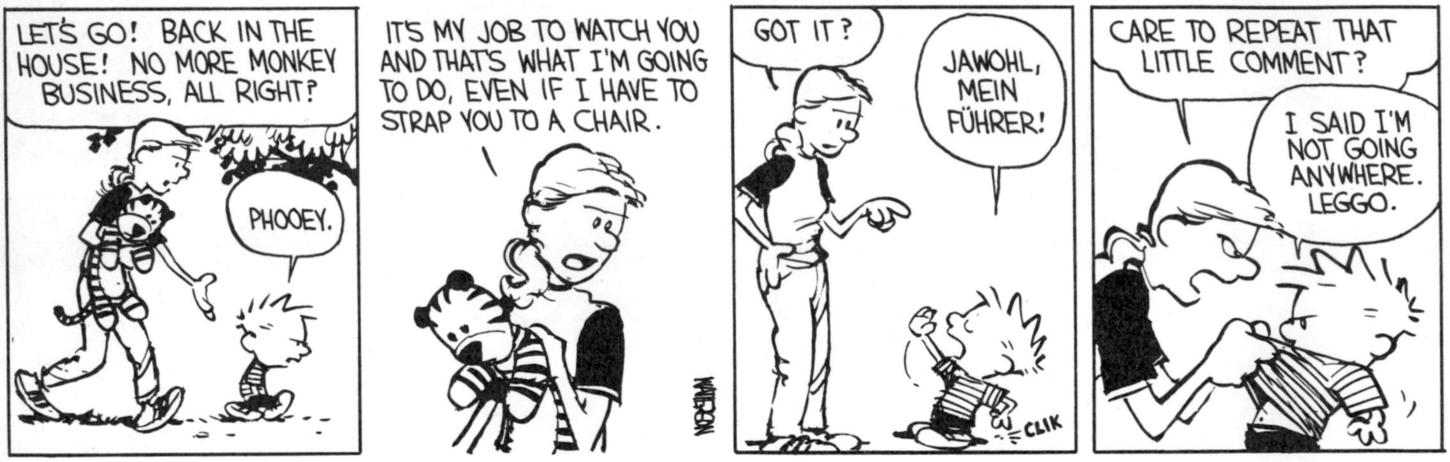
LET'S GO! BACK IN THE HOUSE! NO MORE MONKEY BUSINESS, ALL RIGHT?
PHOOEY.
IT'S MY JOB TO WATCH YOU AND THAT'S WHAT I'M GOING TO DO, EVEN IF I HAVE TO STRAP YOU TO A CHAIR.
GOT IT?
JAWOHL, MEIN FÜHRER!
CLIK
CARE TO REPEAT THAT LITTLE COMMENT?
I SAID I'M NOT GOING ANYWHERE. LEGGO.

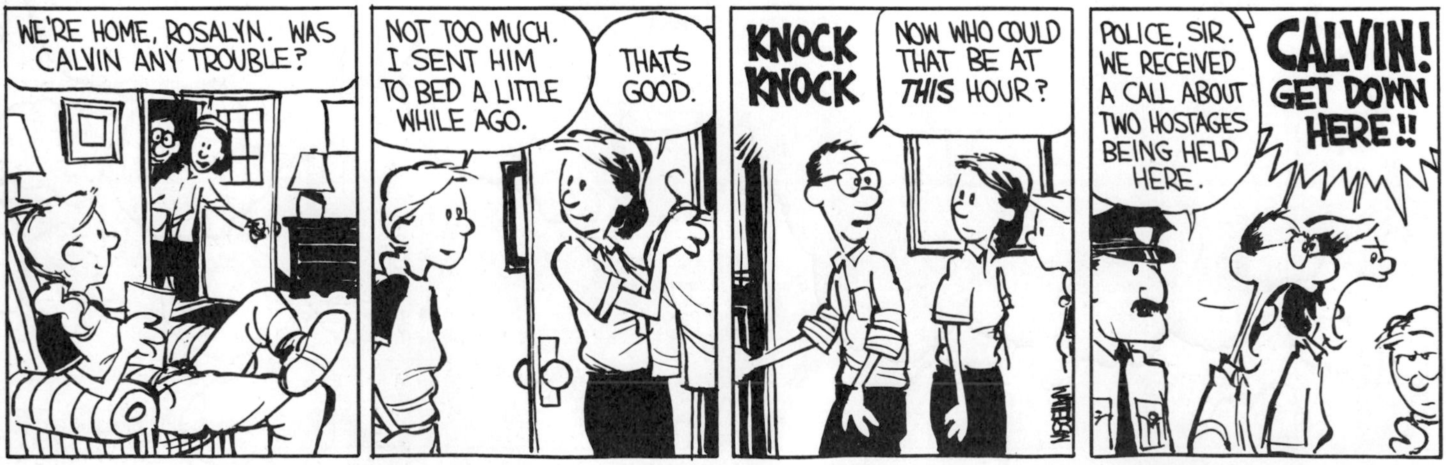
WE'RE HOME, ROSALYN. WAS CALVIN ANY TROUBLE?
NOT TOO MUCH. I SENT HIM TO BED A LITTLE WHILE AGO.
THAT'S GOOD.
KNOCK KNOCK
NOW WHO COULD THAT BE AT THIS HOUR?
POLICE, SIR. WE RECEIVED A CALL ABOUT TWO HOSTAGES BEING HELD HERE.
CALVIN! GET DOWN HERE!!

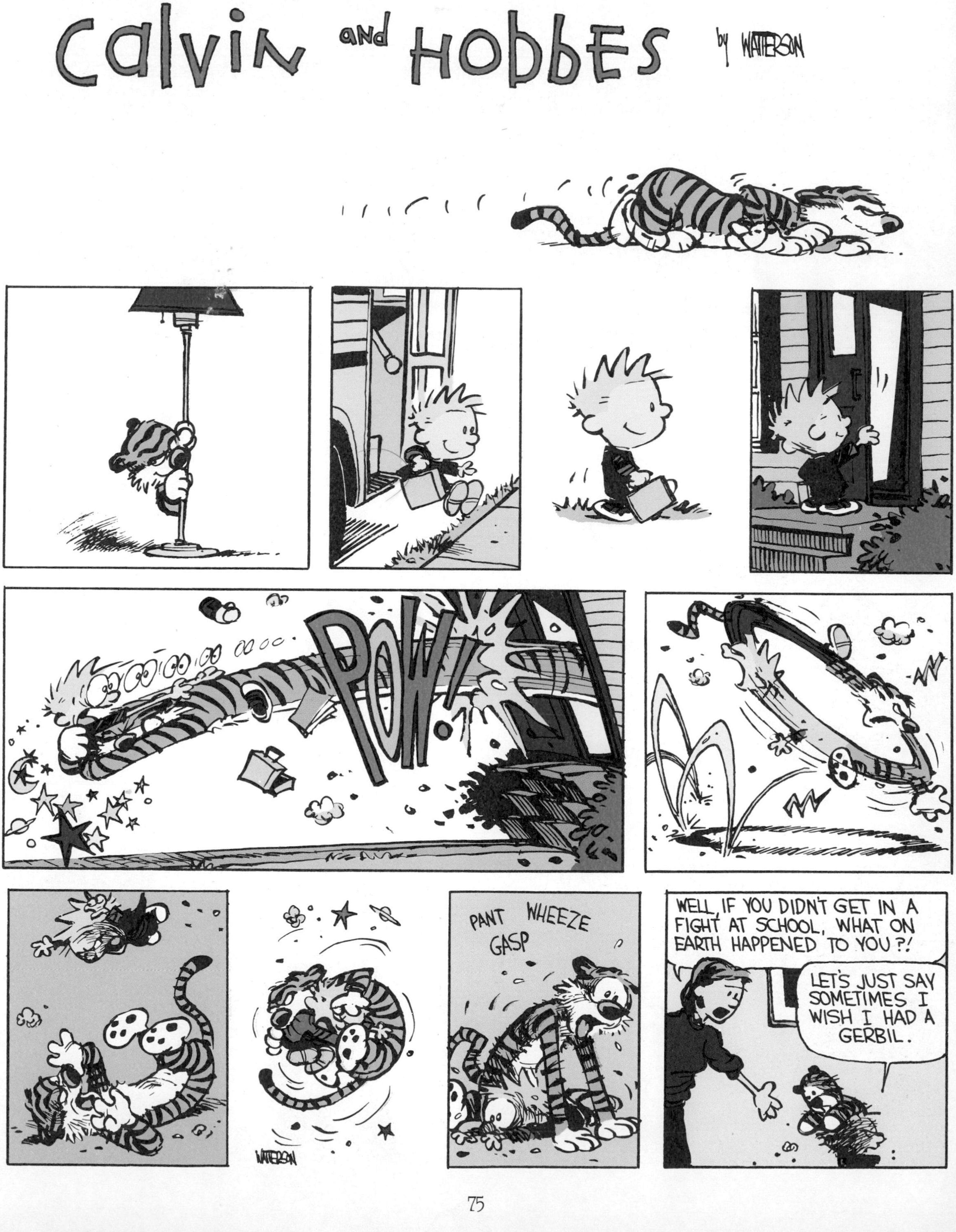
Calvin and HOBBES
by WATTERSON
POW!
WATTERSON
PANT WHEEZE
GASP
WELL, IF YOU DIDN'T GET IN A FIGHT AT SCHOOL, WHAT ON EARTH HAPPENED TO YOU ?!
LET'S JUST SAY SOMETIMES I WISH I HAD A GERBIL.

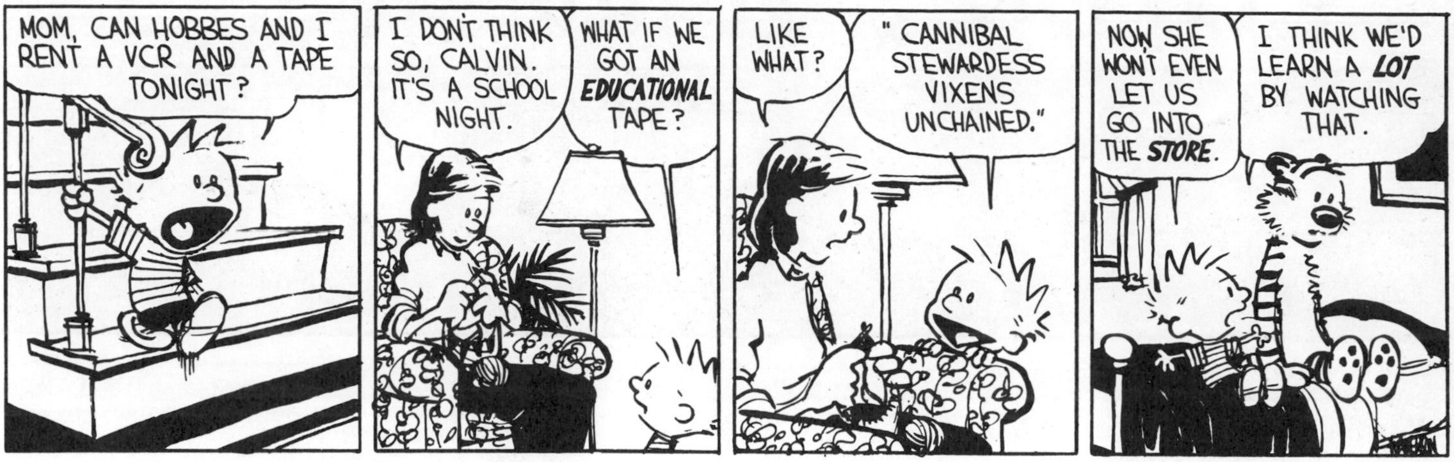

MOM, CAN HOBBES AND I RENT A VCR AND A TAPE TONIGHT?
I DON'T THINK SO, CALVIN. IT'S A SCHOOL NIGHT.
WHAT IF WE GOT AN **EDUCATIONAL** TAPE?
LIKE WHAT?
"CANNIBAL STEWARDESS VIXENS UNCHAINED."
NOW SHE WON'T EVEN LET US GO INTO THE **STORE**.
I THINK WE'D LEARN A **LOT** BY WATCHING THAT.


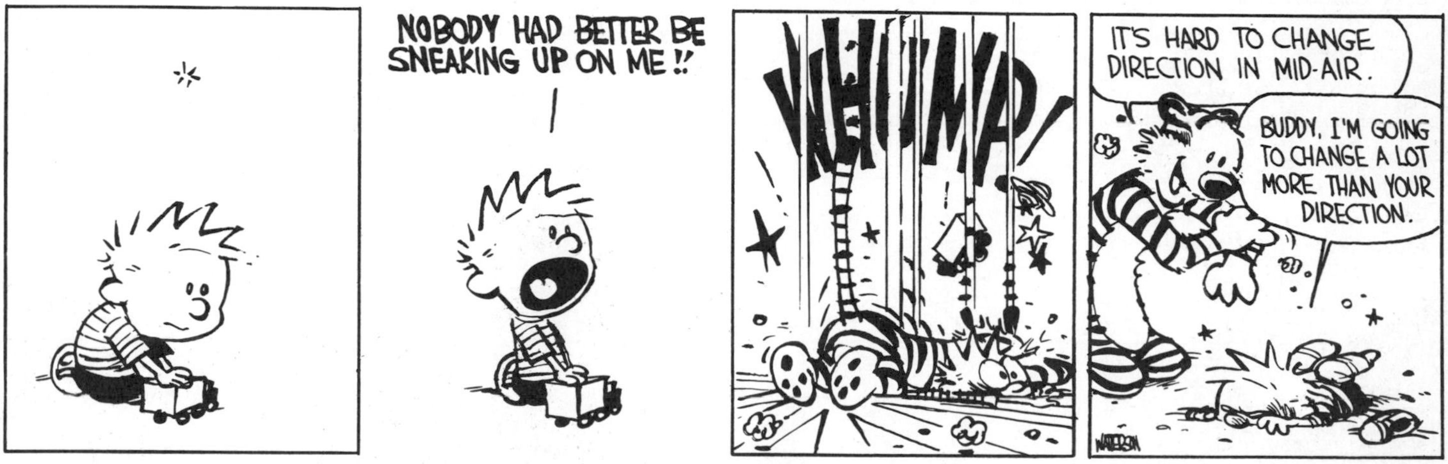

NOBODY HAD BETTER BE SNEAKING UP ON ME!!
WHUMP!
IT'S HARD TO CHANGE DIRECTION IN MID-AIR.
BUDDY, I'M GOING TO CHANGE A LOT MORE THAN YOUR DIRECTION.


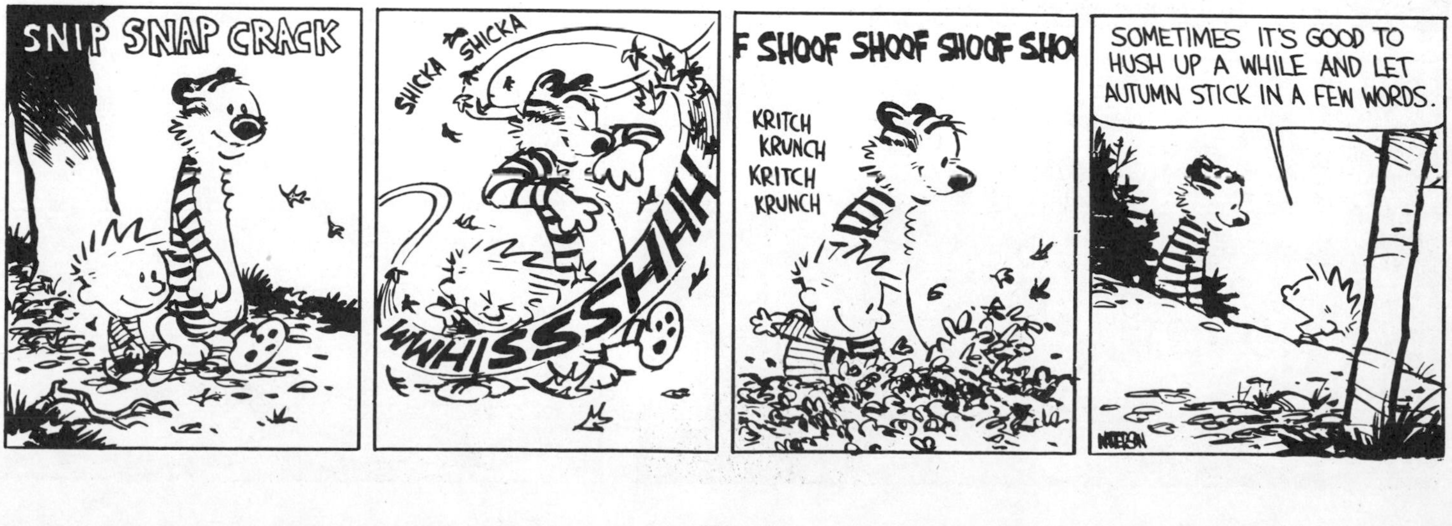

SNIP SNAP CRACK
SHICKA SHICKA
WWHISSSSHHH
SHOOF SHOOF SHOOF
KRITCH KRUNCH KRITCH KRUNCH
SOMETIMES IT'S GOOD TO HUSH UP A WHILE AND LET AUTUMN STICK IN A FEW WORDS.

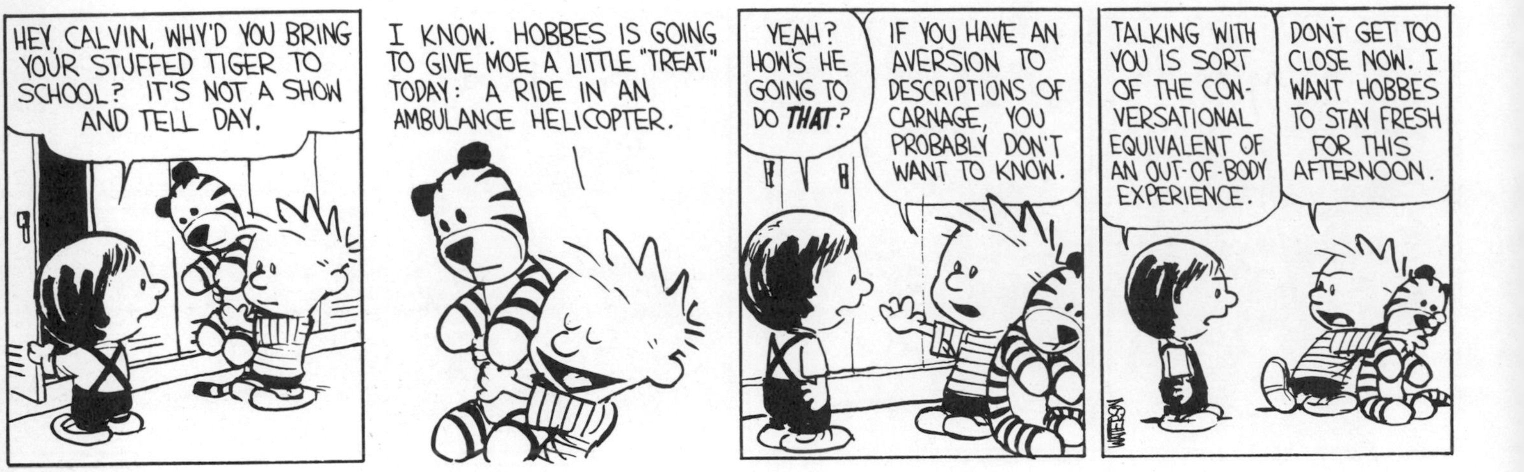
HEY, CALVIN, WHY'D YOU BRING YOUR STUFFED TIGER TO SCHOOL? IT'S NOT A SHOW AND TELL DAY.
I KNOW. HOBBES IS GOING TO GIVE MOE A LITTLE "TREAT" TODAY: A RIDE IN AN AMBULANCE HELICOPTER.
YEAH? HOW'S HE GOING TO DO **THAT**?
IF YOU HAVE AN AVERSION TO DESCRIPTIONS OF CARNAGE, YOU PROBABLY DON'T WANT TO KNOW.
TALKING WITH YOU IS SORT OF THE CONVERSATIONAL EQUIVALENT OF AN OUT-OF-BODY EXPERIENCE.
DON'T GET TOO CLOSE NOW. I WANT HOBBES TO STAY FRESH FOR THIS AFTERNOON.
WATTERSON

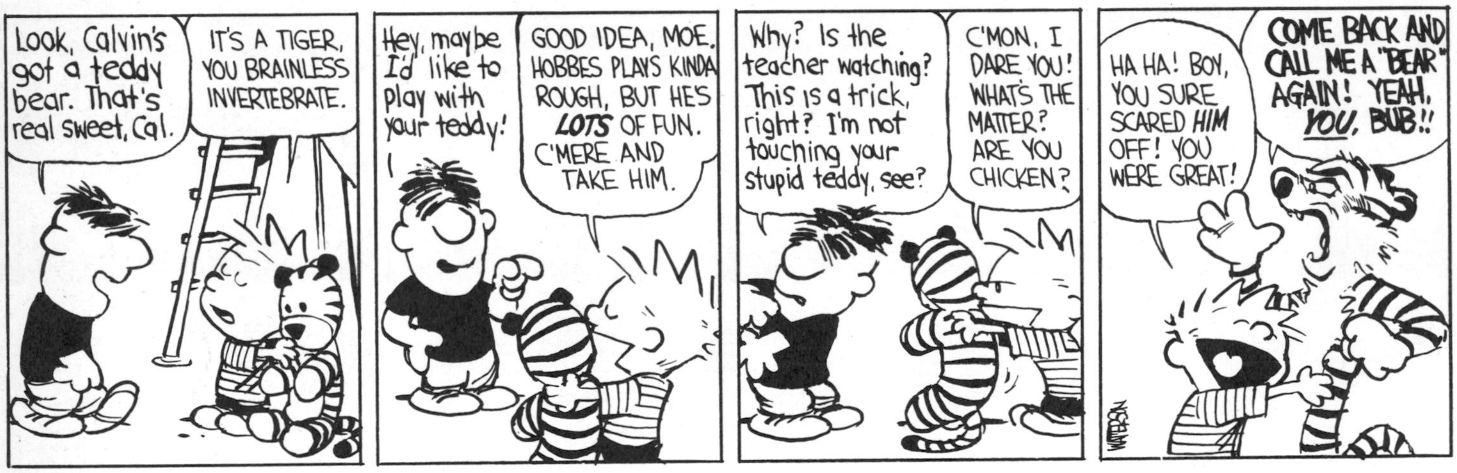
Look, Calvin's got a teddy bear. That's real sweet, Cal.
IT'S A TIGER, YOU BRAINLESS INVERTEBRATE.
Hey, maybe I'd like to play with your teddy!
GOOD IDEA, MOE. HOBBES PLAYS KINDA ROUGH, BUT HE'S **LOTS** OF FUN. C'MERE AND TAKE HIM.
Why? Is the teacher watching? This is a trick, right? I'm not touching your stupid teddy, see?
C'MON, I DARE YOU! WHAT'S THE MATTER? ARE YOU CHICKEN?
HA HA! BOY, YOU SURE SCARED **HIM** OFF! YOU WERE GREAT!
COME BACK AND CALL ME A "BEAR" AGAIN! YEAH, **YOU**, BUB!!
WATTERSON

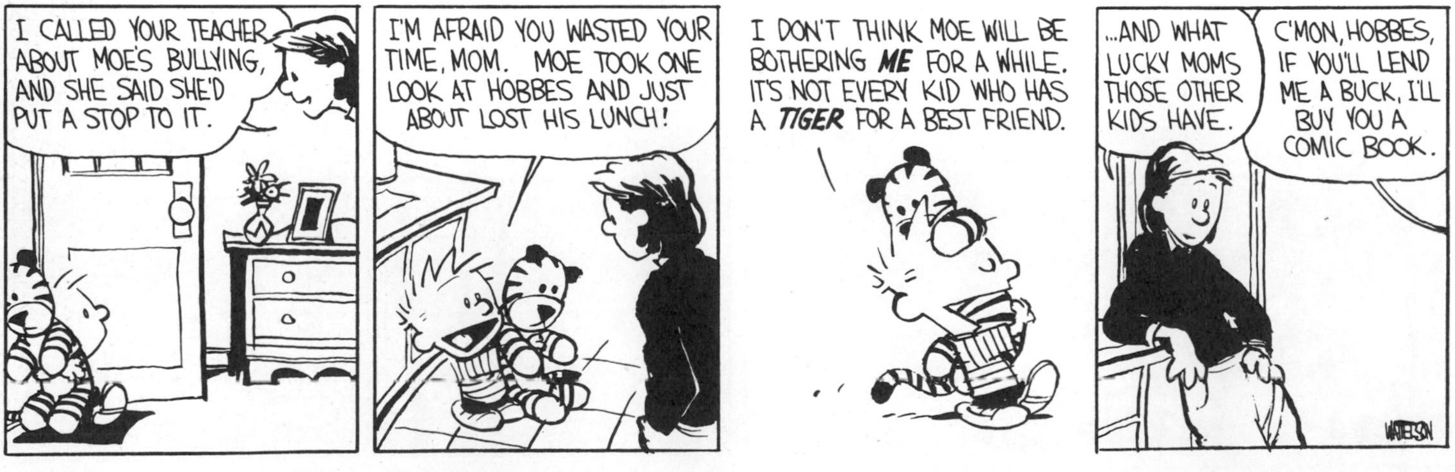
I CALLED YOUR TEACHER ABOUT MOE'S BULLYING, AND SHE SAID SHE'D PUT A STOP TO IT.
I'M AFRAID YOU WASTED YOUR TIME, MOM. MOE TOOK ONE LOOK AT HOBBES AND JUST ABOUT LOST HIS LUNCH!
I DON'T THINK MOE WILL BE BOTHERING **ME** FOR A WHILE. IT'S NOT EVERY KID WHO HAS A **TIGER** FOR A BEST FRIEND.
...AND WHAT LUCKY MOMS THOSE OTHER KIDS HAVE.
C'MON, HOBBES, IF YOU'LL LEND ME A BUCK, I'LL BUY YOU A COMIC BOOK.
WATTERSON

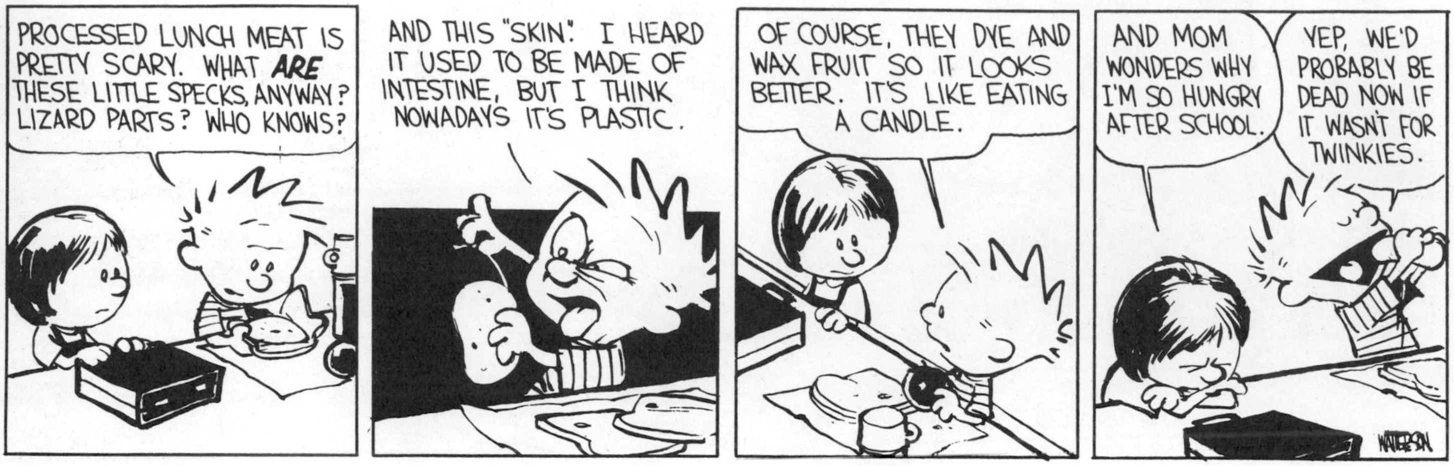
PROCESSED LUNCH MEAT IS PRETTY SCARY. WHAT **ARE** THESE LITTLE SPECKS, ANYWAY? LIZARD PARTS? WHO KNOWS?
AND THIS "SKIN." I HEARD IT USED TO BE MADE OF INTESTINE, BUT I THINK NOWADAYS IT'S PLASTIC.
OF COURSE, THEY DYE AND WAX FRUIT SO IT LOOKS BETTER. IT'S LIKE EATING A CANDLE.
AND MOM WONDERS WHY I'M SO HUNGRY AFTER SCHOOL.
YEP, WE'D PROBABLY BE DEAD NOW IF IT WASN'T FOR TWINKIES.

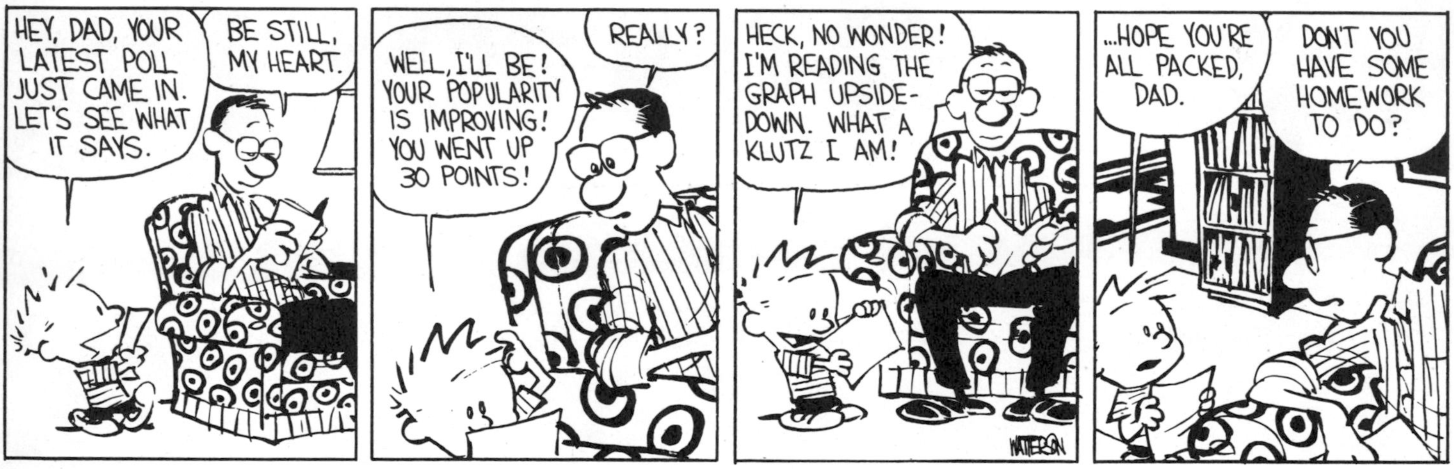
HEY, DAD, YOUR LATEST POLL JUST CAME IN. LET'S SEE WHAT IT SAYS.
BE STILL, MY HEART.
WELL, I'LL BE! YOUR POPULARITY IS IMPROVING! YOU WENT UP 30 POINTS!
REALLY?
HECK, NO WONDER! I'M READING THE GRAPH UPSIDE-DOWN. WHAT A KLUTZ I AM!
...HOPE YOU'RE ALL PACKED, DAD.
DON'T YOU HAVE SOME HOMEWORK TO DO?

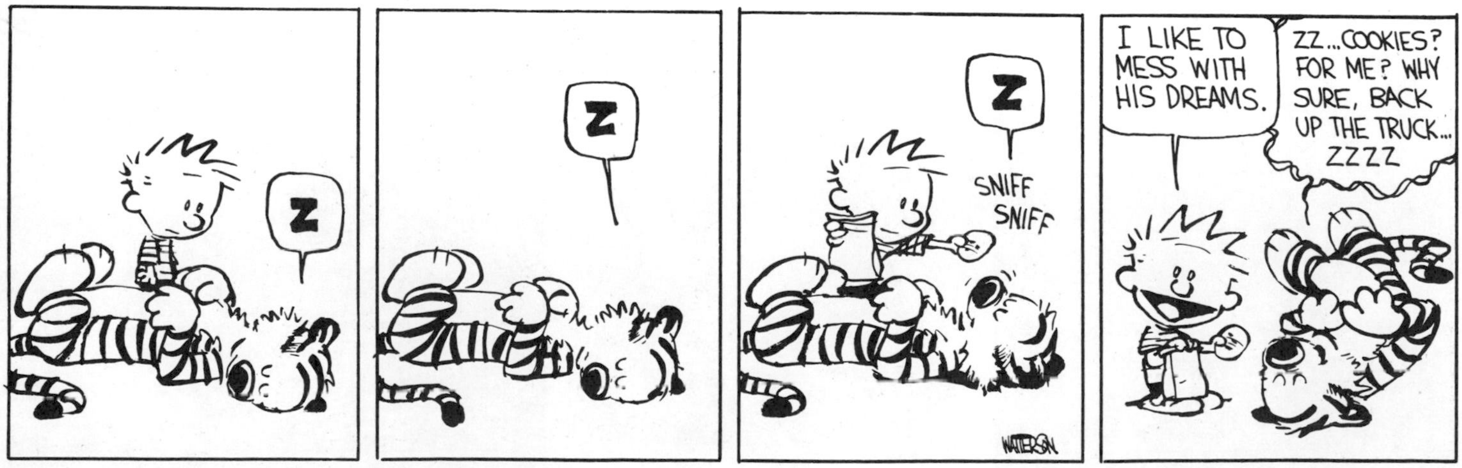
Z
Z
Z
SNIFF SNIFF
I LIKE TO MESS WITH HIS DREAMS.
ZZ...COOKIES? FOR ME? WHY SURE, BACK UP THE TRUCK... ZZZZ

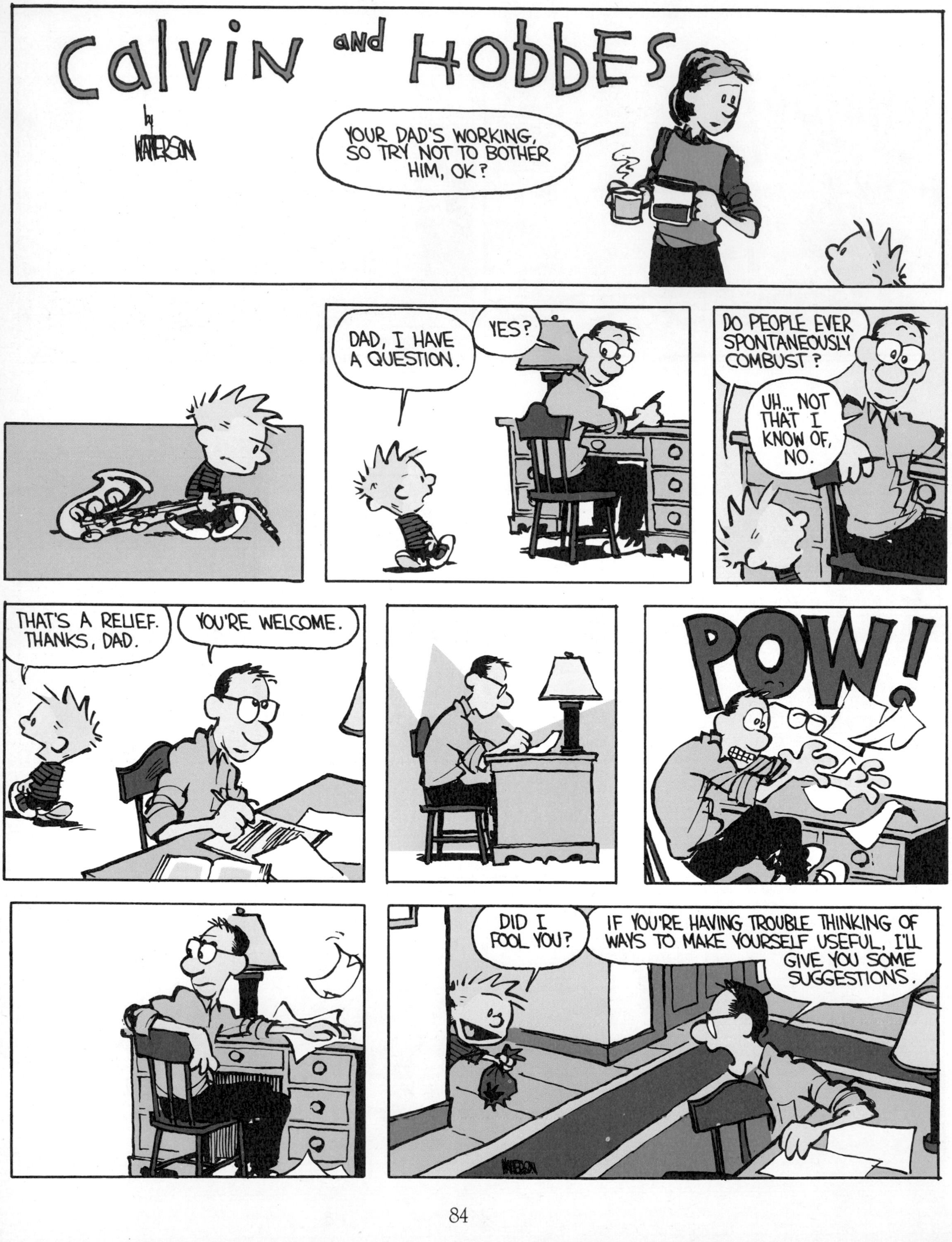
Calvin and HOBBES
by WATTERSON
YOUR DAD'S WORKING, SO TRY NOT TO BOTHER HIM, OK?
DAD, I HAVE A QUESTION.
YES?
DO PEOPLE EVER SPONTANEOUSLY COMBUST?
UH... NOT THAT I KNOW OF, NO.
THAT'S A RELIEF. THANKS, DAD.
YOU'RE WELCOME.
POW!
DID I FOOL YOU?
IF YOU'RE HAVING TROUBLE THINKING OF WAYS TO MAKE YOURSELF USEFUL, I'LL GIVE YOU SOME SUGGESTIONS.
WATTERSON

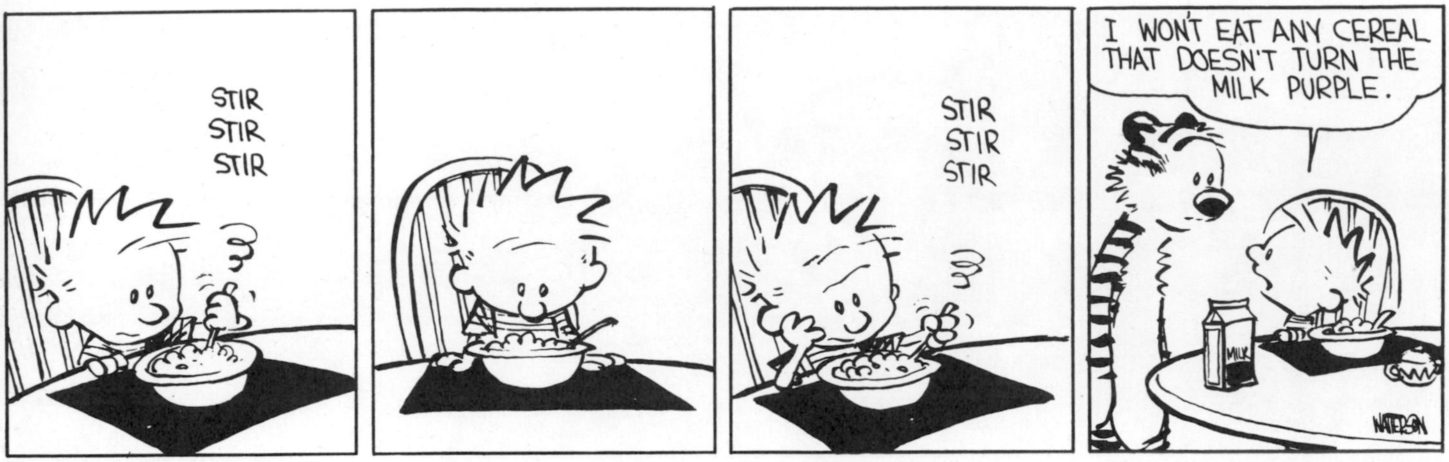
STIR
STIR
STIR
STIR
STIR
STIR
I WON'T EAT ANY CEREAL THAT DOESN'T TURN THE MILK PURPLE.
MILK
WATTERSON

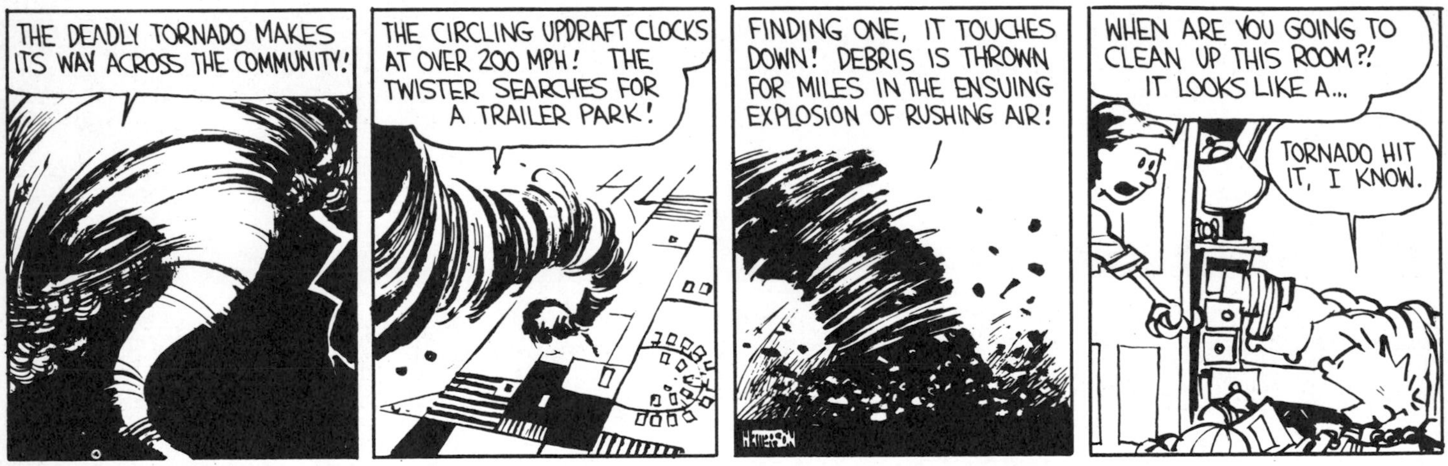
THE DEADLY TORNADO MAKES ITS WAY ACROSS THE COMMUNITY!
THE CIRCLING UPDRAFT CLOCKS AT OVER 200 MPH! THE TWISTER SEARCHES FOR A TRAILER PARK!
FINDING ONE, IT TOUCHES DOWN! DEBRIS IS THROWN FOR MILES IN THE ENSUING EXPLOSION OF RUSHING AIR!
WHEN ARE YOU GOING TO CLEAN UP THIS ROOM?! IT LOOKS LIKE A...
TORNADO HIT IT, I KNOW.

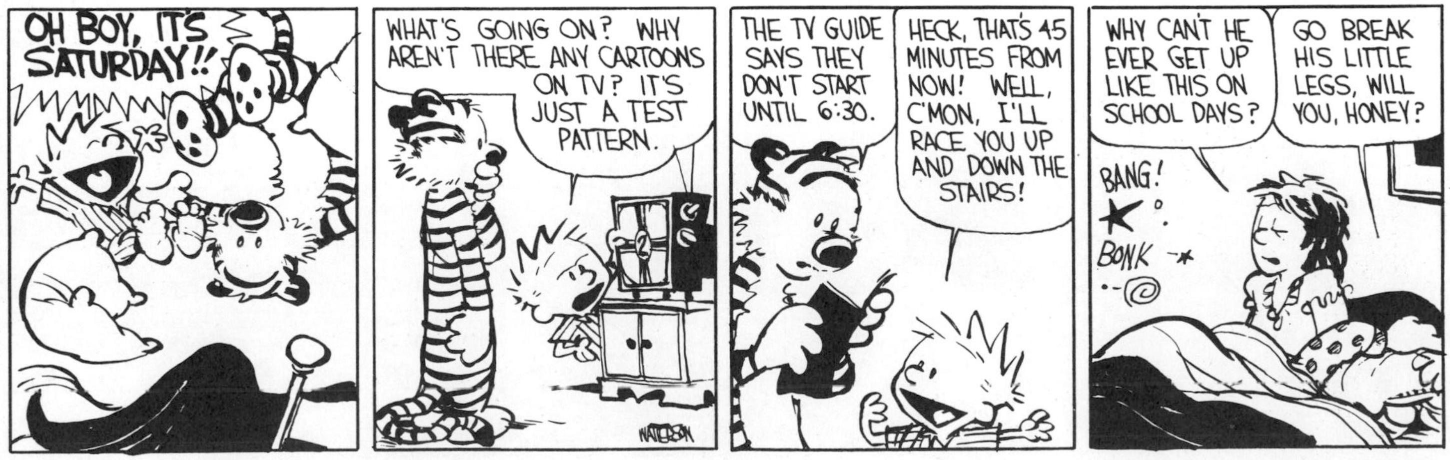
OH BOY, IT'S SATURDAY!!
WHAT'S GOING ON? WHY AREN'T THERE ANY CARTOONS ON TV? IT'S JUST A TEST PATTERN.
WATTERSON
THE TV GUIDE SAYS THEY DON'T START UNTIL 6:30.
HECK, THAT'S 45 MINUTES FROM NOW! WELL, C'MON, I'LL RACE YOU UP AND DOWN THE STAIRS!
WHY CAN'T HE EVER GET UP LIKE THIS ON SCHOOL DAYS?
GO BREAK HIS LITTLE LEGS, WILL YOU, HONEY?
BANG!
BONK

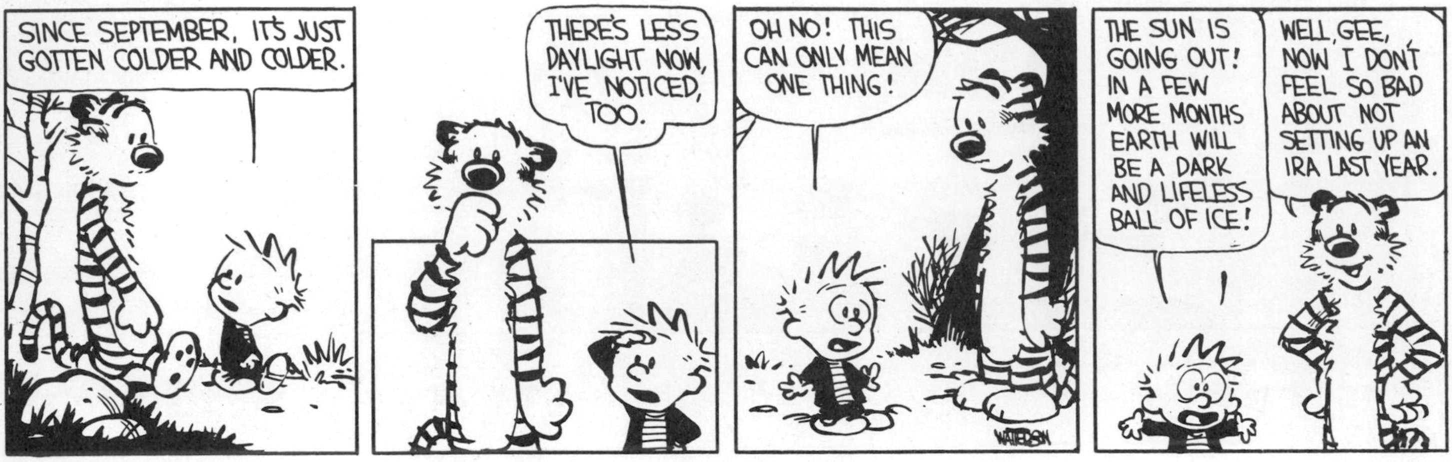

SINCE SEPTEMBER, IT'S JUST GOTTEN COLDER AND COLDER.
THERE'S LESS DAYLIGHT NOW, I'VE NOTICED, TOO.
OH NO! THIS CAN ONLY MEAN ONE THING!
WATTERSON
THE SUN IS GOING OUT! IN A FEW MORE MONTHS EARTH WILL BE A DARK AND LIFELESS BALL OF ICE!
WELL, GEE, NOW I DON'T FEEL SO BAD ABOUT NOT SETTING UP AN IRA LAST YEAR.


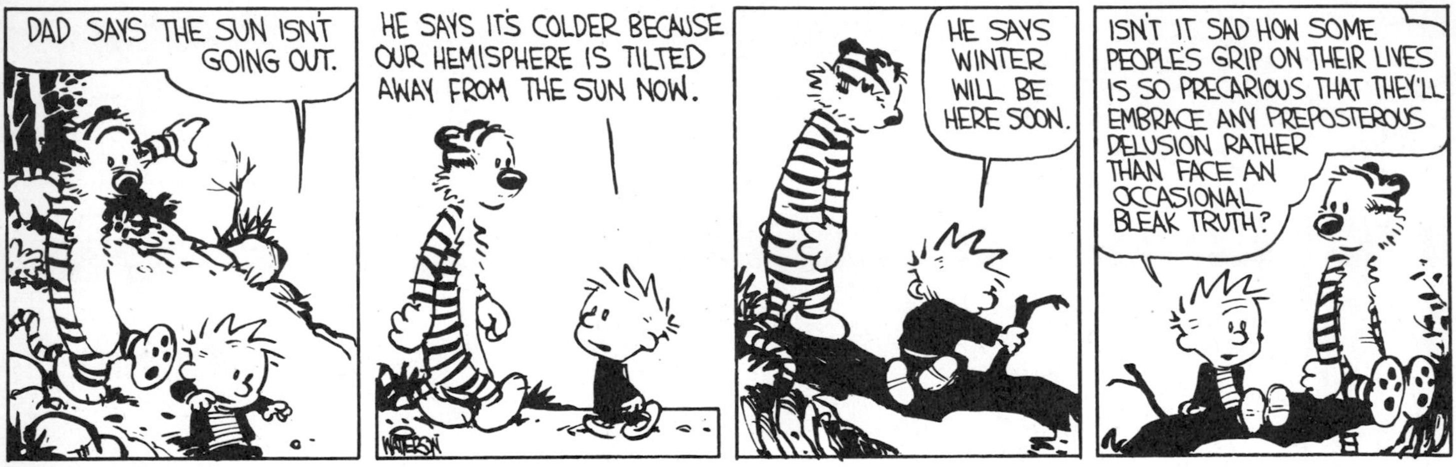

DAD SAYS THE SUN ISN'T GOING OUT.
HE SAYS IT'S COLDER BECAUSE OUR HEMISPHERE IS TILTED AWAY FROM THE SUN NOW.
WATTERSON
HE SAYS WINTER WILL BE HERE SOON.
ISN'T IT SAD HOW SOME PEOPLE'S GRIP ON THEIR LIVES IS SO PRECARIOUS THAT THEY'LL EMBRACE ANY PREPOSTEROUS DELUSION RATHER THAN FACE AN OCCASIONAL BLEAK TRUTH?


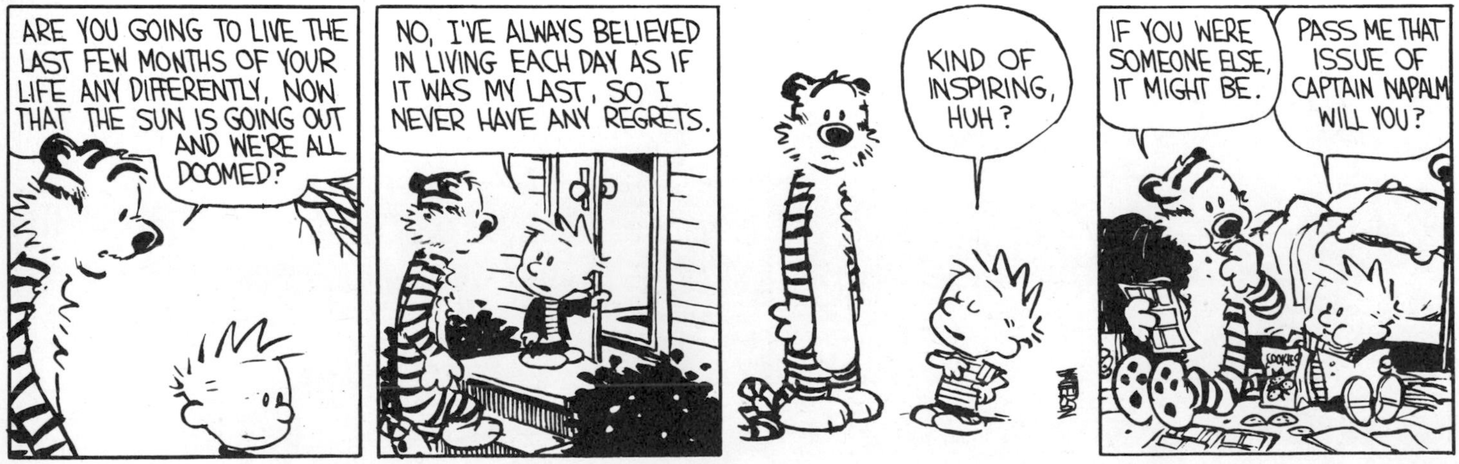

ARE YOU GOING TO LIVE THE LAST FEW MONTHS OF YOUR LIFE ANY DIFFERENTLY, NOW THAT THE SUN IS GOING OUT AND WE'RE ALL DOOMED?
NO, I'VE ALWAYS BELIEVED IN LIVING EACH DAY AS IF IT WAS MY LAST, SO I NEVER HAVE ANY REGRETS.
KIND OF INSPIRING, HUH?
WATTERSON
IF YOU WERE SOMEONE ELSE, IT MIGHT BE.
PASS ME THAT ISSUE OF CAPTAIN NAPALM WILL YOU?
COOKIES

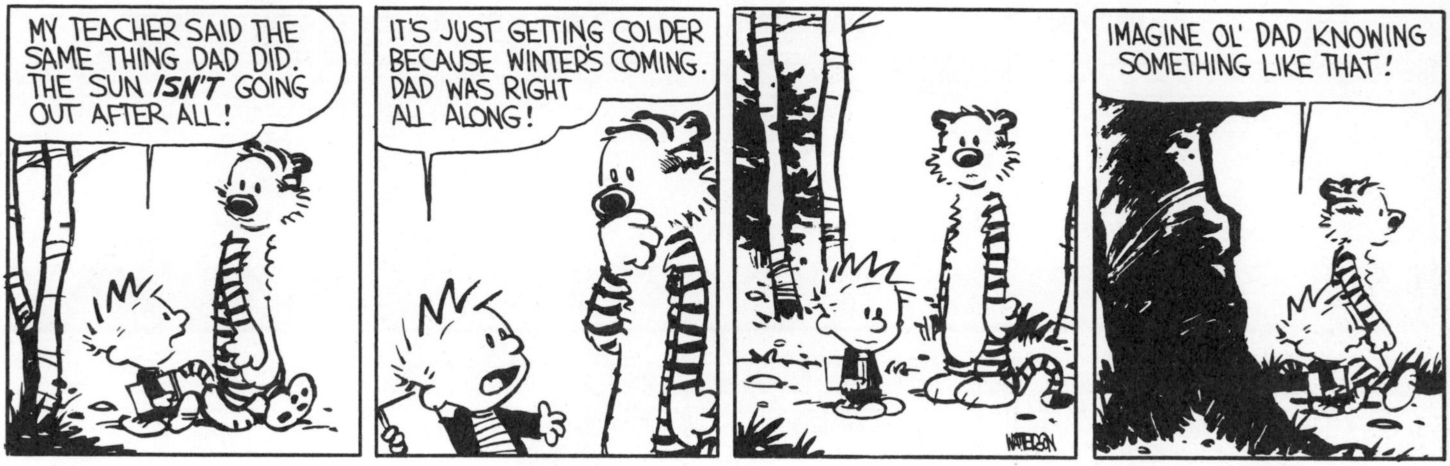
MY TEACHER SAID THE SAME THING DAD DID. THE SUN *ISN'T* GOING OUT AFTER ALL!
IT'S JUST GETTING COLDER BECAUSE WINTER'S COMING. DAD WAS RIGHT ALL ALONG!
WATTERSON
IMAGINE OL' DAD KNOWING SOMETHING LIKE THAT!

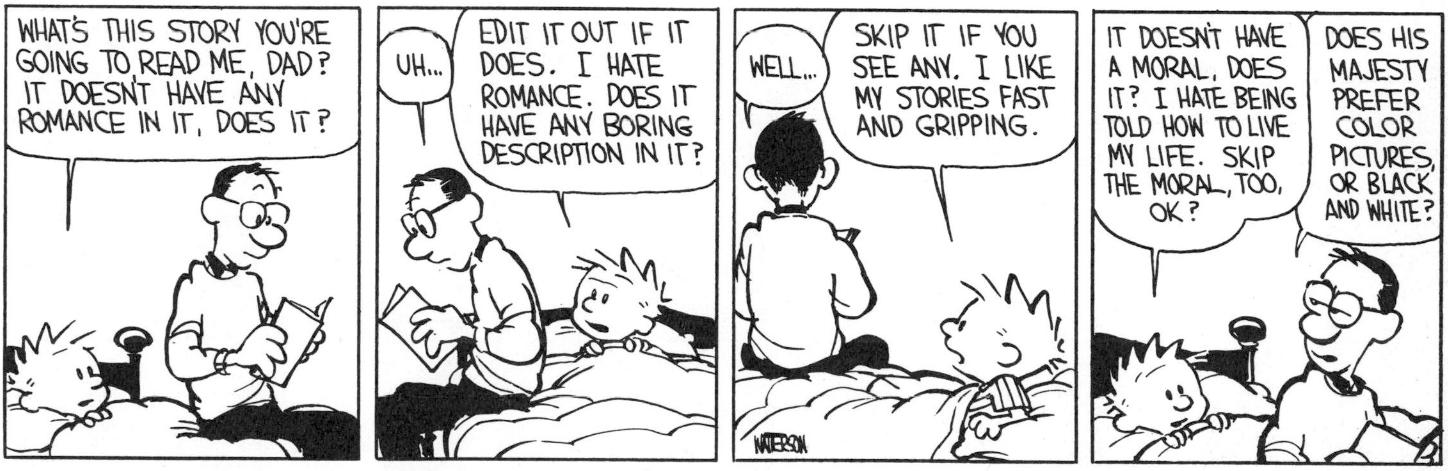
WHAT'S THIS STORY YOU'RE GOING TO READ ME, DAD? IT DOESN'T HAVE ANY ROMANCE IN IT, DOES IT?
UH...
EDIT IT OUT IF IT DOES. I HATE ROMANCE. DOES IT HAVE ANY BORING DESCRIPTION IN IT?
WELL...
SKIP IT IF YOU SEE ANY. I LIKE MY STORIES FAST AND GRIPPING.
WATTERSON
IT DOESN'T HAVE A MORAL, DOES IT? I HATE BEING TOLD HOW TO LIVE MY LIFE. SKIP THE MORAL, TOO, OK?
DOES HIS MAJESTY PREFER COLOR PICTURES, OR BLACK AND WHITE?

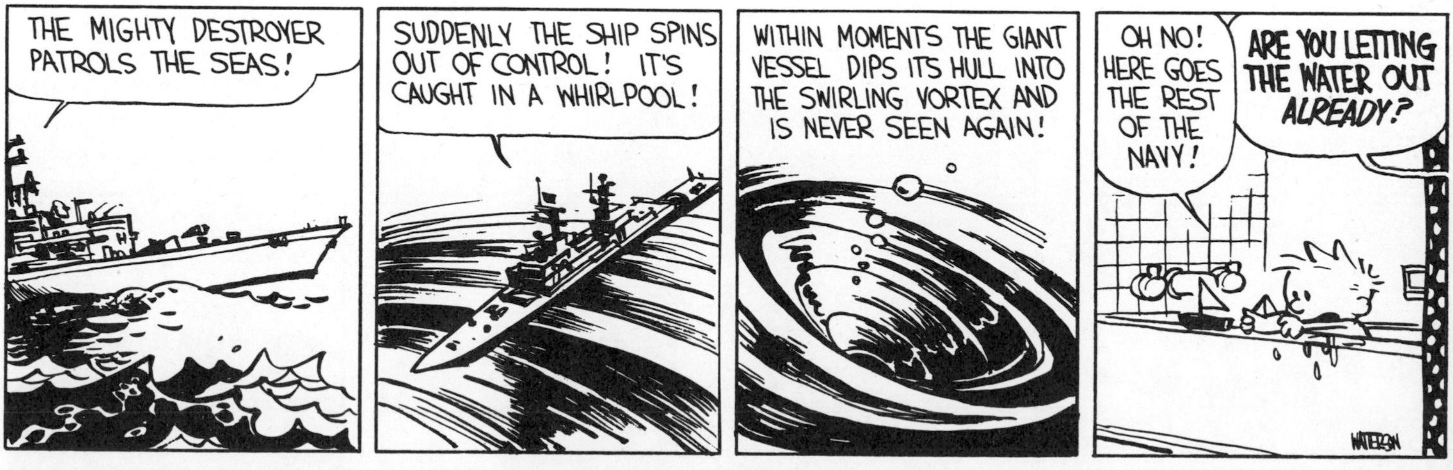
THE MIGHTY DESTROYER PATROLS THE SEAS!
SUDDENLY THE SHIP SPINS OUT OF CONTROL! IT'S CAUGHT IN A WHIRLPOOL!
WITHIN MOMENTS THE GIANT VESSEL DIPS ITS HULL INTO THE SWIRLING VORTEX AND IS NEVER SEEN AGAIN!
OH NO! HERE GOES THE REST OF THE NAVY!
ARE YOU LETTING THE WATER OUT *ALREADY?*
WATTERSON

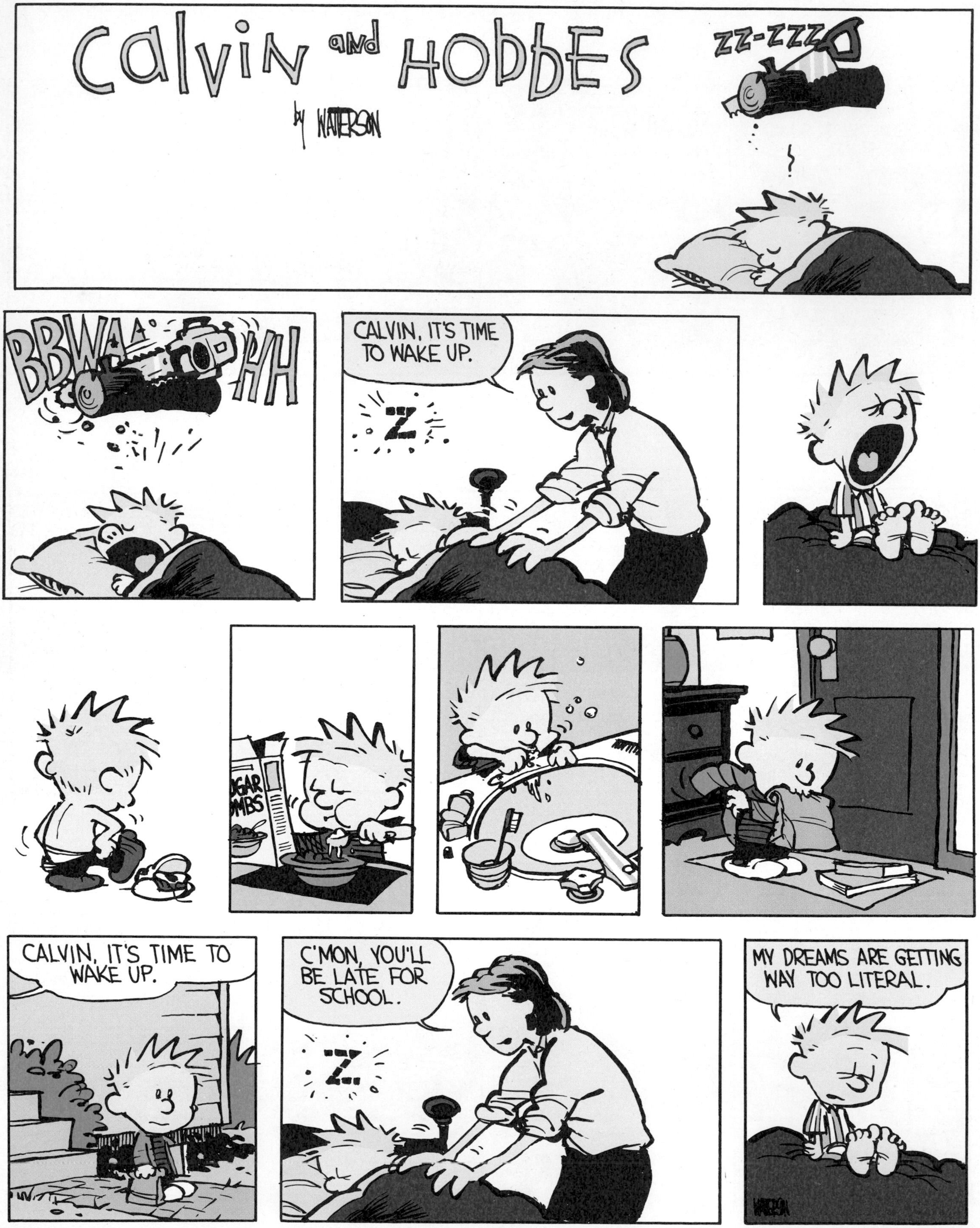
Calvin and HOBBES
by WATTERSON
ZZ-ZZZ
BBWAAAHH
CALVIN, IT'S TIME TO WAKE UP.
Z
SUGAR BOMBS
CALVIN, IT'S TIME TO WAKE UP.
C'MON, YOU'LL BE LATE FOR SCHOOL.
Z
MY DREAMS ARE GETTING WAY TOO LITERAL.

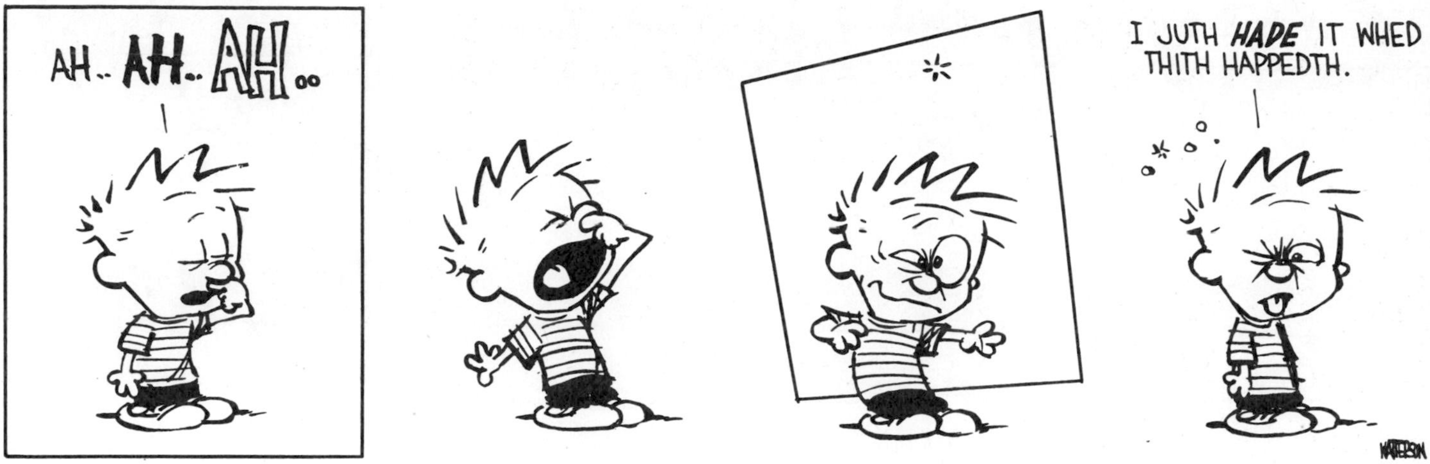
AH.. AH.. AH..
I JUTH HADE IT WHED THITH HAPPEDTH.
WATTERSON

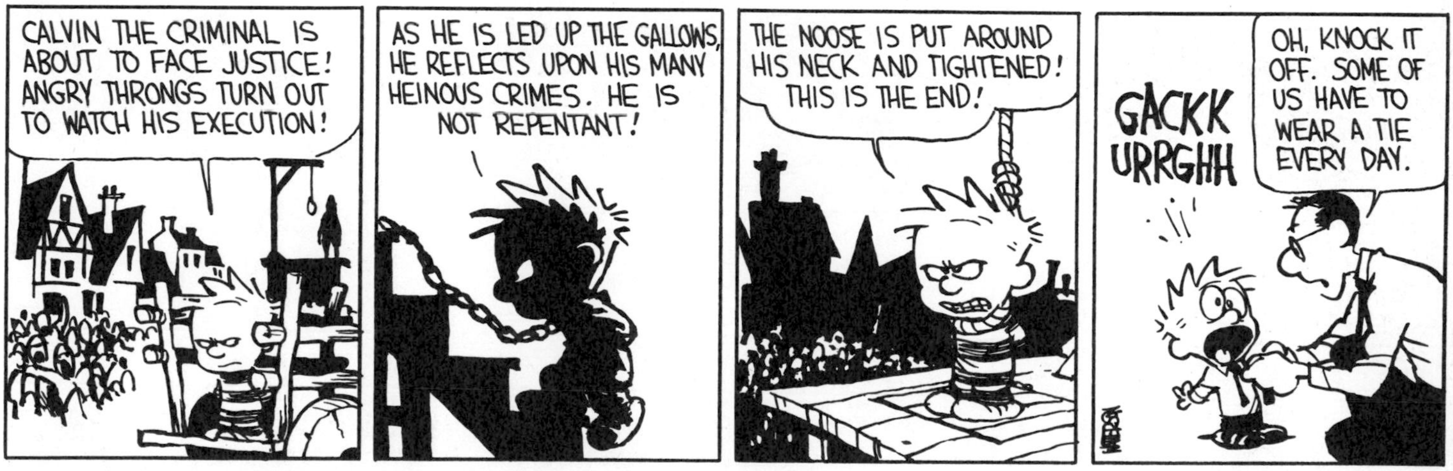
CALVIN THE CRIMINAL IS ABOUT TO FACE JUSTICE! ANGRY THRONGS TURN OUT TO WATCH HIS EXECUTION!
AS HE IS LED UP THE GALLOWS, HE REFLECTS UPON HIS MANY HEINOUS CRIMES. HE IS NOT REPENTANT!
THE NOOSE IS PUT AROUND HIS NECK AND TIGHTENED! THIS IS THE END!
GACKK URRGHH
OH, KNOCK IT OFF. SOME OF US HAVE TO WEAR A TIE EVERY DAY.
WATTERSON

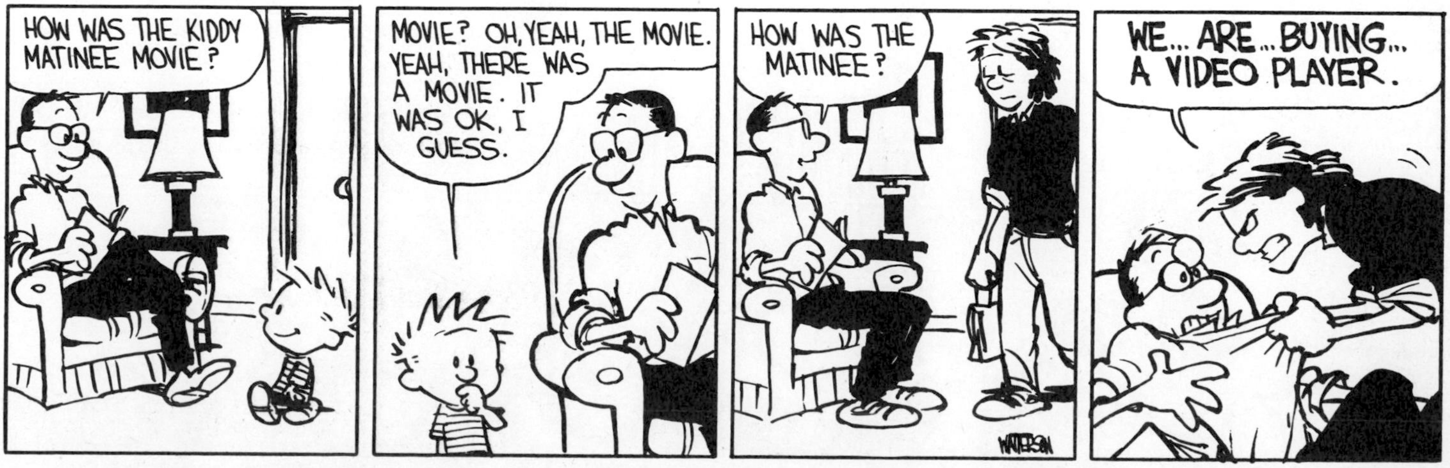
HOW WAS THE KIDDY MATINEE MOVIE?
MOVIE? OH, YEAH, THE MOVIE. YEAH, THERE WAS A MOVIE. IT WAS OK, I GUESS.
HOW WAS THE MATINEE?
WATTERSON
WE... ARE... BUYING... A VIDEO PLAYER.

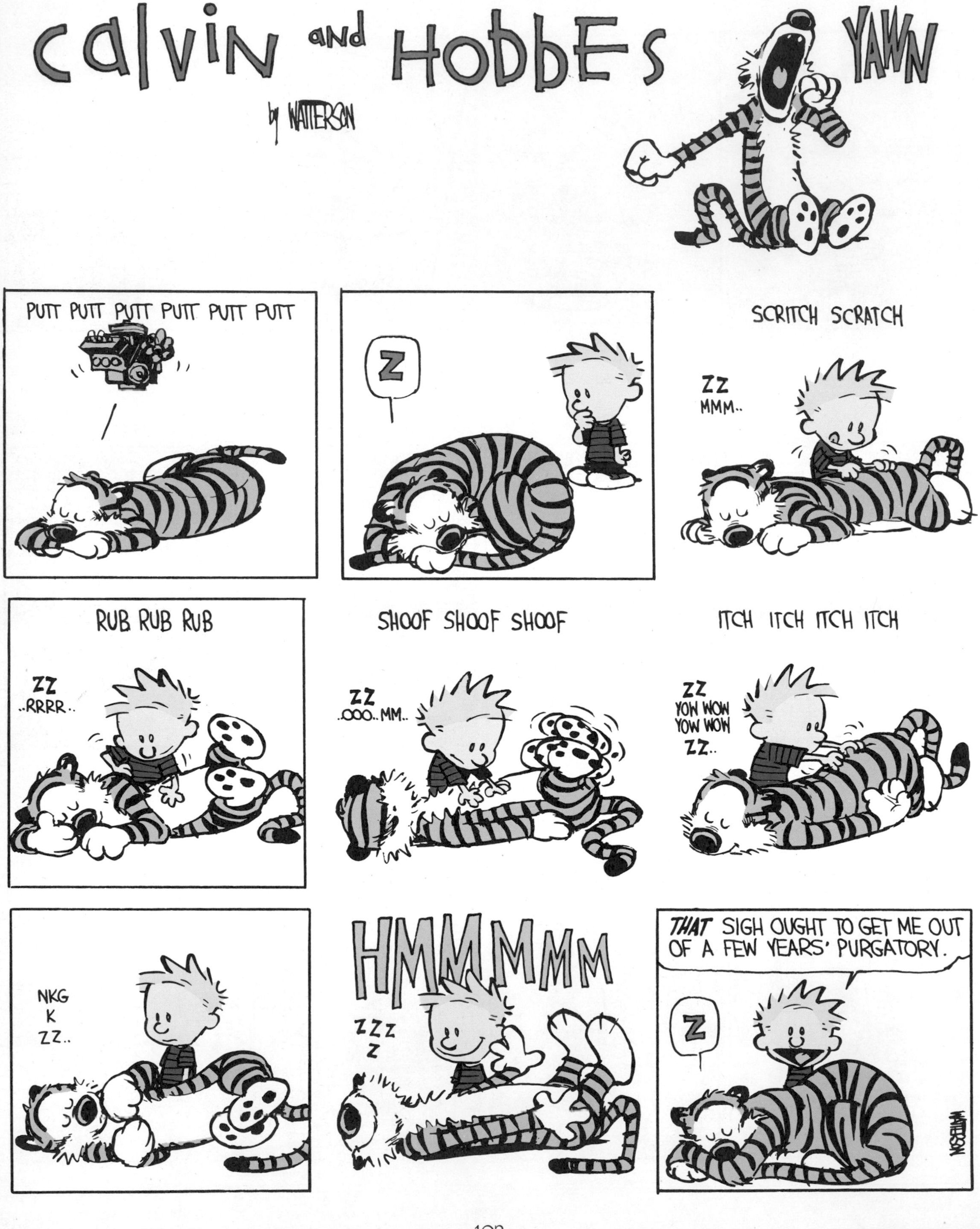

calvin and HOBBES
by WATTERSON
YAWN
PUTT PUTT PUTT PUTT PUTT PUTT
Z
SCRITCH SCRATCH
ZZ
MMM..
RUB RUB RUB
ZZ
..RRRR..
SHOOF SHOOF SHOOF
ZZ
..OOO..MM..
ITCH ITCH ITCH ITCH
ZZ
YOW WOW
YOW WOW
ZZ..
NKG
K
ZZ..
HMMMMMM
ZZZ
Z
THAT SIGH OUGHT TO GET ME OUT OF A FEW YEARS' PURGATORY.
Z
WATTERSON

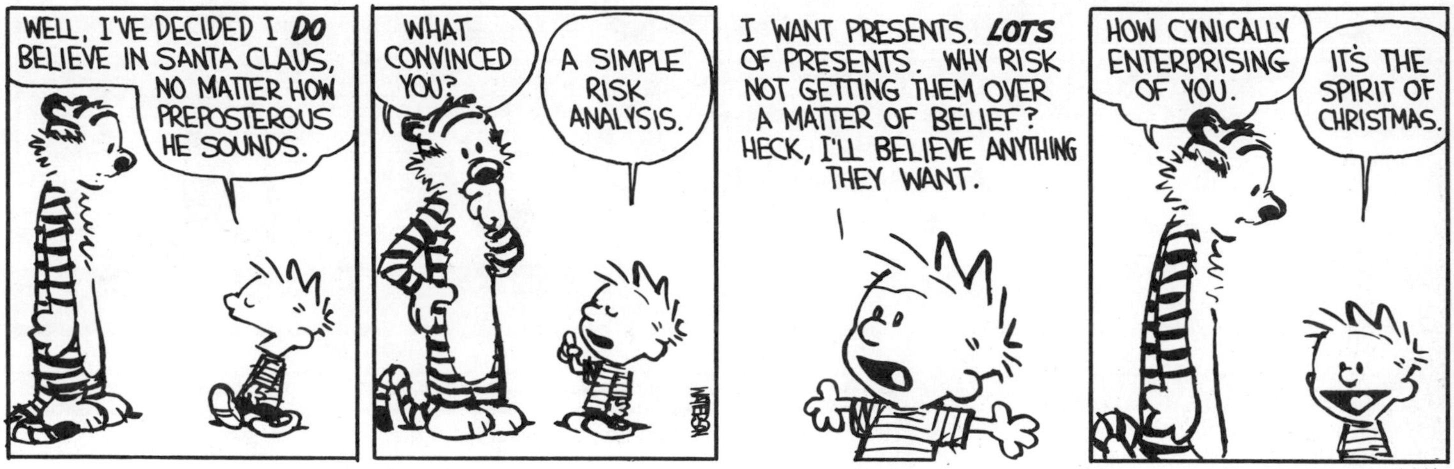
WELL, I'VE DECIDED I **DO** BELIEVE IN SANTA CLAUS, NO MATTER HOW PREPOSTEROUS HE SOUNDS.
WHAT CONVINCED YOU?
A SIMPLE RISK ANALYSIS.
I WANT PRESENTS. **LOTS** OF PRESENTS. WHY RISK NOT GETTING THEM OVER A MATTER OF BELIEF? HECK, I'LL BELIEVE ANYTHING THEY WANT.
HOW CYNICALLY ENTERPRISING OF YOU.
IT'S THE SPIRIT OF CHRISTMAS.

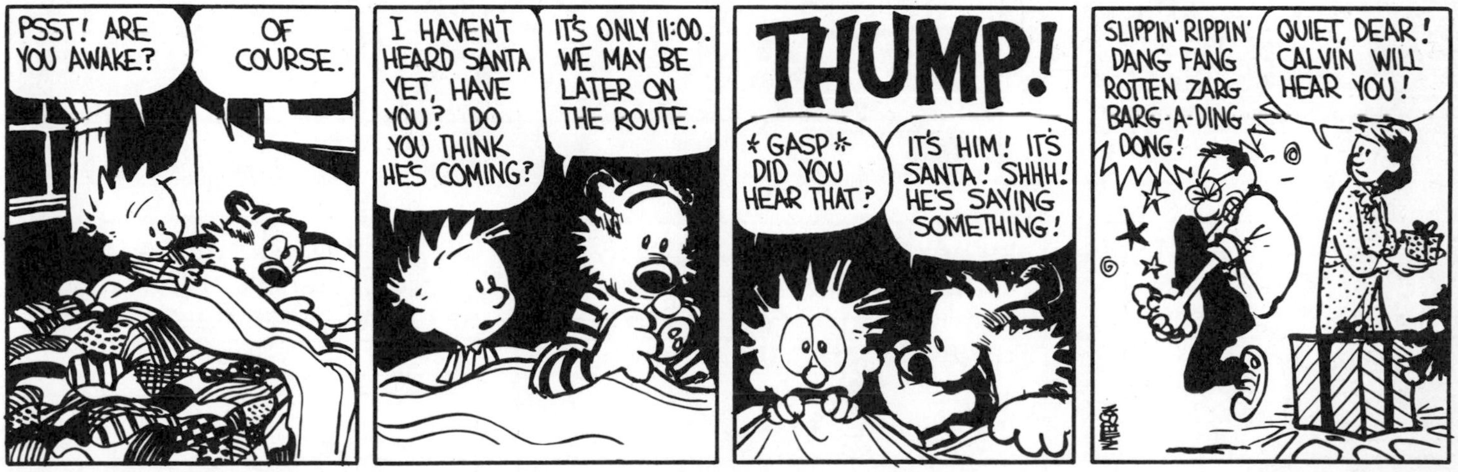
PSST! ARE YOU AWAKE?
OF COURSE.
I HAVEN'T HEARD SANTA YET, HAVE YOU? DO YOU THINK HE'S COMING?
IT'S ONLY 11:00. WE MAY BE LATER ON THE ROUTE.
THUMP!
*GASP* DID YOU HEAR THAT?
IT'S HIM! IT'S SANTA! SHHH! HE'S SAYING SOMETHING!
SLIPPIN' RIPPIN' DANG FANG ROTTEN ZARG BARG-A-DING DONG!
QUIET, DEAR! CALVIN WILL HEAR YOU!

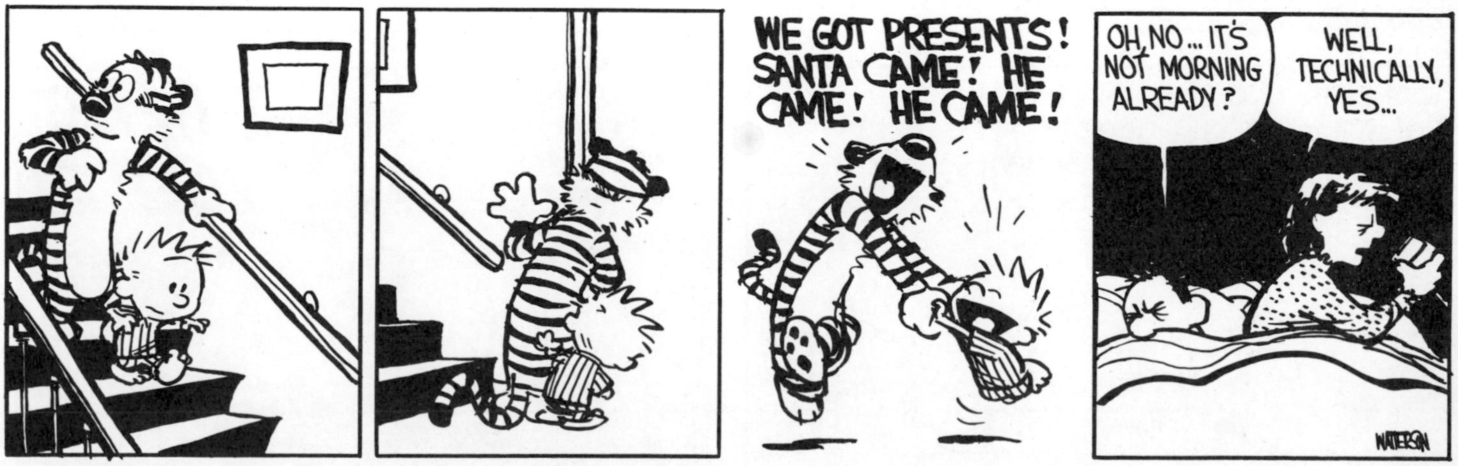
WE GOT PRESENTS! SANTA CAME! HE CAME! HE CAME!
OH, NO... IT'S NOT MORNING ALREADY?
WELL, TECHNICALLY, YES...

108

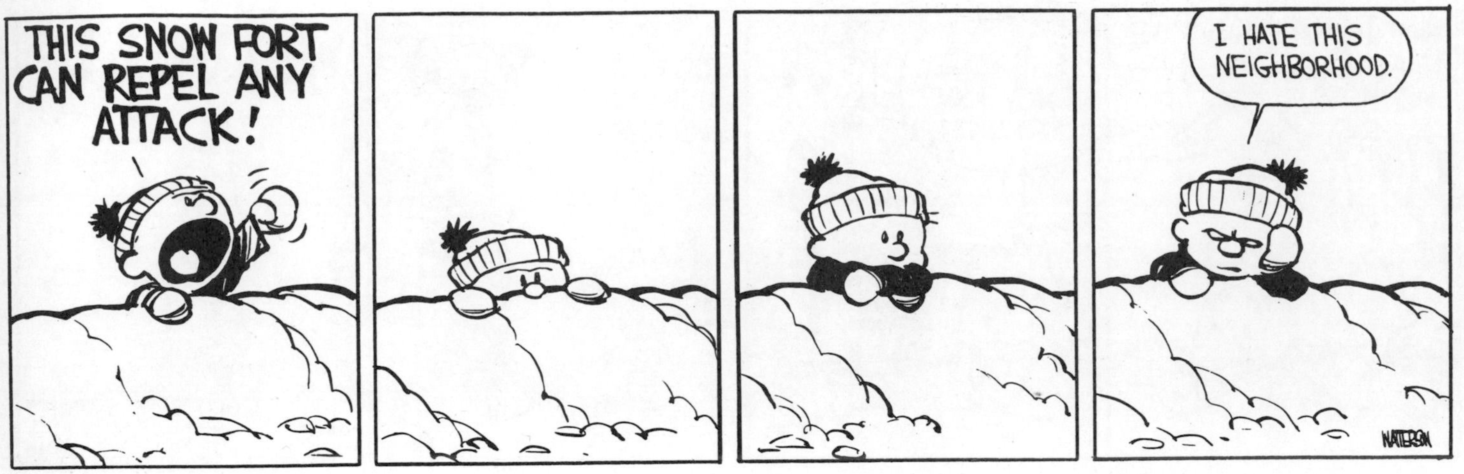
THIS SNOW FORT CAN REPEL ANY ATTACK!
I HATE THIS NEIGHBORHOOD.
WATTERSON

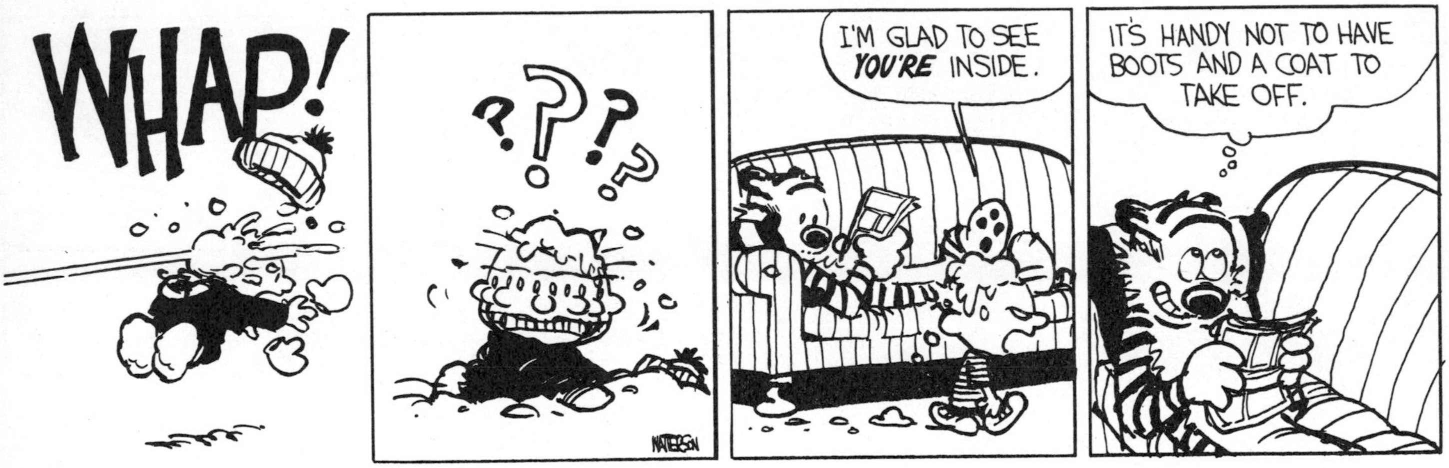
WHAP!
WATTERSON
I'M GLAD TO SEE YOU'RE INSIDE.
IT'S HANDY NOT TO HAVE BOOTS AND A COAT TO TAKE OFF.

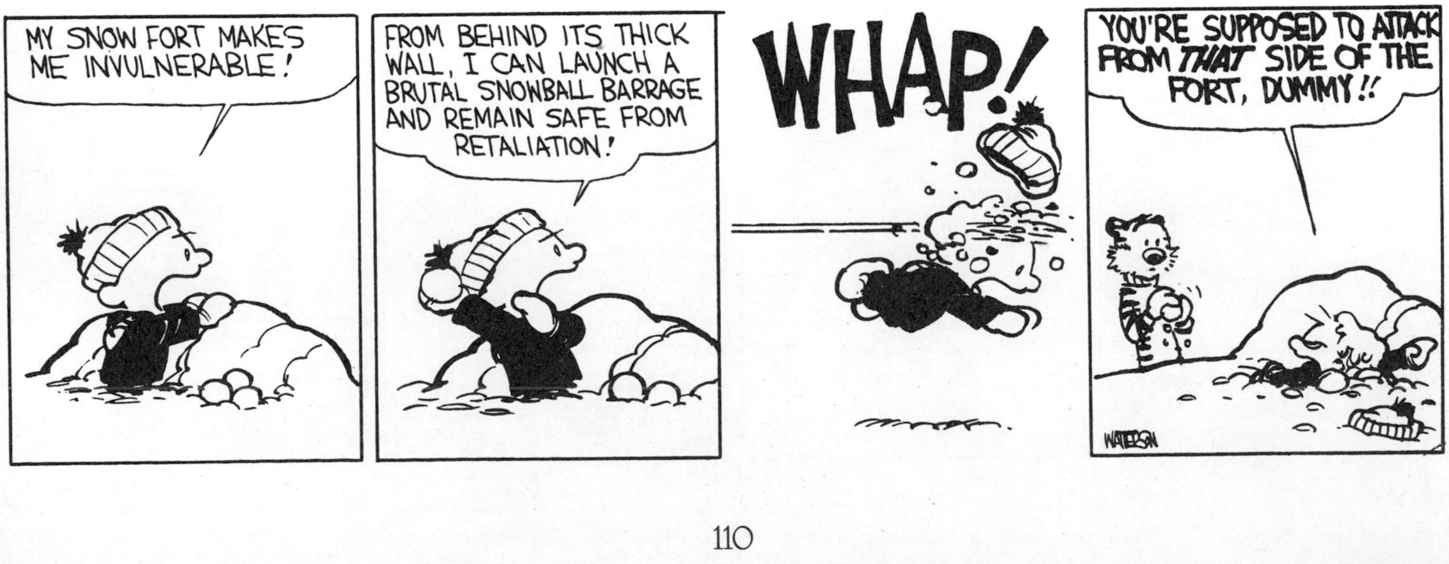
MY SNOW FORT MAKES ME INVULNERABLE!
FROM BEHIND ITS THICK WALL, I CAN LAUNCH A BRUTAL SNOWBALL BARRAGE AND REMAIN SAFE FROM RETALIATION!
WHAP!
YOU'RE SUPPOSED TO ATTACK FROM THAT SIDE OF THE FORT, DUMMY!!
WATTERSON

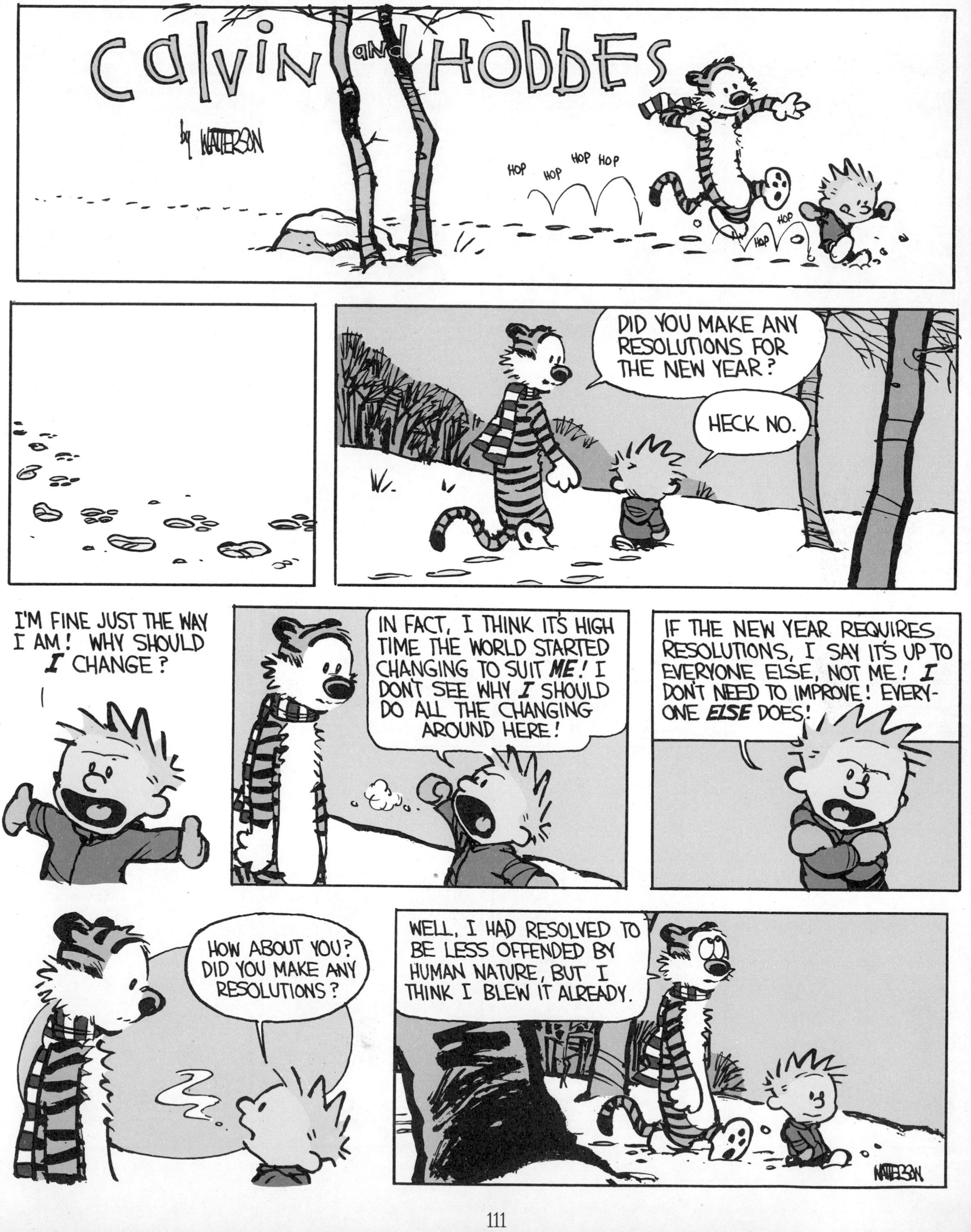
Calvin and HOBBES
by WATTERSON
HOP HOP HOP HOP
HOP HOP
DID YOU MAKE ANY RESOLUTIONS FOR THE NEW YEAR?
HECK NO.
I'M FINE JUST THE WAY I AM! WHY SHOULD *I* CHANGE?
IN FACT, I THINK IT'S HIGH TIME THE WORLD STARTED CHANGING TO SUIT *ME*! I DON'T SEE WHY *I* SHOULD DO ALL THE CHANGING AROUND HERE!
IF THE NEW YEAR REQUIRES RESOLUTIONS, I SAY IT'S UP TO EVERYONE ELSE, NOT ME! *I* DON'T NEED TO IMPROVE! EVERYONE *ELSE* DOES!
HOW ABOUT YOU? DID YOU MAKE ANY RESOLUTIONS?
WELL, I HAD RESOLVED TO BE LESS OFFENDED BY HUMAN NATURE, BUT I THINK I BLEW IT ALREADY.
WATTERSON

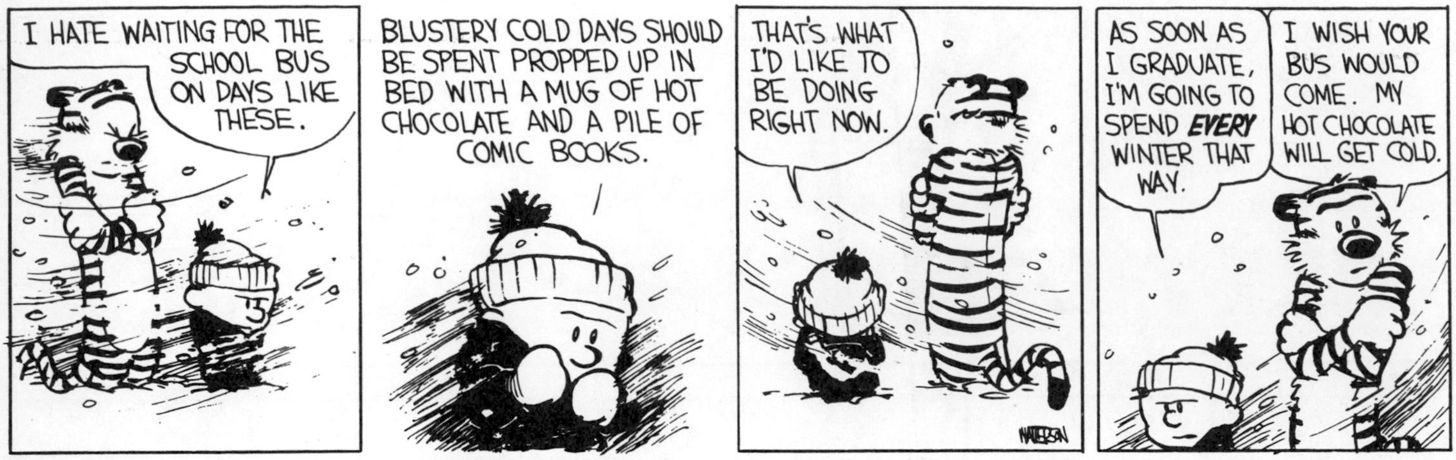
I HATE WAITING FOR THE SCHOOL BUS ON DAYS LIKE THESE.
BLUSTERY COLD DAYS SHOULD BE SPENT PROPPED UP IN BED WITH A MUG OF HOT CHOCOLATE AND A PILE OF COMIC BOOKS.
THAT'S WHAT I'D LIKE TO BE DOING RIGHT NOW.
AS SOON AS I GRADUATE, I'M GOING TO SPEND EVERY WINTER THAT WAY.
I WISH YOUR BUS WOULD COME. MY HOT CHOCOLATE WILL GET COLD.

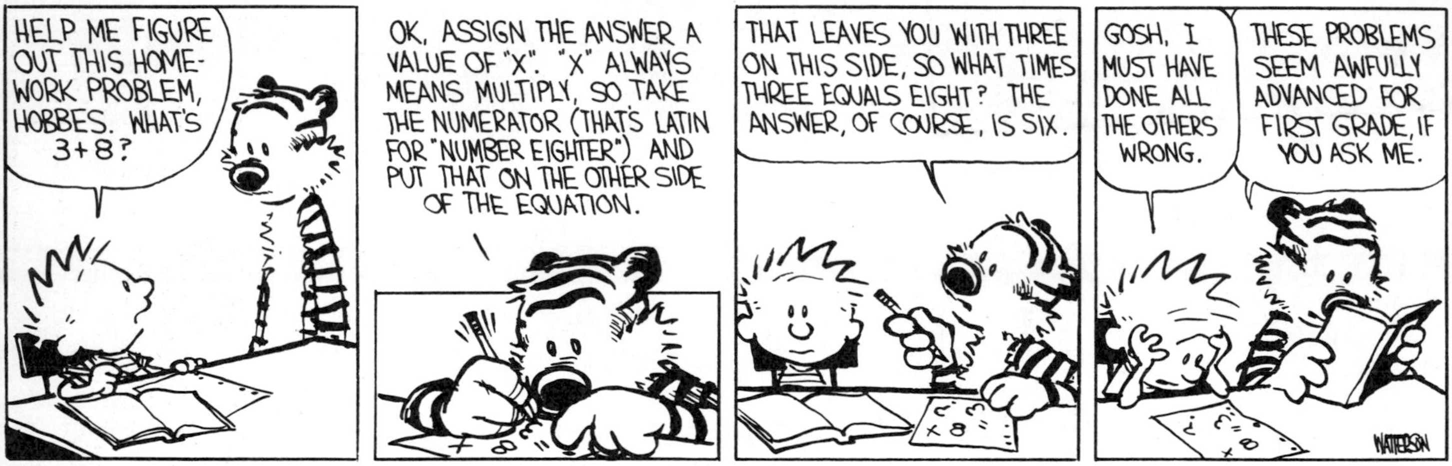
HELP ME FIGURE OUT THIS HOMEWORK PROBLEM, HOBBES. WHAT'S 3+8?
OK, ASSIGN THE ANSWER A VALUE OF "X". "X" ALWAYS MEANS MULTIPLY, SO TAKE THE NUMERATOR (THAT'S LATIN FOR "NUMBER EIGHTER") AND PUT THAT ON THE OTHER SIDE OF THE EQUATION.
THAT LEAVES YOU WITH THREE ON THIS SIDE, SO WHAT TIMES THREE EQUALS EIGHT? THE ANSWER, OF COURSE, IS SIX.
GOSH, I MUST HAVE DONE ALL THE OTHERS WRONG.
THESE PROBLEMS SEEM AWFULLY ADVANCED FOR FIRST GRADE, IF YOU ASK ME.

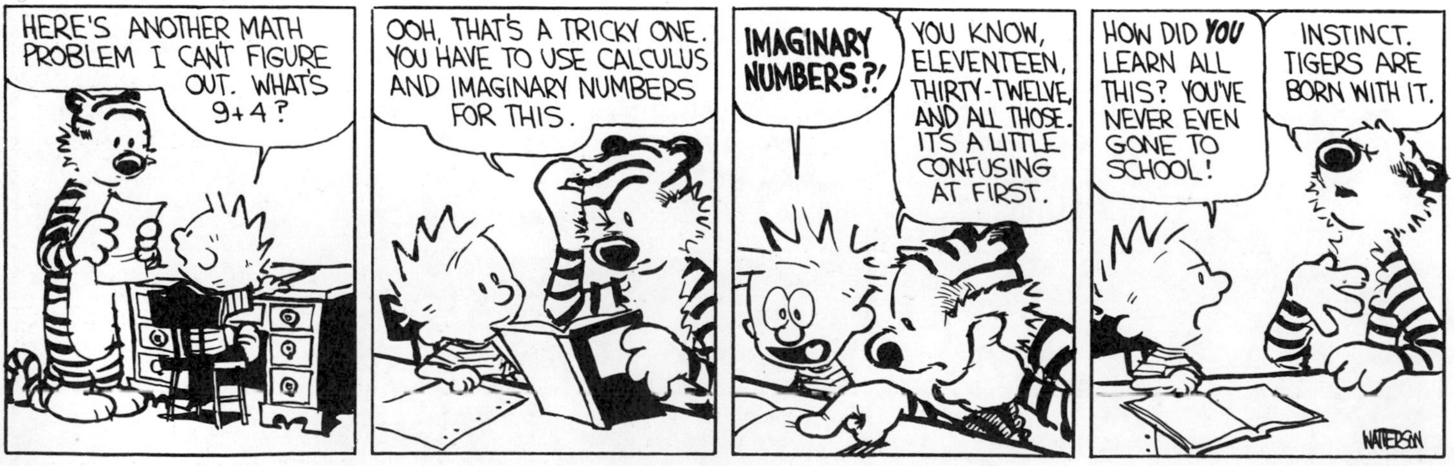
HERE'S ANOTHER MATH PROBLEM I CAN'T FIGURE OUT. WHAT'S 9+4?
OOH, THAT'S A TRICKY ONE. YOU HAVE TO USE CALCULUS AND IMAGINARY NUMBERS FOR THIS.
IMAGINARY NUMBERS ?!
YOU KNOW, ELEVENTEEN, THIRTY-TWELVE, AND ALL THOSE. IT'S A LITTLE CONFUSING AT FIRST.
HOW DID YOU LEARN ALL THIS? YOU'VE NEVER EVEN GONE TO SCHOOL!
INSTINCT. TIGERS ARE BORN WITH IT.

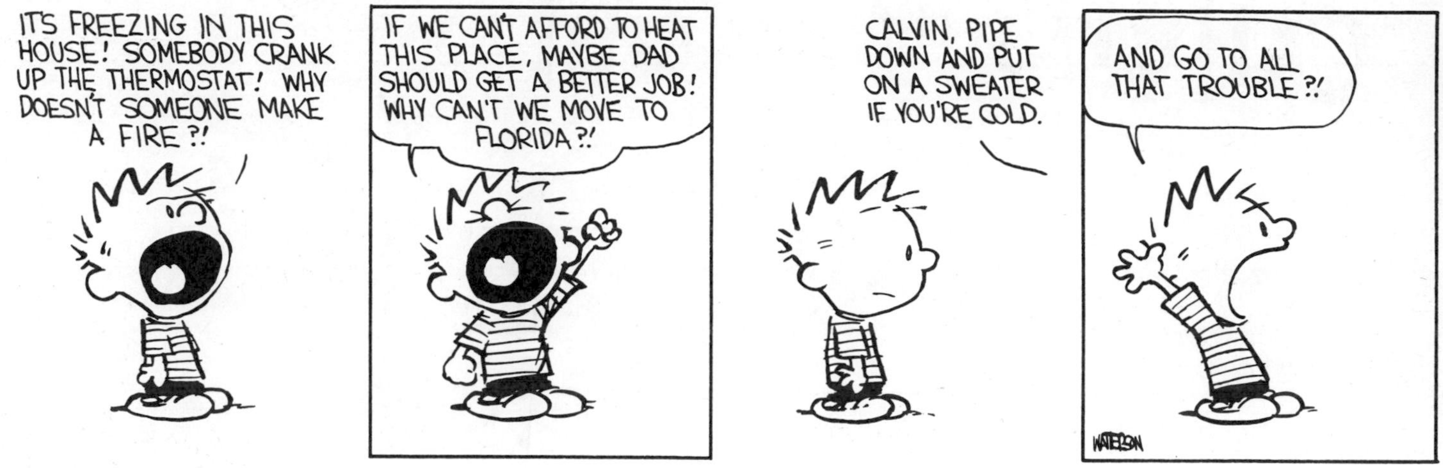
IT'S FREEZING IN THIS HOUSE! SOMEBODY CRANK UP THE THERMOSTAT! WHY DOESN'T SOMEONE MAKE A FIRE?!
IF WE CAN'T AFFORD TO HEAT THIS PLACE, MAYBE DAD SHOULD GET A BETTER JOB! WHY CAN'T WE MOVE TO FLORIDA?!
CALVIN, PIPE DOWN AND PUT ON A SWEATER IF YOU'RE COLD.
AND GO TO ALL THAT TROUBLE?!
WATERSON

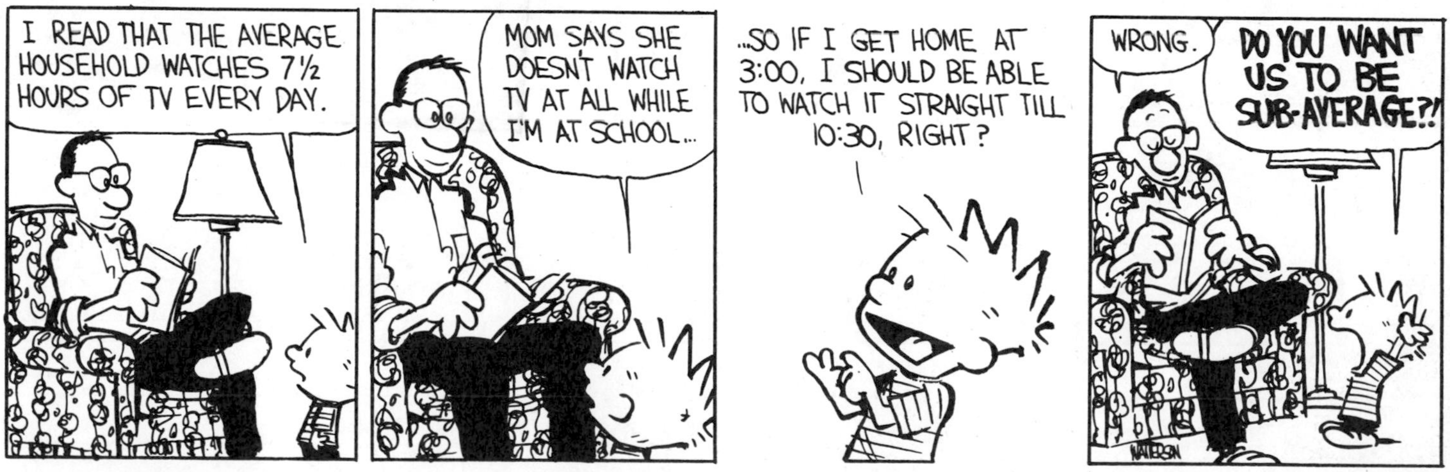
I READ THAT THE AVERAGE HOUSEHOLD WATCHES 7½ HOURS OF TV EVERY DAY.
MOM SAYS SHE DOESN'T WATCH TV AT ALL WHILE I'M AT SCHOOL...
...SO IF I GET HOME AT 3:00, I SHOULD BE ABLE TO WATCH IT STRAIGHT TILL 10:30, RIGHT?
WRONG.
DO YOU WANT US TO BE SUB-AVERAGE?!
WATERSON

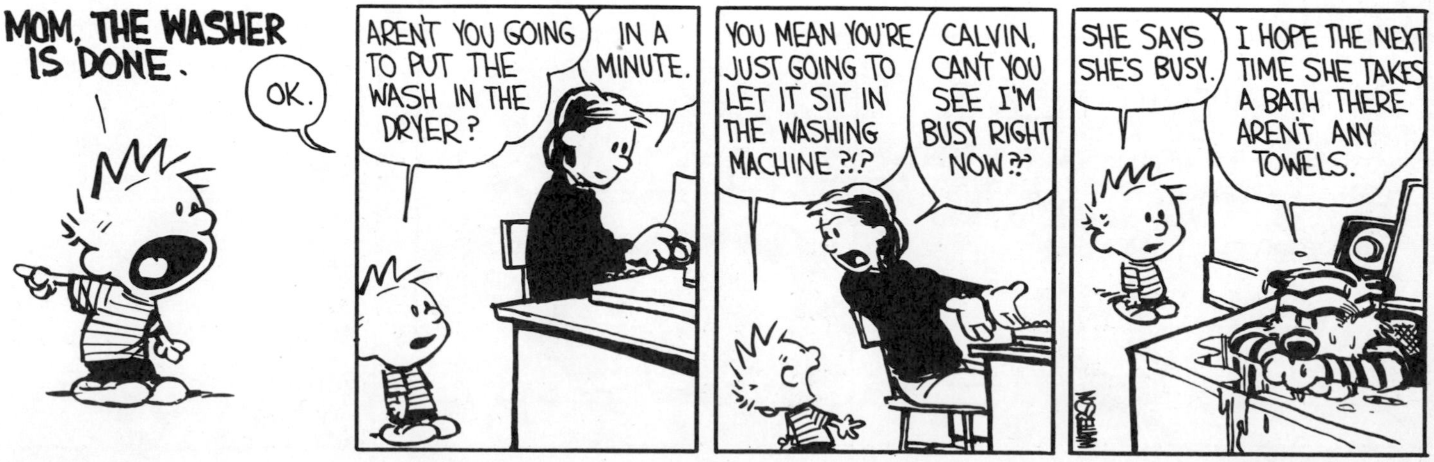
MOM, THE WASHER IS DONE.
OK.
AREN'T YOU GOING TO PUT THE WASH IN THE DRYER?
IN A MINUTE.
YOU MEAN YOU'RE JUST GOING TO LET IT SIT IN THE WASHING MACHINE?!?
CALVIN, CAN'T YOU SEE I'M BUSY RIGHT NOW?!
SHE SAYS SHE'S BUSY.
I HOPE THE NEXT TIME SHE TAKES A BATH THERE AREN'T ANY TOWELS.
WATERSON

# CALVIN and HOBBES

by WATTERSON

TWO PARTS SLUSH...
ONE PART SOLID ICE...
ONE PART HARD-PACKED SNOW...
A DASH OF ASSORTED DEBRIS...

SCULPT INTO SPHERE, AND SERVE AT HIGH VELOCITY WITHOUT WARNING.

OH, BOY, HERE COMES SUSIE!

HEY, SUSIE!

WHAP!

HA HA! I GOTCHA, YOU DUMB GIRL!!

AUGHH!

MY EYEBALL! WHERE'S MY EYEBALL?!

WHAT ARE YOU TALKING ABOUT? I HIT YOU IN THE BACK.

IT KNOCKED MY EYEBALL OUT! FIND IT AND PACK IT IN SNOW SO THEY CAN SAVE IT! OW! OW!

GOSH, DID YOU REALLY LOSE YOUR EYEBALL? I DIDN'T KNOW THEY CAME OUT! WOW. I'M REALLY SORRY. I DIDN'T MEAN TO KNOCK IT OUT. CAN I SEE THE SOCKET? BOY, WHERE DO YOU SUPPOSE IT ROLLED?

SOMEWHERE OVER THERE, POOP HEAD!!

BOOT

WATTERSON

WHAT ARE YOU DOING?

MY EYEBALL FELL OUT. HELP ME LOOK FOR IT.

114

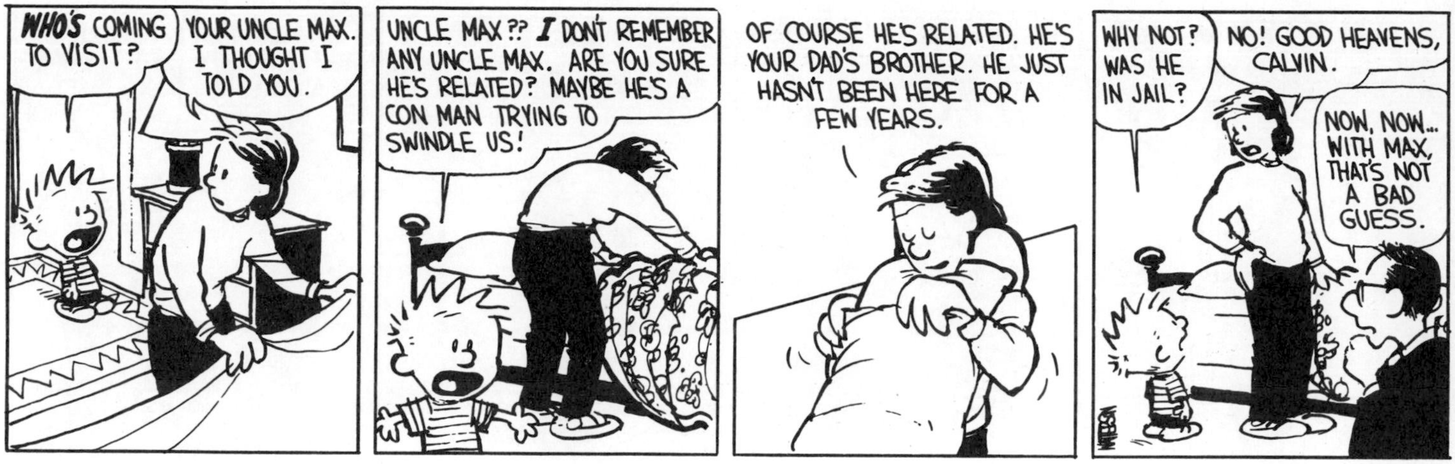
WHO'S COMING TO VISIT?
YOUR UNCLE MAX. I THOUGHT I TOLD YOU.
UNCLE MAX?? I DON'T REMEMBER ANY UNCLE MAX. ARE YOU SURE HE'S RELATED? MAYBE HE'S A CON MAN TRYING TO SWINDLE US!
OF COURSE HE'S RELATED. HE'S YOUR DAD'S BROTHER. HE JUST HASN'T BEEN HERE FOR A FEW YEARS.
WHY NOT? WAS HE IN JAIL?
NO! GOOD HEAVENS, CALVIN.
NOW, NOW... WITH MAX, THAT'S NOT A BAD GUESS.

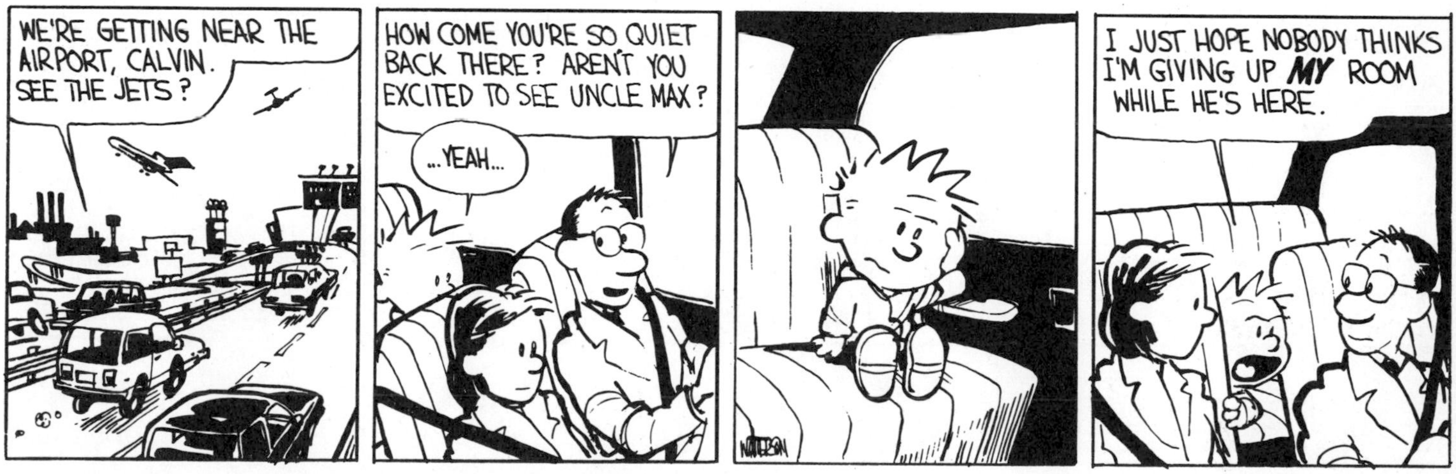
WE'RE GETTING NEAR THE AIRPORT, CALVIN. SEE THE JETS?
HOW COME YOU'RE SO QUIET BACK THERE? AREN'T YOU EXCITED TO SEE UNCLE MAX?
...YEAH...
I JUST HOPE NOBODY THINKS I'M GIVING UP MY ROOM WHILE HE'S HERE.

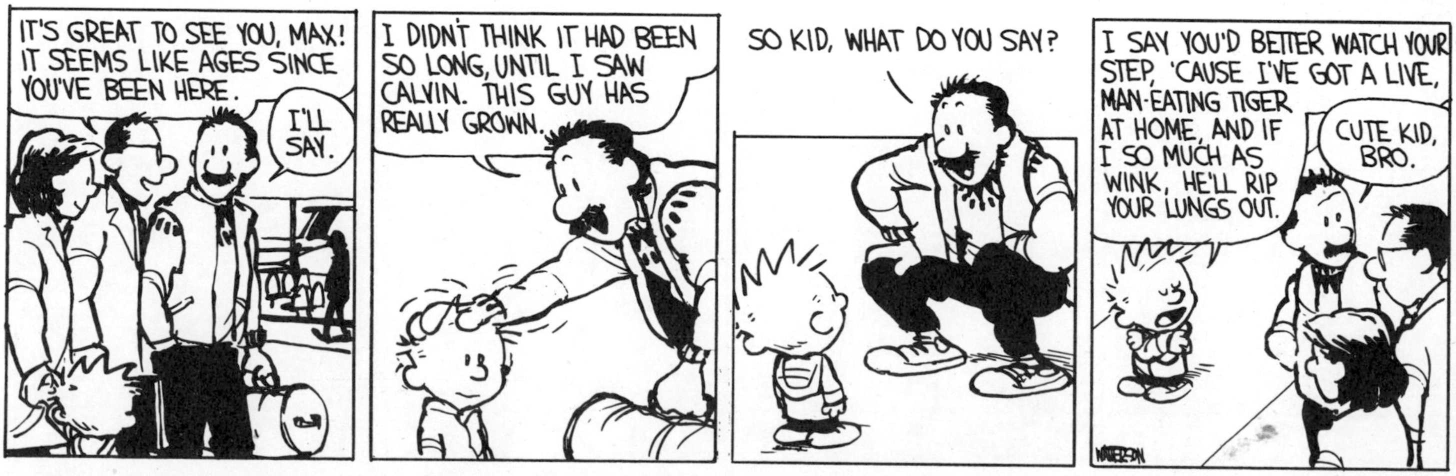
IT'S GREAT TO SEE YOU, MAX! IT SEEMS LIKE AGES SINCE YOU'VE BEEN HERE.
I'LL SAY.
I DIDN'T THINK IT HAD BEEN SO LONG, UNTIL I SAW CALVIN. THIS GUY HAS REALLY GROWN.
SO KID, WHAT DO YOU SAY?
I SAY YOU'D BETTER WATCH YOUR STEP, 'CAUSE I'VE GOT A LIVE, MAN-EATING TIGER AT HOME, AND IF I SO MUCH AS WINK, HE'LL RIP YOUR LUNGS OUT.
CUTE KID, BRO.

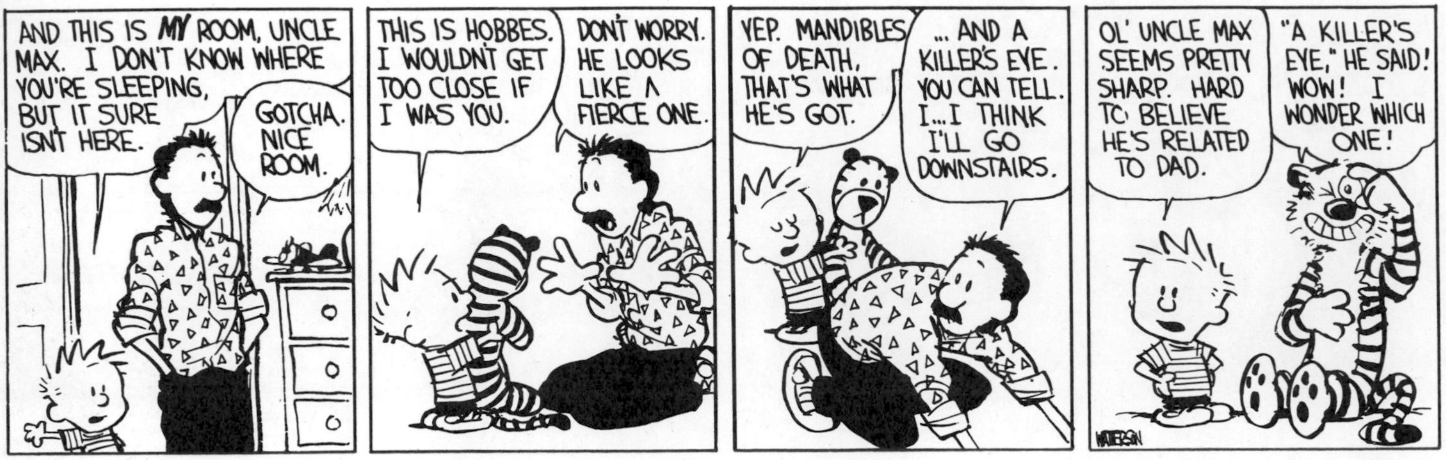
AND THIS IS MY ROOM, UNCLE MAX. I DON'T KNOW WHERE YOU'RE SLEEPING, BUT IT SURE ISN'T HERE.
GOTCHA. NICE ROOM.
THIS IS HOBBES. I WOULDN'T GET TOO CLOSE IF I WAS YOU.
DON'T WORRY. HE LOOKS LIKE A FIERCE ONE.
YEP. MANDIBLES OF DEATH. THAT'S WHAT HE'S GOT.
... AND A KILLER'S EYE. YOU CAN TELL. I...I THINK I'LL GO DOWNSTAIRS.
OL' UNCLE MAX SEEMS PRETTY SHARP. HARD TO BELIEVE HE'S RELATED TO DAD.
"A KILLER'S EYE," HE SAID! WOW! I WONDER WHICH ONE!

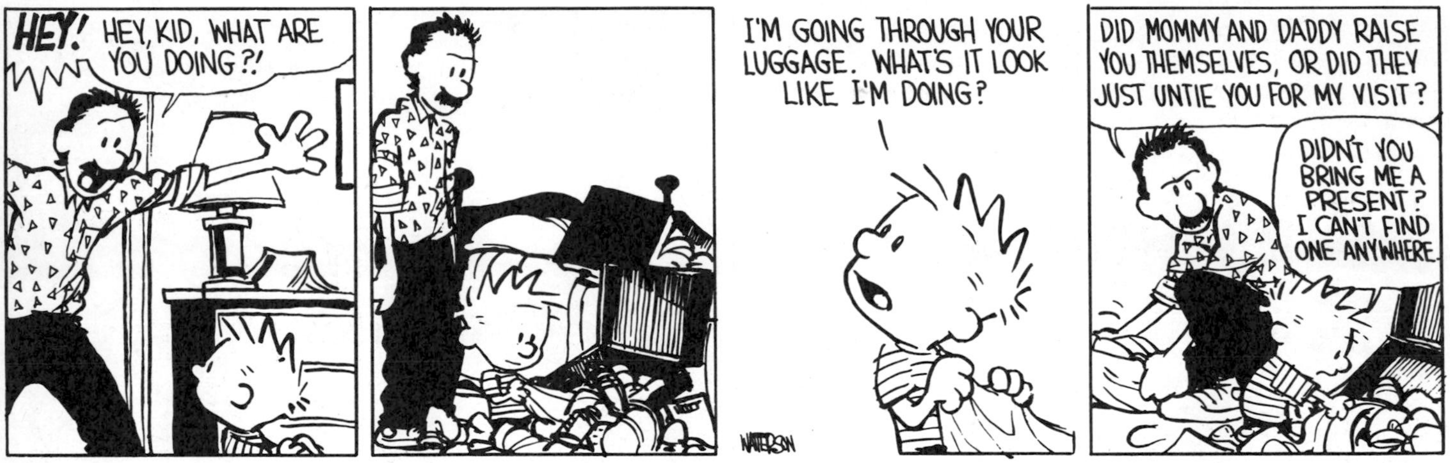
HEY!
HEY, KID, WHAT ARE YOU DOING?!
I'M GOING THROUGH YOUR LUGGAGE. WHAT'S IT LOOK LIKE I'M DOING?
DID MOMMY AND DADDY RAISE YOU THEMSELVES, OR DID THEY JUST UNTIE YOU FOR MY VISIT?
DIDN'T YOU BRING ME A PRESENT? I CAN'T FIND ONE ANYWHERE.

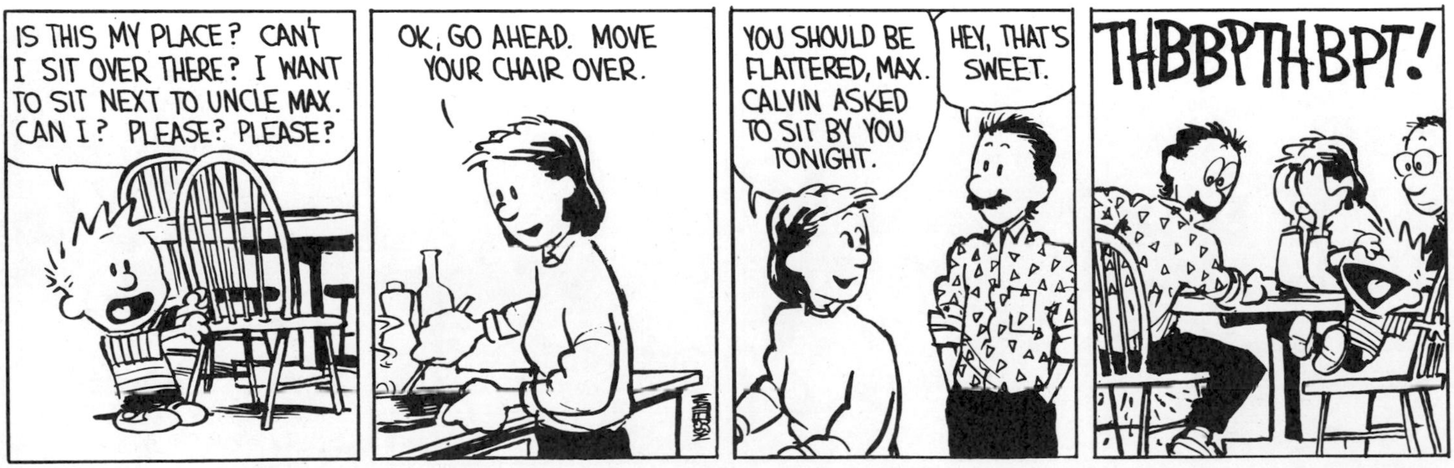
IS THIS MY PLACE? CAN'T I SIT OVER THERE? I WANT TO SIT NEXT TO UNCLE MAX. CAN I? PLEASE? PLEASE?
OK, GO AHEAD. MOVE YOUR CHAIR OVER.
YOU SHOULD BE FLATTERED, MAX. CALVIN ASKED TO SIT BY YOU TONIGHT.
HEY, THAT'S SWEET.
THBBPTHBPT!

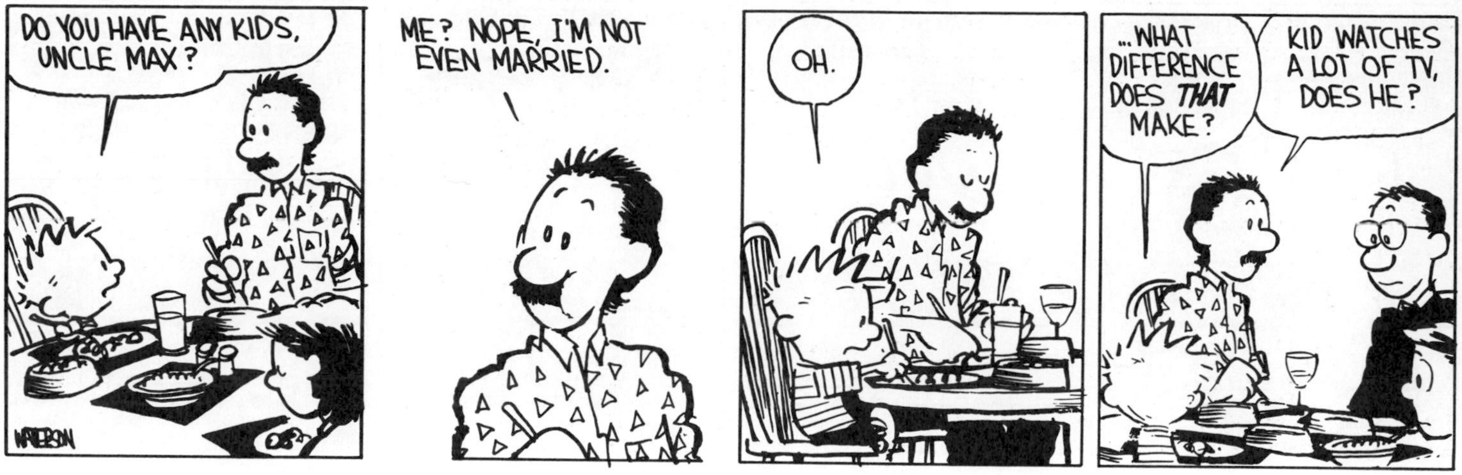
DO YOU HAVE ANY KIDS, UNCLE MAX?
ME? NOPE, I'M NOT EVEN MARRIED.
OH.
...WHAT DIFFERENCE DOES **THAT** MAKE?
KID WATCHES A LOT OF TV, DOES HE?
WATTERSON

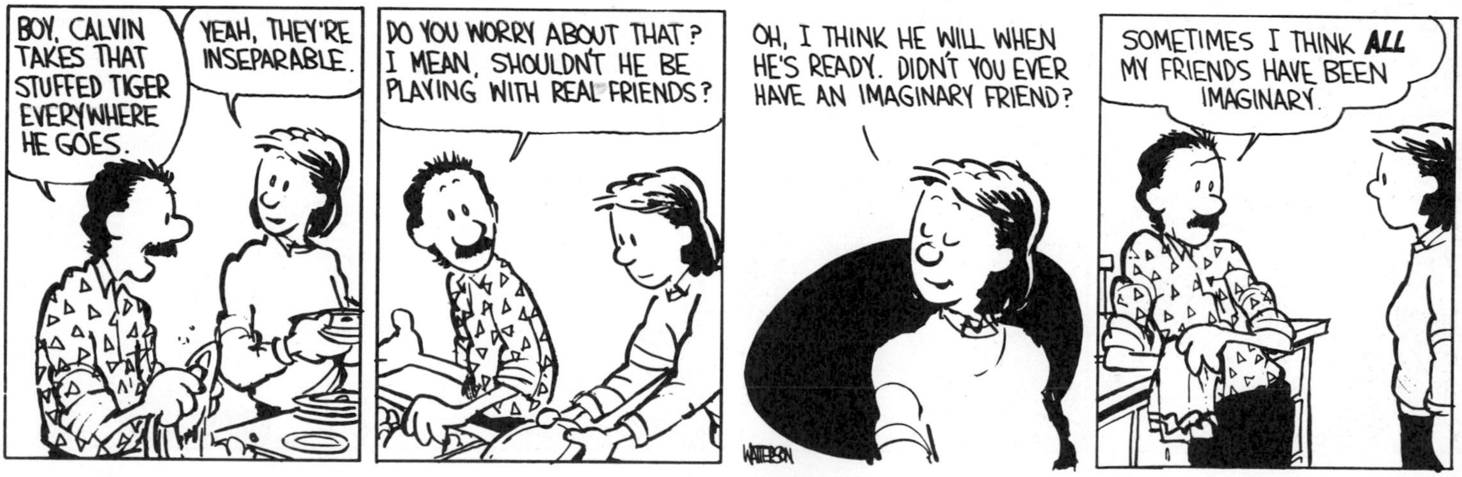
BOY, CALVIN TAKES THAT STUFFED TIGER EVERYWHERE HE GOES.
YEAH, THEY'RE INSEPARABLE.
DO YOU WORRY ABOUT THAT? I MEAN, SHOULDN'T HE BE PLAYING WITH REAL FRIENDS?
OH, I THINK HE WILL WHEN HE'S READY. DIDN'T YOU EVER HAVE AN IMAGINARY FRIEND?
WATTERSON
SOMETIMES I THINK **ALL** MY FRIENDS HAVE BEEN IMAGINARY.

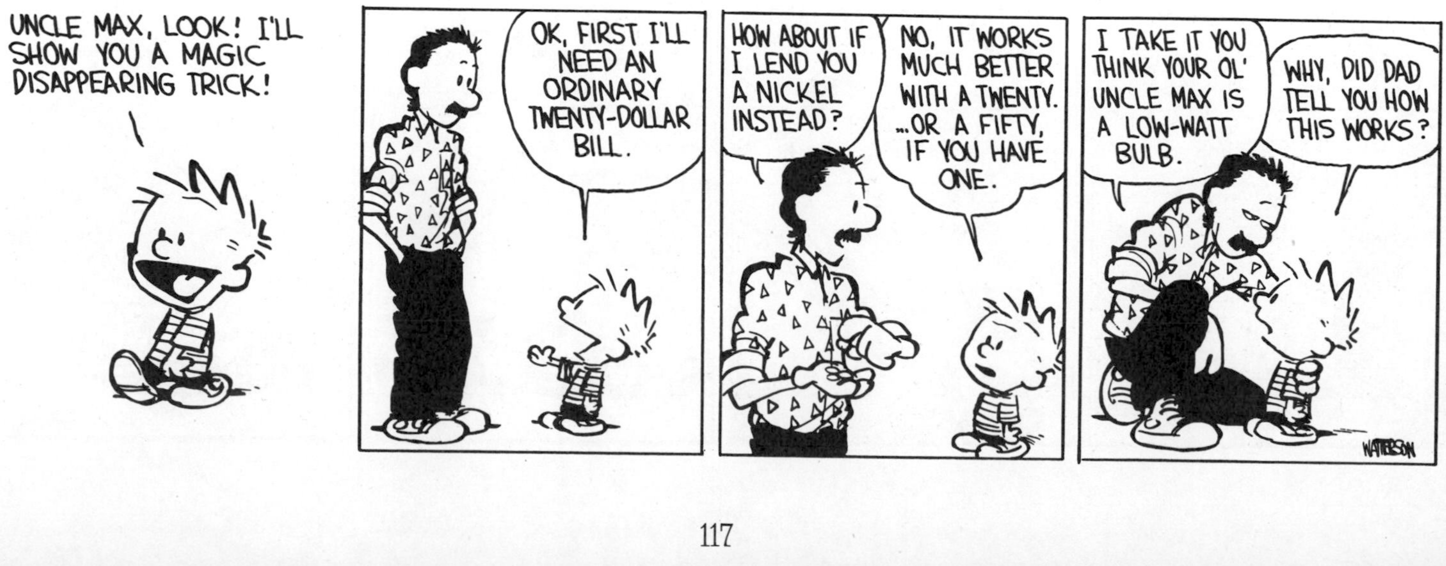
UNCLE MAX, LOOK! I'LL SHOW YOU A MAGIC DISAPPEARING TRICK!
OK, FIRST I'LL NEED AN ORDINARY TWENTY-DOLLAR BILL.
HOW ABOUT IF I LEND YOU A NICKEL INSTEAD?
NO, IT WORKS MUCH BETTER WITH A TWENTY. ...OR A FIFTY, IF YOU HAVE ONE.
I TAKE IT YOU THINK YOUR OL' UNCLE MAX IS A LOW-WATT BULB.
WHY, DID DAD TELL YOU HOW THIS WORKS?
WATTERSON

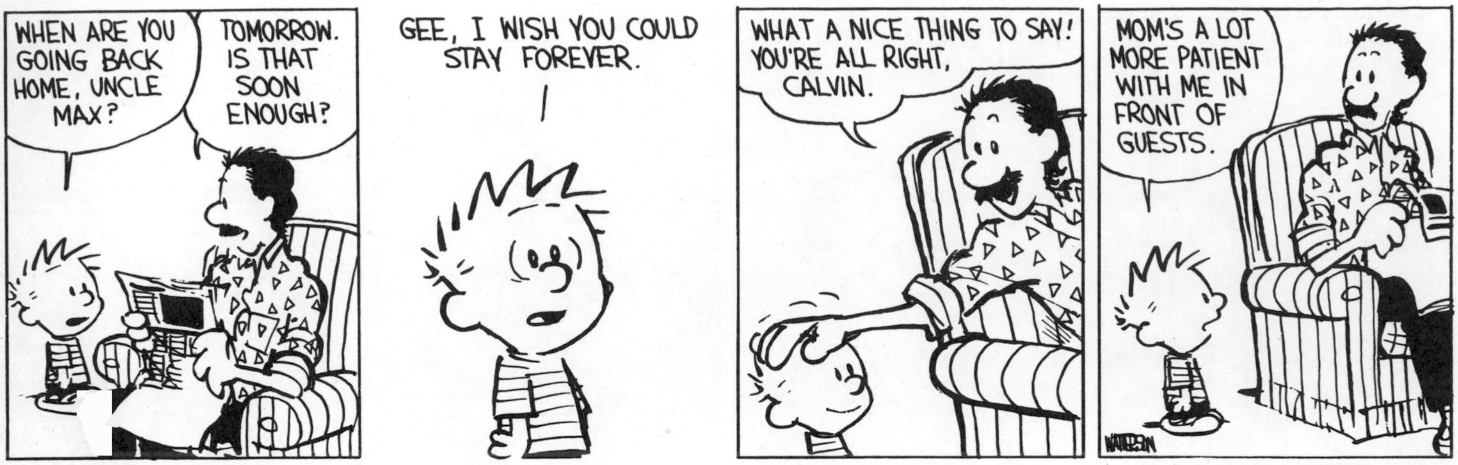
WHEN ARE YOU GOING BACK HOME, UNCLE MAX?
TOMORROW. IS THAT SOON ENOUGH?
GEE, I WISH YOU COULD STAY FOREVER.
WHAT A NICE THING TO SAY! YOU'RE ALL RIGHT, CALVIN.
MOM'S A LOT MORE PATIENT WITH ME IN FRONT OF GUESTS.
WATTERSON

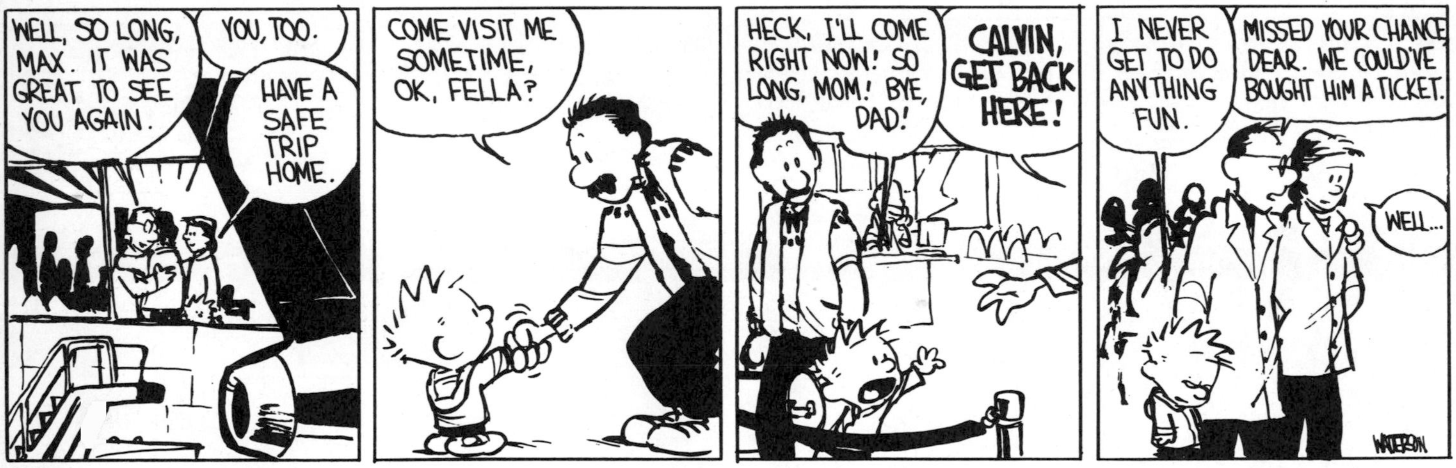
WELL, SO LONG, MAX. IT WAS GREAT TO SEE YOU AGAIN.
YOU, TOO.
HAVE A SAFE TRIP HOME.
COME VISIT ME SOMETIME, OK, FELLA?
HECK, I'LL COME RIGHT NOW! SO LONG, MOM! BYE, DAD!
CALVIN, GET BACK HERE!
I NEVER GET TO DO ANYTHING FUN.
MISSED YOUR CHANCE DEAR. WE COULD'VE BOUGHT HIM A TICKET.
WELL...
WATTERSON

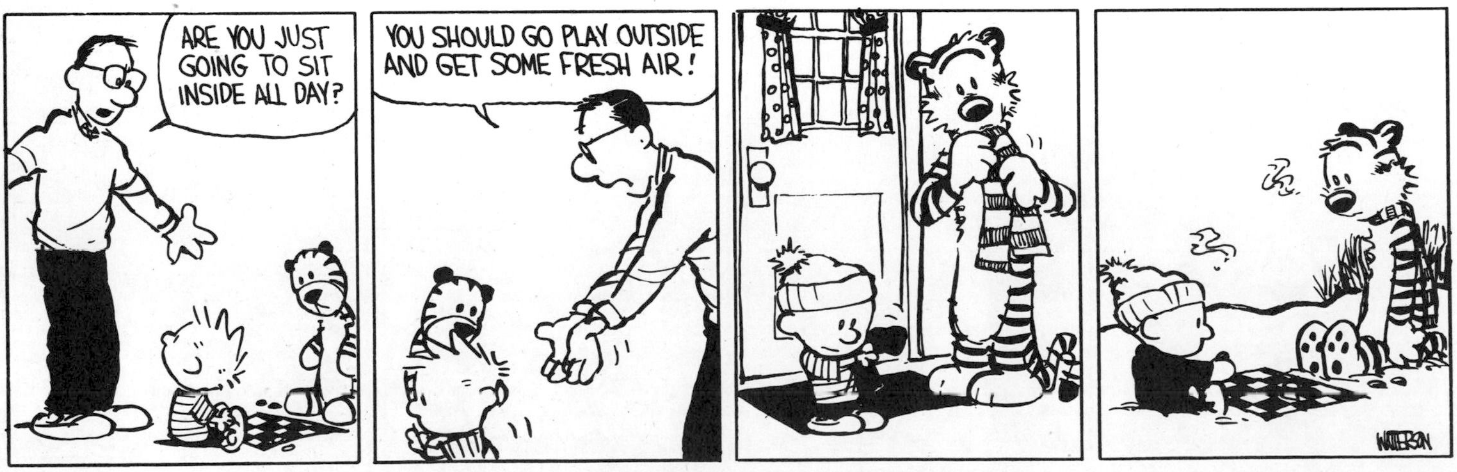
ARE YOU JUST GOING TO SIT INSIDE ALL DAY?
YOU SHOULD GO PLAY OUTSIDE AND GET SOME FRESH AIR!
WATTERSON

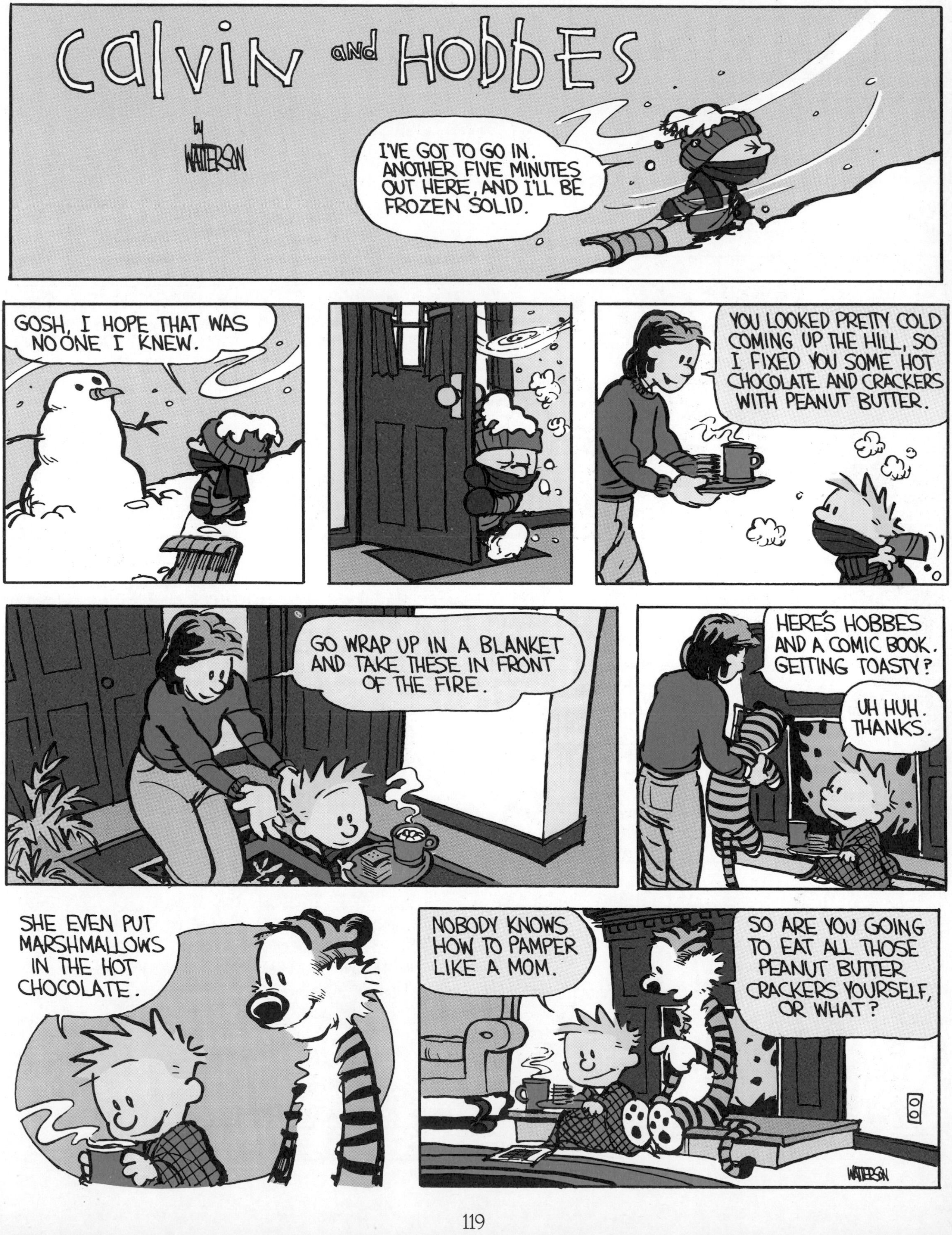
Calvin and HOBBES
by WATTERSON
I'VE GOT TO GO IN. ANOTHER FIVE MINUTES OUT HERE, AND I'LL BE FROZEN SOLID.
GOSH, I HOPE THAT WAS NO ONE I KNEW.
YOU LOOKED PRETTY COLD COMING UP THE HILL, SO I FIXED YOU SOME HOT CHOCOLATE AND CRACKERS WITH PEANUT BUTTER.
GO WRAP UP IN A BLANKET AND TAKE THESE IN FRONT OF THE FIRE.
HERE'S HOBBES AND A COMIC BOOK. GETTING TOASTY?
UH HUH. THANKS.
SHE EVEN PUT MARSHMALLOWS IN THE HOT CHOCOLATE.
NOBODY KNOWS HOW TO PAMPER LIKE A MOM.
SO ARE YOU GOING TO EAT ALL THOSE PEANUT BUTTER CRACKERS YOURSELF, OR WHAT?
WATTERSON

AAGHH, I CAN'T BELIEVE WE WERE ASSIGNED TO DO A REPORT TOGETHER.

ALL I CAN SAY IS YOU'D BETTER DO A GREAT JOB! I DON'T WANT TO FLUNK JUST BECAUSE I WAS ASSIGNED A DOOFUS FOR A PARTNER.

A **DOOFUS**?? WHO TAKES HER SANDWICHES APART AND EATS EACH INGREDIENT SEPARATELY?

**WHAT'S WRONG WITH THAT?!**

IT CERTIFIES YOU AS A GRADE "A" NIMROD.

**IT DOES NOT!**

OK, LOOK. WE'VE GOT TO DO THIS DUMB PROJECT TOGETHER, SO WE MIGHT AS WELL GET IT OVER WITH. WHAT ARE WE SUPPOSED TO BE DOING?

WEREN'T YOU EVEN PAYING ATTENTION?! WHAT WOULD YOU DO IF I WASN'T HERE TO ASK?? YOU'D FLUNK AND BE SENT BACK TO KINDERGARTEN, THAT'S WHAT!

SAYS YOU! I HEARD THAT SOMETIMES KIDS DON'T PAY ATTENTION BECAUSE THE CLASS GOES AT TOO SLOW OF A PACE FOR THEM. SOME OF US ARE TOO SMART FOR THE CLASS.

OH, RIGHT. YOU'RE **TOO** SMART.

BELIEVE IT, LADY. YOU KNOW HOW EINSTEIN GOT BAD GRADES AS A KID? WELL, **MINE** ARE EVEN **WORSE!**

SO WHAT ARE WE SUPPOSED TO BE DOING?

WE'RE **SUPPOSED** TO BE RESEARCHING THE PLANET MERCURY.

SO WHAT HAVE WE FOUND OUT?

**NOTHING!** I'M NOT GOING TO DO THIS WHOLE THING MYSELF!

YOU'D PROBABLY GOOF IT ALL UP IF YOU DID. LET'S GET STARTED.

YES! **LET'S!**

I'LL BE THE MANAGEMENT, AND YOU CAN BE THE LABOR. FIRST, GET SOME BOOKS.

**DOES ANYONE WANT TO TRADE PARTNERS?**

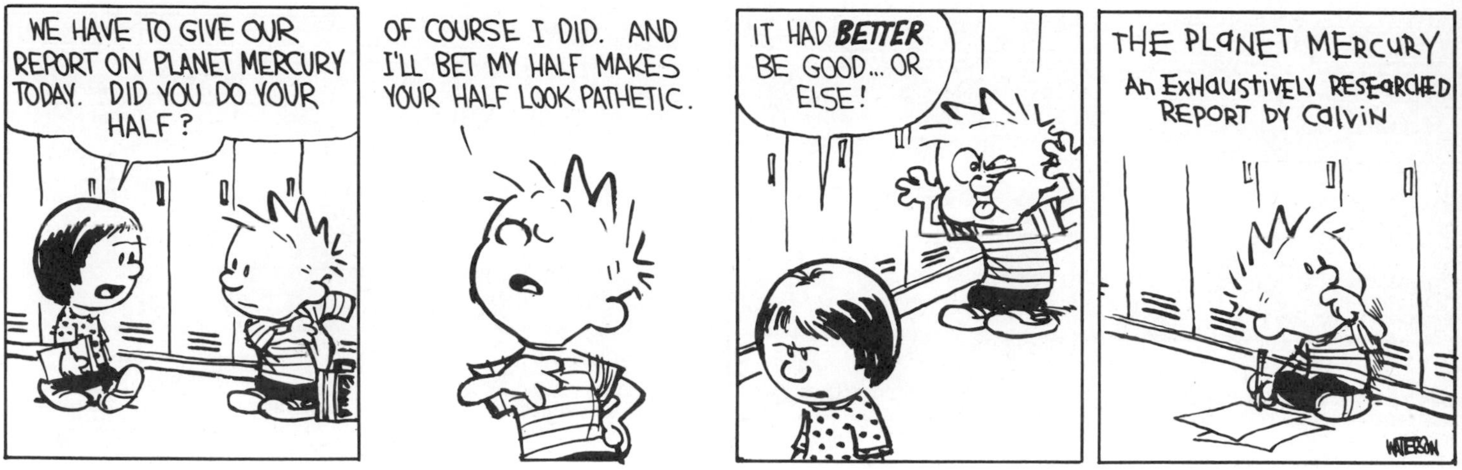
WE HAVE TO GIVE OUR REPORT ON PLANET MERCURY TODAY. DID YOU DO YOUR HALF?
OF COURSE I DID. AND I'LL BET MY HALF MAKES YOUR HALF LOOK PATHETIC.
IT HAD **BETTER** BE GOOD... OR ELSE!
THE PLANET MERCURY
An EXHAUSTIVELY RESEARCHED REPORT BY CALVIN
WATTERSON

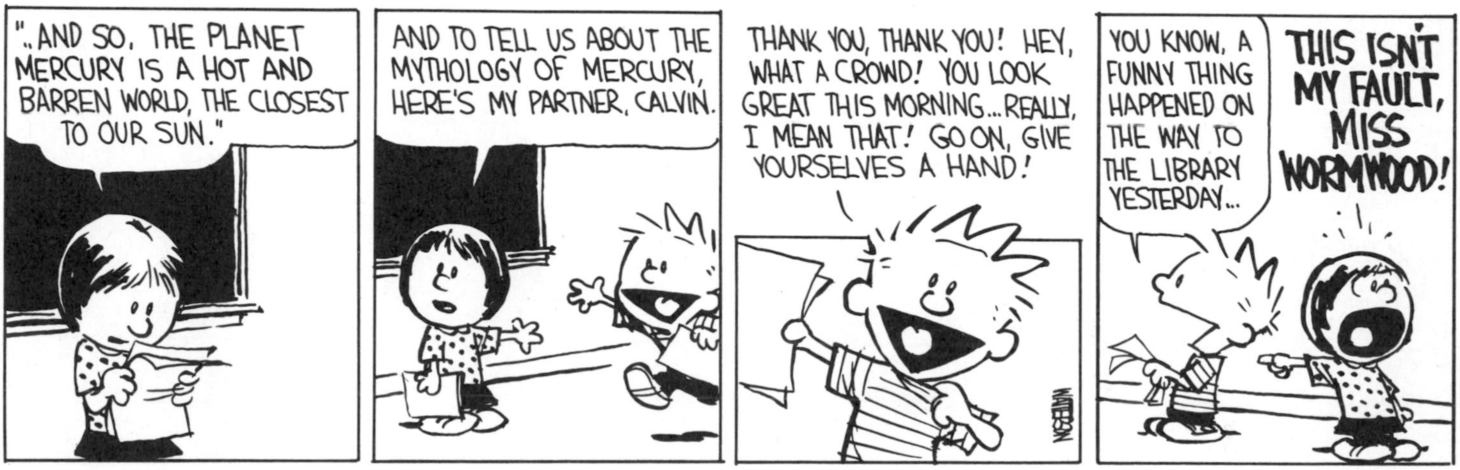
"..AND SO, THE PLANET MERCURY IS A HOT AND BARREN WORLD, THE CLOSEST TO OUR SUN."
AND TO TELL US ABOUT THE MYTHOLOGY OF MERCURY, HERE'S MY PARTNER, CALVIN.
THANK YOU, THANK YOU! HEY, WHAT A CROWD! YOU LOOK GREAT THIS MORNING...REALLY, I MEAN THAT! GO ON, GIVE YOURSELVES A HAND!
YOU KNOW, A FUNNY THING HAPPENED ON THE WAY TO THE LIBRARY YESTERDAY...
THIS ISN'T MY FAULT, MISS WORMWOOD!

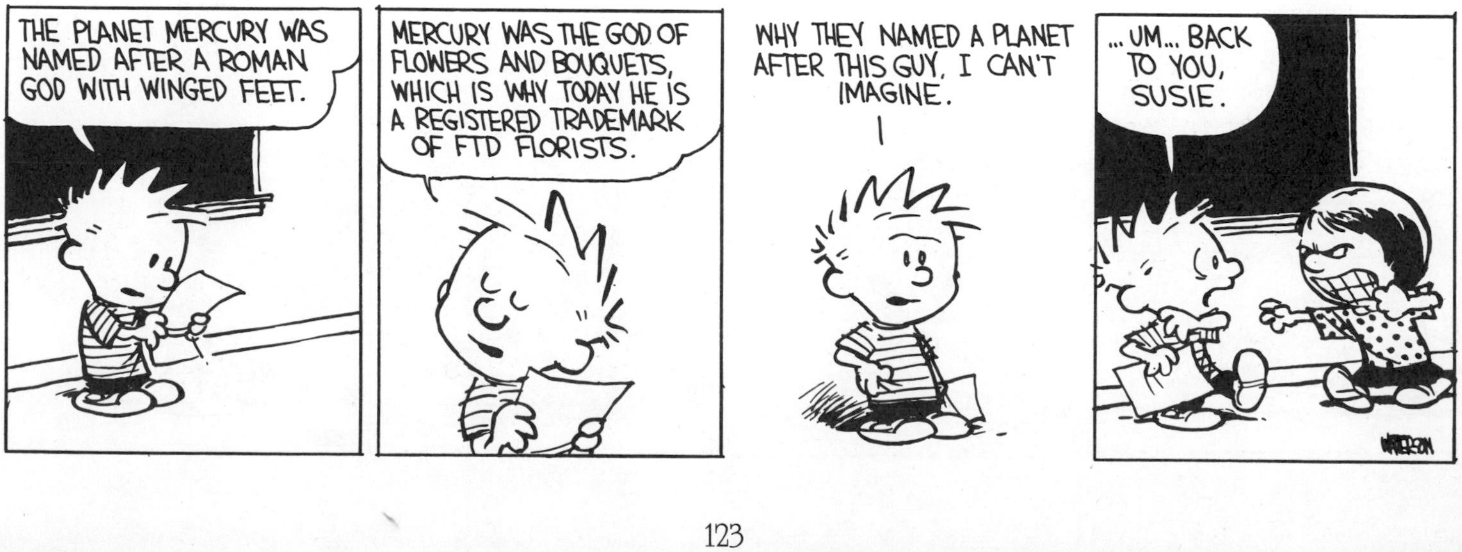
THE PLANET MERCURY WAS NAMED AFTER A ROMAN GOD WITH WINGED FEET.
MERCURY WAS THE GOD OF FLOWERS AND BOUQUETS, WHICH IS WHY TODAY HE IS A REGISTERED TRADEMARK OF FTD FLORISTS.
WHY THEY NAMED A PLANET AFTER THIS GUY, I CAN'T IMAGINE.
... UM... BACK TO YOU, SUSIE.
WATTERSON

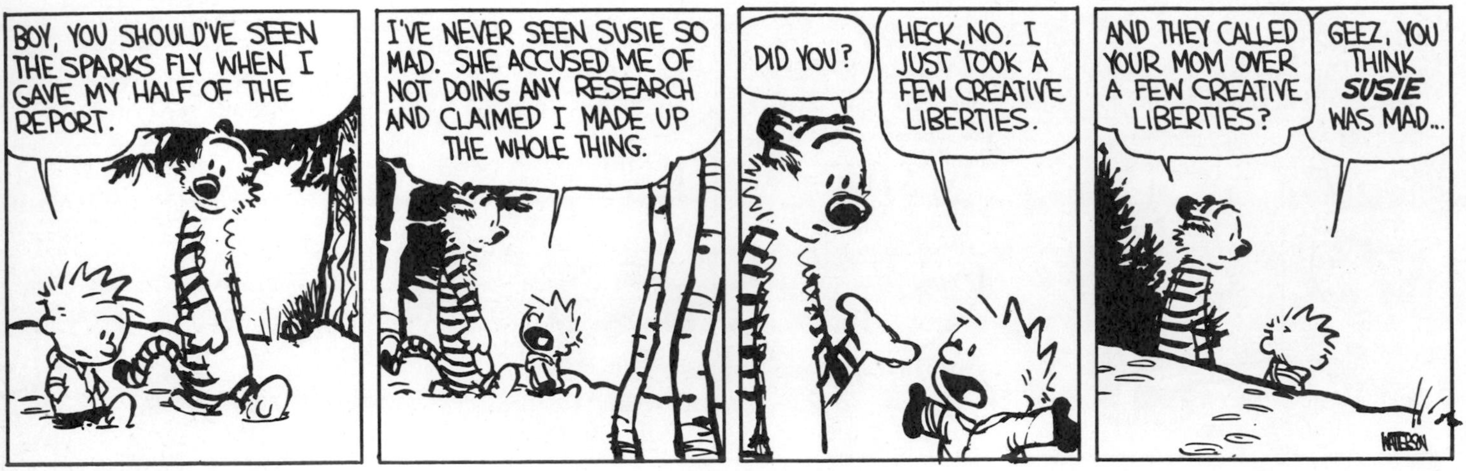
BOY, YOU SHOULD'VE SEEN THE SPARKS FLY WHEN I GAVE MY HALF OF THE REPORT.
I'VE NEVER SEEN SUSIE SO MAD. SHE ACCUSED ME OF NOT DOING ANY RESEARCH AND CLAIMED I MADE UP THE WHOLE THING.
DID YOU?
HECK, NO. I JUST TOOK A FEW CREATIVE LIBERTIES.
AND THEY CALLED YOUR MOM OVER A FEW CREATIVE LIBERTIES?
GEEZ, YOU THINK *SUSIE* WAS MAD...

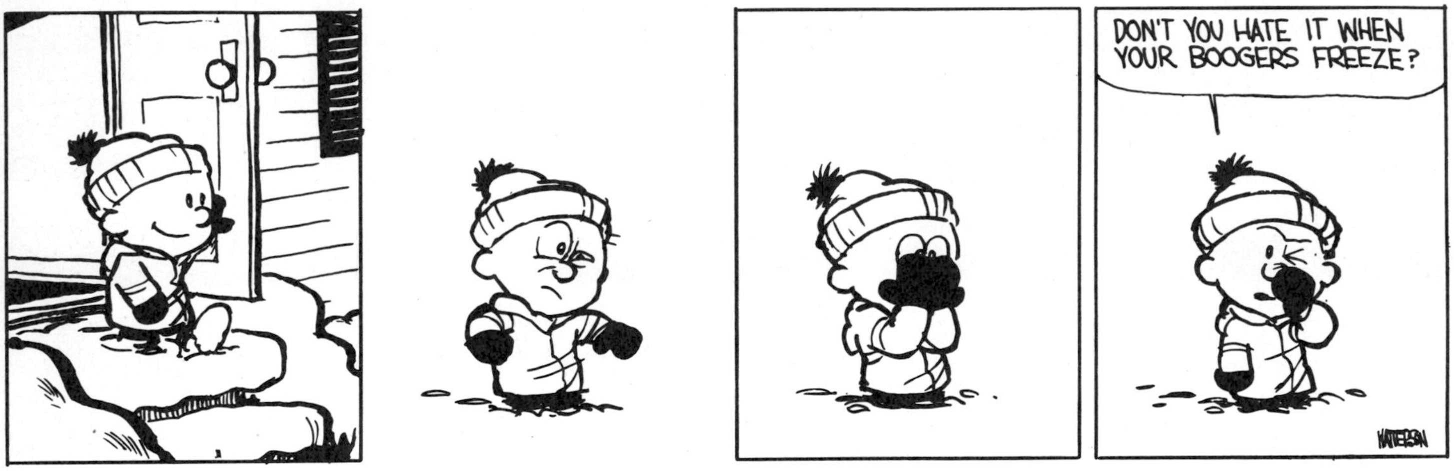
DON'T YOU HATE IT WHEN YOUR BOOGERS FREEZE?

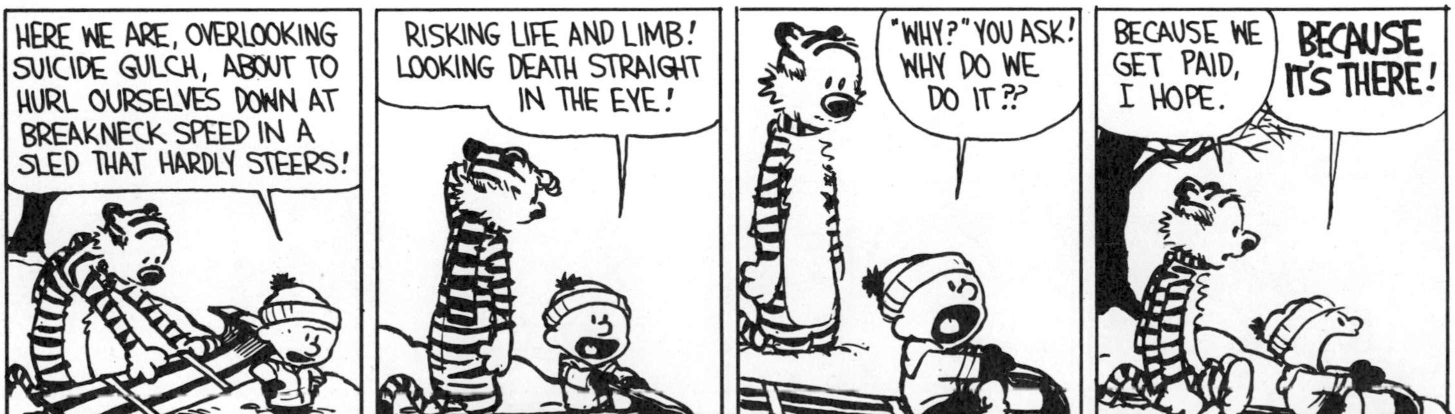
HERE WE ARE, OVERLOOKING SUICIDE GULCH, ABOUT TO HURL OURSELVES DOWN AT BREAKNECK SPEED IN A SLED THAT HARDLY STEERS!
RISKING LIFE AND LIMB! LOOKING DEATH STRAIGHT IN THE EYE!
"WHY?" YOU ASK! WHY DO WE DO IT??
BECAUSE WE GET PAID, I HOPE.
**BECAUSE IT'S THERE!**

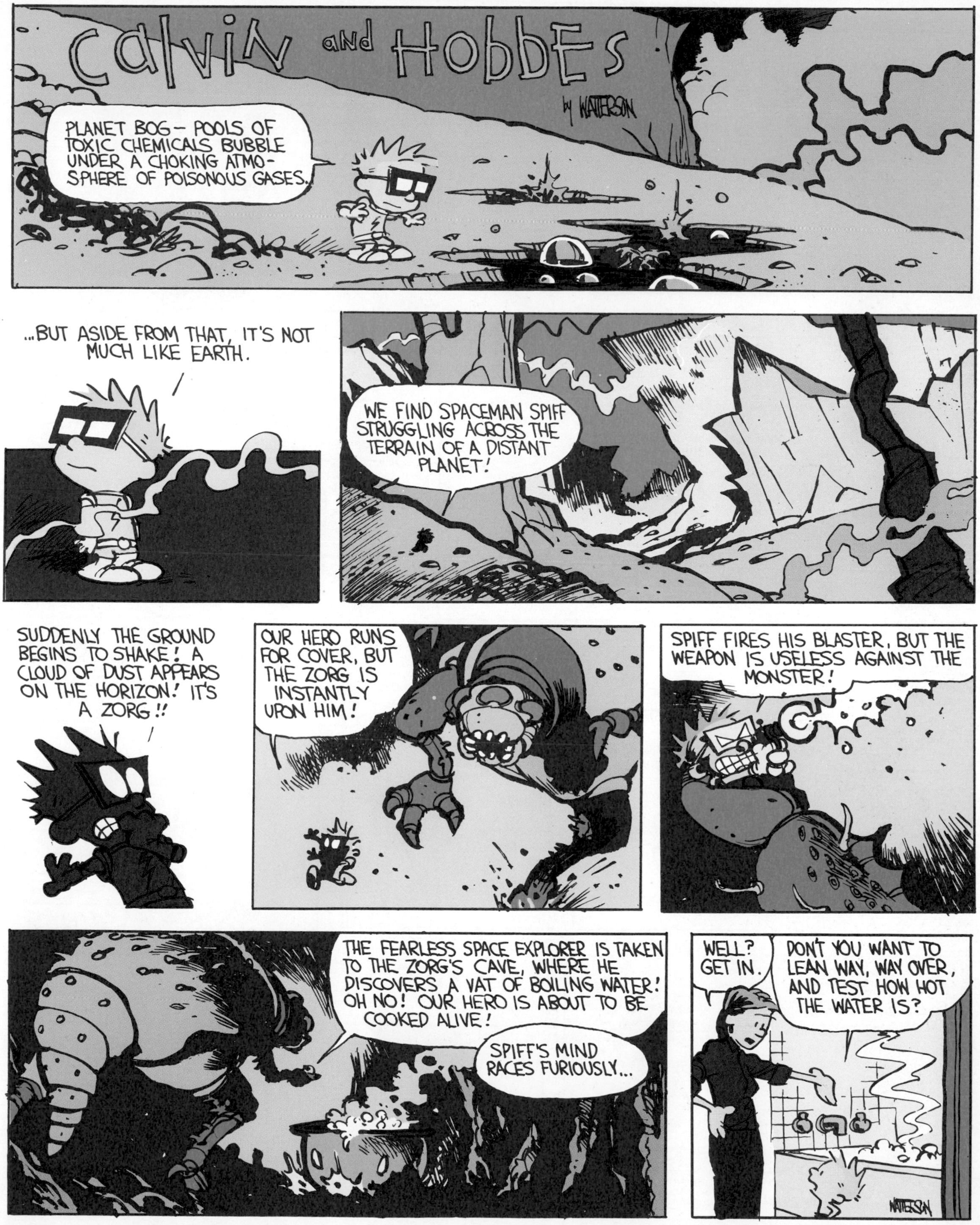
Calvin and Hobbes
by WATTERSON
PLANET BOG — POOLS OF TOXIC CHEMICALS BUBBLE UNDER A CHOKING ATMO-SPHERE OF POISONOUS GASES.
...BUT ASIDE FROM THAT, IT'S NOT MUCH LIKE EARTH.
WE FIND SPACEMAN SPIFF STRUGGLING ACROSS THE TERRAIN OF A DISTANT PLANET!
SUDDENLY THE GROUND BEGINS TO SHAKE! A CLOUD OF DUST APPEARS ON THE HORIZON! IT'S A ZORG!!
OUR HERO RUNS FOR COVER, BUT THE ZORG IS INSTANTLY UPON HIM!
SPIFF FIRES HIS BLASTER, BUT THE WEAPON IS USELESS AGAINST THE MONSTER!
THE FEARLESS SPACE EXPLORER IS TAKEN TO THE ZORG'S CAVE, WHERE HE DISCOVERS A VAT OF BOILING WATER! OH NO! OUR HERO IS ABOUT TO BE COOKED ALIVE!
SPIFF'S MIND RACES FURIOUSLY...
WELL? GET IN.
DON'T YOU WANT TO LEAN WAY, WAY OVER, AND TEST HOW HOT THE WATER IS?
WATTERSON

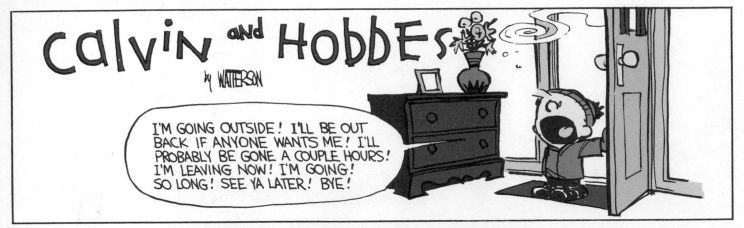

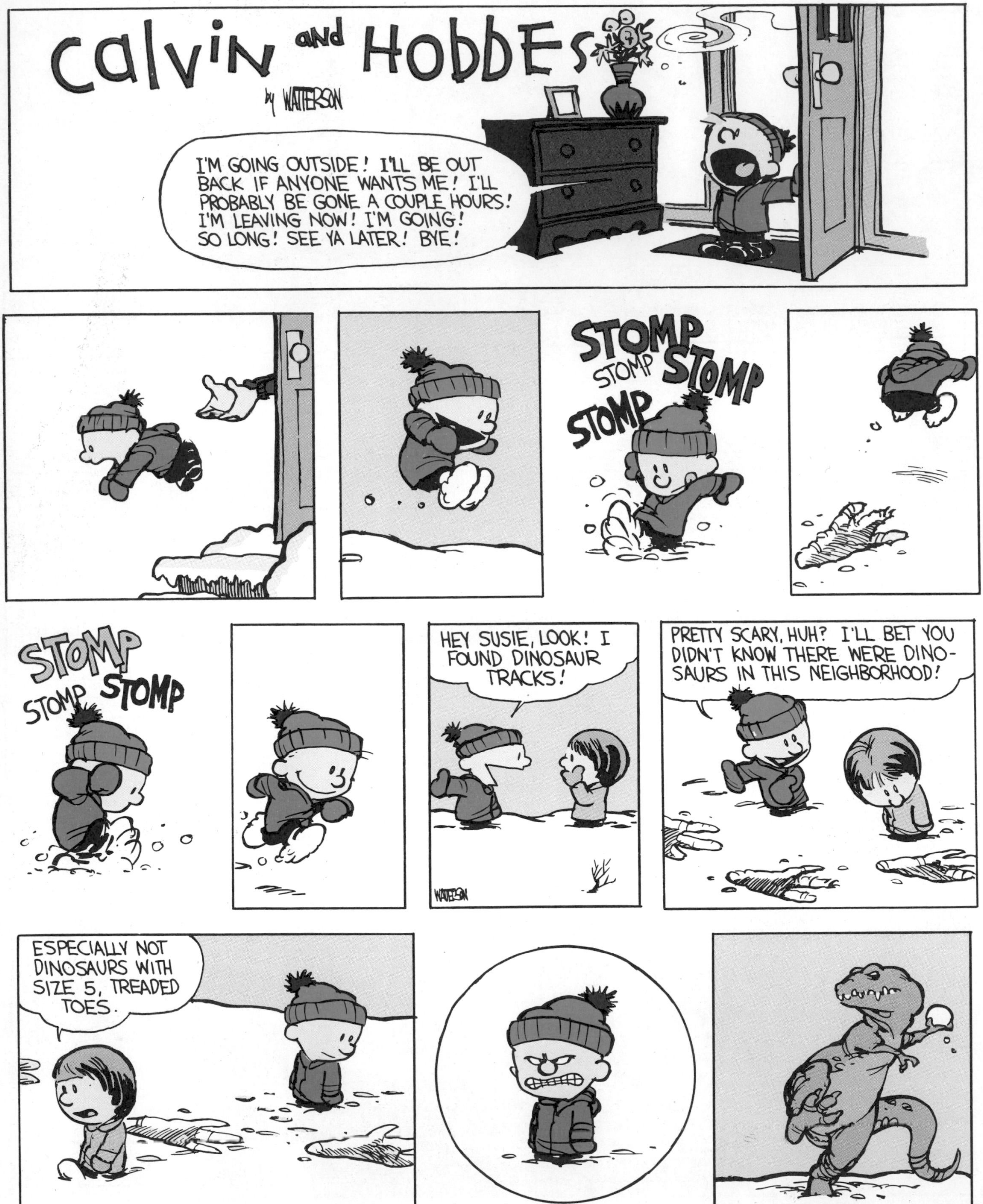
Calvin and HobbEs
by WATTERSON
I'M GOING OUTSIDE! I'LL BE OUT BACK IF ANYONE WANTS ME! I'LL PROBABLY BE GONE A COUPLE HOURS! I'M LEAVING NOW! I'M GOING! SO LONG! SEE YA LATER! BYE!
STOMP STOMP STOMP STOMP
STOMP STOMP STOMP
HEY SUSIE, LOOK! I FOUND DINOSAUR TRACKS!
WATTERSON
PRETTY SCARY, HUH? I'LL BET YOU DIDN'T KNOW THERE WERE DINOSAURS IN THIS NEIGHBORHOOD!
ESPECIALLY NOT DINOSAURS WITH SIZE 5, TREADED TOES.

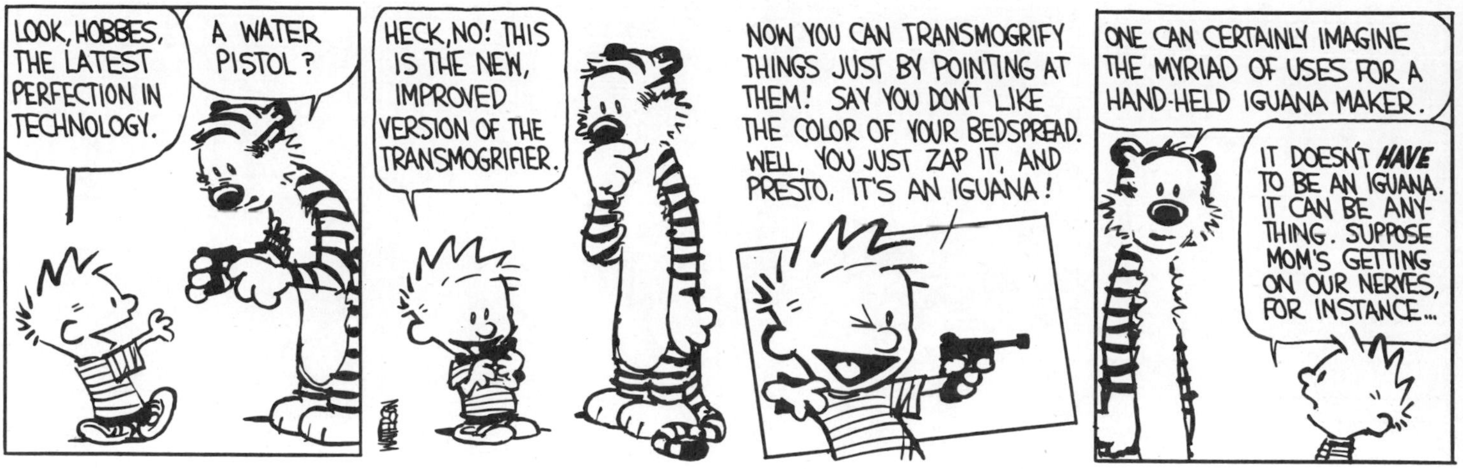
LOOK, HOBBES, THE LATEST PERFECTION IN TECHNOLOGY.
A WATER PISTOL?
HECK, NO! THIS IS THE NEW, IMPROVED VERSION OF THE TRANSMOGRIFIER.
NOW YOU CAN TRANSMOGRIFY THINGS JUST BY POINTING AT THEM! SAY YOU DON'T LIKE THE COLOR OF YOUR BEDSPREAD. WELL, YOU JUST ZAP IT, AND PRESTO, IT'S AN IGUANA!
ONE CAN CERTAINLY IMAGINE THE MYRIAD OF USES FOR A HAND-HELD IGUANA MAKER.
IT DOESN'T HAVE TO BE AN IGUANA. IT CAN BE ANYTHING. SUPPOSE MOM'S GETTING ON OUR NERVES, FOR INSTANCE...

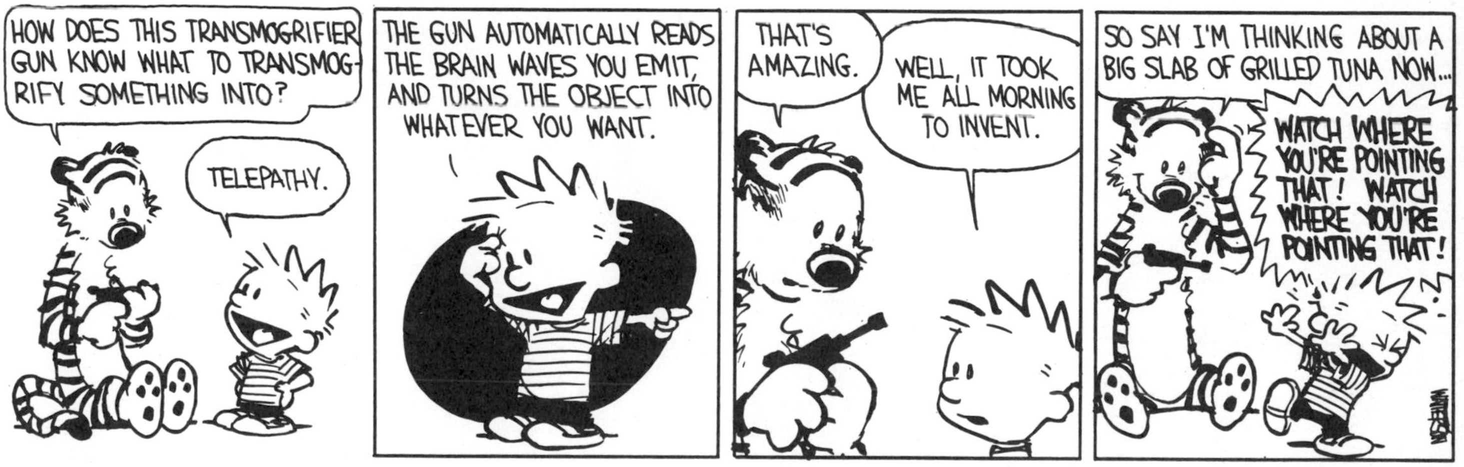
HOW DOES THIS TRANSMOGRIFIER GUN KNOW WHAT TO TRANSMOGRIFY SOMETHING INTO?
TELEPATHY.
THE GUN AUTOMATICALLY READS THE BRAIN WAVES YOU EMIT, AND TURNS THE OBJECT INTO WHATEVER YOU WANT.
THAT'S AMAZING.
WELL, IT TOOK ME ALL MORNING TO INVENT.
SO SAY I'M THINKING ABOUT A BIG SLAB OF GRILLED TUNA NOW...
WATCH WHERE YOU'RE POINTING THAT! WATCH WHERE YOU'RE POINTING THAT!

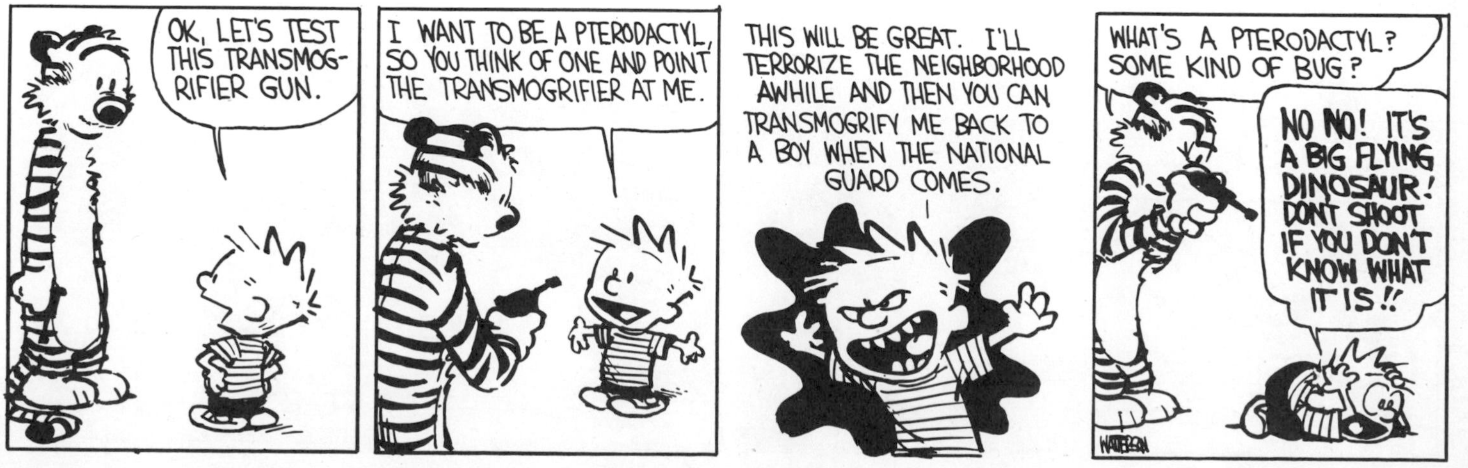
OK, LET'S TEST THIS TRANSMOGRIFIER GUN.
I WANT TO BE A PTERODACTYL, SO YOU THINK OF ONE AND POINT THE TRANSMOGRIFIER AT ME.
THIS WILL BE GREAT. I'LL TERRORIZE THE NEIGHBORHOOD AWHILE AND THEN YOU CAN TRANSMOGRIFY ME BACK TO A BOY WHEN THE NATIONAL GUARD COMES.
WHAT'S A PTERODACTYL? SOME KIND OF BUG?
NO NO! IT'S A BIG FLYING DINOSAUR! DON'T SHOOT IF YOU DON'T KNOW WHAT IT IS!!

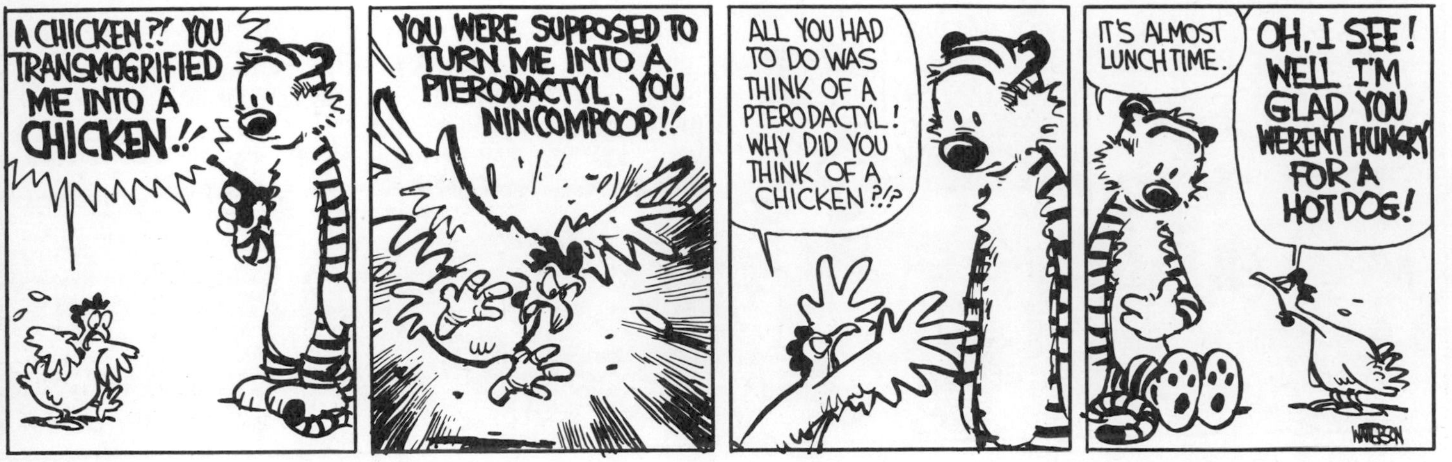
A CHICKEN?!' YOU TRANSMOGRIFIED ME INTO A CHICKEN!!'
YOU WERE SUPPOSED TO TURN ME INTO A PTERODACTYL, YOU NINCOMPOOP!!'
ALL YOU HAD TO DO WAS THINK OF A PTERODACTYL! WHY DID YOU THINK OF A CHICKEN?!?
IT'S ALMOST LUNCHTIME.
OH, I SEE! WELL I'M GLAD YOU WEREN'T HUNGRY FOR A HOT DOG!
WATTERSON

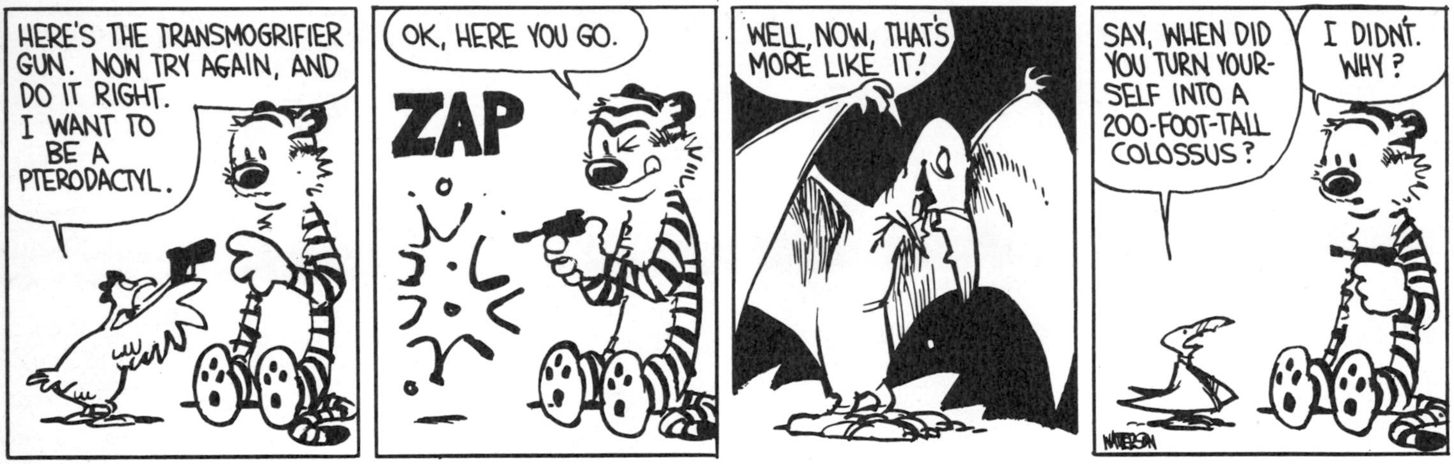
HERE'S THE TRANSMOGRIFIER GUN. NOW TRY AGAIN, AND DO IT RIGHT. I WANT TO BE A PTERODACTYL.
OK, HERE YOU GO.
ZAP
WELL, NOW, THAT'S MORE LIKE IT!
SAY, WHEN DID YOU TURN YOURSELF INTO A 200-FOOT-TALL COLOSSUS?
I DIDN'T. WHY?
WATTERSON

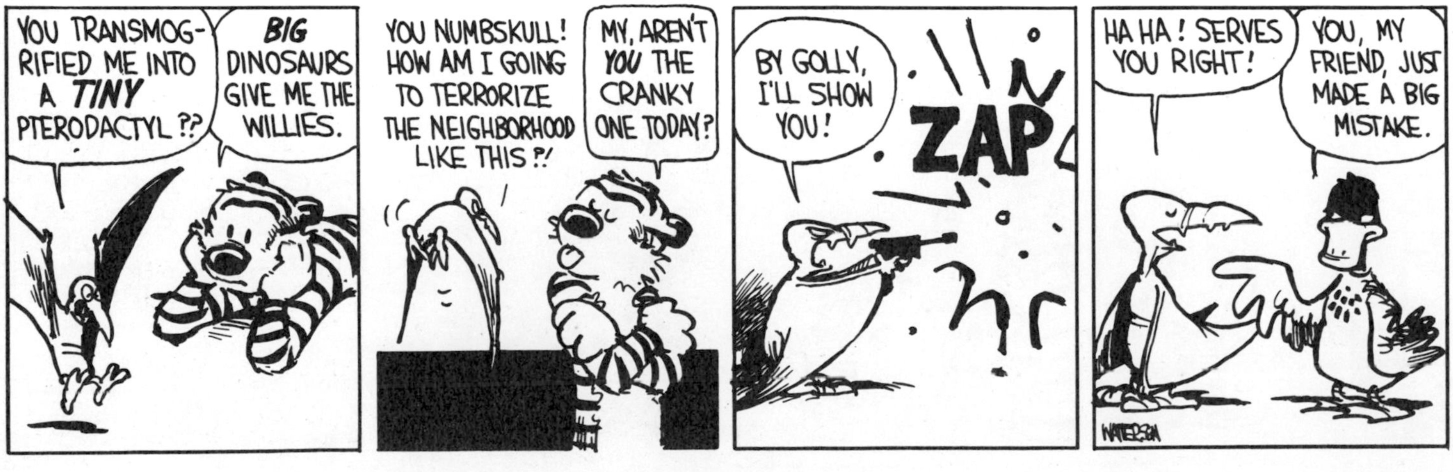
YOU TRANSMOGRIFIED ME INTO A TINY PTERODACTYL?!?
BIG DINOSAURS GIVE ME THE WILLIES.
YOU NUMBSKULL! HOW AM I GOING TO TERRORIZE THE NEIGHBORHOOD LIKE THIS?!
MY, AREN'T YOU THE CRANKY ONE TODAY?
BY GOLLY, I'LL SHOW YOU!
ZAP
HA HA! SERVES YOU RIGHT!
YOU, MY FRIEND, JUST MADE A BIG MISTAKE.
WATTERSON

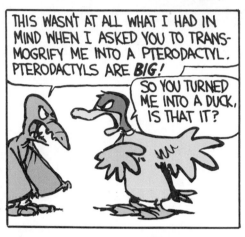

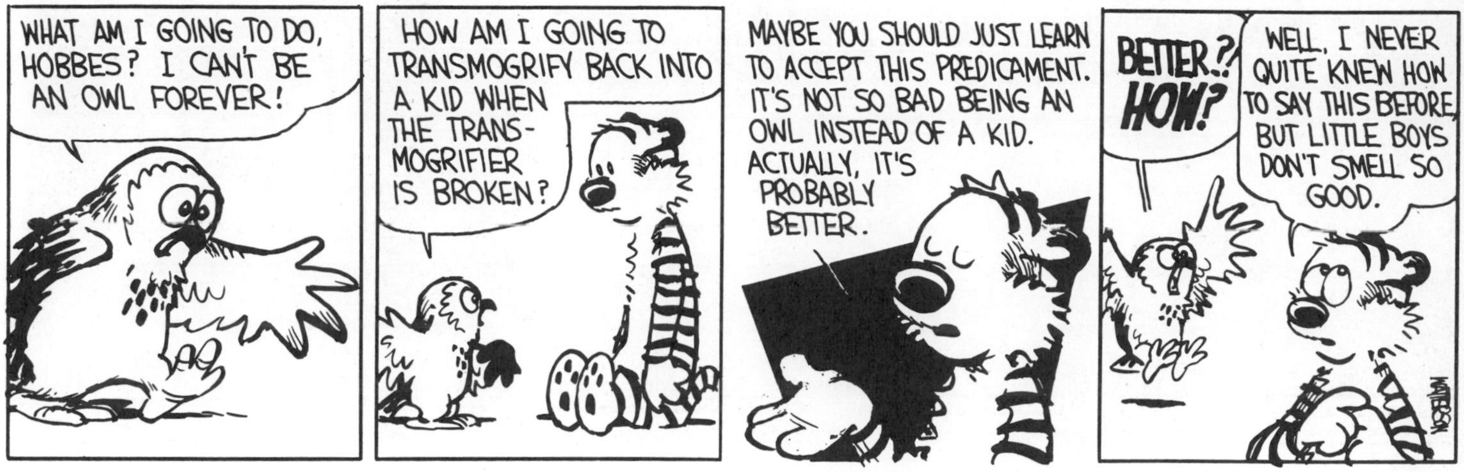
WHAT AM I GOING TO DO, HOBBES? I CAN'T BE AN OWL FOREVER!
HOW AM I GOING TO TRANSMOGRIFY BACK INTO A KID WHEN THE TRANS-MOGRIFIER IS BROKEN?
MAYBE YOU SHOULD JUST LEARN TO ACCEPT THIS PREDICAMENT. IT'S NOT SO BAD BEING AN OWL INSTEAD OF A KID. ACTUALLY, IT'S PROBABLY BETTER.
BETTER?! HOW?
WELL, I NEVER QUITE KNEW HOW TO SAY THIS BEFORE, BUT LITTLE BOYS DON'T SMELL SO GOOD.
WATTERSON

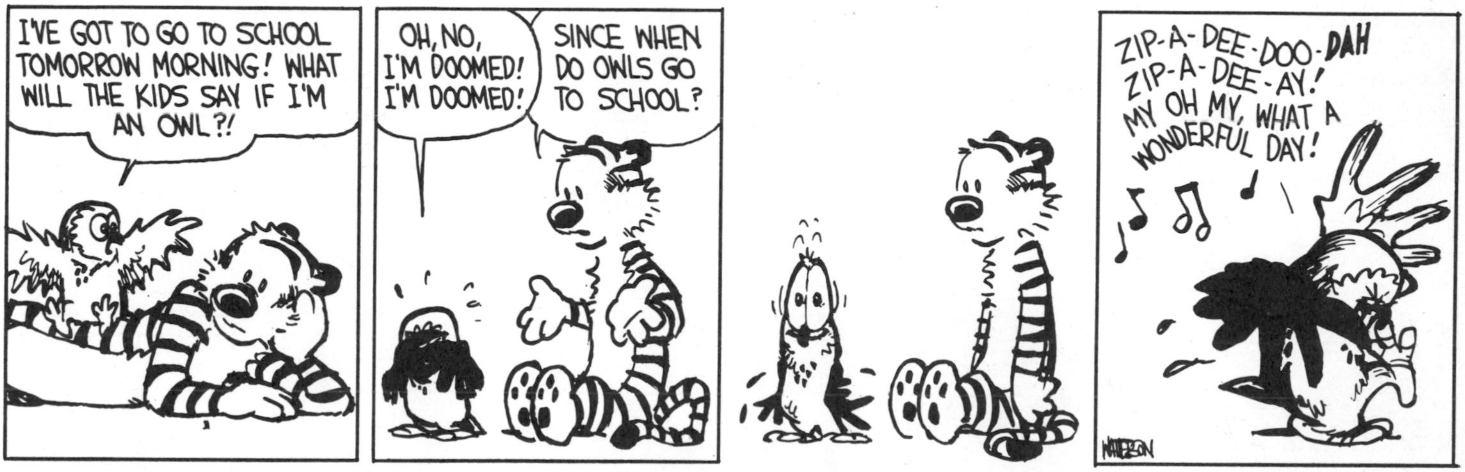
I'VE GOT TO GO TO SCHOOL TOMORROW MORNING! WHAT WILL THE KIDS SAY IF I'M AN OWL?!
OH, NO, I'M DOOMED! I'M DOOMED!
SINCE WHEN DO OWLS GO TO SCHOOL?
ZIP-A-DEE-DOO-DAH ZIP-A-DEE-AY! MY OH MY, WHAT A WONDERFUL DAY!
WATERSON

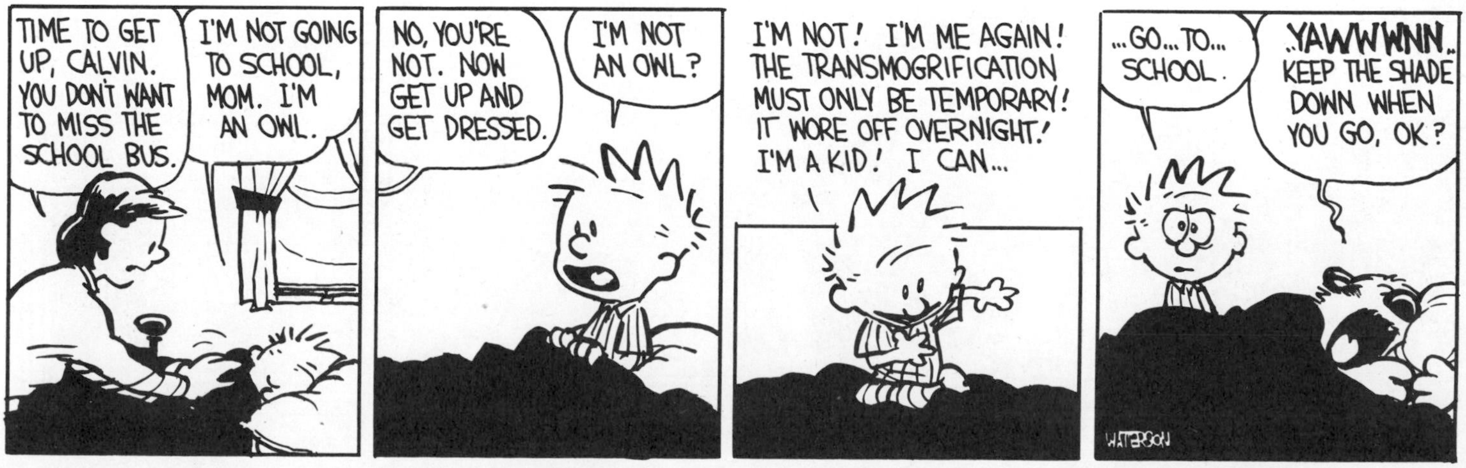
TIME TO GET UP, CALVIN. YOU DON'T WANT TO MISS THE SCHOOL BUS.
I'M NOT GOING TO SCHOOL, MOM. I'M AN OWL.
NO, YOU'RE NOT. NOW GET UP AND GET DRESSED.
I'M NOT AN OWL?
I'M NOT! I'M ME AGAIN! THE TRANSMOGRIFICATION MUST ONLY BE TEMPORARY! IT WORE OFF OVERNIGHT! I'M A KID! I CAN...
...GO... TO... SCHOOL.
..YAWWWNN.. KEEP THE SHADE DOWN WHEN YOU GO, OK?
WATTERSON

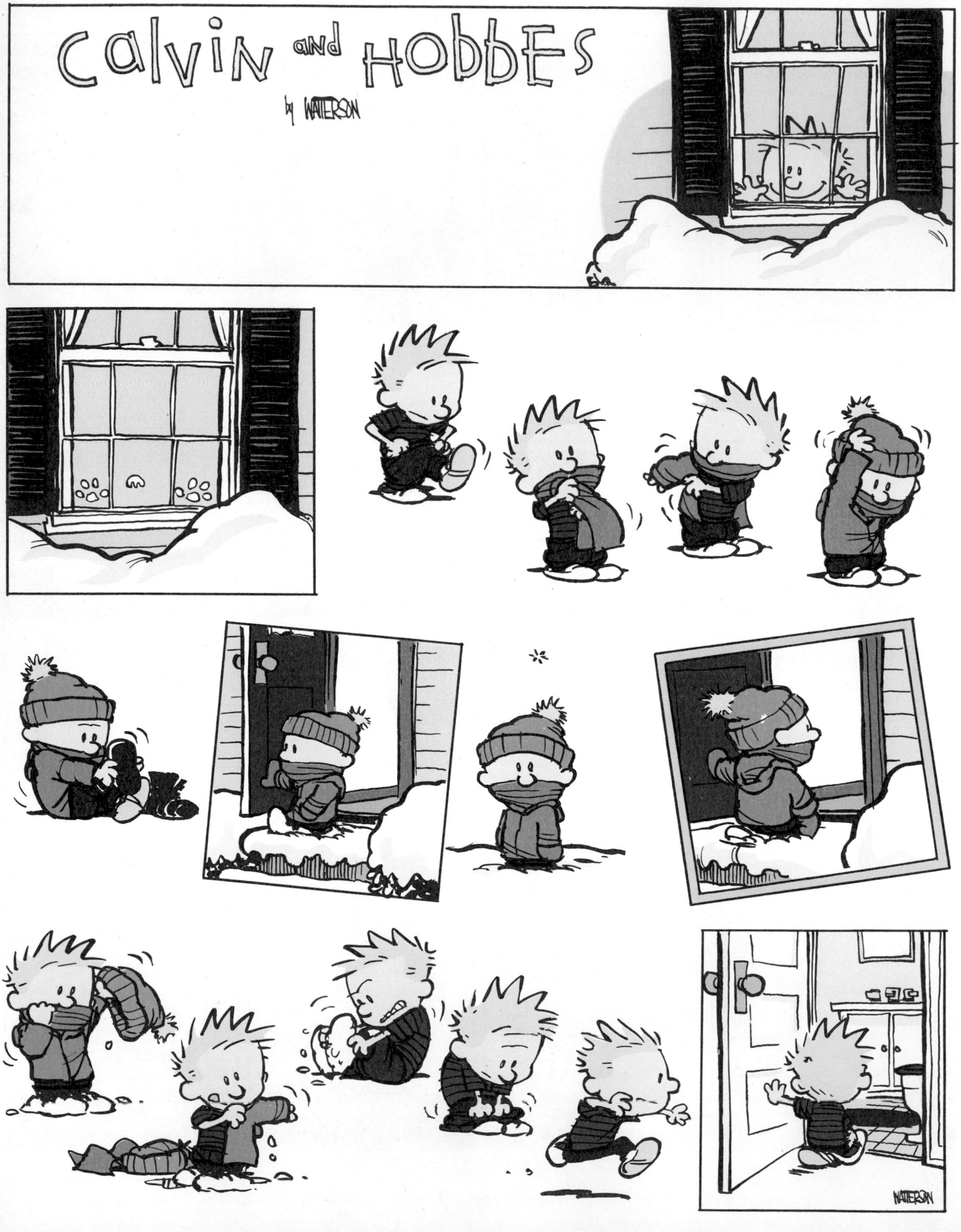
Calvin and HOBBES
by WATTERSON
WATTERSON

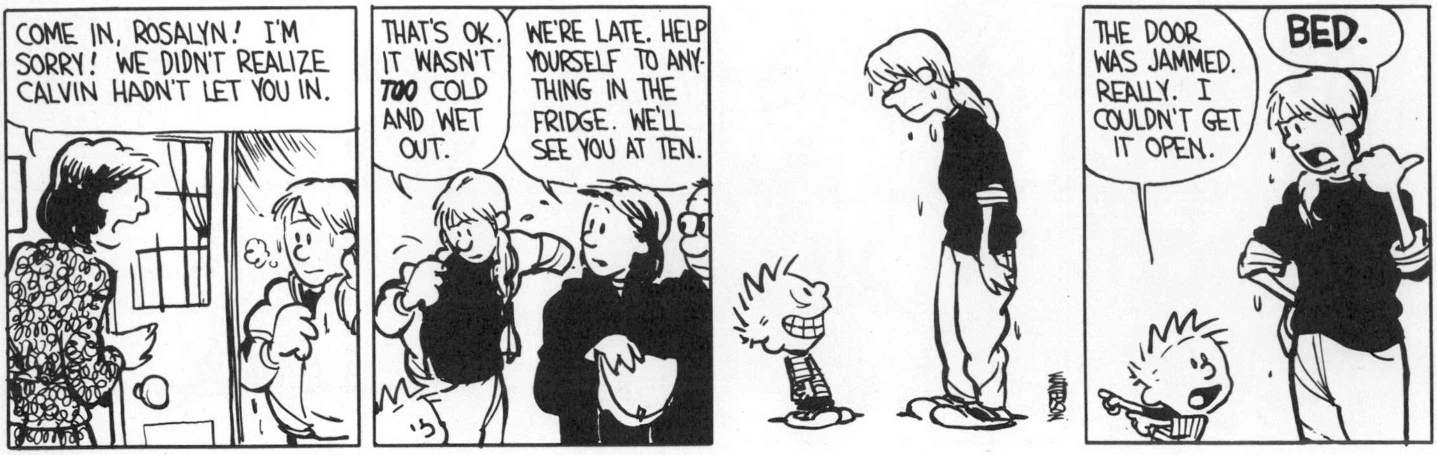
COME IN, ROSALYN! I'M SORRY! WE DIDN'T REALIZE CALVIN HADN'T LET YOU IN.
THAT'S OK. IT WASN'T *TOO* COLD AND WET OUT.
WE'RE LATE. HELP YOURSELF TO ANYTHING IN THE FRIDGE. WE'LL SEE YOU AT TEN.
THE DOOR WAS JAMMED. REALLY. I COULDN'T GET IT OPEN.
BED.

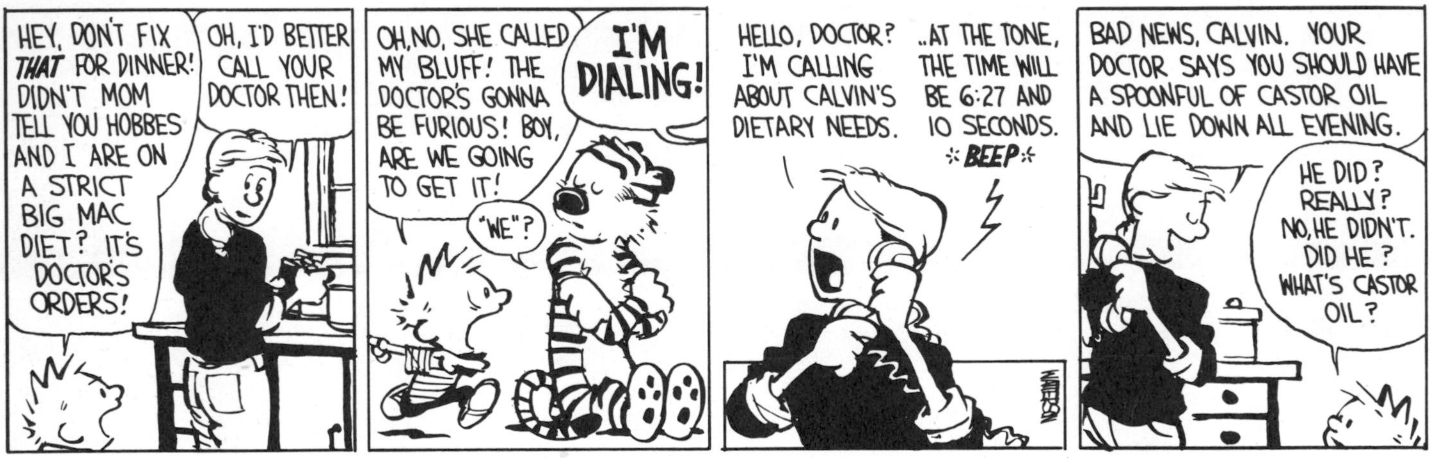
HEY, DON'T FIX *THAT* FOR DINNER! DIDN'T MOM TELL YOU HOBBES AND I ARE ON A STRICT BIG MAC DIET? IT'S DOCTOR'S ORDERS!
OH, I'D BETTER CALL YOUR DOCTOR THEN!
OH, NO, SHE CALLED MY BLUFF! THE DOCTOR'S GONNA BE FURIOUS! BOY, ARE WE GOING TO GET IT!
I'M DIALING!
"WE"?
HELLO, DOCTOR? I'M CALLING ABOUT CALVIN'S DIETARY NEEDS.
..AT THE TONE, THE TIME WILL BE 6:27 AND 10 SECONDS.
BEEP
BAD NEWS, CALVIN. YOUR DOCTOR SAYS YOU SHOULD HAVE A SPOONFUL OF CASTOR OIL AND LIE DOWN ALL EVENING.
HE DID? REALLY? NO, HE DIDN'T. DID HE? WHAT'S CASTOR OIL?

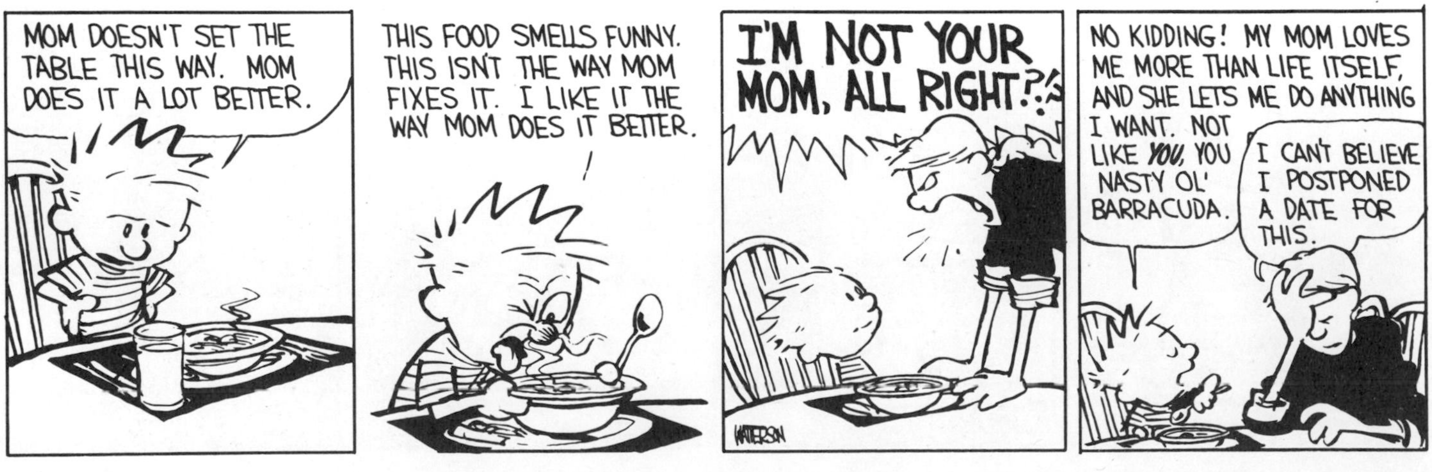
MOM DOESN'T SET THE TABLE THIS WAY. MOM DOES IT A LOT BETTER.
THIS FOOD SMELLS FUNNY. THIS ISN'T THE WAY MOM FIXES IT. I LIKE IT THE WAY MOM DOES IT BETTER.
I'M NOT YOUR MOM, ALL RIGHT?!
NO KIDDING! MY MOM LOVES ME MORE THAN LIFE ITSELF, AND SHE LETS ME DO ANYTHING I WANT. NOT LIKE *YOU*, YOU NASTY OL' BARRACUDA.
I CAN'T BELIEVE I POSTPONED A DATE FOR THIS.

135

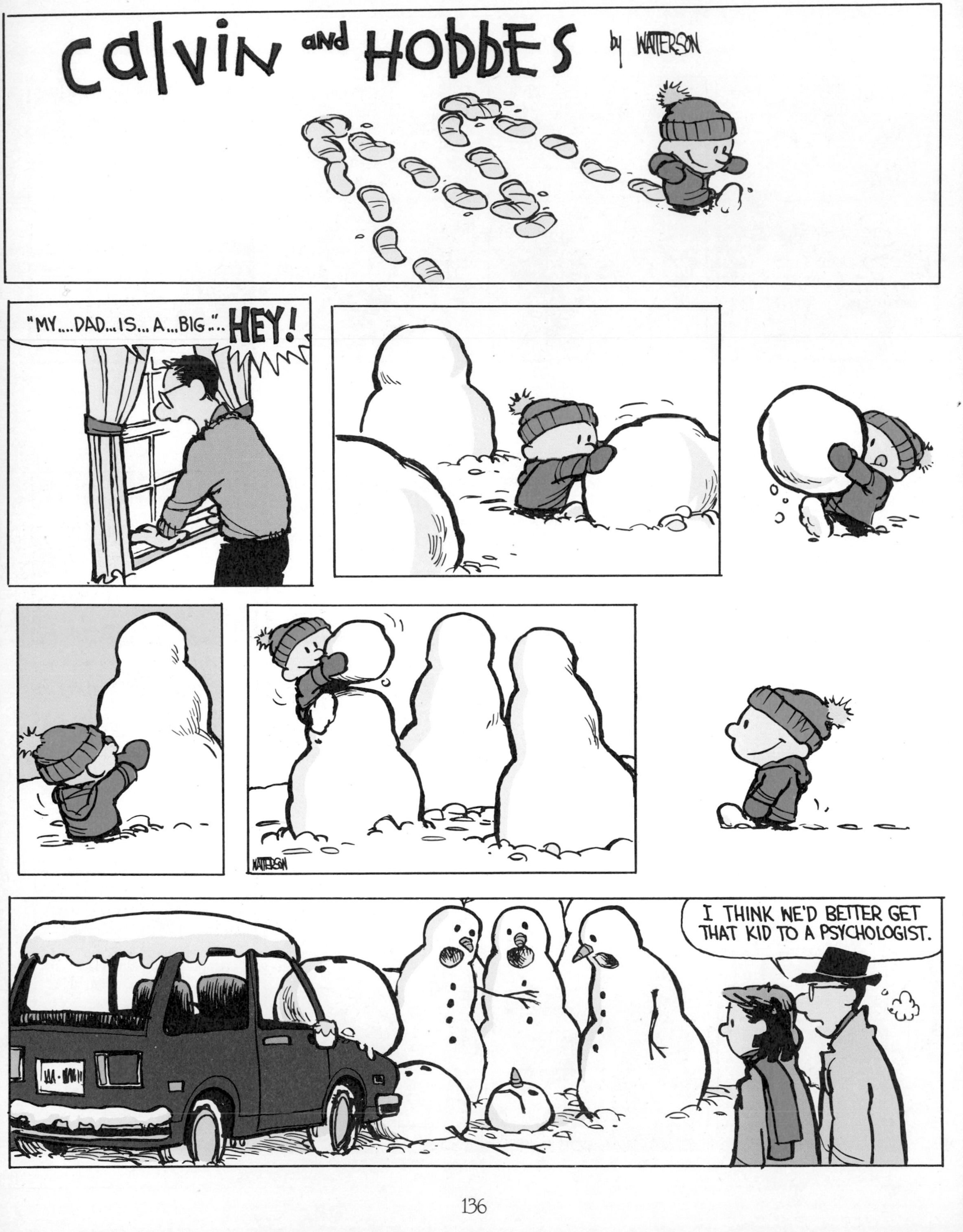
Calvin and HOBBES
by WATTERSON
"MY....DAD...IS... A...BIG..."..
HEY!
WATTERSON
I THINK WE'D BETTER GET THAT KID TO A PSYCHOLOGIST.

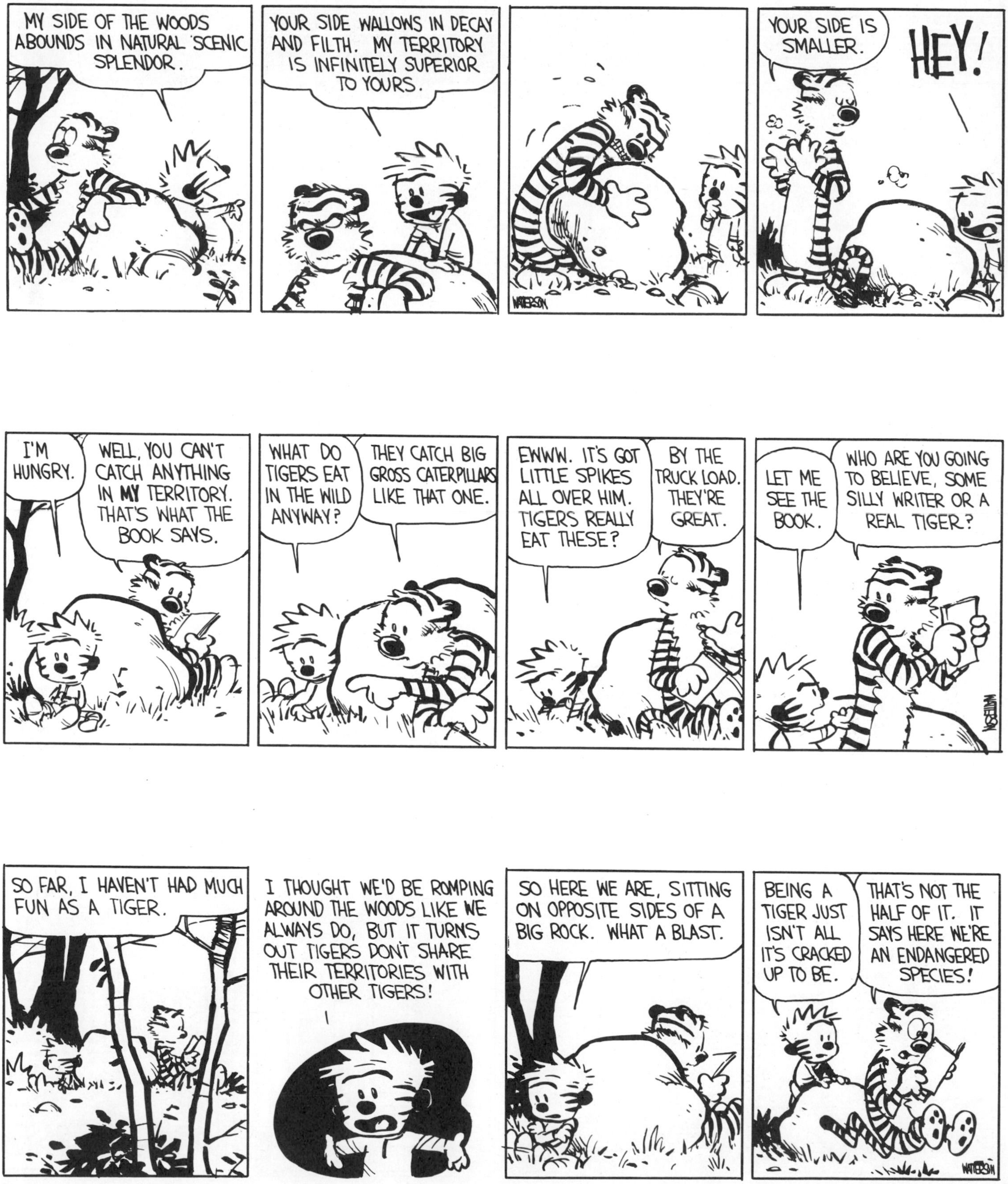
MY SIDE OF THE WOODS ABOUNDS IN NATURAL SCENIC SPLENDOR.
YOUR SIDE WALLOWS IN DECAY AND FILTH. MY TERRITORY IS INFINITELY SUPERIOR TO YOURS.
YOUR SIDE IS SMALLER.
HEY!
I'M HUNGRY.
WELL, YOU CAN'T CATCH ANYTHING IN MY TERRITORY. THAT'S WHAT THE BOOK SAYS.
WHAT DO TIGERS EAT IN THE WILD ANYWAY?
THEY CATCH BIG GROSS CATERPILLARS LIKE THAT ONE.
EWWW. IT'S GOT LITTLE SPIKES ALL OVER HIM. TIGERS REALLY EAT THESE?
BY THE TRUCK LOAD. THEY'RE GREAT.
LET ME SEE THE BOOK.
WHO ARE YOU GOING TO BELIEVE, SOME SILLY WRITER OR A REAL TIGER?
SO FAR, I HAVEN'T HAD MUCH FUN AS A TIGER.
I THOUGHT WE'D BE ROMPING AROUND THE WOODS LIKE WE ALWAYS DO, BUT IT TURNS OUT TIGERS DON'T SHARE THEIR TERRITORIES WITH OTHER TIGERS!
SO HERE WE ARE, SITTING ON OPPOSITE SIDES OF A BIG ROCK. WHAT A BLAST.
BEING A TIGER JUST ISN'T ALL IT'S CRACKED UP TO BE.
THAT'S NOT THE HALF OF IT. IT SAYS HERE WE'RE AN ENDANGERED SPECIES!

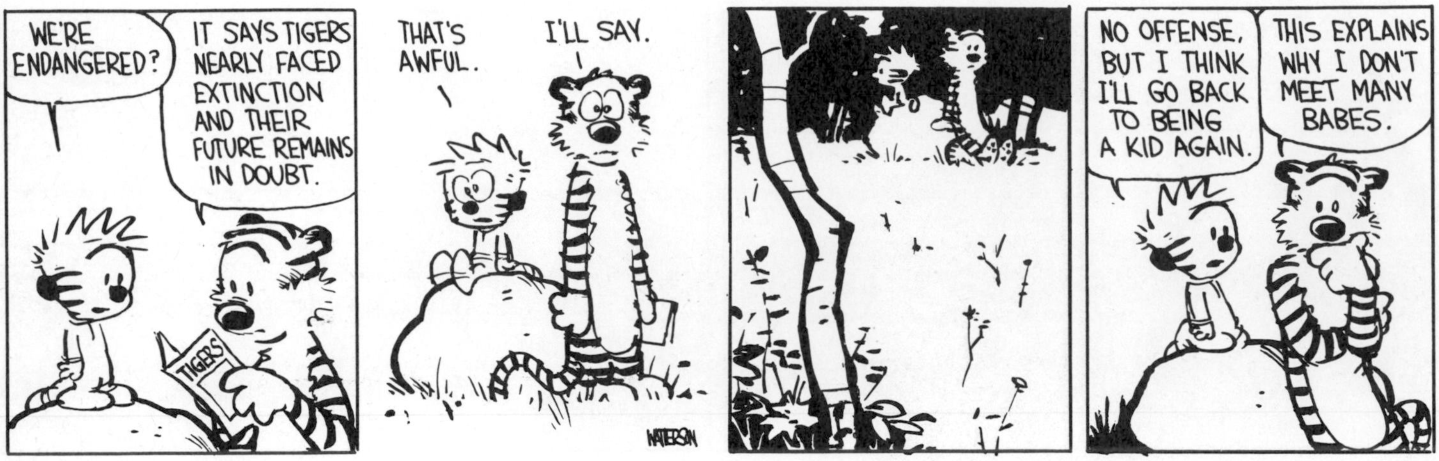
WE'RE ENDANGERED?
IT SAYS TIGERS NEARLY FACED EXTINCTION AND THEIR FUTURE REMAINS IN DOUBT.
TIGERS
THAT'S AWFUL.
I'LL SAY.
NO OFFENSE, BUT I THINK I'LL GO BACK TO BEING A KID AGAIN.
THIS EXPLAINS WHY I DON'T MEET MANY BABES.

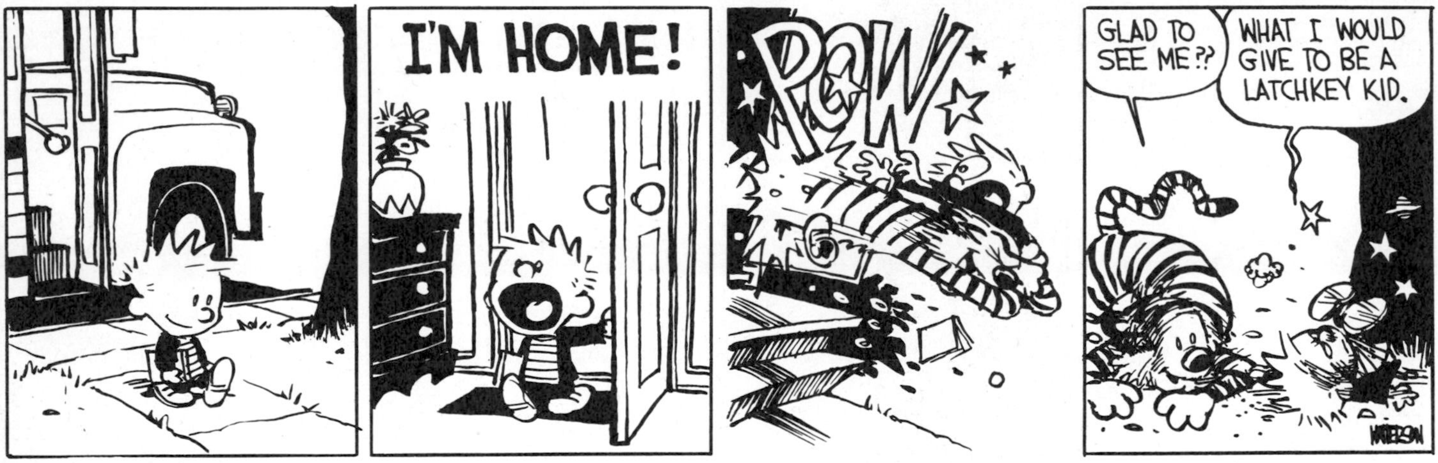
I'M HOME!
POW
GLAD TO SEE ME??
WHAT I WOULD GIVE TO BE A LATCHKEY KID.

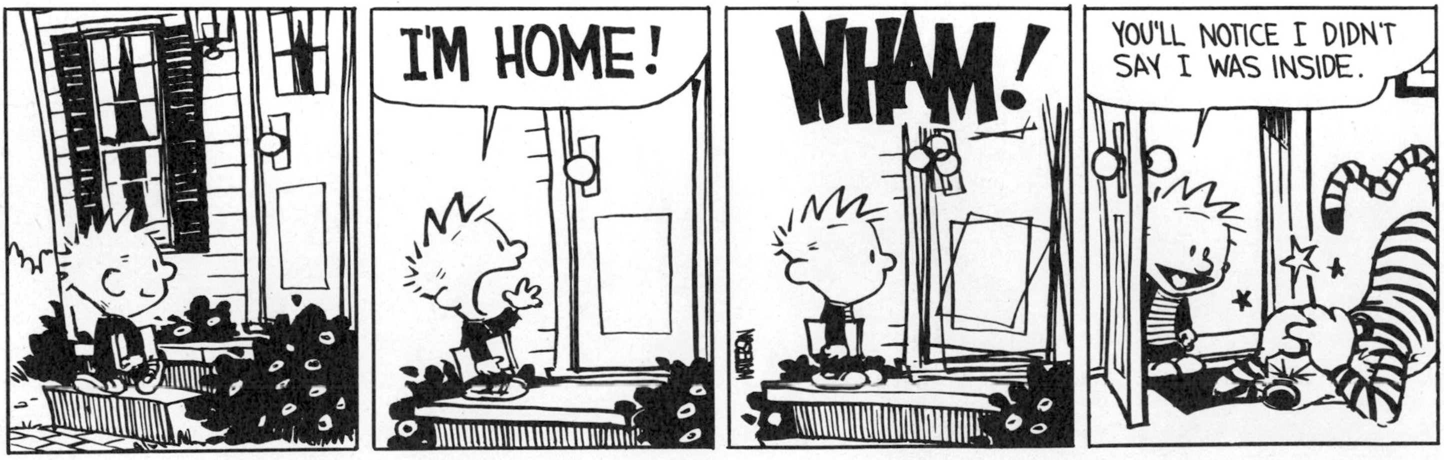
I'M HOME!
WHAM!
YOU'LL NOTICE I DIDN'T SAY I WAS INSIDE.

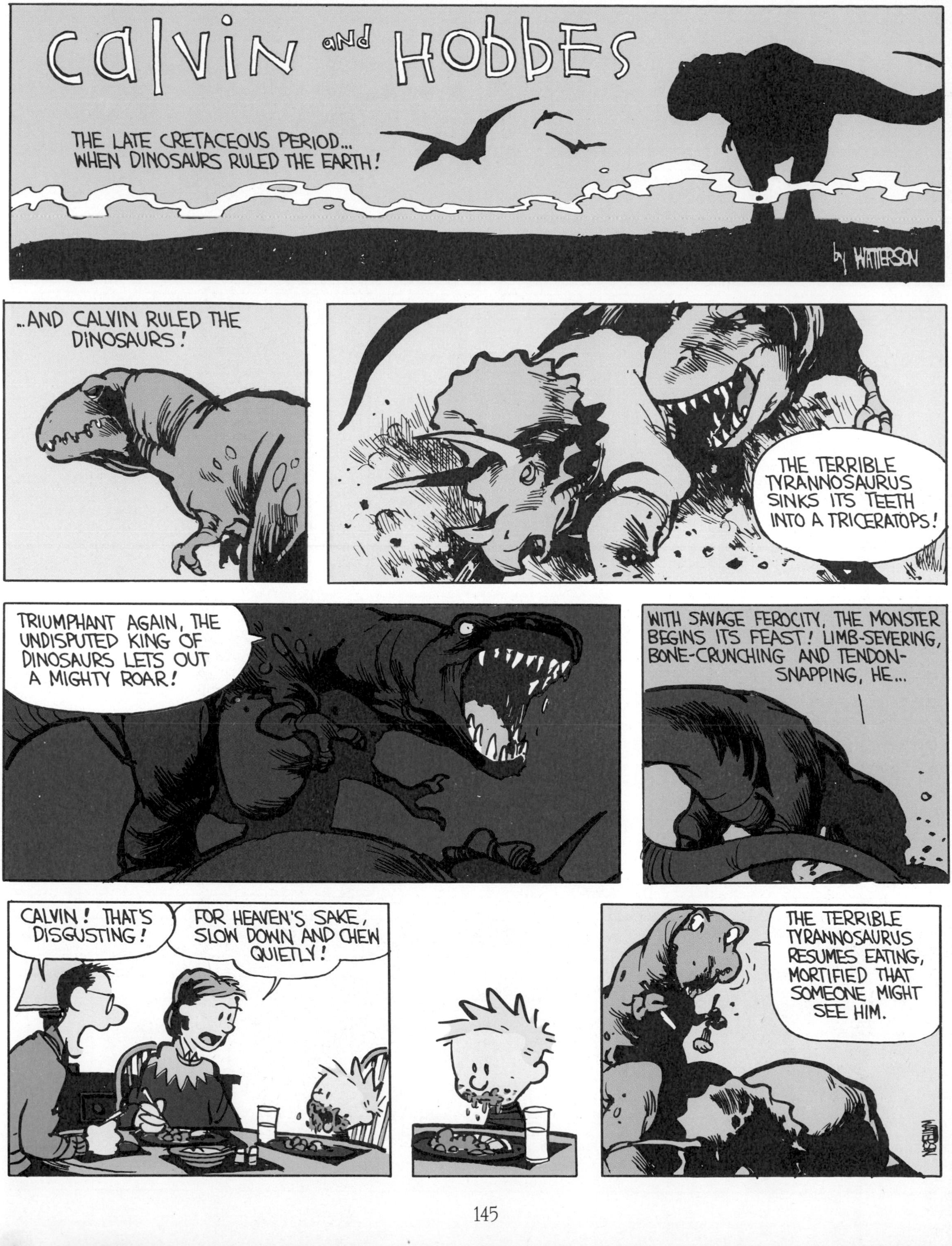

Calvin and HOBBES
THE LATE CRETACEOUS PERIOD... WHEN DINOSAURS RULED THE EARTH!
by WATTERSON
..AND CALVIN RULED THE DINOSAURS!
THE TERRIBLE TYRANNOSAURUS SINKS ITS TEETH INTO A TRICERATOPS!
TRIUMPHANT AGAIN, THE UNDISPUTED KING OF DINOSAURS LETS OUT A MIGHTY ROAR!
WITH SAVAGE FEROCITY, THE MONSTER BEGINS ITS FEAST! LIMB-SEVERING, BONE-CRUNCHING AND TENDON-SNAPPING, HE...
CALVIN! THAT'S DISGUSTING!
FOR HEAVEN'S SAKE, SLOW DOWN AND CHEW QUIETLY!
THE TERRIBLE TYRANNOSAURUS RESUMES EATING, MORTIFIED THAT SOMEONE MIGHT SEE HIM.

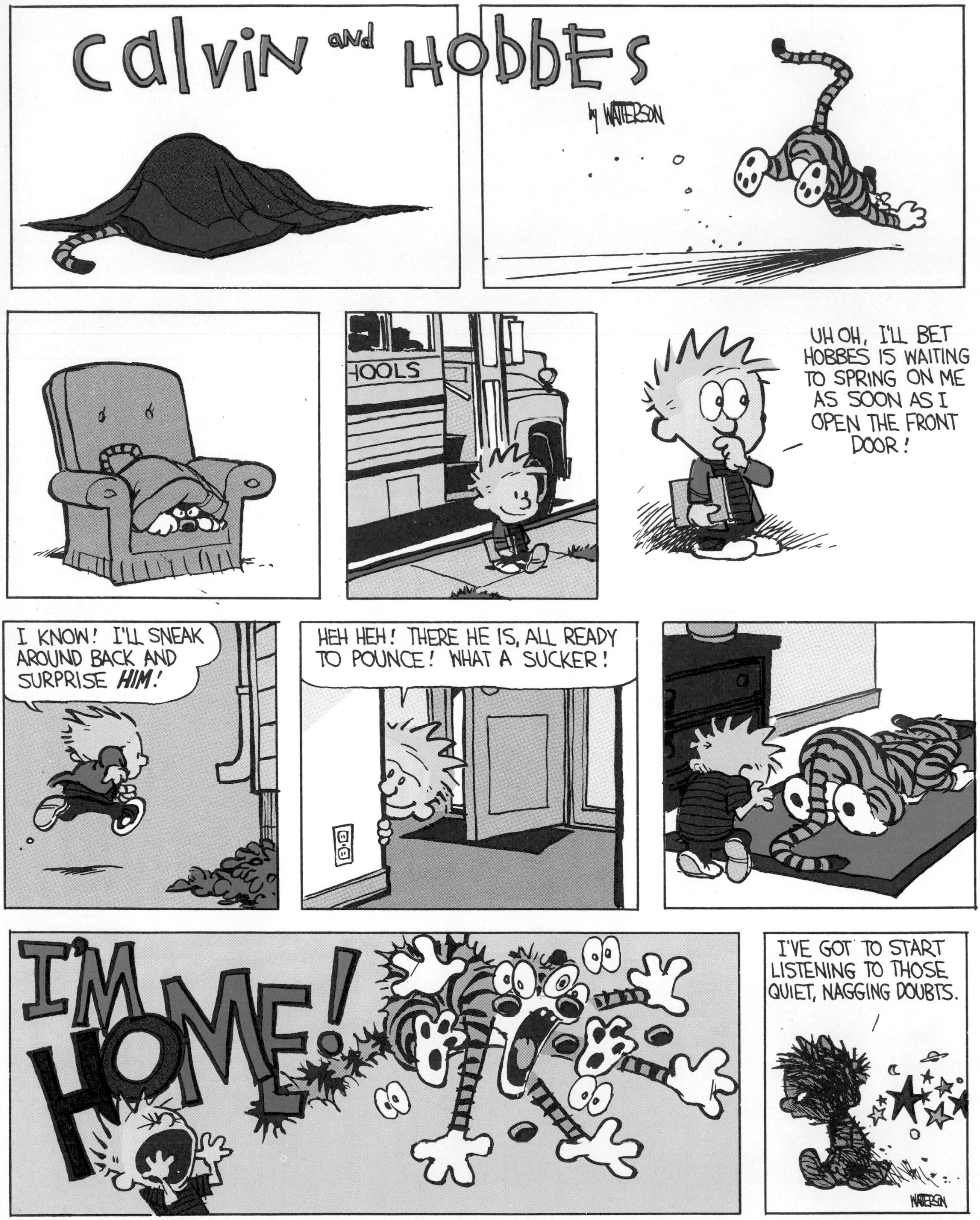
Calvin and HOBBES
by WATTERSON
HOOLS
UH OH, I'LL BET HOBBES IS WAITING TO SPRING ON ME AS SOON AS I OPEN THE FRONT DOOR!
I KNOW! I'LL SNEAK AROUND BACK AND SURPRISE HIM!
HEH HEH! THERE HE IS, ALL READY TO POUNCE! WHAT A SUCKER!
I'M HOME!
I'VE GOT TO START LISTENING TO THOSE QUIET, NAGGING DOUBTS.
WATTERSON

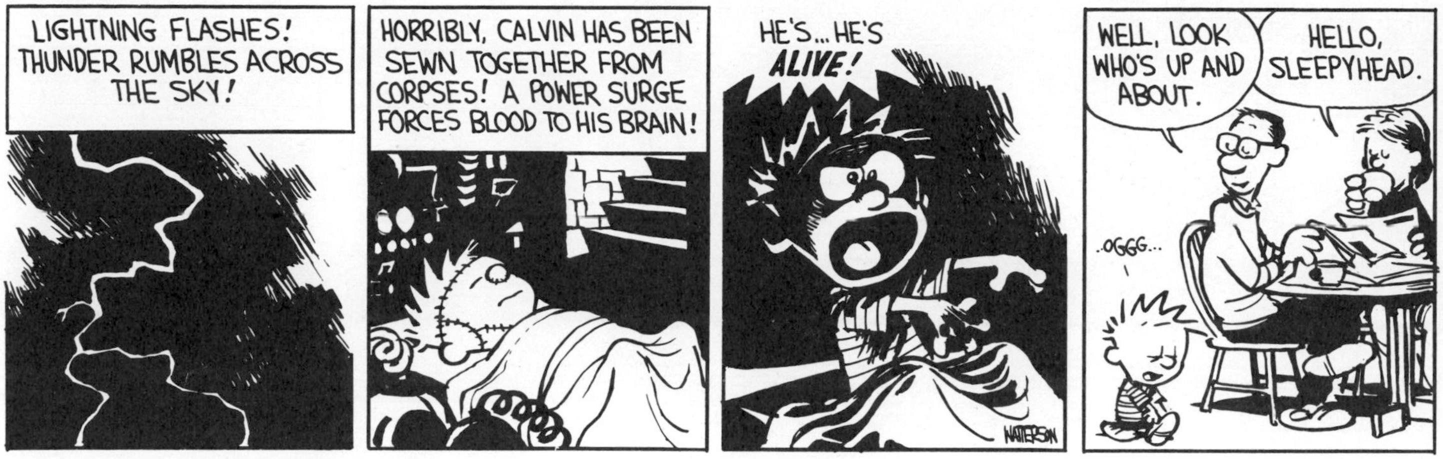
LIGHTNING FLASHES! THUNDER RUMBLES ACROSS THE SKY!
HORRIBLY, CALVIN HAS BEEN SEWN TOGETHER FROM CORPSES! A POWER SURGE FORCES BLOOD TO HIS BRAIN!
HE'S... HE'S *ALIVE!*
WATTERSON
WELL, LOOK WHO'S UP AND ABOUT.
HELLO, SLEEPYHEAD.
..OGGG...

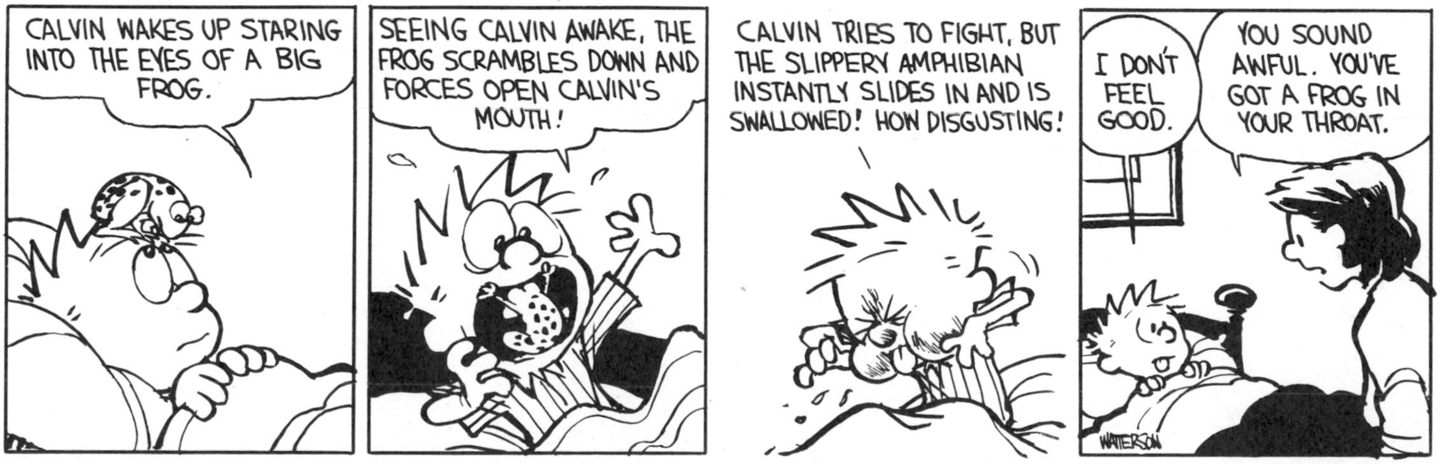
CALVIN WAKES UP STARING INTO THE EYES OF A BIG FROG.
SEEING CALVIN AWAKE, THE FROG SCRAMBLES DOWN AND FORCES OPEN CALVIN'S MOUTH!
CALVIN TRIES TO FIGHT, BUT THE SLIPPERY AMPHIBIAN INSTANTLY SLIDES IN AND IS SWALLOWED! HOW DISGUSTING!
I DON'T FEEL GOOD.
YOU SOUND AWFUL. YOU'VE GOT A FROG IN YOUR THROAT.
WATTERSON

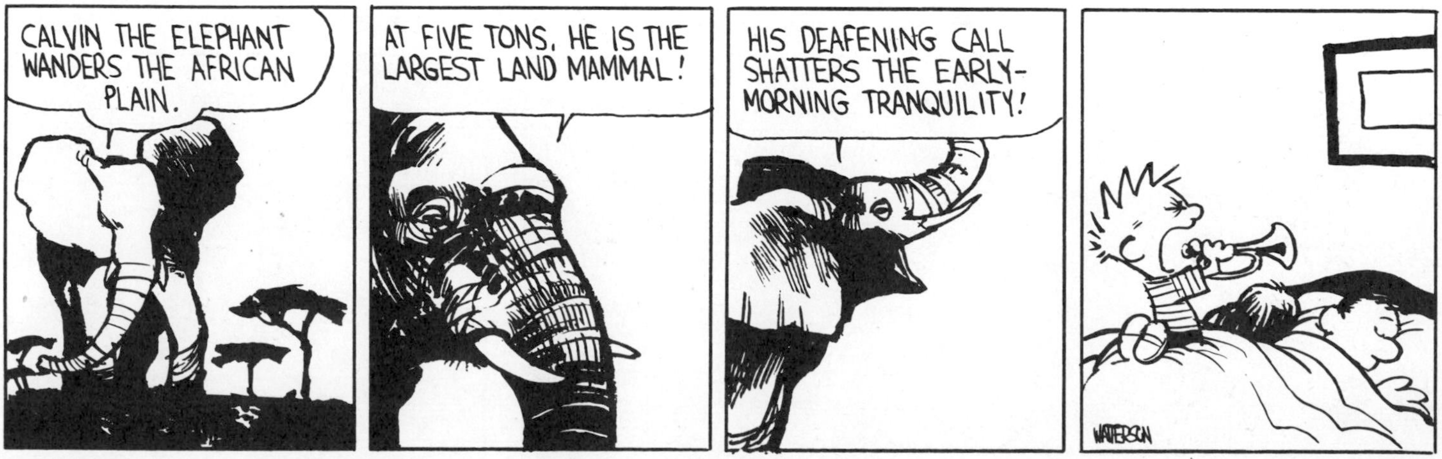
CALVIN THE ELEPHANT WANDERS THE AFRICAN PLAIN.
AT FIVE TONS, HE IS THE LARGEST LAND MAMMAL!
HIS DEAFENING CALL SHATTERS THE EARLY-MORNING TRANQUILITY!
WATTERSON

148

**Calvin:** AHH! LUNCH, MY FAVORITE MEAL! AND TODAY'S LUNCH IS *EXTRA* SPECIAL!

**Calvin:** EVER SINCE THE WEATHER GOT WARM I'VE BEEN SWATTING FLIES AND SAVING THEM IN A JAR.

**Calvin:** FINALLY I GOT ENOUGH BUGS TO MASH THEM INTO A GOOEY PASTE WITH A SPOON.

**Calvin:** I CALL IT "BUG BUTTER." CARE FOR A TASTE?

**Susie:** TELL ME, CALVIN, DO YOU HAVE ANY FRIENDS AT *ALL*?

**Teacher:** OK, YOU'VE ALL READ THE CHAPTER, SO WHO CAN TELL ME WHAT'S IMPORTANT ABOUT THE BATTLE OF LEXINGTON?

**Teacher:** ANYONE?

**Teacher:** CALVIN, HOW ABOUT YOU?

**Calvin:** HARD TO SAY, MA'AM. I THINK MY CEREBELLUM JUST FUSED.

**Calvin:** HEY, MOM, CAN WE GO OUT FOR HAMBURGERS TONIGHT?

**Mom:** NOT TONIGHT, DEAR.

**Calvin:** AW, MOM! WHY NOT?

**Mom:** BECAUSE I'M ALREADY FIXING SOMETHING FOR DINNER.

**Calvin:** YEAH... I KNOW.

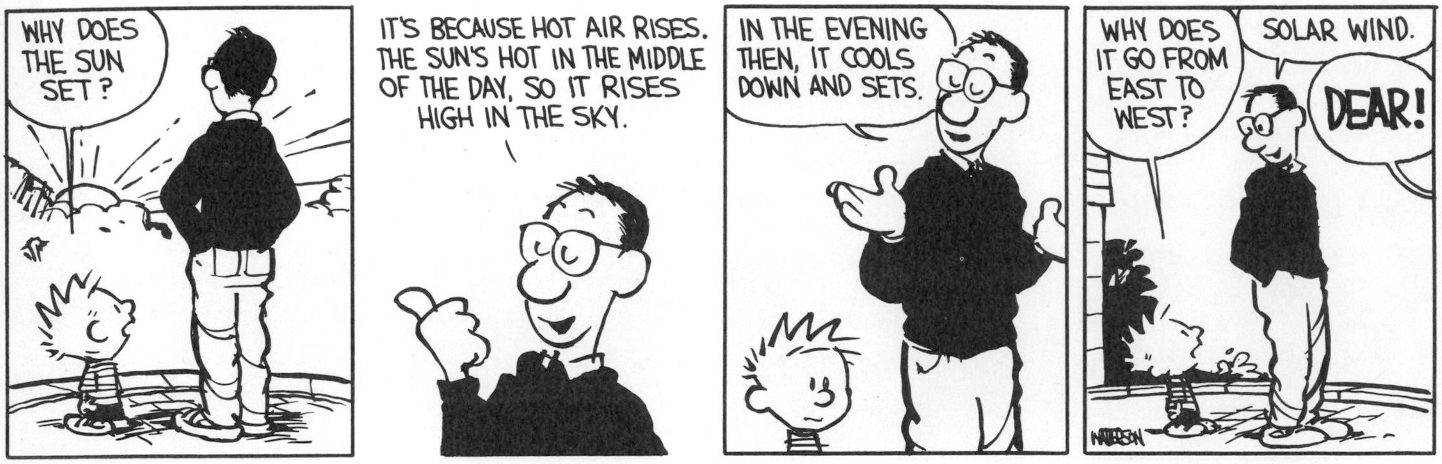
WHY DOES THE SUN SET?
IT'S BECAUSE HOT AIR RISES. THE SUN'S HOT IN THE MIDDLE OF THE DAY, SO IT RISES HIGH IN THE SKY.
IN THE EVENING THEN, IT COOLS DOWN AND SETS.
WHY DOES IT GO FROM EAST TO WEST?
SOLAR WIND.
DEAR!

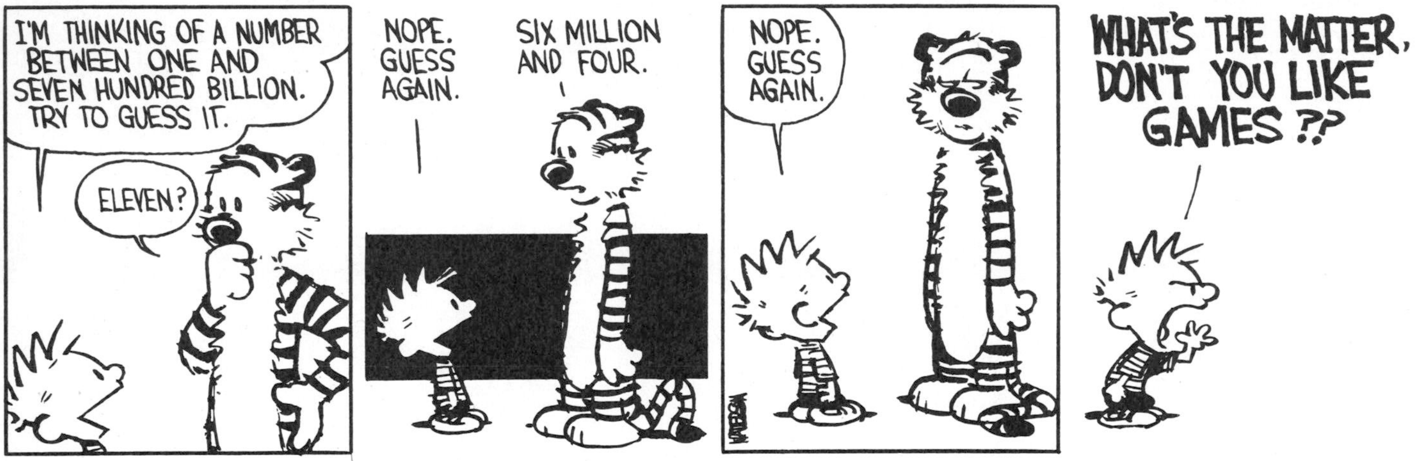
I'M THINKING OF A NUMBER BETWEEN ONE AND SEVEN HUNDRED BILLION. TRY TO GUESS IT.
ELEVEN?
NOPE. GUESS AGAIN.
SIX MILLION AND FOUR.
NOPE. GUESS AGAIN.
WHAT'S THE MATTER, DON'T YOU LIKE GAMES ??

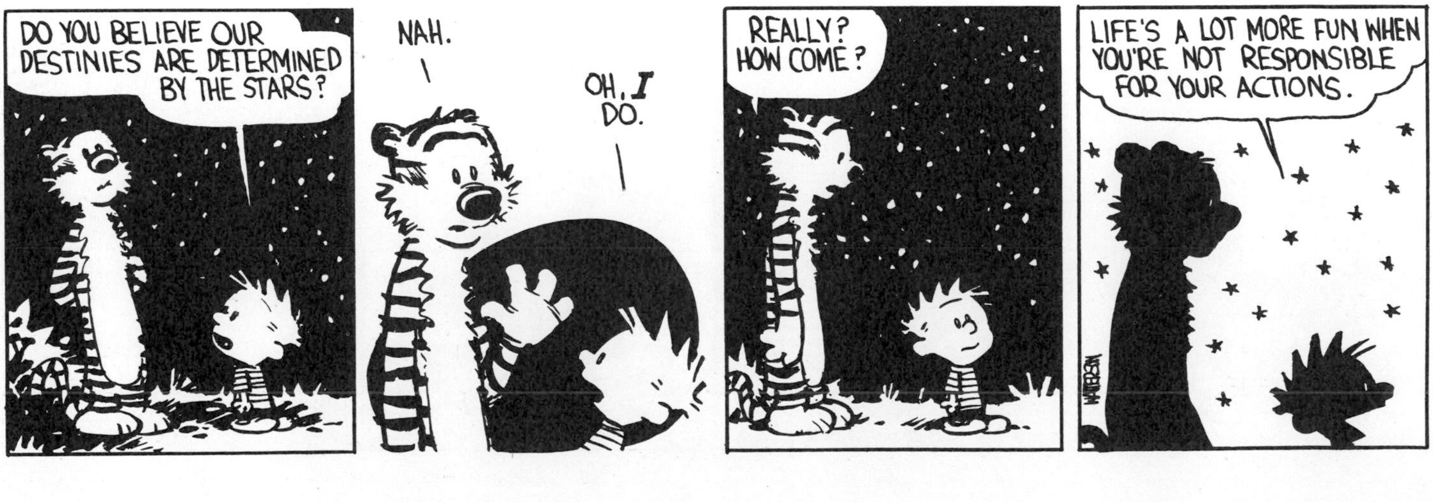
DO YOU BELIEVE OUR DESTINIES ARE DETERMINED BY THE STARS?
NAH.
OH, I DO.
REALLY? HOW COME?
LIFE'S A LOT MORE FUN WHEN YOU'RE NOT RESPONSIBLE FOR YOUR ACTIONS.

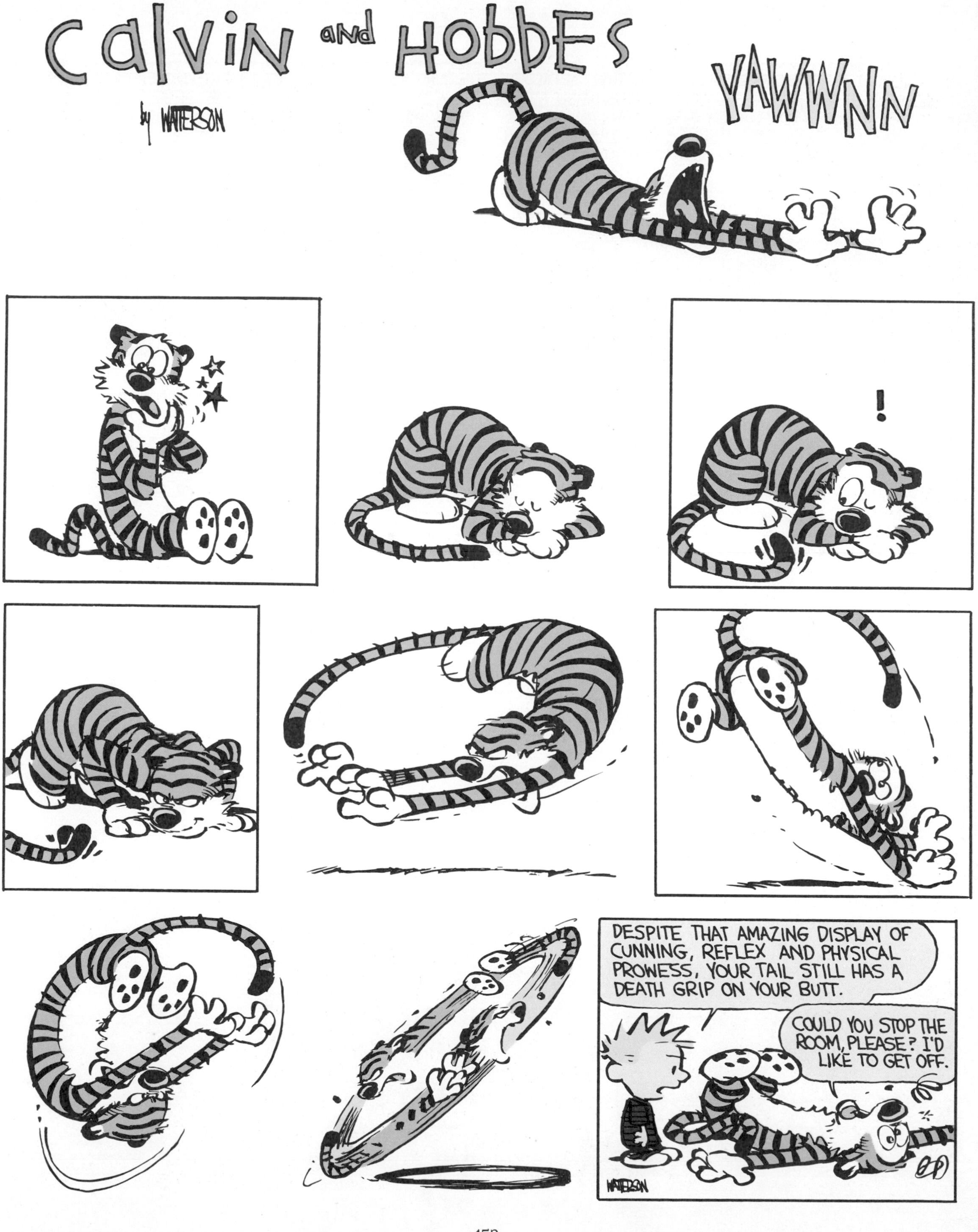
Calvin and HOBBES
by WATTERSON
YAWWNN
!
DESPITE THAT AMAZING DISPLAY OF CUNNING, REFLEX AND PHYSICAL PROWESS, YOUR TAIL STILL HAS A DEATH GRIP ON YOUR BUTT.
COULD YOU STOP THE ROOM, PLEASE? I'D LIKE TO GET OFF.
WATTERSON

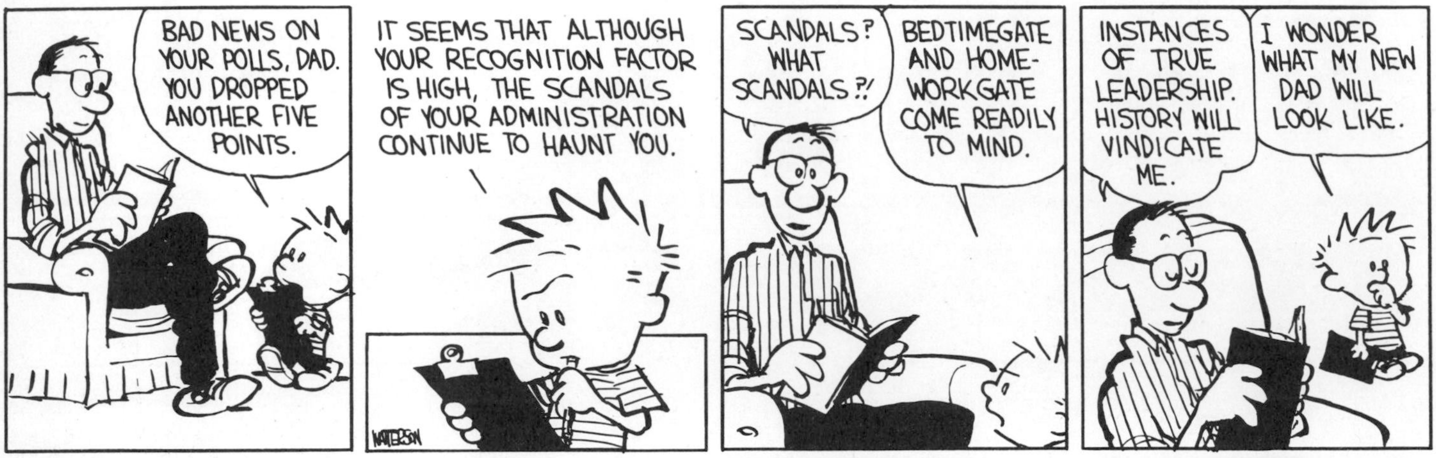
BAD NEWS ON YOUR POLLS, DAD. YOU DROPPED ANOTHER FIVE POINTS.
IT SEEMS THAT ALTHOUGH YOUR RECOGNITION FACTOR IS HIGH, THE SCANDALS OF YOUR ADMINISTRATION CONTINUE TO HAUNT YOU.
WATTERSON
SCANDALS? WHAT SCANDALS?!
BEDTIMEGATE AND HOME-WORKGATE COME READILY TO MIND.
INSTANCES OF TRUE LEADERSHIP. HISTORY WILL VINDICATE ME.
I WONDER WHAT MY NEW DAD WILL LOOK LIKE.

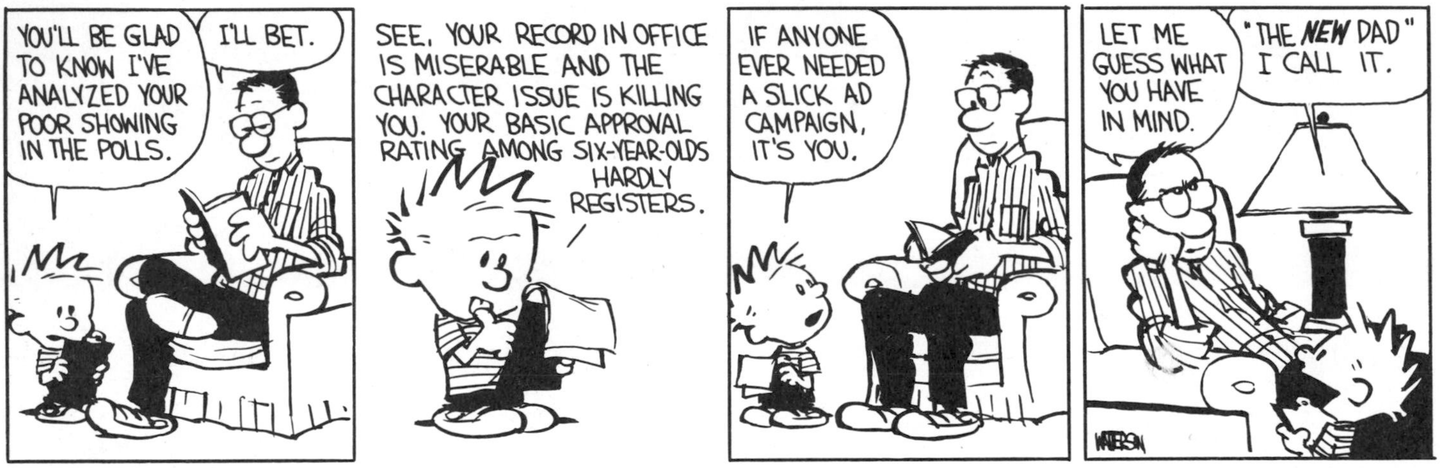
YOU'LL BE GLAD TO KNOW I'VE ANALYZED YOUR POOR SHOWING IN THE POLLS.
I'LL BET.
SEE, YOUR RECORD IN OFFICE IS MISERABLE AND THE CHARACTER ISSUE IS KILLING YOU. YOUR BASIC APPROVAL RATING AMONG SIX-YEAR-OLDS HARDLY REGISTERS.
IF ANYONE EVER NEEDED A SLICK AD CAMPAIGN, IT'S YOU.
LET ME GUESS WHAT YOU HAVE IN MIND.
"THE NEW DAD" I CALL IT.
WATTERSON

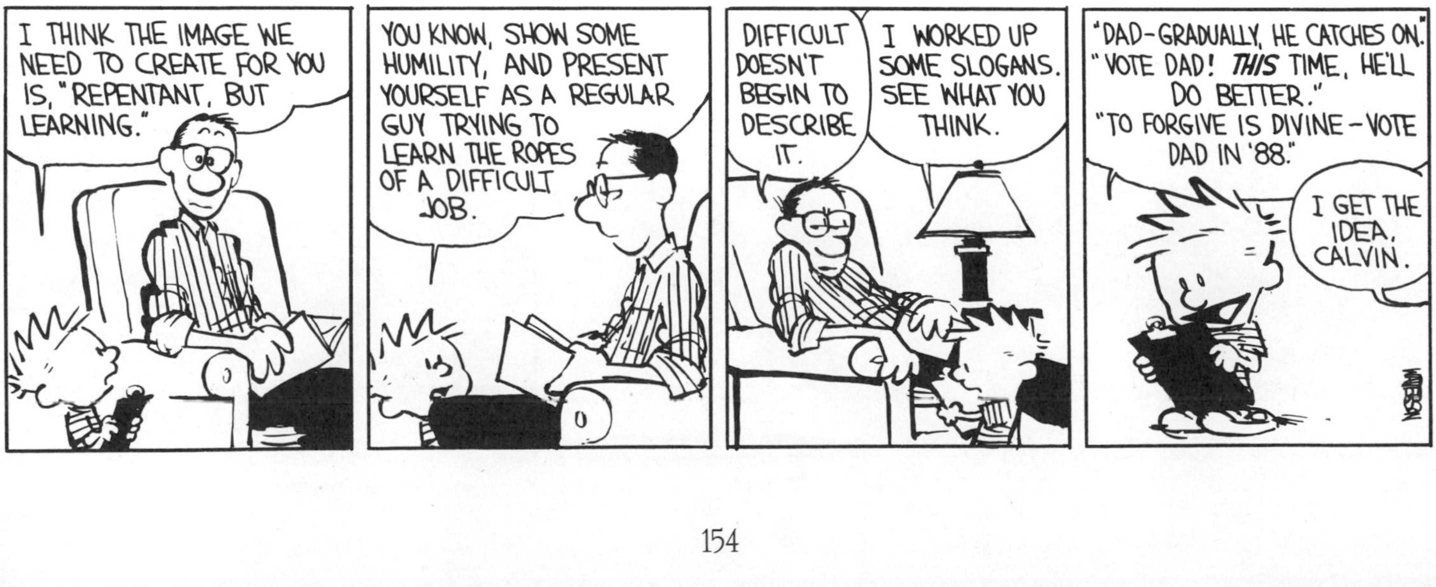
I THINK THE IMAGE WE NEED TO CREATE FOR YOU IS, "REPENTANT, BUT LEARNING."
YOU KNOW, SHOW SOME HUMILITY, AND PRESENT YOURSELF AS A REGULAR GUY TRYING TO LEARN THE ROPES OF A DIFFICULT JOB.
DIFFICULT DOESN'T BEGIN TO DESCRIBE IT.
I WORKED UP SOME SLOGANS. SEE WHAT YOU THINK.
"DAD-GRADUALLY, HE CATCHES ON." "VOTE DAD! THIS TIME, HE'LL DO BETTER." "TO FORGIVE IS DIVINE-VOTE DAD IN '88."
I GET THE IDEA, CALVIN.
WATTERSON

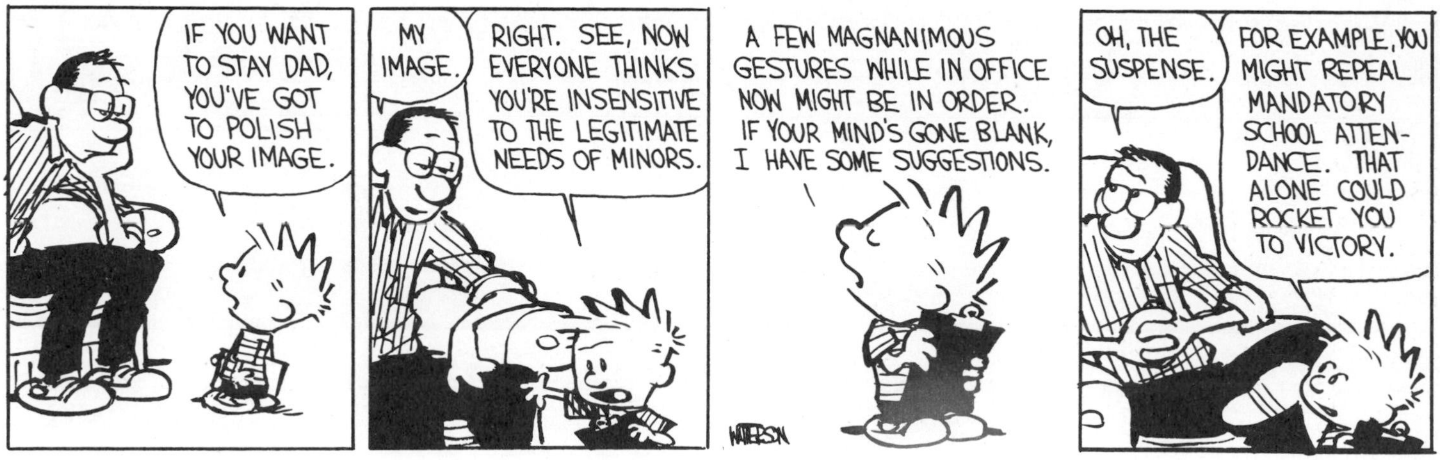
IF YOU WANT TO STAY DAD, YOU'VE GOT TO POLISH YOUR IMAGE.
MY IMAGE.
RIGHT. SEE, NOW EVERYONE THINKS YOU'RE INSENSITIVE TO THE LEGITIMATE NEEDS OF MINORS.
A FEW MAGNANIMOUS GESTURES WHILE IN OFFICE NOW MIGHT BE IN ORDER. IF YOUR MIND'S GONE BLANK, I HAVE SOME SUGGESTIONS.
OH, THE SUSPENSE.
FOR EXAMPLE, YOU MIGHT REPEAL MANDATORY SCHOOL ATTENDANCE. THAT ALONE COULD ROCKET YOU TO VICTORY.

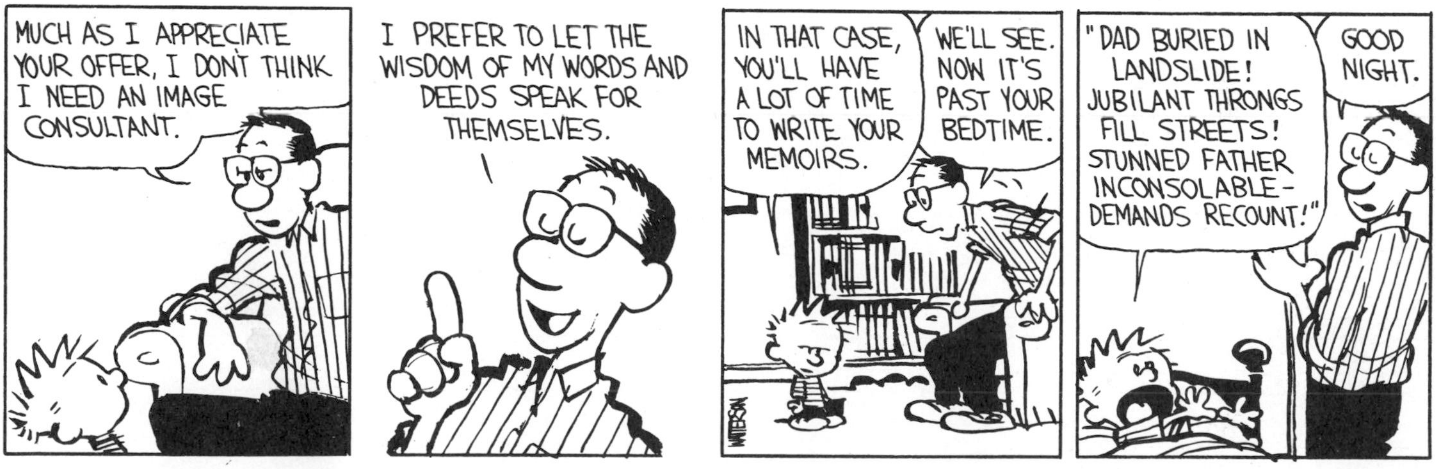
MUCH AS I APPRECIATE YOUR OFFER, I DON'T THINK I NEED AN IMAGE CONSULTANT.
I PREFER TO LET THE WISDOM OF MY WORDS AND DEEDS SPEAK FOR THEMSELVES.
IN THAT CASE, YOU'LL HAVE A LOT OF TIME TO WRITE YOUR MEMOIRS.
WE'LL SEE. NOW IT'S PAST YOUR BEDTIME.
"DAD BURIED IN LANDSLIDE! JUBILANT THRONGS FILL STREETS! STUNNED FATHER INCONSOLABLE– DEMANDS RECOUNT!"
GOOD NIGHT.

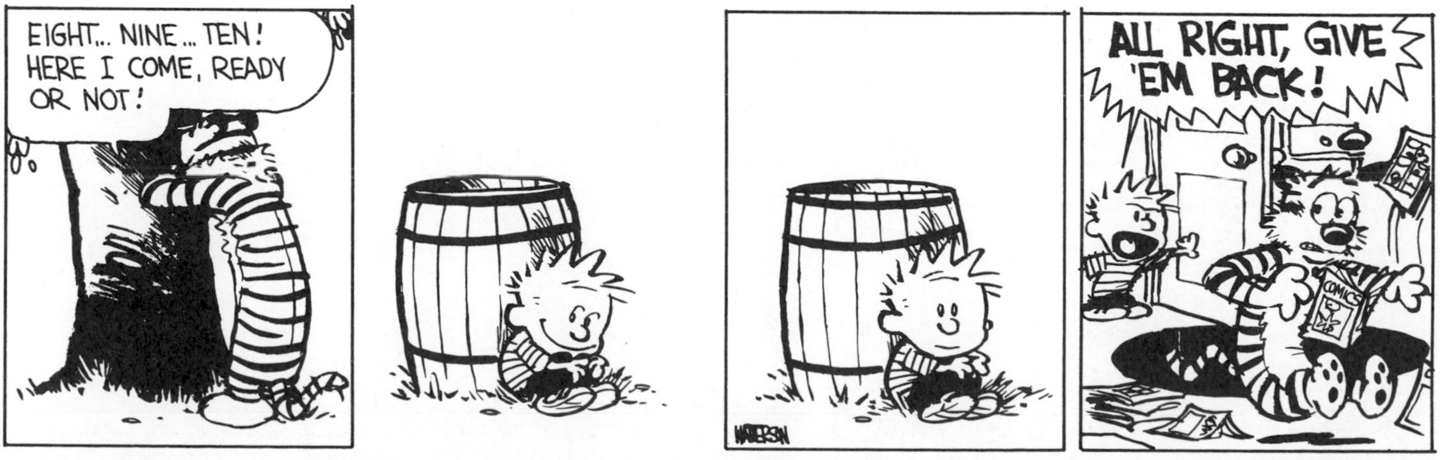
EIGHT... NINE... TEN! HERE I COME, READY OR NOT!
ALL RIGHT, GIVE 'EM BACK!

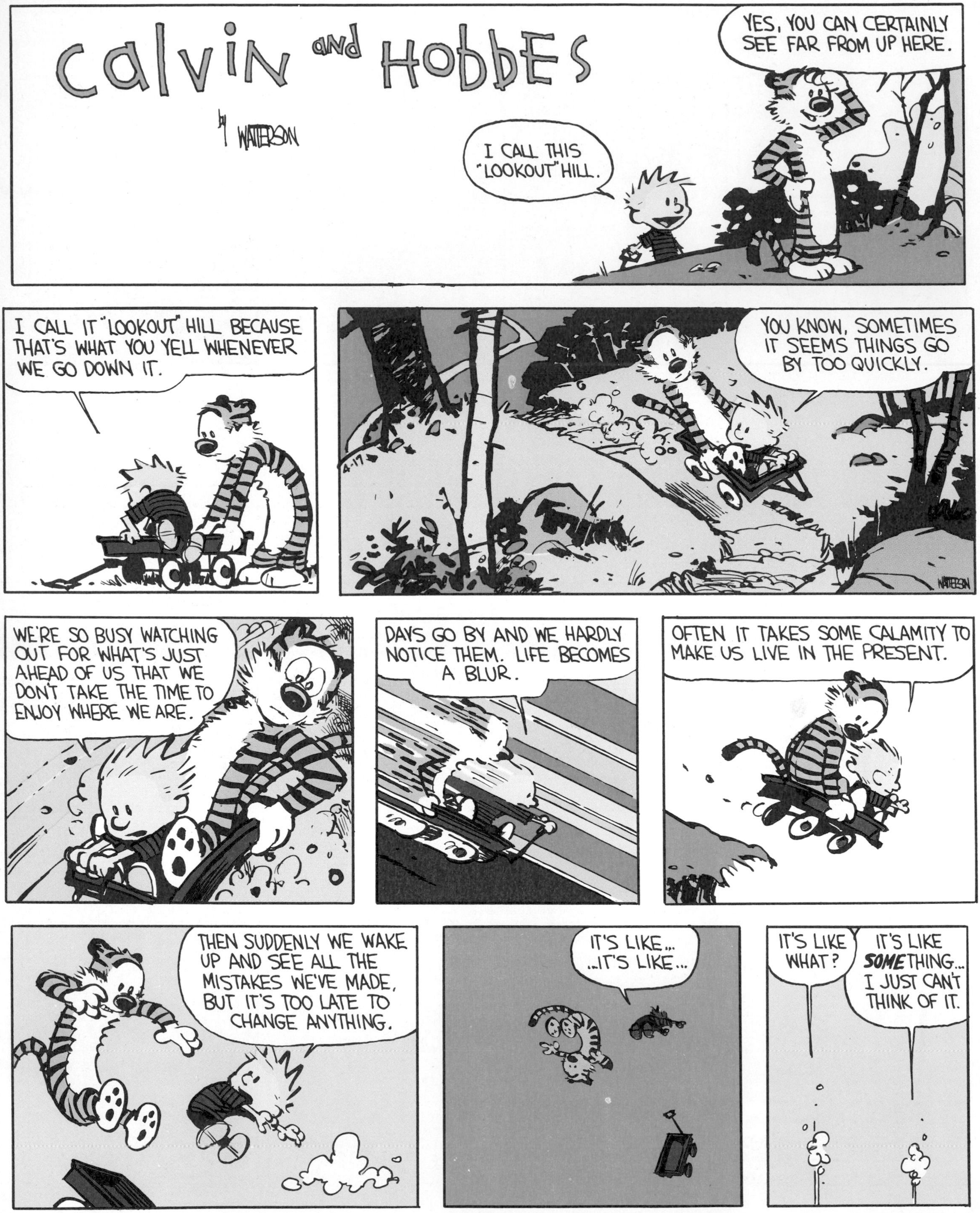
Calvin and Hobbes
by WATTERSON
I CALL THIS "LOOKOUT" HILL.
YES, YOU CAN CERTAINLY SEE FAR FROM UP HERE.
I CALL IT "LOOKOUT" HILL BECAUSE THAT'S WHAT YOU YELL WHENEVER WE GO DOWN IT.
YOU KNOW, SOMETIMES IT SEEMS THINGS GO BY TOO QUICKLY.
WE'RE SO BUSY WATCHING OUT FOR WHAT'S JUST AHEAD OF US THAT WE DON'T TAKE THE TIME TO ENJOY WHERE WE ARE.
DAYS GO BY AND WE HARDLY NOTICE THEM. LIFE BECOMES A BLUR.
OFTEN IT TAKES SOME CALAMITY TO MAKE US LIVE IN THE PRESENT.
THEN SUDDENLY WE WAKE UP AND SEE ALL THE MISTAKES WE'VE MADE, BUT IT'S TOO LATE TO CHANGE ANYTHING.
IT'S LIKE... ...IT'S LIKE...
IT'S LIKE WHAT?
IT'S LIKE SOMETHING... I JUST CAN'T THINK OF IT.

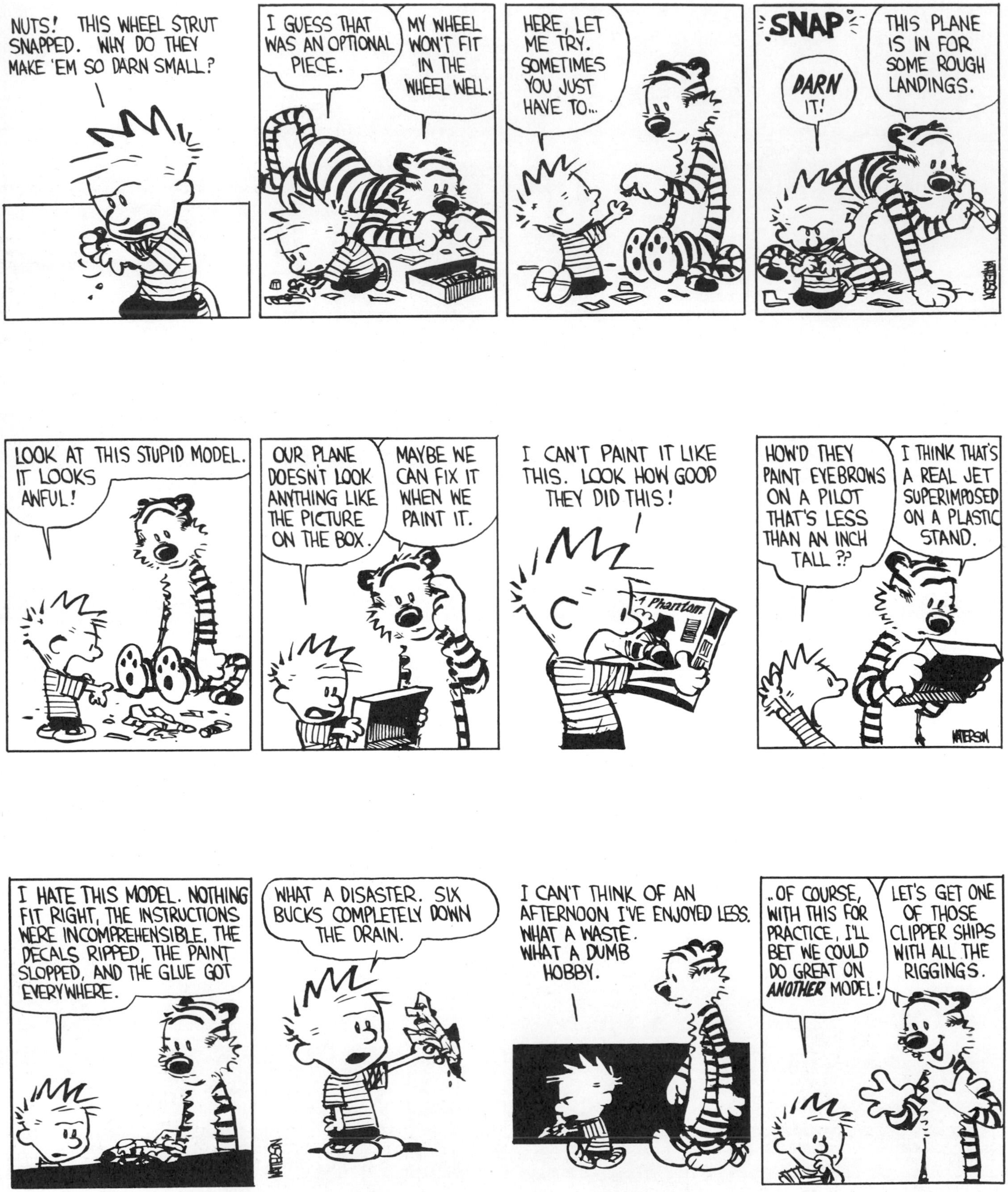
NUTS! THIS WHEEL STRUT SNAPPED. WHY DO THEY MAKE 'EM SO DARN SMALL?
I GUESS THAT WAS AN OPTIONAL PIECE.
MY WHEEL WON'T FIT IN THE WHEEL WELL.
HERE, LET ME TRY. SOMETIMES YOU JUST HAVE TO...
SNAP
DARN IT!
THIS PLANE IS IN FOR SOME ROUGH LANDINGS.
LOOK AT THIS STUPID MODEL. IT LOOKS AWFUL!
OUR PLANE DOESN'T LOOK ANYTHING LIKE THE PICTURE ON THE BOX.
MAYBE WE CAN FIX IT WHEN WE PAINT IT.
I CAN'T PAINT IT LIKE THIS. LOOK HOW GOOD THEY DID THIS!
Phantom
HOW'D THEY PAINT EYEBROWS ON A PILOT THAT'S LESS THAN AN INCH TALL ??
I THINK THAT'S A REAL JET SUPERIMPOSED ON A PLASTIC STAND.
I HATE THIS MODEL. NOTHING FIT RIGHT, THE INSTRUCTIONS WERE INCOMPREHENSIBLE, THE DECALS RIPPED, THE PAINT SLOPPED, AND THE GLUE GOT EVERYWHERE.
WHAT A DISASTER. SIX BUCKS COMPLETELY DOWN THE DRAIN.
I CAN'T THINK OF AN AFTERNOON I'VE ENJOYED LESS. WHAT A WASTE. WHAT A DUMB HOBBY.
..OF COURSE, WITH THIS FOR PRACTICE, I'LL BET WE COULD DO GREAT ON ANOTHER MODEL!
LET'S GET ONE OF THOSE CLIPPER SHIPS WITH ALL THE RIGGINGS.

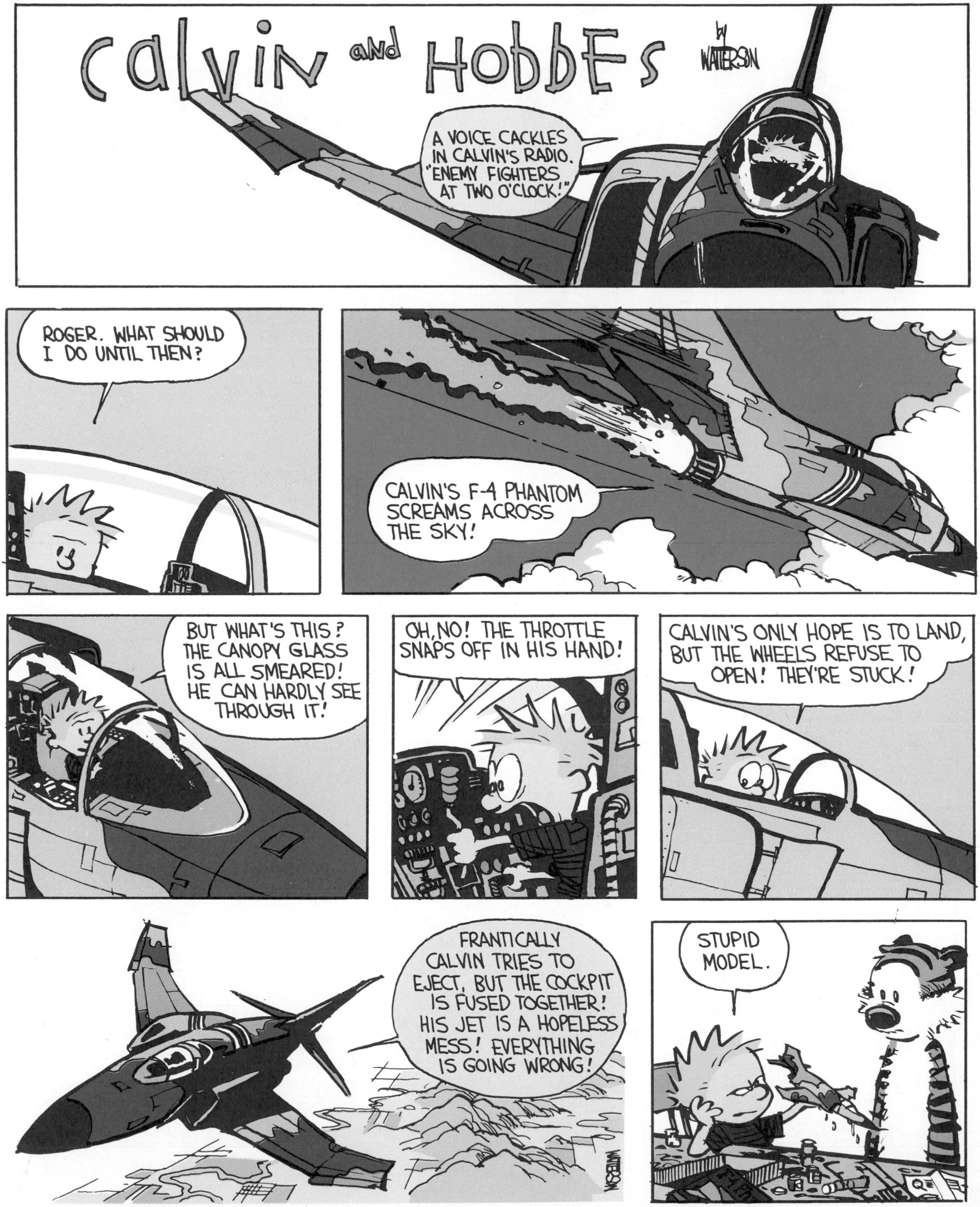
Calvin and HOBBES
by WATTERSON
A VOICE CACKLES IN CALVIN'S RADIO. "ENEMY FIGHTERS AT TWO O'CLOCK!"
ROGER. WHAT SHOULD I DO UNTIL THEN?
CALVIN'S F-4 PHANTOM SCREAMS ACROSS THE SKY!
BUT WHAT'S THIS? THE CANOPY GLASS IS ALL SMEARED! HE CAN HARDLY SEE THROUGH IT!
OH, NO! THE THROTTLE SNAPS OFF IN HIS HAND!
CALVIN'S ONLY HOPE IS TO LAND, BUT THE WHEELS REFUSE TO OPEN! THEY'RE STUCK!
FRANTICALLY CALVIN TRIES TO EJECT, BUT THE COCKPIT IS FUSED TOGETHER! HIS JET IS A HOPELESS MESS! EVERYTHING IS GOING WRONG!
STUPID MODEL.

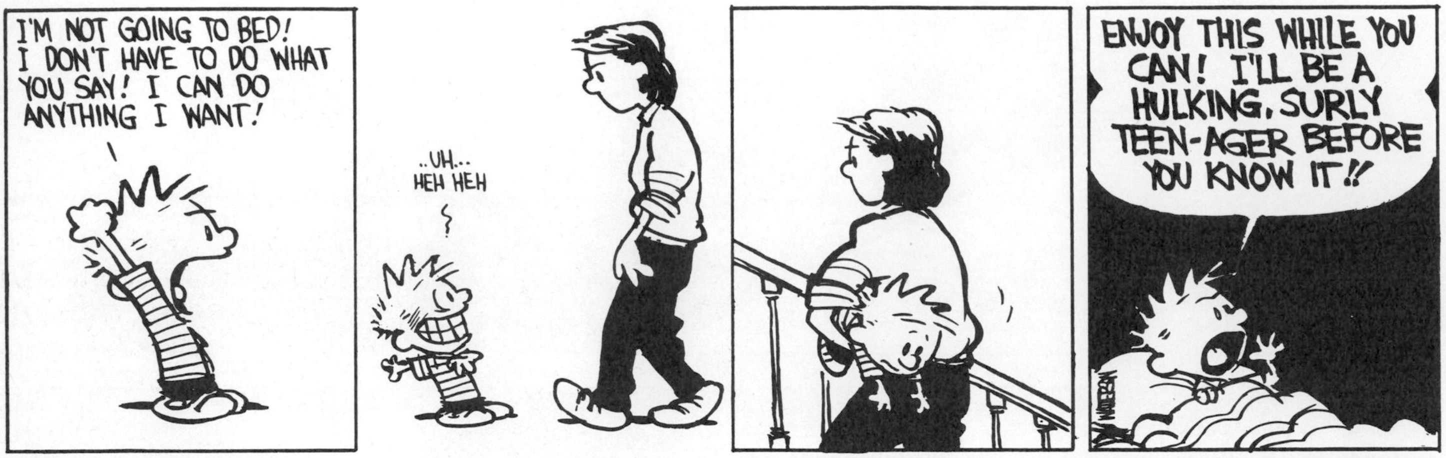
I'M NOT GOING TO BED! I DON'T HAVE TO DO WHAT YOU SAY! I CAN DO ANYTHING I WANT!
..UH... HEH HEH
ENJOY THIS WHILE YOU CAN! I'LL BE A HULKING, SURLY TEEN-AGER BEFORE YOU KNOW IT!!

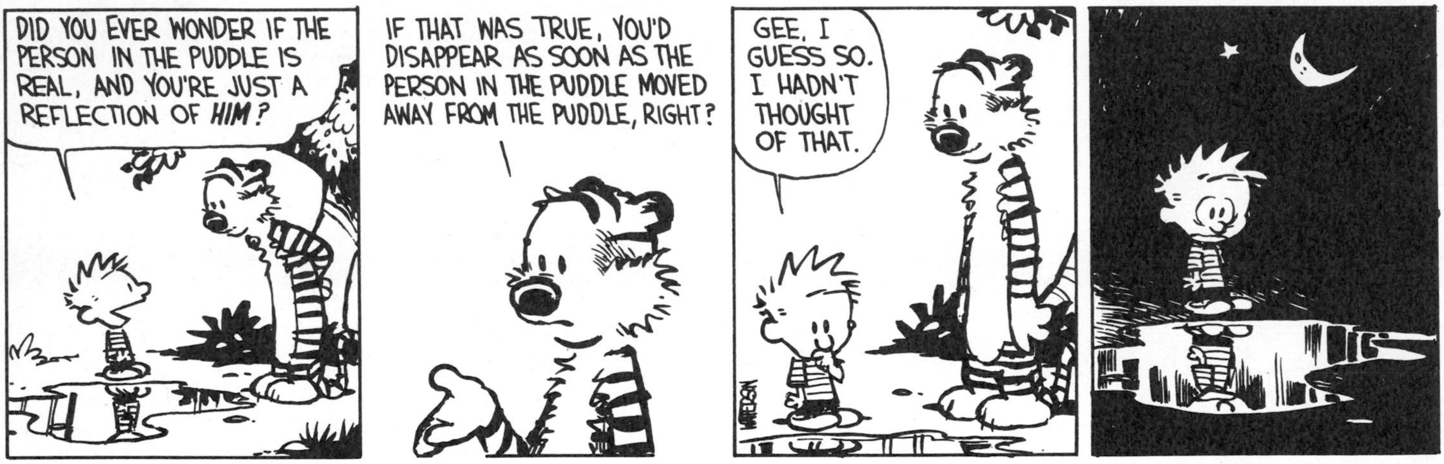
DID YOU EVER WONDER IF THE PERSON IN THE PUDDLE IS REAL, AND YOU'RE JUST A REFLECTION OF HIM?
IF THAT WAS TRUE, YOU'D DISAPPEAR AS SOON AS THE PERSON IN THE PUDDLE MOVED AWAY FROM THE PUDDLE, RIGHT?
GEE, I GUESS SO. I HADN'T THOUGHT OF THAT.

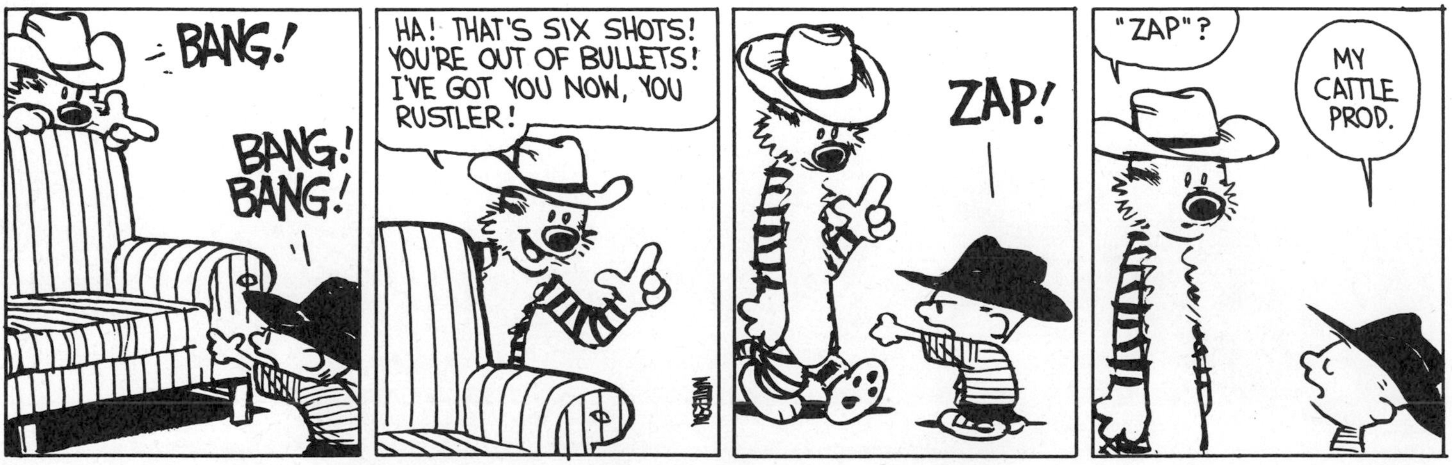
BANG!
BANG! BANG!
HA! THAT'S SIX SHOTS! YOU'RE OUT OF BULLETS! I'VE GOT YOU NOW, YOU RUSTLER!
ZAP!
"ZAP"?
MY CATTLE PROD.

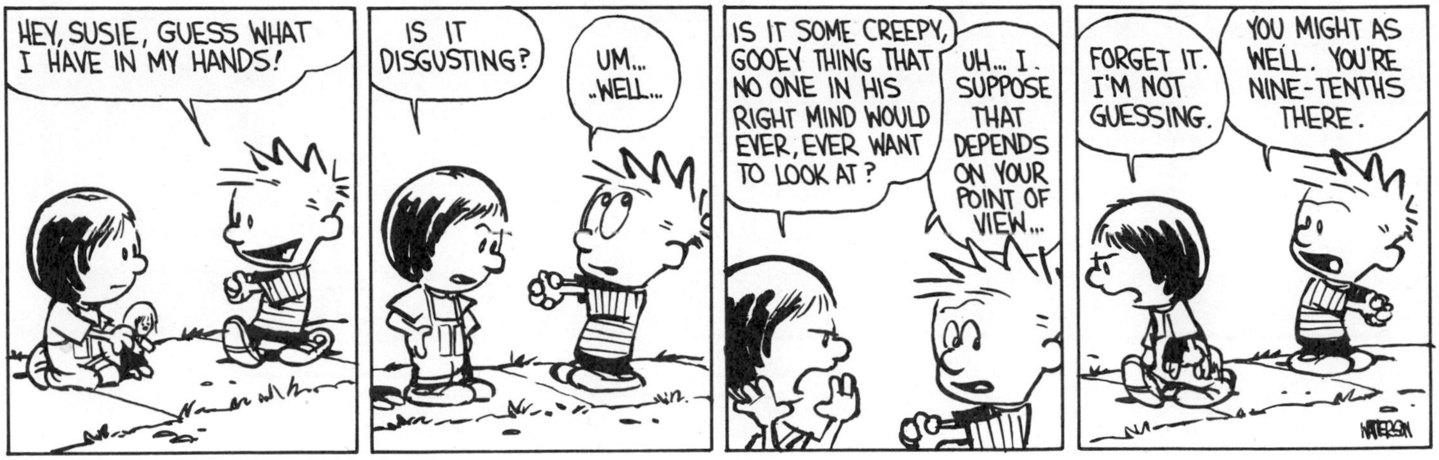
HEY, SUSIE, GUESS WHAT I HAVE IN MY HANDS!
IS IT DISGUSTING?
UM... ..WELL...
IS IT SOME CREEPY, GOOEY THING THAT NO ONE IN HIS RIGHT MIND WOULD EVER, EVER WANT TO LOOK AT?
UH... I. SUPPOSE THAT DEPENDS ON YOUR POINT OF VIEW...
FORGET IT. I'M NOT GUESSING.
YOU MIGHT AS WELL. YOU'RE NINE-TENTHS THERE.
WATTERSON

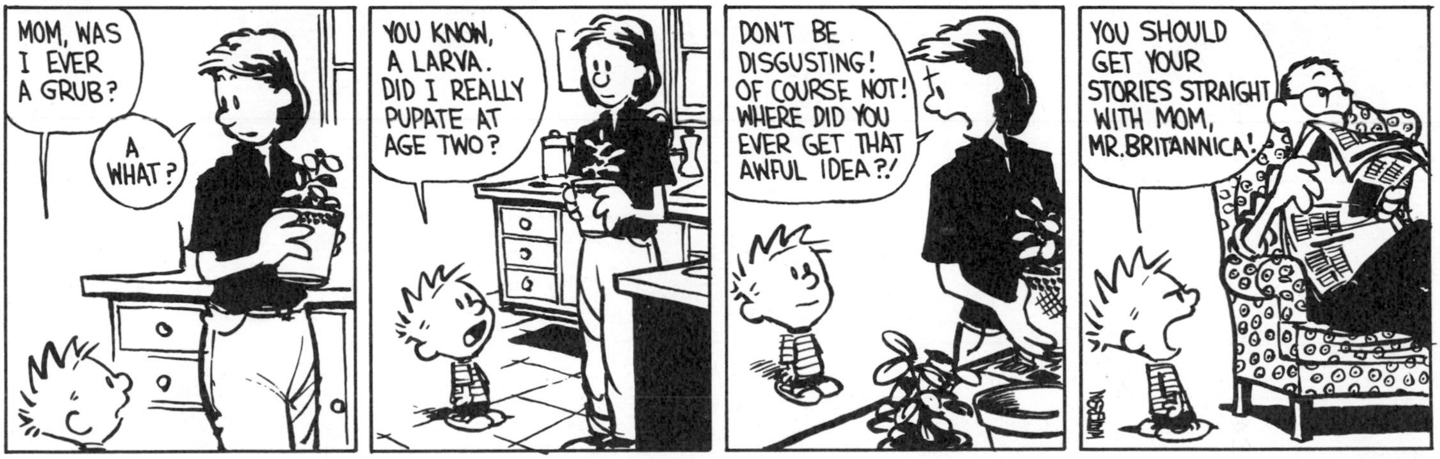
MOM, WAS I EVER A GRUB?
A WHAT?
YOU KNOW, A LARVA. DID I REALLY PUPATE AT AGE TWO?
DON'T BE DISGUSTING! OF COURSE NOT! WHERE DID YOU EVER GET THAT AWFUL IDEA?!
YOU SHOULD GET YOUR STORIES STRAIGHT WITH MOM, MR. BRITANNICA!
WATTERSON

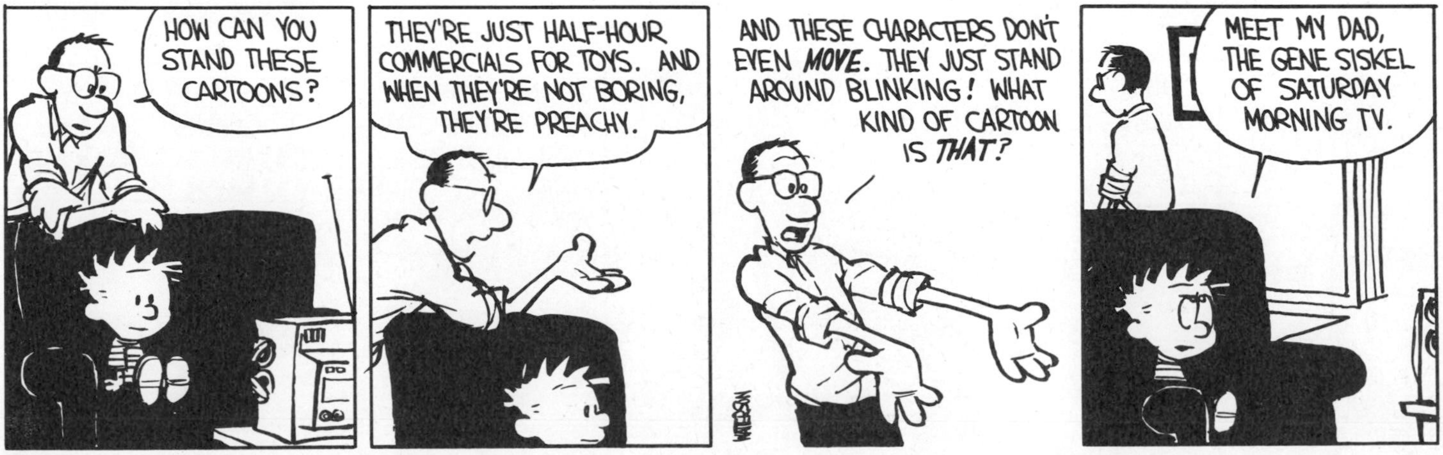
HOW CAN YOU STAND THESE CARTOONS?
THEY'RE JUST HALF-HOUR COMMERCIALS FOR TOYS. AND WHEN THEY'RE NOT BORING, THEY'RE PREACHY.
AND THESE CHARACTERS DON'T EVEN MOVE. THEY JUST STAND AROUND BLINKING! WHAT KIND OF CARTOON IS THAT?
WATTERSON
MEET MY DAD, THE GENE SISKEL OF SATURDAY MORNING TV.

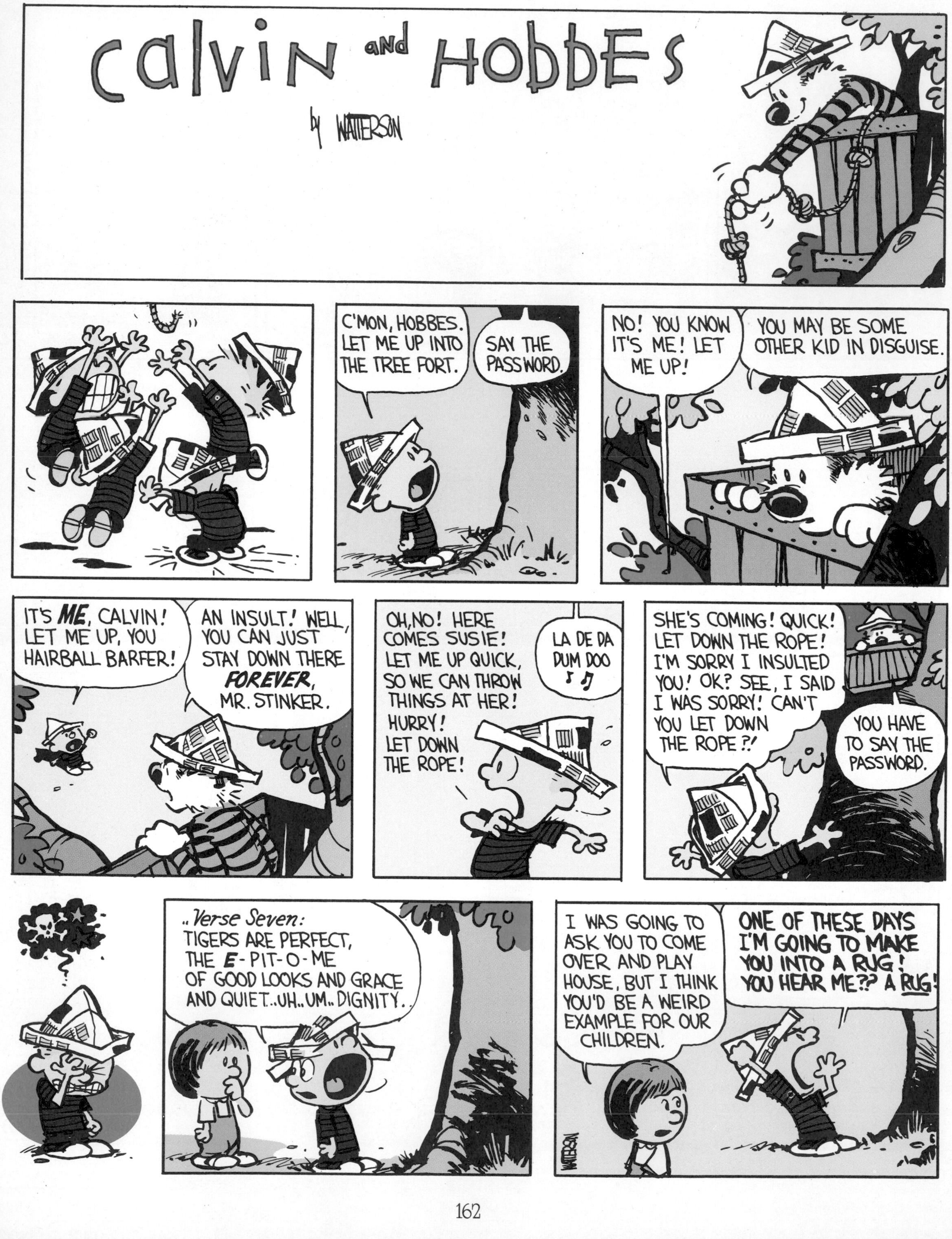
Calvin and HOBBES
by WATTERSON
C'MON, HOBBES. LET ME UP INTO THE TREE FORT.
SAY THE PASSWORD.
NO! YOU KNOW IT'S ME! LET ME UP!
YOU MAY BE SOME OTHER KID IN DISGUISE.
IT'S ME, CALVIN! LET ME UP, YOU HAIRBALL BARFER!
AN INSULT! WELL, YOU CAN JUST STAY DOWN THERE FOREVER, MR. STINKER.
OH, NO! HERE COMES SUSIE! LET ME UP QUICK, SO WE CAN THROW THINGS AT HER! HURRY! LET DOWN THE ROPE!
LA DE DA DUM DOO
SHE'S COMING! QUICK! LET DOWN THE ROPE! I'M SORRY I INSULTED YOU! OK? SEE, I SAID I WAS SORRY! CAN'T YOU LET DOWN THE ROPE?!
YOU HAVE TO SAY THE PASSWORD.
..Verse Seven: TIGERS ARE PERFECT, THE E-PIT-O-ME OF GOOD LOOKS AND GRACE AND QUIET..UH..UM..DIGNITY..
I WAS GOING TO ASK YOU TO COME OVER AND PLAY HOUSE, BUT I THINK YOU'D BE A WEIRD EXAMPLE FOR OUR CHILDREN.
ONE OF THESE DAYS I'M GOING TO MAKE YOU INTO A RUG! YOU HEAR ME?? A RUG!
WATTERSON

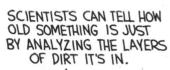

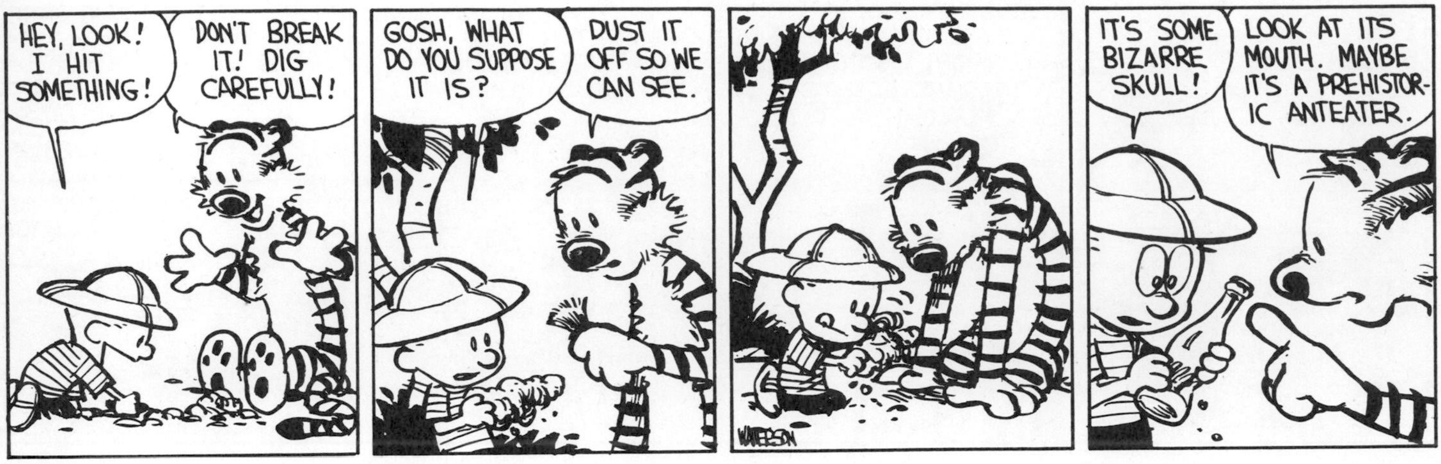
HEY, LOOK! I HIT SOMETHING!
DON'T BREAK IT! DIG CAREFULLY!
GOSH, WHAT DO YOU SUPPOSE IT IS?
DUST IT OFF SO WE CAN SEE.
IT'S SOME BIZARRE SKULL!
LOOK AT ITS MOUTH. MAYBE IT'S A PREHISTORIC ANTEATER.

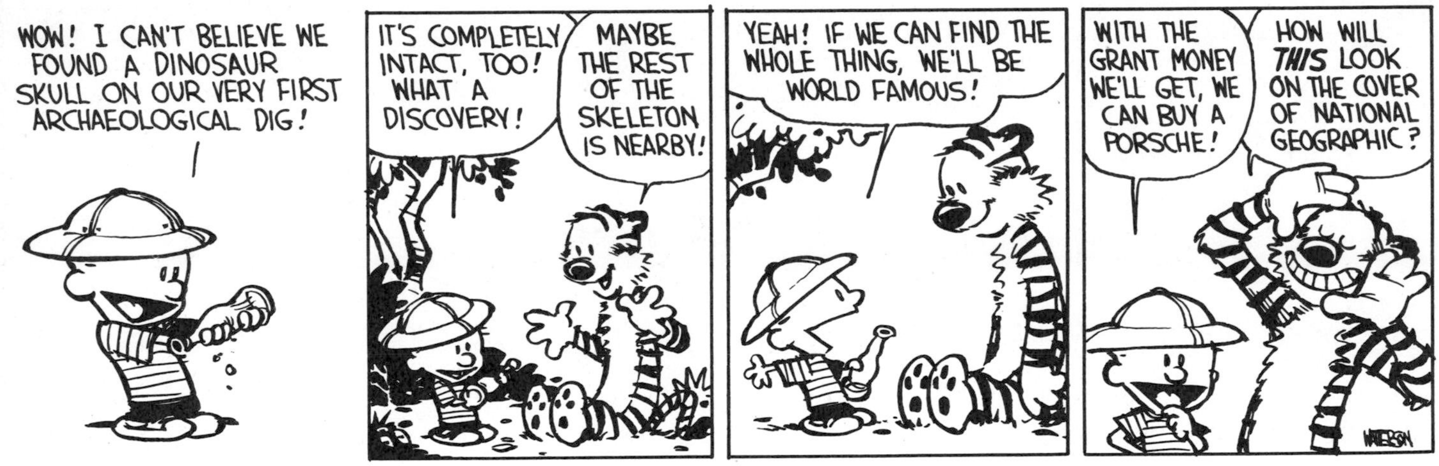
WOW! I CAN'T BELIEVE WE FOUND A DINOSAUR SKULL ON OUR VERY FIRST ARCHAEOLOGICAL DIG!
IT'S COMPLETELY INTACT, TOO! WHAT A DISCOVERY!
MAYBE THE REST OF THE SKELETON IS NEARBY!
YEAH! IF WE CAN FIND THE WHOLE THING, WE'LL BE WORLD FAMOUS!
WITH THE GRANT MONEY WE'LL GET, WE CAN BUY A PORSCHE!
HOW WILL THIS LOOK ON THE COVER OF NATIONAL GEOGRAPHIC?

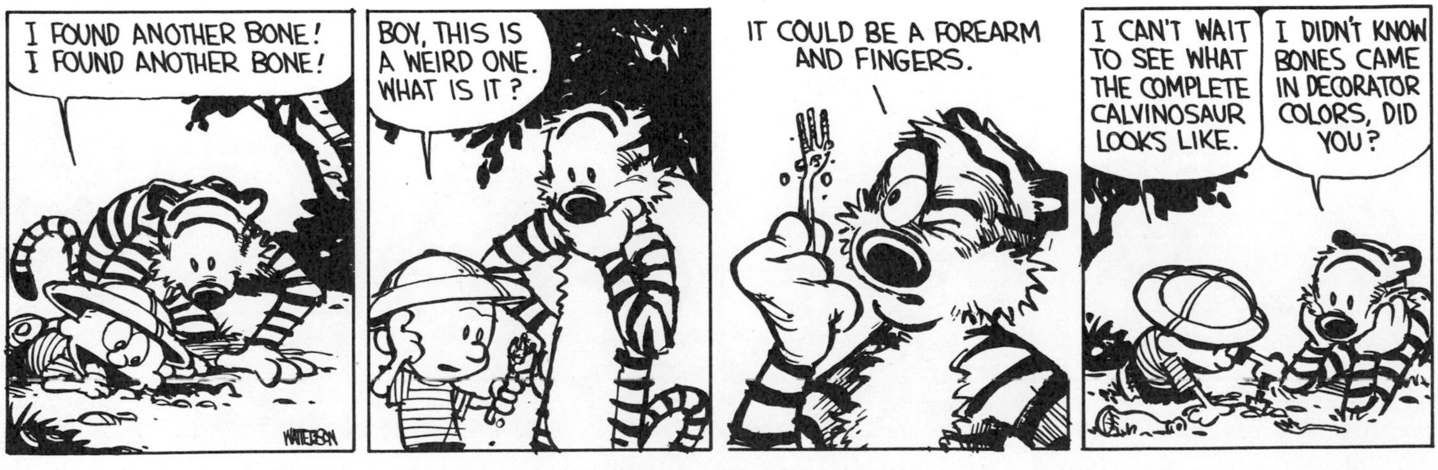
I FOUND ANOTHER BONE! I FOUND ANOTHER BONE!
BOY, THIS IS A WEIRD ONE. WHAT IS IT?
IT COULD BE A FOREARM AND FINGERS.
I CAN'T WAIT TO SEE WHAT THE COMPLETE CALVINOSAUR LOOKS LIKE.
I DIDN'T KNOW BONES CAME IN DECORATOR COLORS, DID YOU?

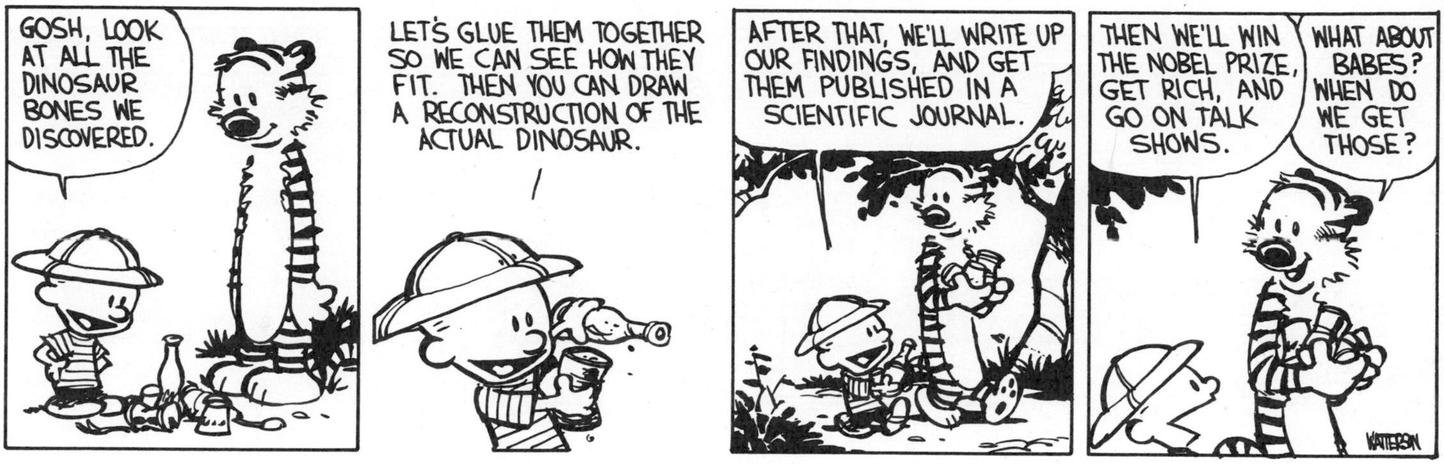
GOSH, LOOK AT ALL THE DINOSAUR BONES WE DISCOVERED.
LET'S GLUE THEM TOGETHER SO WE CAN SEE HOW THEY FIT. THEN YOU CAN DRAW A RECONSTRUCTION OF THE ACTUAL DINOSAUR.
AFTER THAT, WE'LL WRITE UP OUR FINDINGS, AND GET THEM PUBLISHED IN A SCIENTIFIC JOURNAL.
THEN WE'LL WIN THE NOBEL PRIZE, GET RICH, AND GO ON TALK SHOWS.
WHAT ABOUT BABES? WHEN DO WE GET THOSE?
WATTERSON

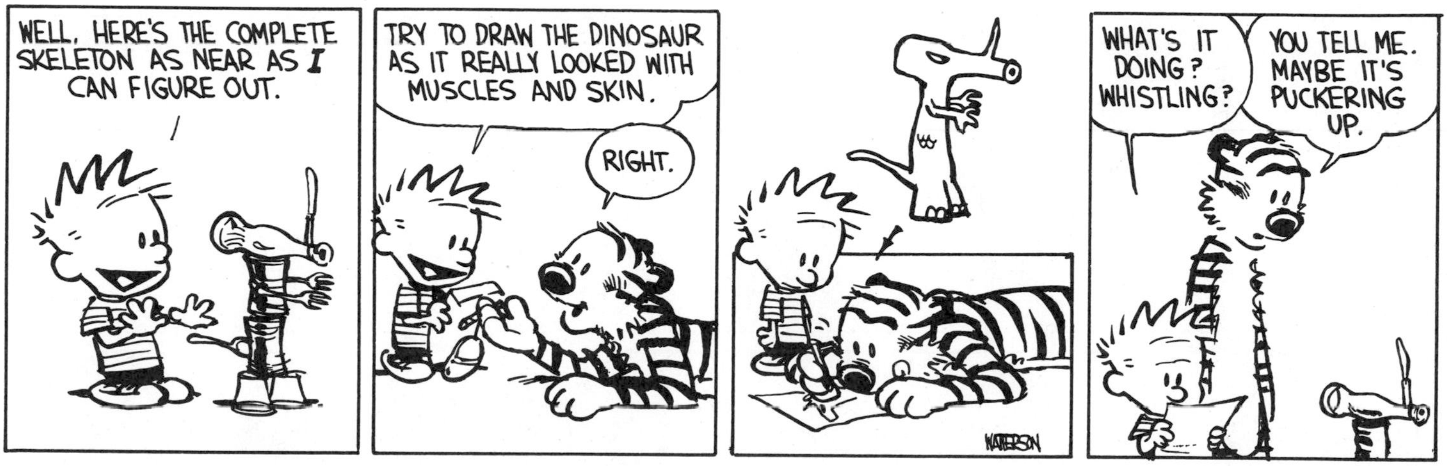
WELL, HERE'S THE COMPLETE SKELETON AS NEAR AS *I* CAN FIGURE OUT.
TRY TO DRAW THE DINOSAUR AS IT REALLY LOOKED WITH MUSCLES AND SKIN.
RIGHT.
WATTERSON
WHAT'S IT DOING? WHISTLING?
YOU TELL ME. MAYBE IT'S PUCKERING UP.

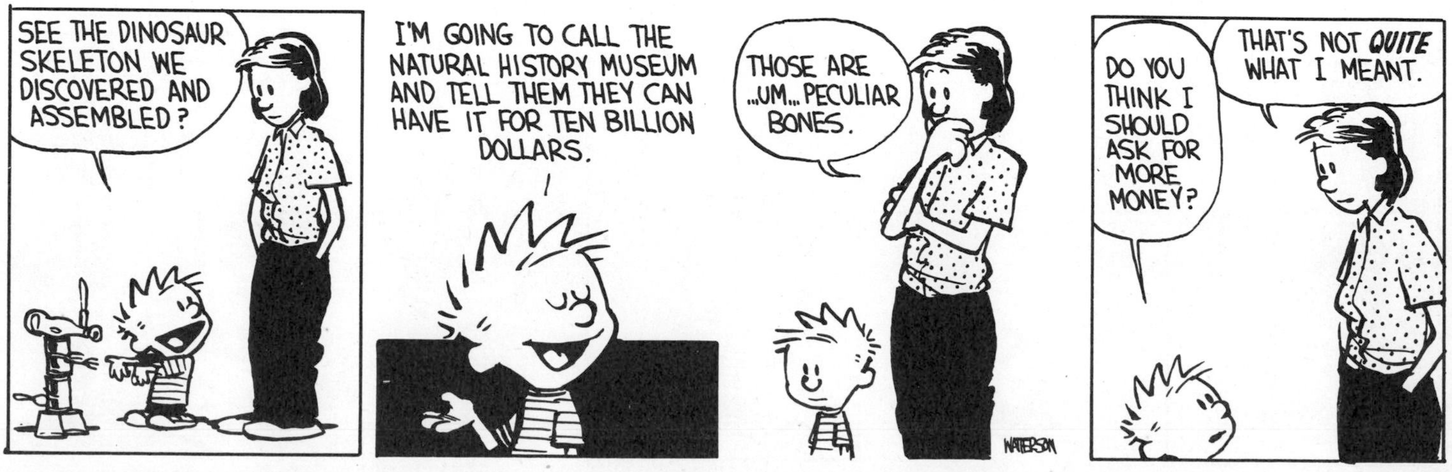
SEE THE DINOSAUR SKELETON WE DISCOVERED AND ASSEMBLED?
I'M GOING TO CALL THE NATURAL HISTORY MUSEUM AND TELL THEM THEY CAN HAVE IT FOR TEN BILLION DOLLARS.
THOSE ARE ...UM... PECULIAR BONES.
WATTERSON
DO YOU THINK I SHOULD ASK FOR MORE MONEY?
THAT'S NOT ***QUITE*** WHAT I MEANT.

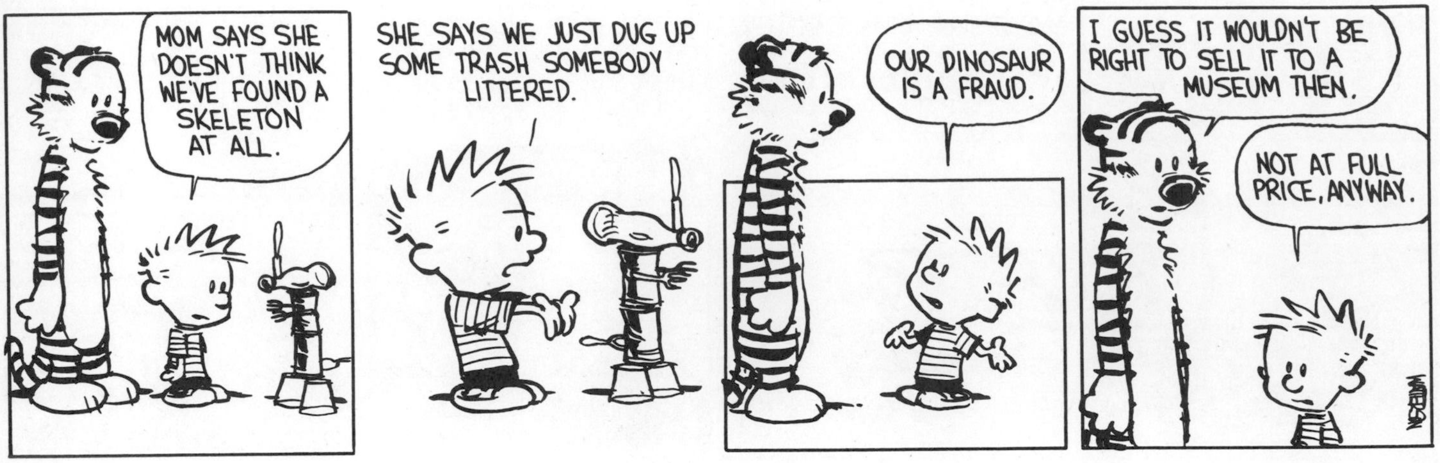
MOM SAYS SHE DOESN'T THINK WE'VE FOUND A SKELETON AT ALL.
SHE SAYS WE JUST DUG UP SOME TRASH SOMEBODY LITTERED.
OUR DINOSAUR IS A FRAUD.
I GUESS IT WOULDN'T BE RIGHT TO SELL IT TO A MUSEUM THEN.
NOT AT FULL PRICE, ANYWAY.

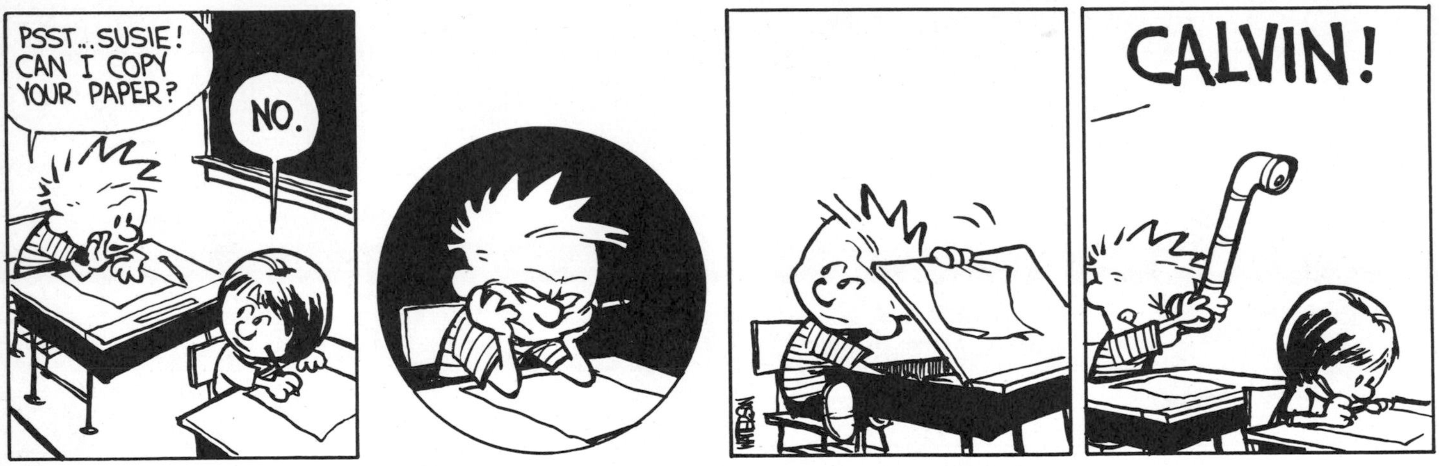
PSST...SUSIE! CAN I COPY YOUR PAPER?
NO.
CALVIN!

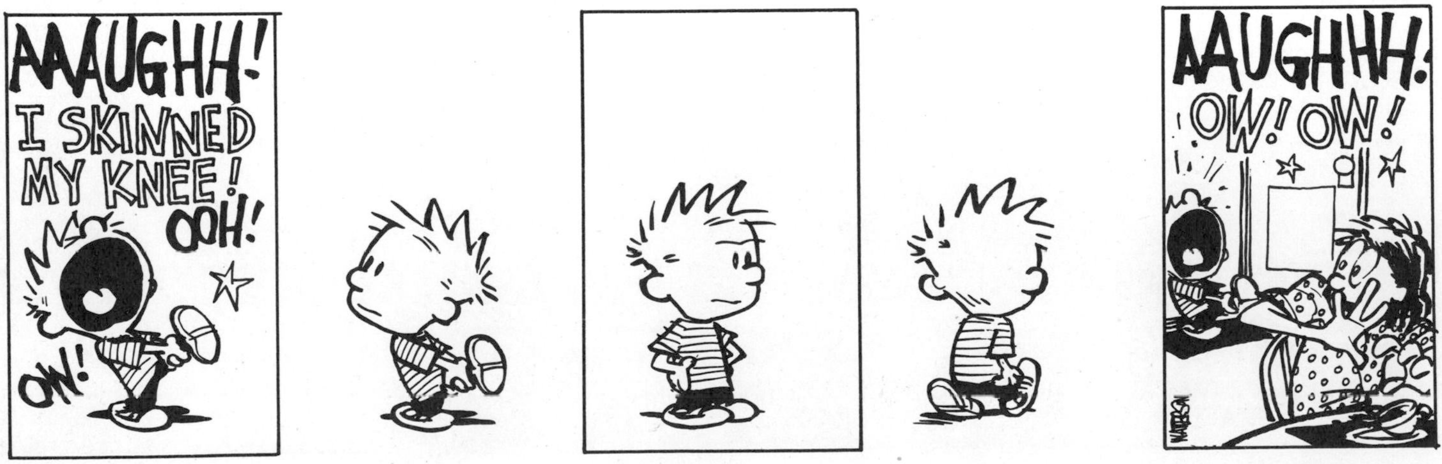
AAAUGHH! I SKINNED MY KNEE! OOH! OW!
AAUGHHH! OW! OW!

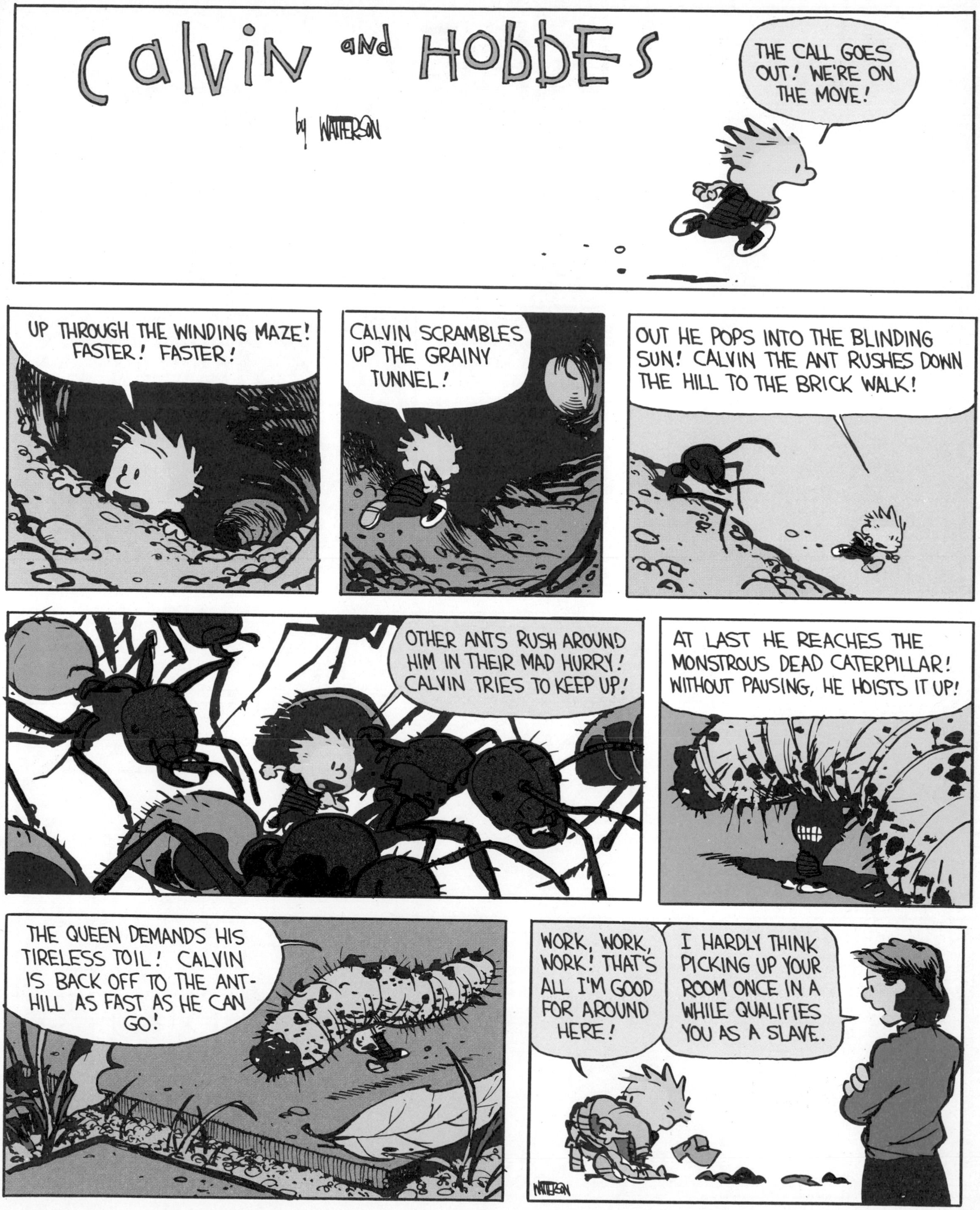

Calvin and HobbEs
by WATTERSON
THE CALL GOES OUT! WE'RE ON THE MOVE!
UP THROUGH THE WINDING MAZE! FASTER! FASTER!
CALVIN SCRAMBLES UP THE GRAINY TUNNEL!
OUT HE POPS INTO THE BLINDING SUN! CALVIN THE ANT RUSHES DOWN THE HILL TO THE BRICK WALK!
OTHER ANTS RUSH AROUND HIM IN THEIR MAD HURRY! CALVIN TRIES TO KEEP UP!
AT LAST HE REACHES THE MONSTROUS DEAD CATERPILLAR! WITHOUT PAUSING, HE HOISTS IT UP!
THE QUEEN DEMANDS HIS TIRELESS TOIL! CALVIN IS BACK OFF TO THE ANT-HILL AS FAST AS HE CAN GO!
WORK, WORK, WORK! THAT'S ALL I'M GOOD FOR AROUND HERE!
I HARDLY THINK PICKING UP YOUR ROOM ONCE IN A WHILE QUALIFIES YOU AS A SLAVE.
WATTERSON

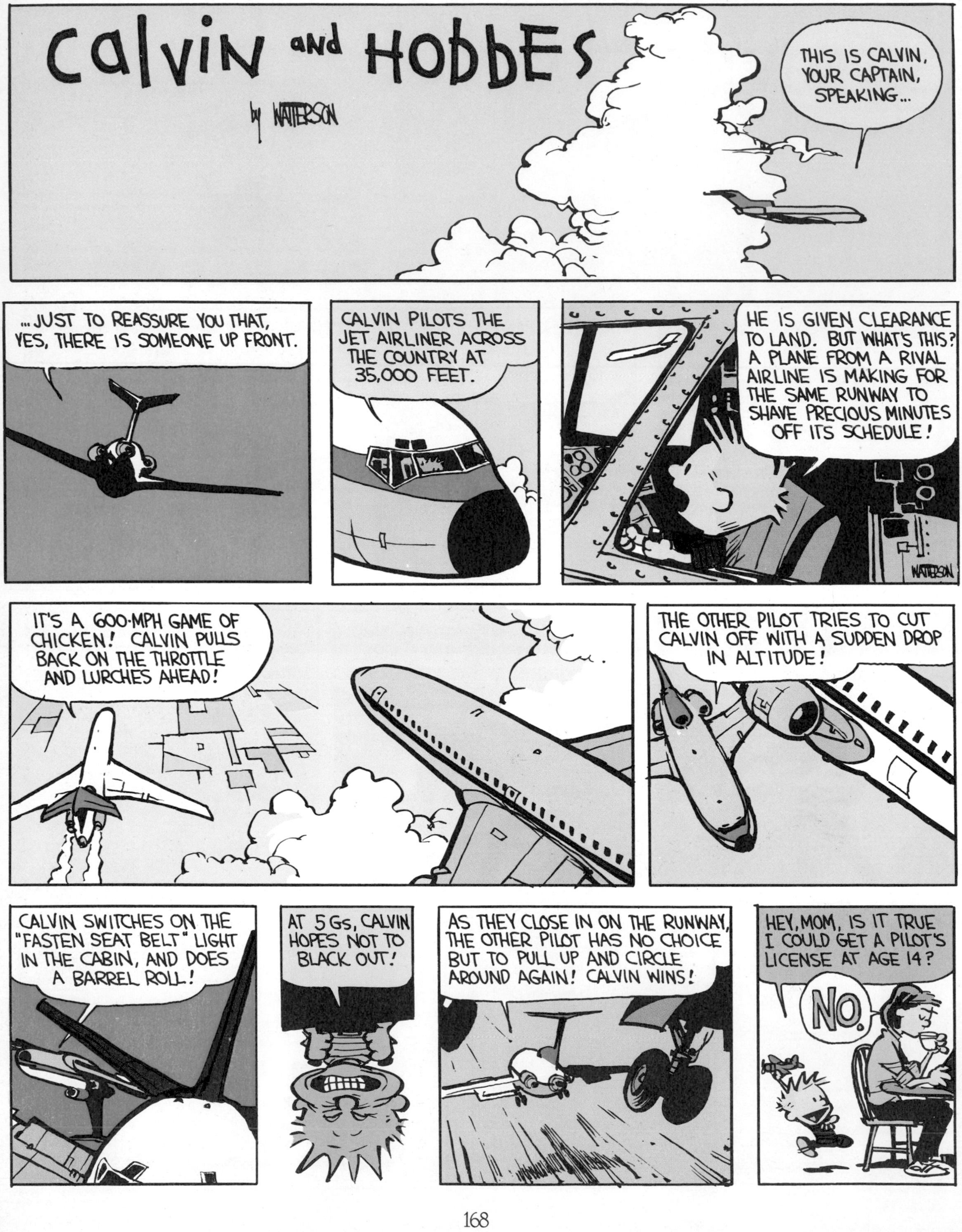
Calvin and HOBBES
by WATTERSON
THIS IS CALVIN, YOUR CAPTAIN, SPEAKING...
...JUST TO REASSURE YOU THAT, YES, THERE IS SOMEONE UP FRONT.
CALVIN PILOTS THE JET AIRLINER ACROSS THE COUNTRY AT 35,000 FEET.
HE IS GIVEN CLEARANCE TO LAND. BUT WHAT'S THIS? A PLANE FROM A RIVAL AIRLINE IS MAKING FOR THE SAME RUNWAY TO SHAVE PRECIOUS MINUTES OFF ITS SCHEDULE!
WATTERSON
IT'S A 600-MPH GAME OF CHICKEN! CALVIN PULLS BACK ON THE THROTTLE AND LURCHES AHEAD!
THE OTHER PILOT TRIES TO CUT CALVIN OFF WITH A SUDDEN DROP IN ALTITUDE!
CALVIN SWITCHES ON THE "FASTEN SEAT BELT" LIGHT IN THE CABIN, AND DOES A BARREL ROLL!
AT 5 Gs, CALVIN HOPES NOT TO BLACK OUT!
AS THEY CLOSE IN ON THE RUNWAY, THE OTHER PILOT HAS NO CHOICE BUT TO PULL UP AND CIRCLE AROUND AGAIN! CALVIN WINS!
HEY, MOM, IS IT TRUE I COULD GET A PILOT'S LICENSE AT AGE 14?
NO.

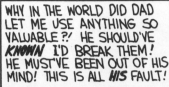

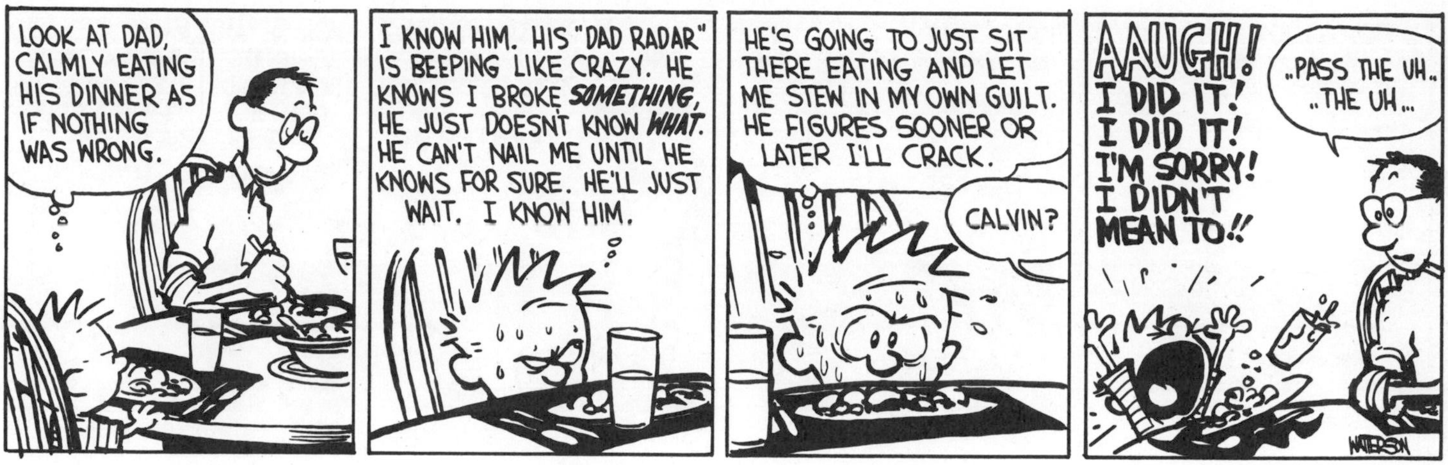

LOOK AT DAD, CALMLY EATING HIS DINNER AS IF NOTHING WAS WRONG.
I KNOW HIM. HIS "DAD RADAR" IS BEEPING LIKE CRAZY. HE KNOWS I BROKE *SOMETHING*, HE JUST DOESN'T KNOW *WHAT*. HE CAN'T NAIL ME UNTIL HE KNOWS FOR SURE. HE'LL JUST WAIT. I KNOW HIM.
HE'S GOING TO JUST SIT THERE EATING AND LET ME STEW IN MY OWN GUILT. HE FIGURES SOONER OR LATER I'LL CRACK.
CALVIN?
AAUGH! I DID IT! I DID IT! I'M SORRY! I DIDN'T MEAN TO!!
..PASS THE UH.. ..THE UH...
WATTERSON


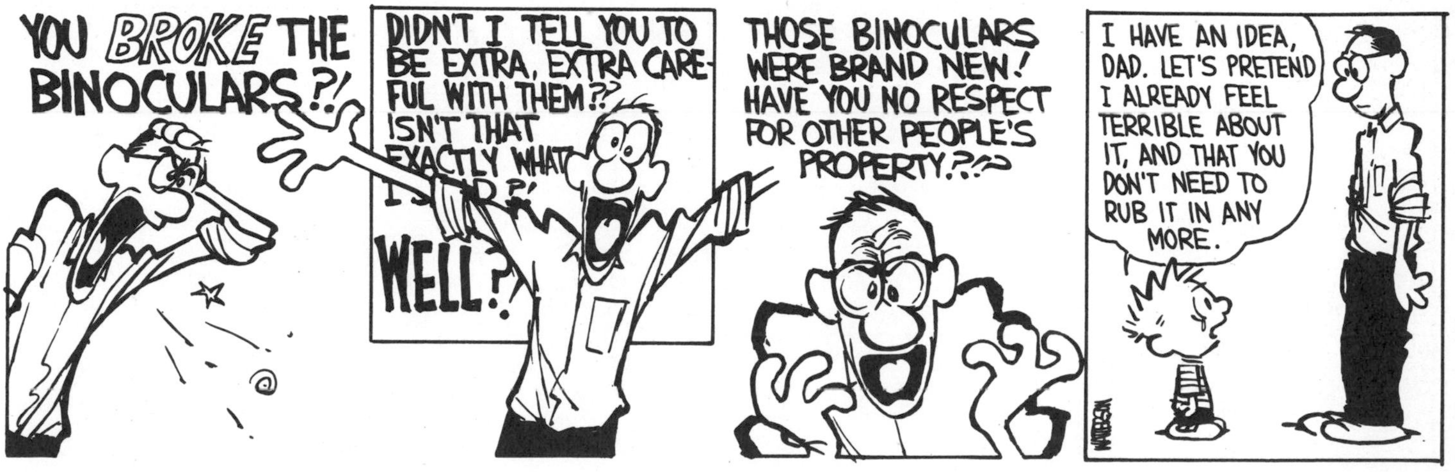

YOU *BROKE* THE BINOCULARS?!
DIDN'T I TELL YOU TO BE EXTRA, EXTRA CAREFUL WITH THEM?? ISN'T THAT EXACTLY WHAT
WELL?!
THOSE BINOCULARS WERE BRAND NEW! HAVE YOU NO RESPECT FOR OTHER PEOPLE'S PROPERTY?!?!
I HAVE AN IDEA, DAD. LET'S PRETEND I ALREADY FEEL TERRIBLE ABOUT IT, AND THAT YOU DON'T NEED TO RUB IT IN ANY MORE.
WATTERSON


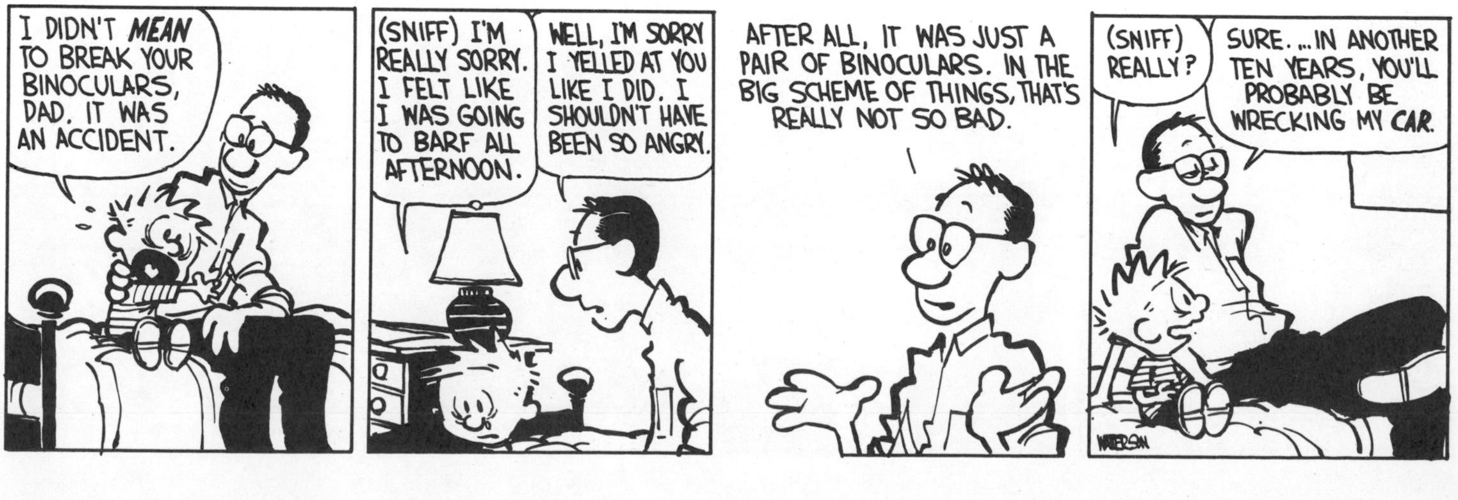

I DIDN'T *MEAN* TO BREAK YOUR BINOCULARS, DAD. IT WAS AN ACCIDENT.
(SNIFF) I'M REALLY SORRY. I FELT LIKE I WAS GOING TO BARF ALL AFTERNOON.
WELL, I'M SORRY I YELLED AT YOU LIKE I DID. I SHOULDN'T HAVE BEEN SO ANGRY.
AFTER ALL, IT WAS JUST A PAIR OF BINOCULARS. IN THE BIG SCHEME OF THINGS, THAT'S REALLY NOT SO BAD.
(SNIFF) REALLY?
SURE. ...IN ANOTHER TEN YEARS, YOU'LL PROBABLY BE WRECKING MY *CAR*.
WATTERSON

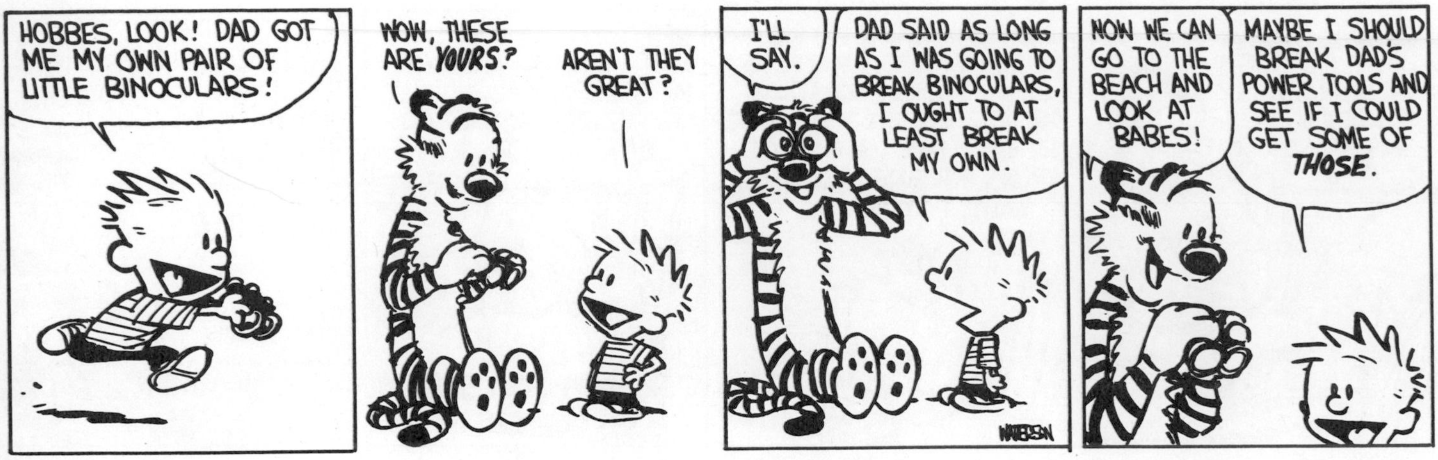

HOBBES, LOOK! DAD GOT ME MY OWN PAIR OF LITTLE BINOCULARS!
WOW, THESE ARE *YOURS*?
AREN'T THEY GREAT?
I'LL SAY.
DAD SAID AS LONG AS I WAS GOING TO BREAK BINOCULARS, I OUGHT TO AT LEAST BREAK MY OWN.
NOW WE CAN GO TO THE BEACH AND LOOK AT BABES!
MAYBE I SHOULD BREAK DAD'S POWER TOOLS AND SEE IF I COULD GET SOME OF *THOSE*.
WATTERSON


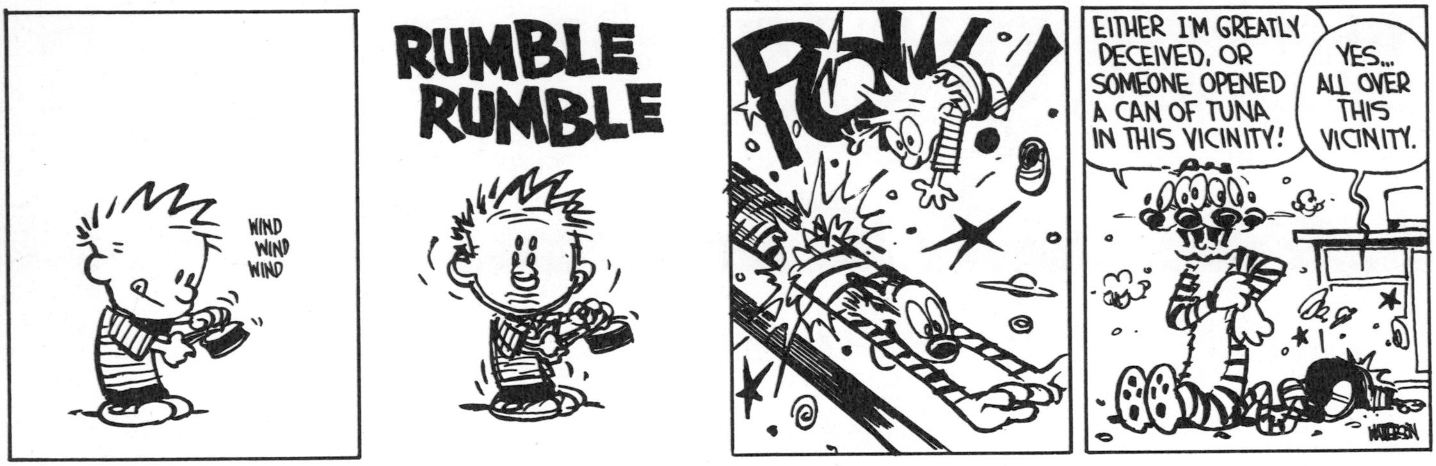

WIND WIND WIND
RUMBLE RUMBLE
POW!
EITHER I'M GREATLY DECEIVED, OR SOMEONE OPENED A CAN OF TUNA IN THIS VICINITY!
YES... ALL OVER THIS VICINITY.
WATTERSON


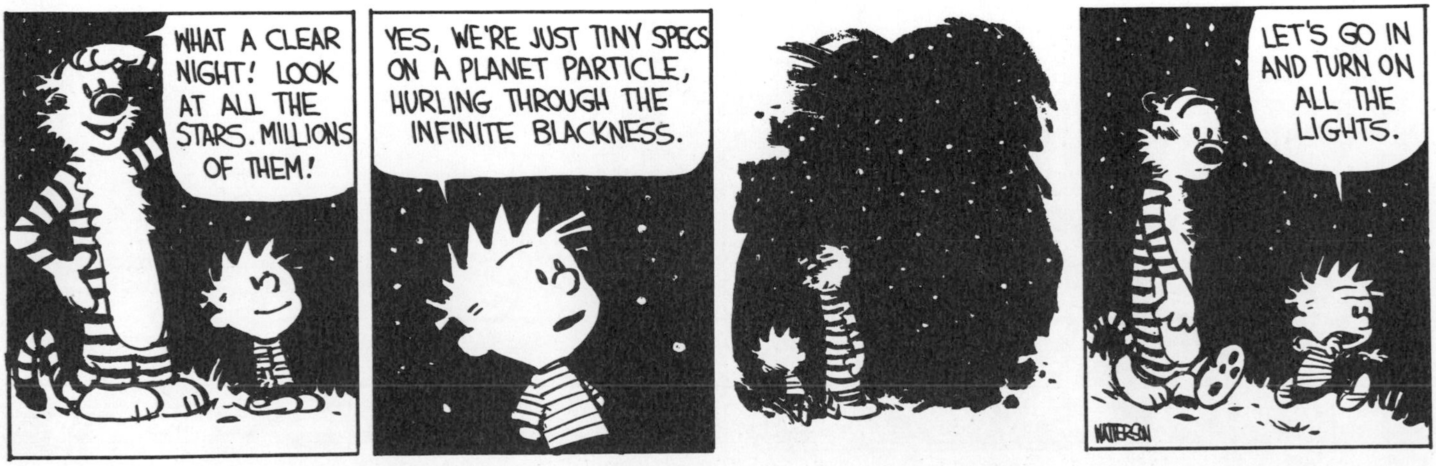

WHAT A CLEAR NIGHT! LOOK AT ALL THE STARS. MILLIONS OF THEM!
YES, WE'RE JUST TINY SPECS ON A PLANET PARTICLE, HURLING THROUGH THE INFINITE BLACKNESS.
LET'S GO IN AND TURN ON ALL THE LIGHTS.
WATTERSON

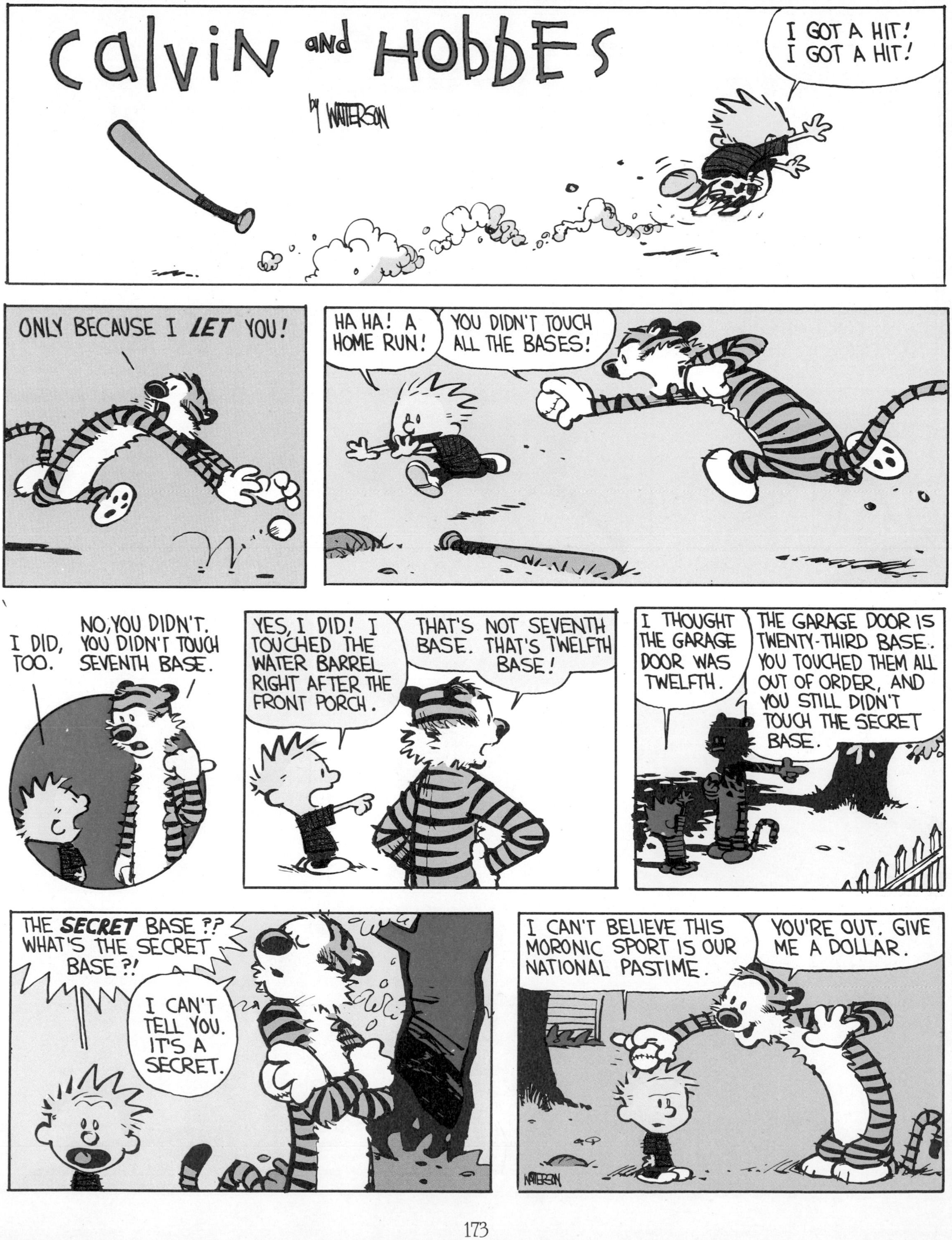
Calvin and HobbEs
by WATTERSON
I GOT A HIT! I GOT A HIT!
ONLY BECAUSE I *LET* YOU!
HA HA! A HOME RUN!
YOU DIDN'T TOUCH ALL THE BASES!
I DID, TOO.
NO, YOU DIDN'T. YOU DIDN'T TOUCH SEVENTH BASE.
YES, I DID! I TOUCHED THE WATER BARREL RIGHT AFTER THE FRONT PORCH.
THAT'S NOT SEVENTH BASE. THAT'S TWELFTH BASE!
I THOUGHT THE GARAGE DOOR WAS TWELFTH.
THE GARAGE DOOR IS TWENTY-THIRD BASE. YOU TOUCHED THEM ALL OUT OF ORDER, AND YOU STILL DIDN'T TOUCH THE SECRET BASE.
THE *SECRET* BASE ?? WHAT'S THE SECRET BASE ?!
I CAN'T TELL YOU. IT'S A SECRET.
I CAN'T BELIEVE THIS MORONIC SPORT IS OUR NATIONAL PASTIME.
YOU'RE OUT. GIVE ME A DOLLAR.
WATTERSON

# Calvin and Hobbes by WATTERSON

ZZZZZZZZZZZZZZ 🪰

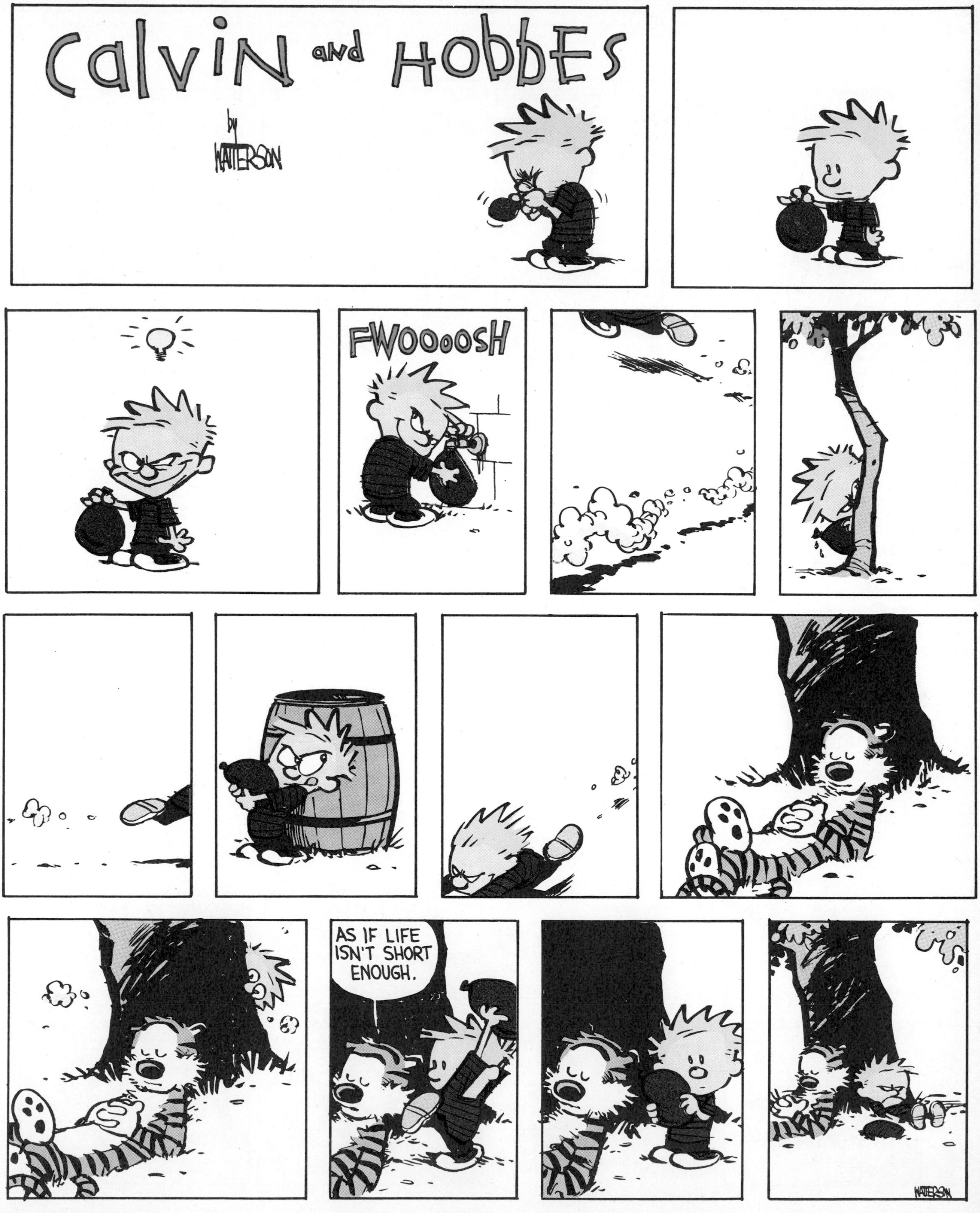
Calvin and HOBBES
by WATTERSON
FWOOooSH
AS IF LIFE ISN'T SHORT ENOUGH.
WATTERSON

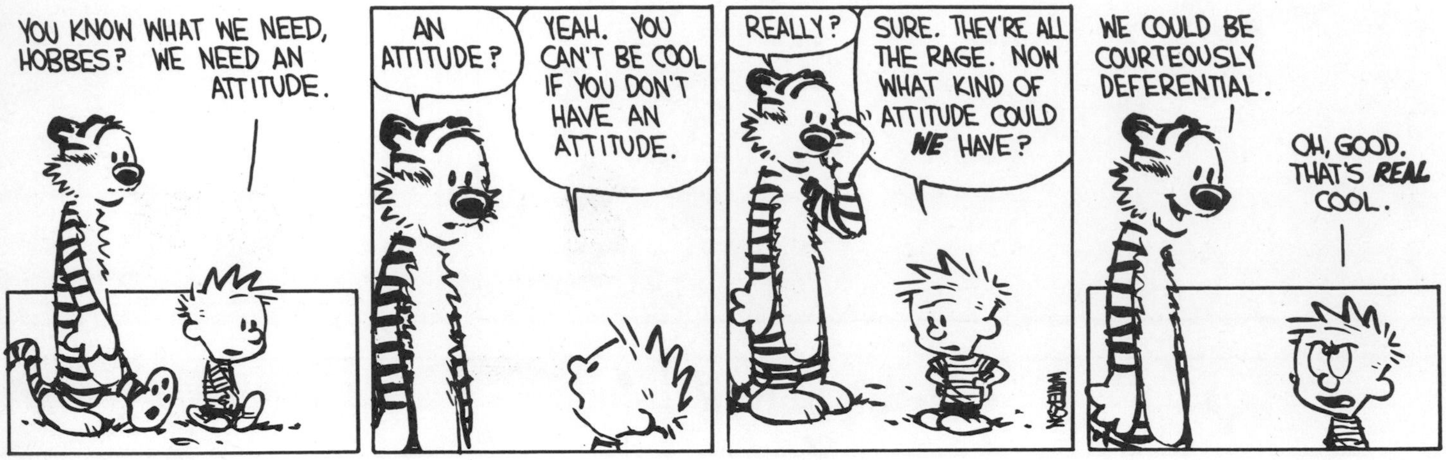
YOU KNOW WHAT WE NEED, HOBBES? WE NEED AN ATTITUDE.
AN ATTITUDE?
YEAH. YOU CAN'T BE COOL IF YOU DON'T HAVE AN ATTITUDE.
REALLY?
SURE. THEY'RE ALL THE RAGE. NOW WHAT KIND OF ATTITUDE COULD **WE** HAVE?
WE COULD BE COURTEOUSLY DEFERENTIAL.
OH, GOOD. THAT'S **REAL** COOL.

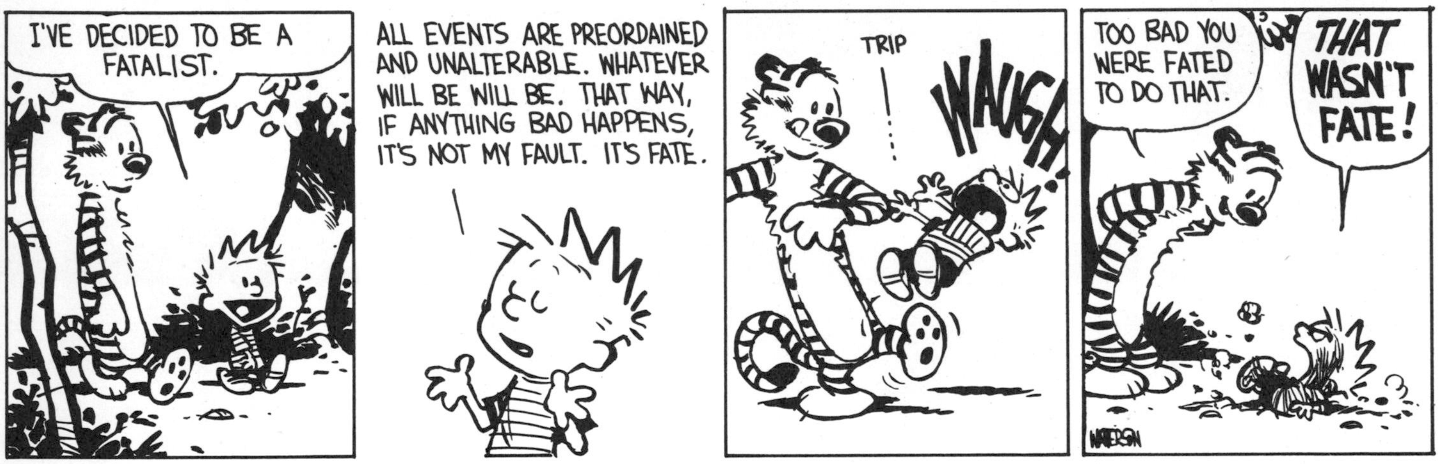
I'VE DECIDED TO BE A FATALIST.
ALL EVENTS ARE PREORDAINED AND UNALTERABLE. WHATEVER WILL BE WILL BE. THAT WAY, IF ANYTHING BAD HAPPENS, IT'S NOT MY FAULT. IT'S FATE.
TRIP
WAUGH!
TOO BAD YOU WERE FATED TO DO THAT.
**THAT WASN'T FATE!**

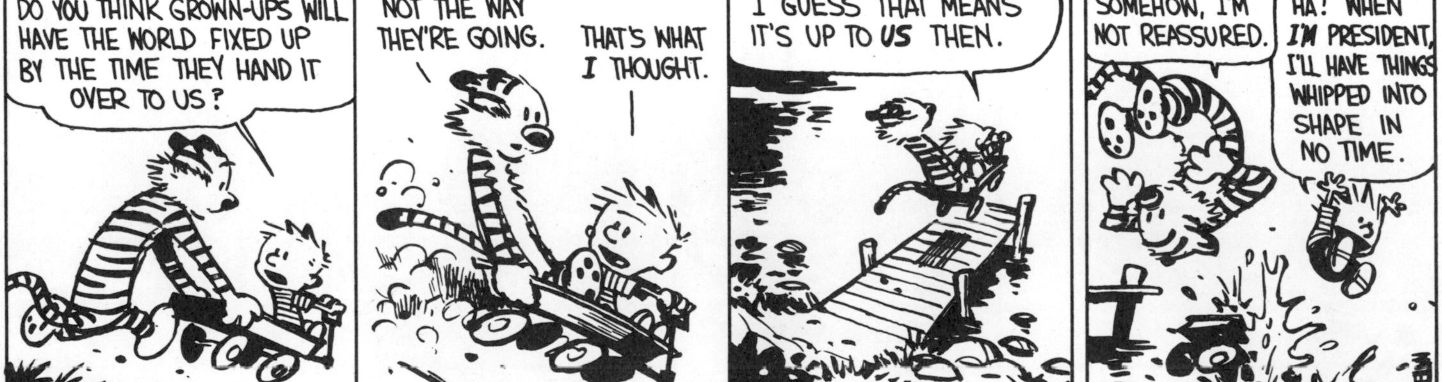
DO YOU THINK GROWN-UPS WILL HAVE THE WORLD FIXED UP BY THE TIME THEY HAND IT OVER TO US?
NOT THE WAY THEY'RE GOING.
THAT'S WHAT **I** THOUGHT.
I GUESS THAT MEANS IT'S UP TO **US** THEN.
SOMEHOW, I'M NOT REASSURED.
HA! WHEN **I'M** PRESIDENT, I'LL HAVE THINGS WHIPPED INTO SHAPE IN NO TIME.

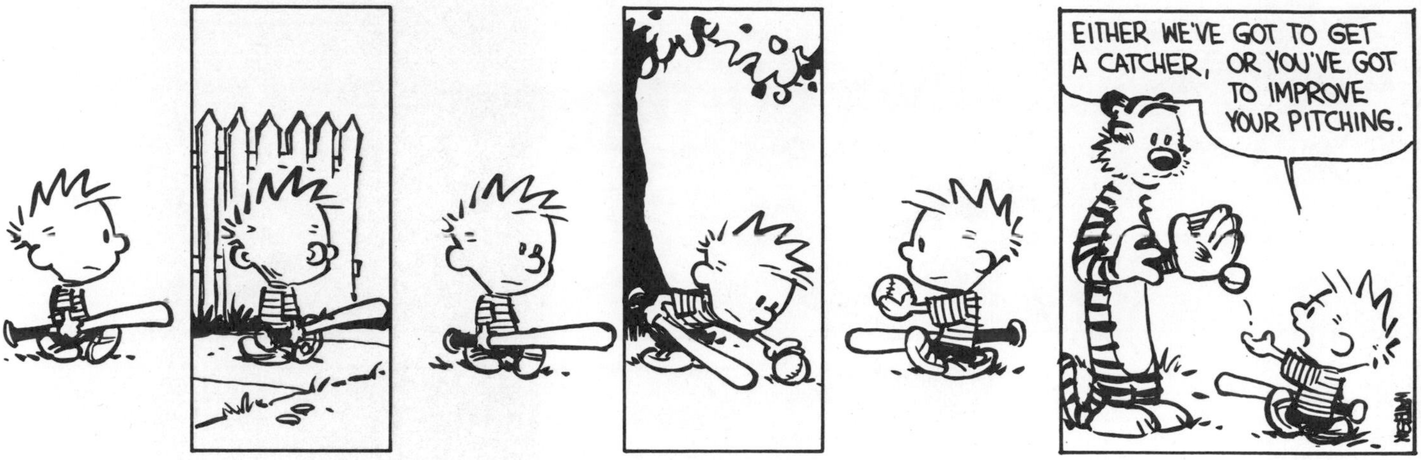
EITHER WE'VE GOT TO GET A CATCHER, OR YOU'VE GOT TO IMPROVE YOUR PITCHING.

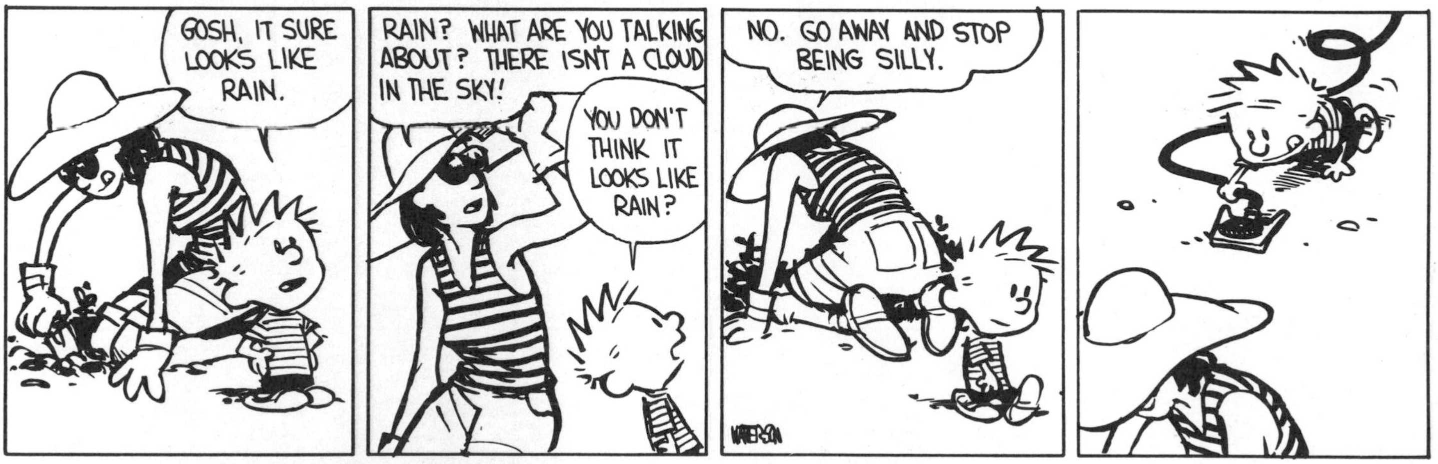
GOSH, IT SURE LOOKS LIKE RAIN.
RAIN? WHAT ARE YOU TALKING ABOUT? THERE ISN'T A CLOUD IN THE SKY!
YOU DON'T THINK IT LOOKS LIKE RAIN?
NO. GO AWAY AND STOP BEING SILLY.

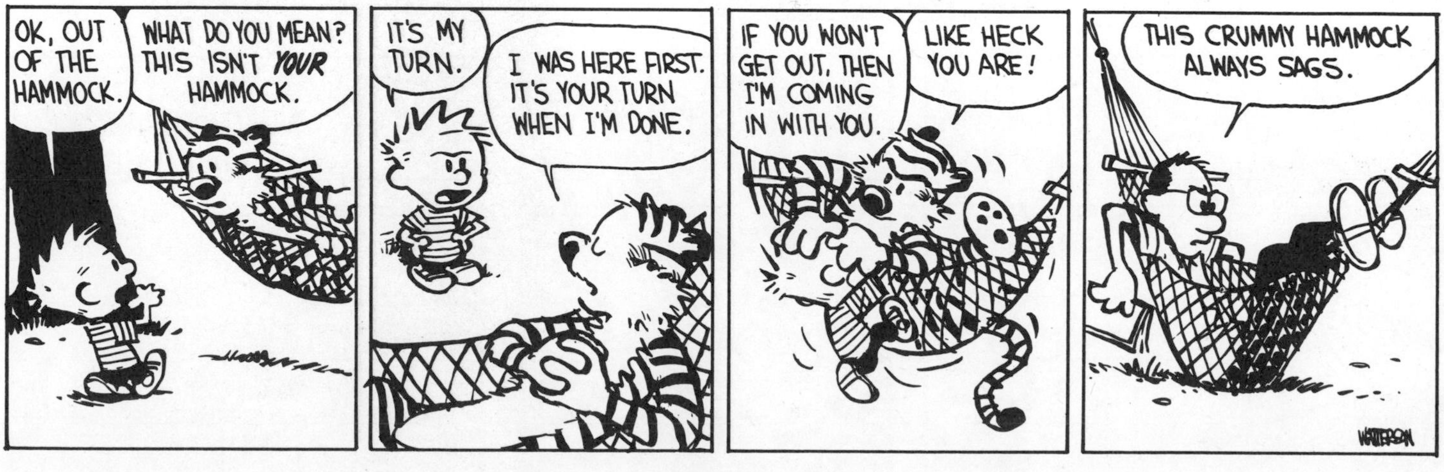
OK, OUT OF THE HAMMOCK.
WHAT DO YOU MEAN? THIS ISN'T *YOUR* HAMMOCK.
IT'S MY TURN.
I WAS HERE FIRST. IT'S YOUR TURN WHEN I'M DONE.
IF YOU WON'T GET OUT, THEN I'M COMING IN WITH YOU.
LIKE HECK YOU ARE!
THIS CRUMMY HAMMOCK ALWAYS SAGS.

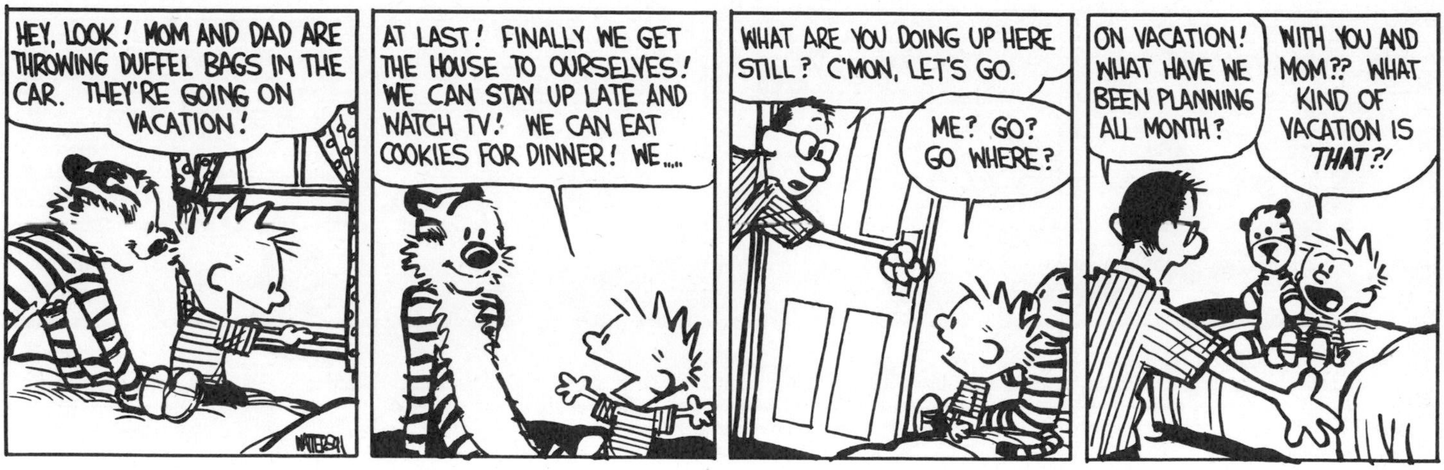
HEY, LOOK! MOM AND DAD ARE THROWING DUFFEL BAGS IN THE CAR. THEY'RE GOING ON VACATION!
AT LAST! FINALLY WE GET THE HOUSE TO OURSELVES! WE CAN STAY UP LATE AND WATCH TV! WE CAN EAT COOKIES FOR DINNER! WE....
WHAT ARE YOU DOING UP HERE STILL? C'MON, LET'S GO.
ME? GO? GO WHERE?
ON VACATION! WHAT HAVE WE BEEN PLANNING ALL MONTH?
WITH YOU AND MOM?? WHAT KIND OF VACATION IS *THAT*?!

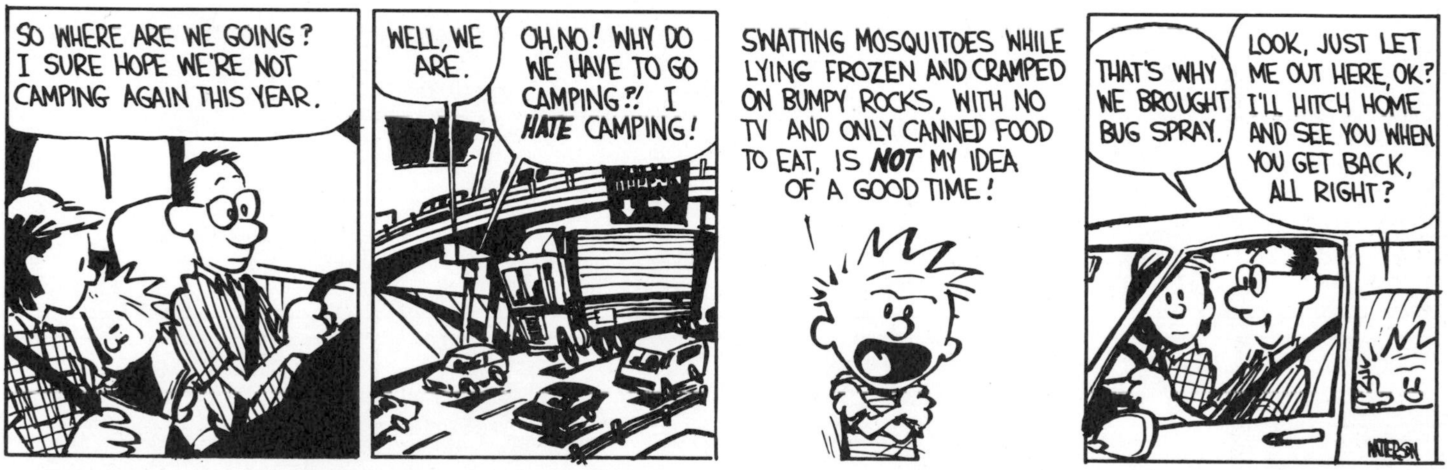
SO WHERE ARE WE GOING? I SURE HOPE WE'RE NOT CAMPING AGAIN THIS YEAR.
WELL, WE ARE.
OH, NO! WHY DO WE HAVE TO GO CAMPING?! I *HATE* CAMPING!
SWATTING MOSQUITOES WHILE LYING FROZEN AND CRAMPED ON BUMPY ROCKS, WITH NO TV AND ONLY CANNED FOOD TO EAT, IS *NOT* MY IDEA OF A GOOD TIME!
THAT'S WHY WE BROUGHT BUG SPRAY.
LOOK, JUST LET ME OUT HERE, OK? I'LL HITCH HOME AND SEE YOU WHEN YOU GET BACK, ALL RIGHT?

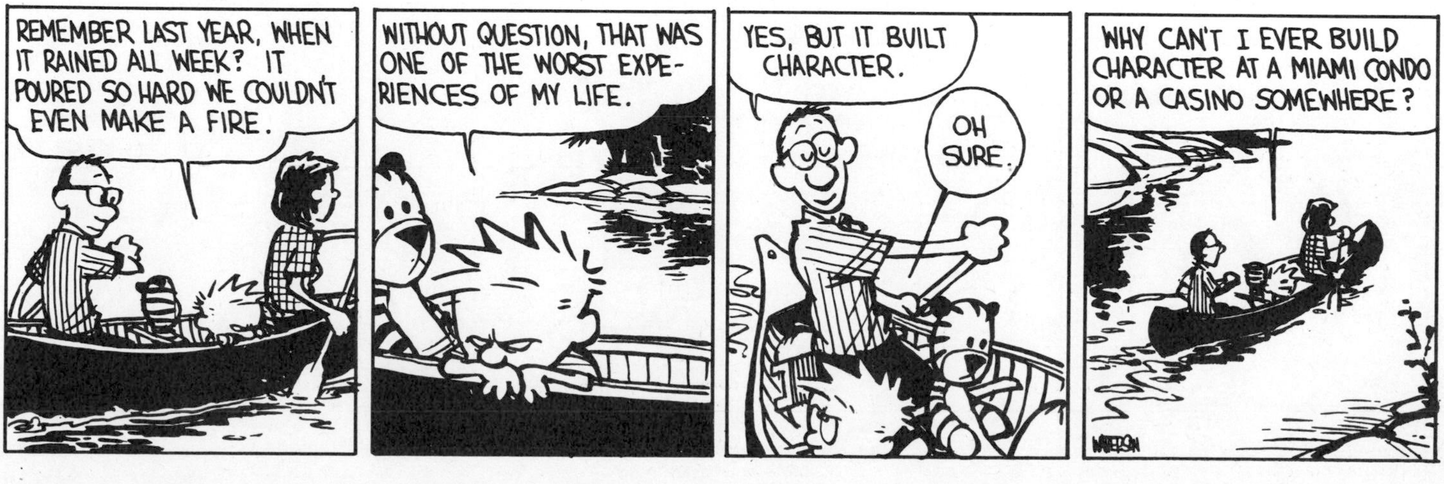
REMEMBER LAST YEAR, WHEN IT RAINED ALL WEEK? IT POURED SO HARD WE COULDN'T EVEN MAKE A FIRE.
WITHOUT QUESTION, THAT WAS ONE OF THE WORST EXPERIENCES OF MY LIFE.
YES, BUT IT BUILT CHARACTER.
OH SURE.
WHY CAN'T I EVER BUILD CHARACTER AT A MIAMI CONDO OR A CASINO SOMEWHERE?

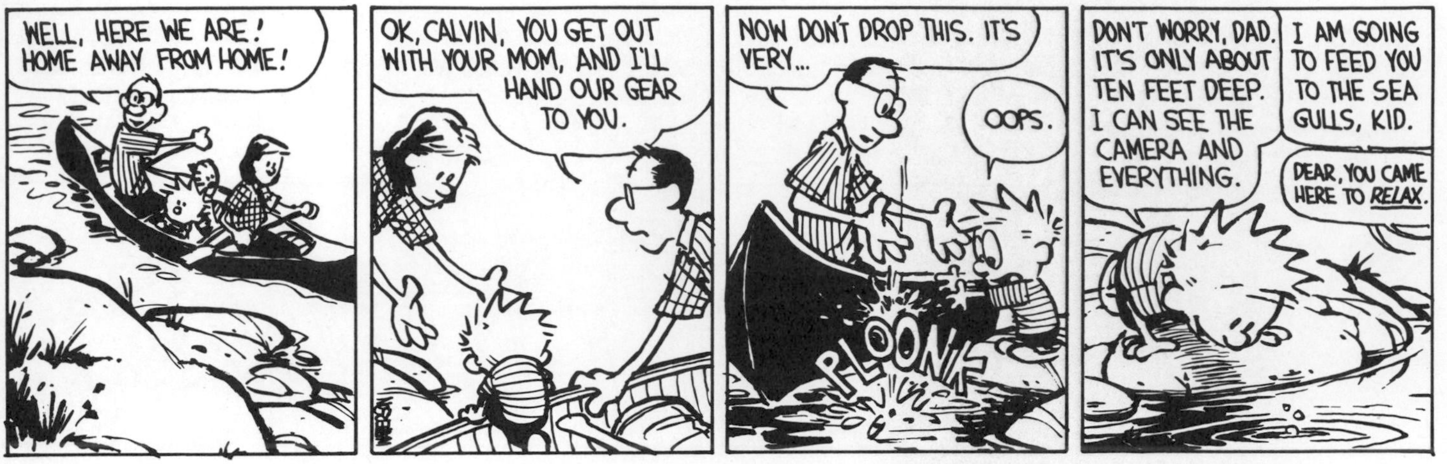
WELL, HERE WE ARE! HOME AWAY FROM HOME!
OK, CALVIN, YOU GET OUT WITH YOUR MOM, AND I'LL HAND OUR GEAR TO YOU.
NOW DON'T DROP THIS. IT'S VERY...
OOPS.
PLOONK
DON'T WORRY, DAD. IT'S ONLY ABOUT TEN FEET DEEP. I CAN SEE THE CAMERA AND EVERYTHING.
I AM GOING TO FEED YOU TO THE SEA GULLS, KID.
DEAR, YOU CAME HERE TO RELAX.

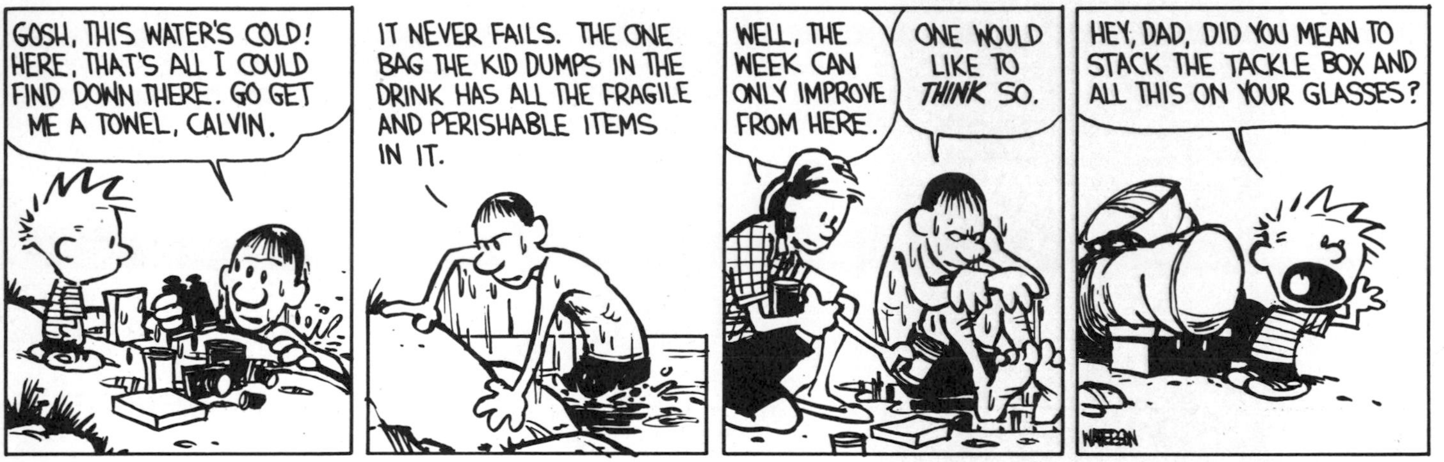
GOSH, THIS WATER'S COLD! HERE, THAT'S ALL I COULD FIND DOWN THERE. GO GET ME A TOWEL, CALVIN.
IT NEVER FAILS. THE ONE BAG THE KID DUMPS IN THE DRINK HAS ALL THE FRAGILE AND PERISHABLE ITEMS IN IT.
WELL, THE WEEK CAN ONLY IMPROVE FROM HERE.
ONE WOULD LIKE TO THINK SO.
HEY, DAD, DID YOU MEAN TO STACK THE TACKLE BOX AND ALL THIS ON YOUR GLASSES?

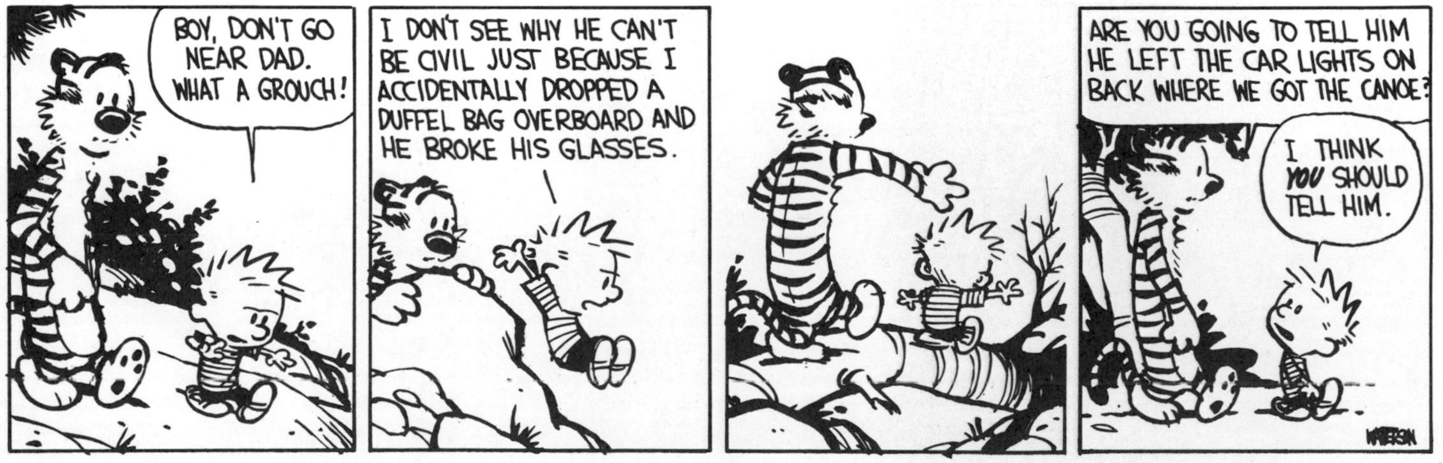
BOY, DON'T GO NEAR DAD. WHAT A GROUCH!
I DON'T SEE WHY HE CAN'T BE CIVIL JUST BECAUSE I ACCIDENTALLY DROPPED A DUFFEL BAG OVERBOARD AND HE BROKE HIS GLASSES.
ARE YOU GOING TO TELL HIM HE LEFT THE CAR LIGHTS ON BACK WHERE WE GOT THE CANOE?
I THINK YOU SHOULD TELL HIM.

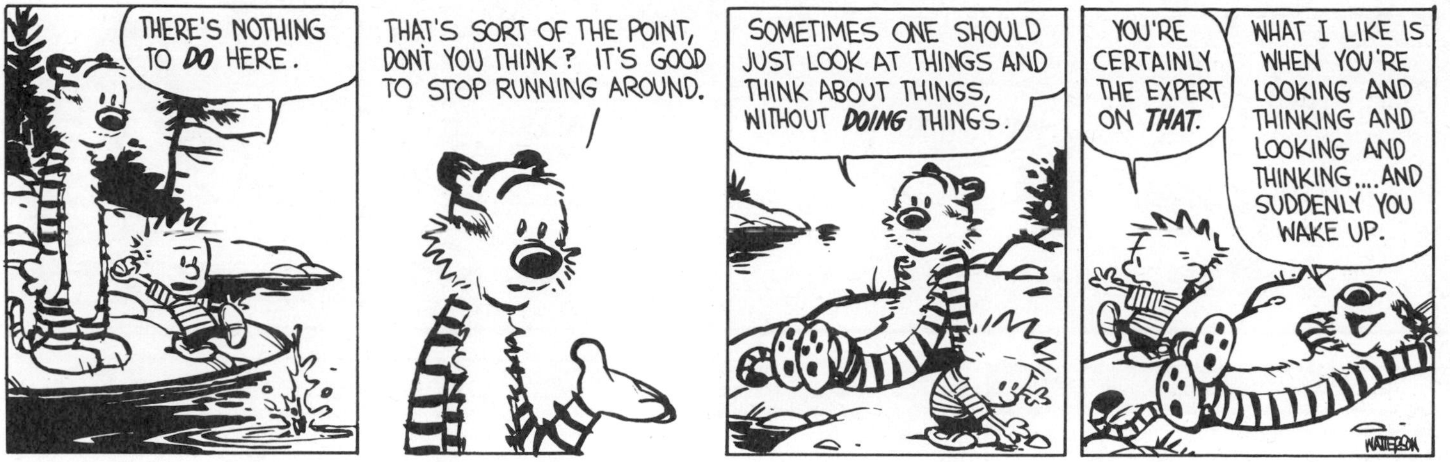
THERE'S NOTHING TO ***DO*** HERE.
THAT'S SORT OF THE POINT, DON'T YOU THINK? IT'S GOOD TO STOP RUNNING AROUND.
SOMETIMES ONE SHOULD JUST LOOK AT THINGS AND THINK ABOUT THINGS, WITHOUT ***DOING*** THINGS.
YOU'RE CERTAINLY THE EXPERT ON ***THAT.***
WHAT I LIKE IS WHEN YOU'RE LOOKING AND THINKING AND LOOKING AND THINKING.....AND SUDDENLY YOU WAKE UP.
WATTERSON

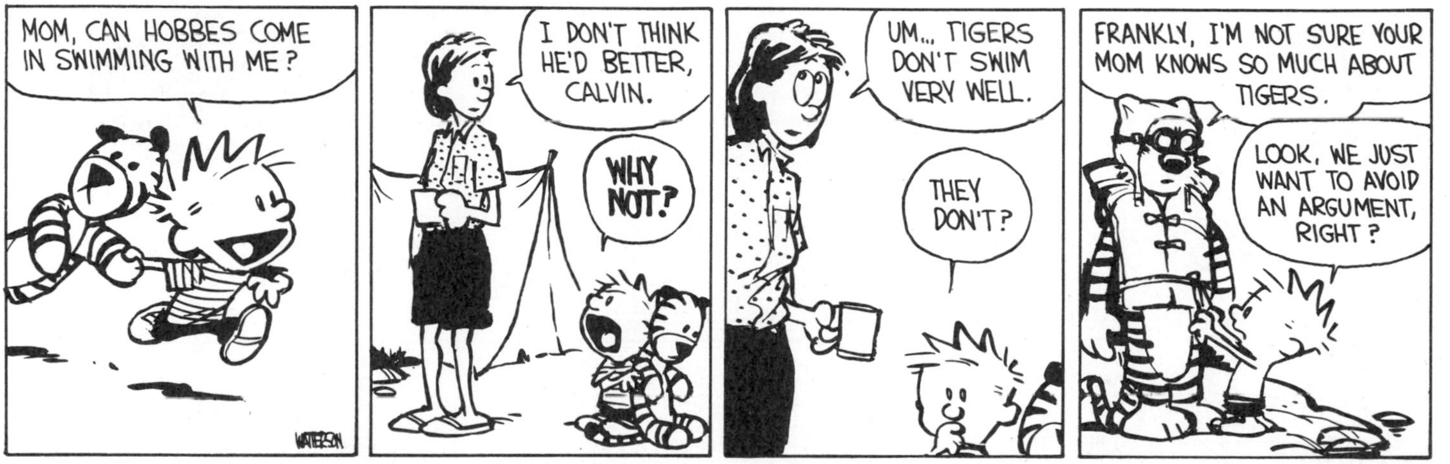
MOM, CAN HOBBES COME IN SWIMMING WITH ME?
WATTERSON
I DON'T THINK HE'D BETTER, CALVIN.
WHY NOT?
UM... TIGERS DON'T SWIM VERY WELL.
THEY DON'T?
FRANKLY, I'M NOT SURE YOUR MOM KNOWS SO MUCH ABOUT TIGERS.
LOOK, WE JUST WANT TO AVOID AN ARGUMENT, RIGHT?

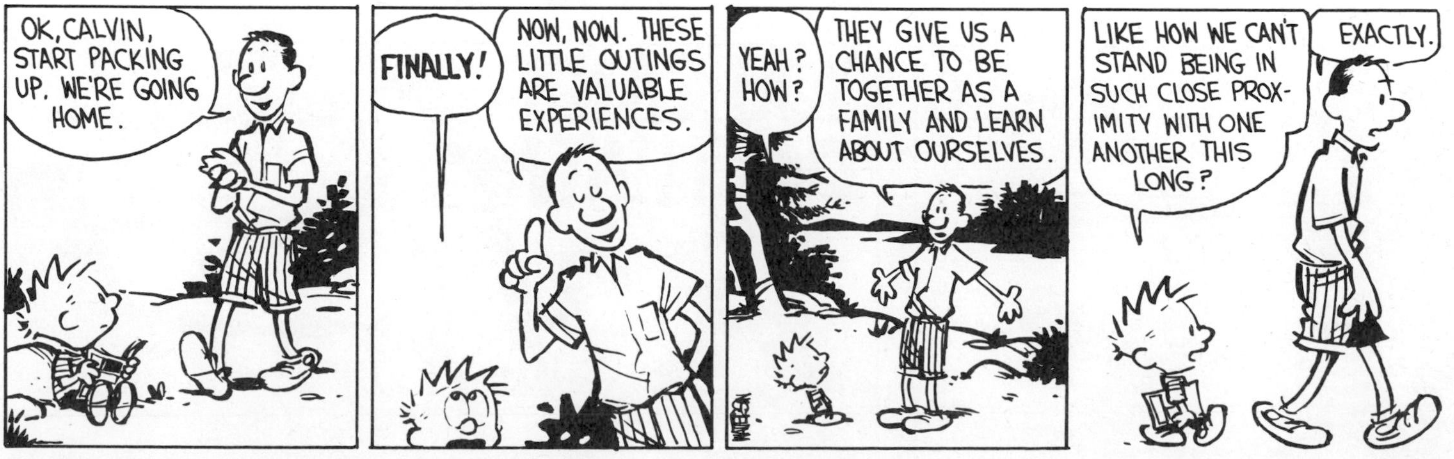
OK, CALVIN, START PACKING UP. WE'RE GOING HOME.
FINALLY!
NOW, NOW. THESE LITTLE OUTINGS ARE VALUABLE EXPERIENCES.
YEAH? HOW?
THEY GIVE US A CHANCE TO BE TOGETHER AS A FAMILY AND LEARN ABOUT OURSELVES.
WATTERSON
LIKE HOW WE CAN'T STAND BEING IN SUCH CLOSE PROXIMITY WITH ONE ANOTHER THIS LONG?
EXACTLY.

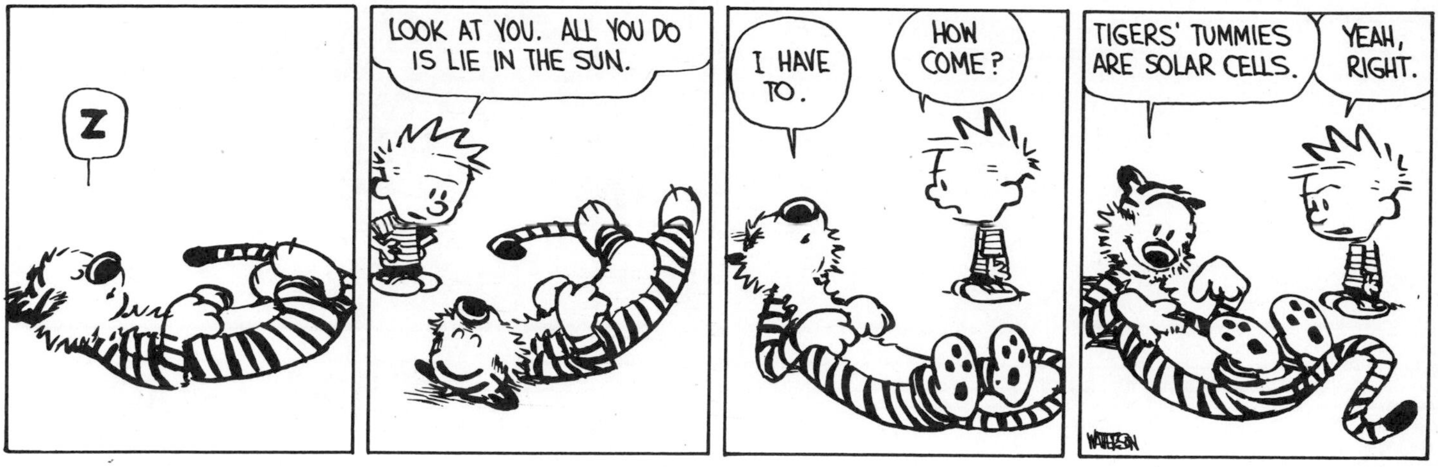
Z
LOOK AT YOU. ALL YOU DO IS LIE IN THE SUN.
I HAVE TO.
HOW COME?
TIGERS' TUMMIES ARE SOLAR CELLS.
YEAH, RIGHT.

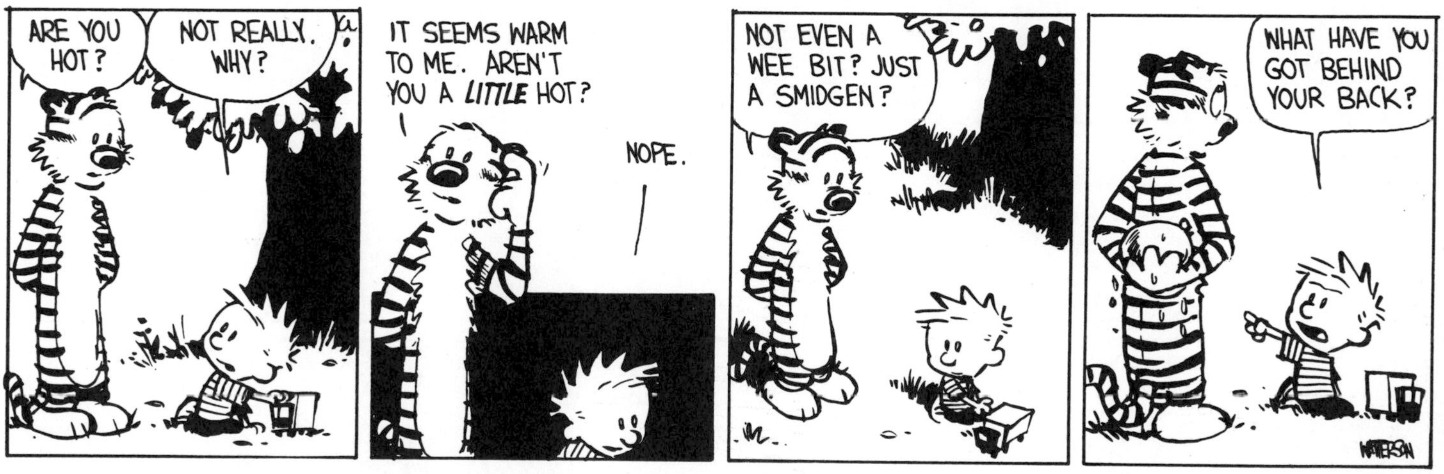
ARE YOU HOT?
NOT REALLY. WHY?
IT SEEMS WARM TO ME. AREN'T YOU A *LITTLE* HOT?
NOPE.
NOT EVEN A WEE BIT? JUST A SMIDGEN?
WHAT HAVE YOU GOT BEHIND YOUR BACK?

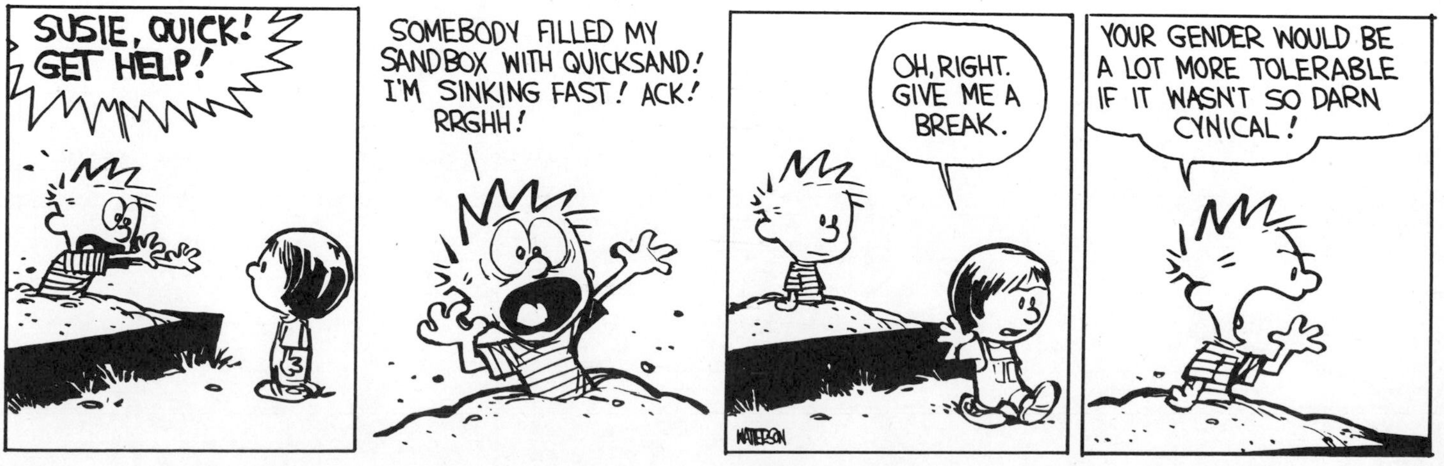
SUSIE, QUICK! GET HELP!
SOMEBODY FILLED MY SANDBOX WITH QUICKSAND! I'M SINKING FAST! ACK! RRGHH!
OH, RIGHT. GIVE ME A BREAK.
YOUR GENDER WOULD BE A LOT MORE TOLERABLE IF IT WASN'T SO DARN CYNICAL!

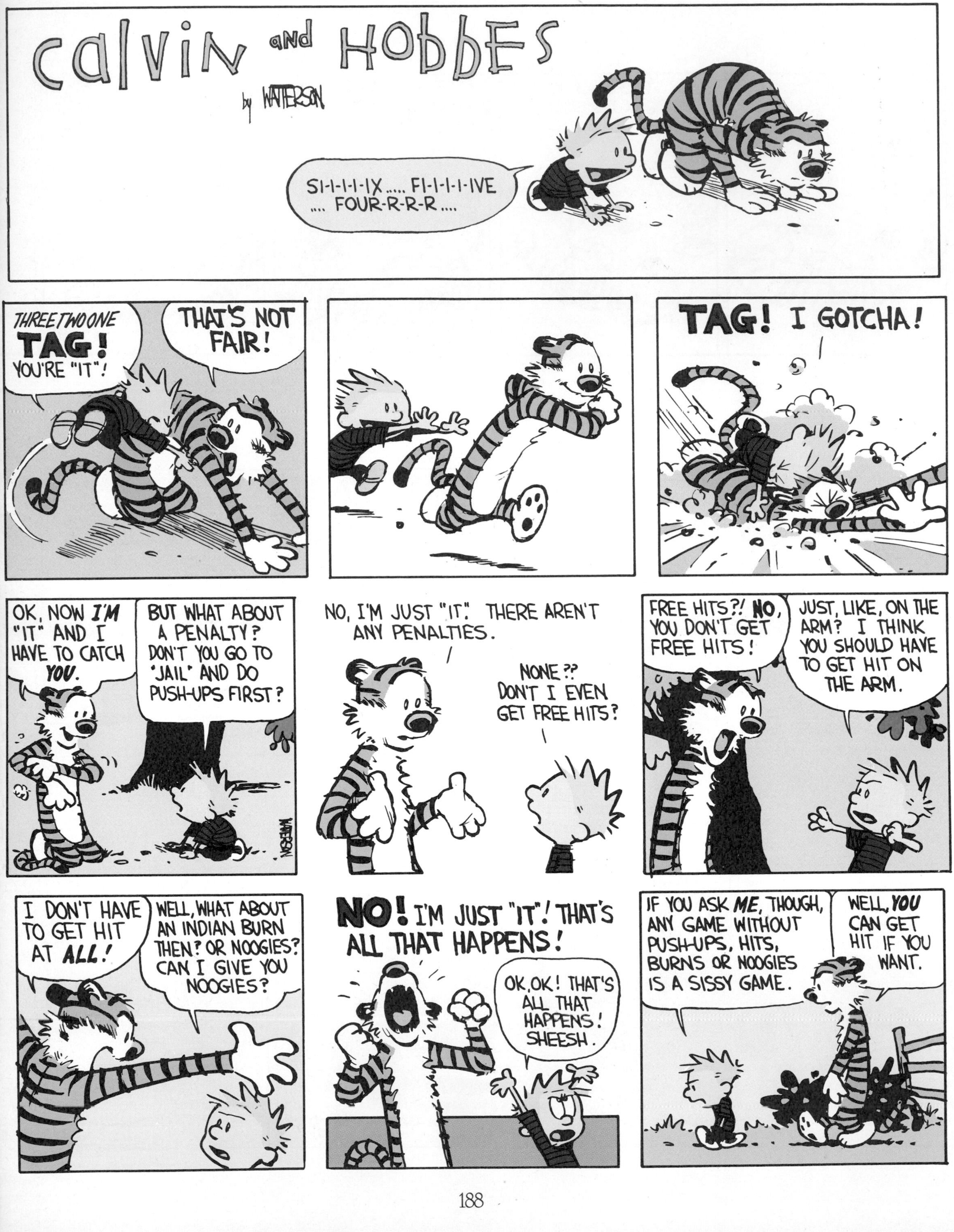
Calvin and HOBBES
by WATTERSON
SI-I-I-I-IX ..... FI-I-I-I-IVE .... FOUR-R-R-R ....
THREETWOONE TAG! YOU'RE "IT"!
THAT'S NOT FAIR!
TAG! I GOTCHA!
OK, NOW I'M "IT" AND I HAVE TO CATCH YOU.
BUT WHAT ABOUT A PENALTY? DON'T YOU GO TO "JAIL" AND DO PUSH-UPS FIRST?
NO, I'M JUST "IT". THERE AREN'T ANY PENALTIES.
NONE?? DON'T I EVEN GET FREE HITS?
FREE HITS?! NO, YOU DON'T GET FREE HITS!
JUST, LIKE, ON THE ARM? I THINK YOU SHOULD HAVE TO GET HIT ON THE ARM.
I DON'T HAVE TO GET HIT AT ALL!
WELL, WHAT ABOUT AN INDIAN BURN THEN? OR NOOGIES? CAN I GIVE YOU NOOGIES?
NO! I'M JUST "IT"! THAT'S ALL THAT HAPPENS!
OK, OK! THAT'S ALL THAT HAPPENS! SHEESH.
IF YOU ASK ME, THOUGH, ANY GAME WITHOUT PUSH-UPS, HITS, BURNS OR NOOGIES IS A SISSY GAME.
WELL, YOU CAN GET HIT IF YOU WANT.

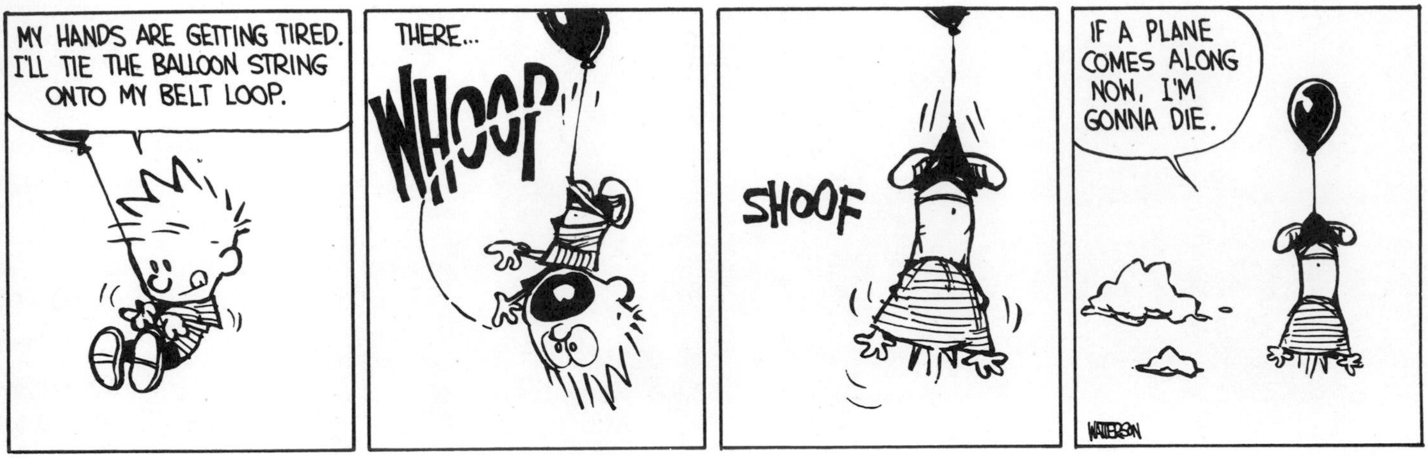
MY HANDS ARE GETTING TIRED. I'LL TIE THE BALLOON STRING ONTO MY BELT LOOP.
THERE...
WHOOP
SHOOF
IF A PLANE COMES ALONG NOW, I'M GONNA DIE.
WATTERSON

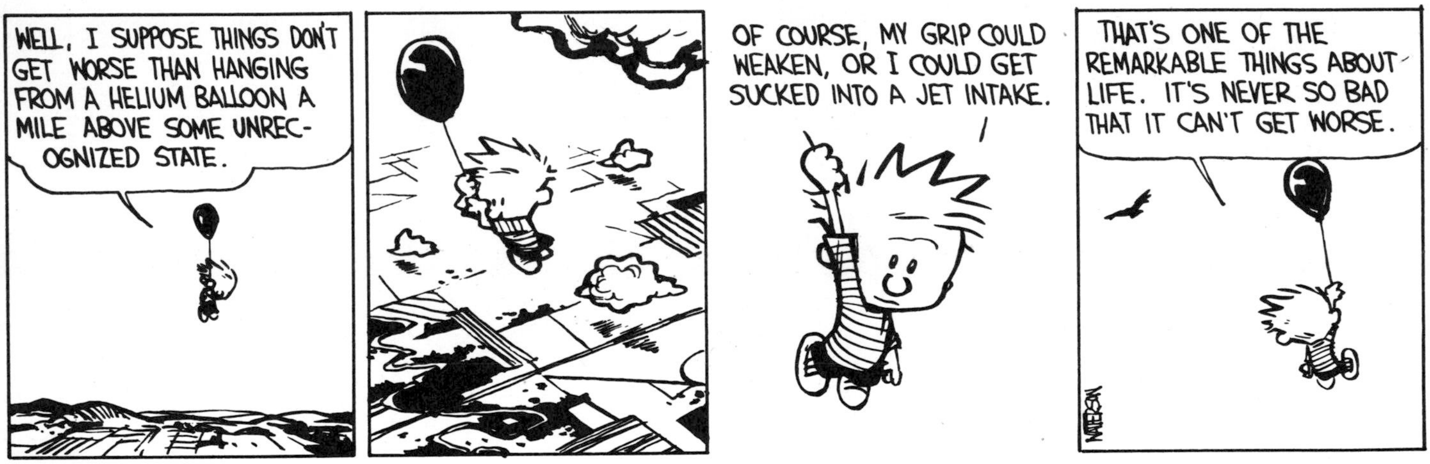
WELL, I SUPPOSE THINGS DON'T GET WORSE THAN HANGING FROM A HELIUM BALLOON A MILE ABOVE SOME UNRECOGNIZED STATE.
OF COURSE, MY GRIP COULD WEAKEN, OR I COULD GET SUCKED INTO A JET INTAKE.
THAT'S ONE OF THE REMARKABLE THINGS ABOUT LIFE. IT'S NEVER SO BAD THAT IT CAN'T GET WORSE.
WATTERSON

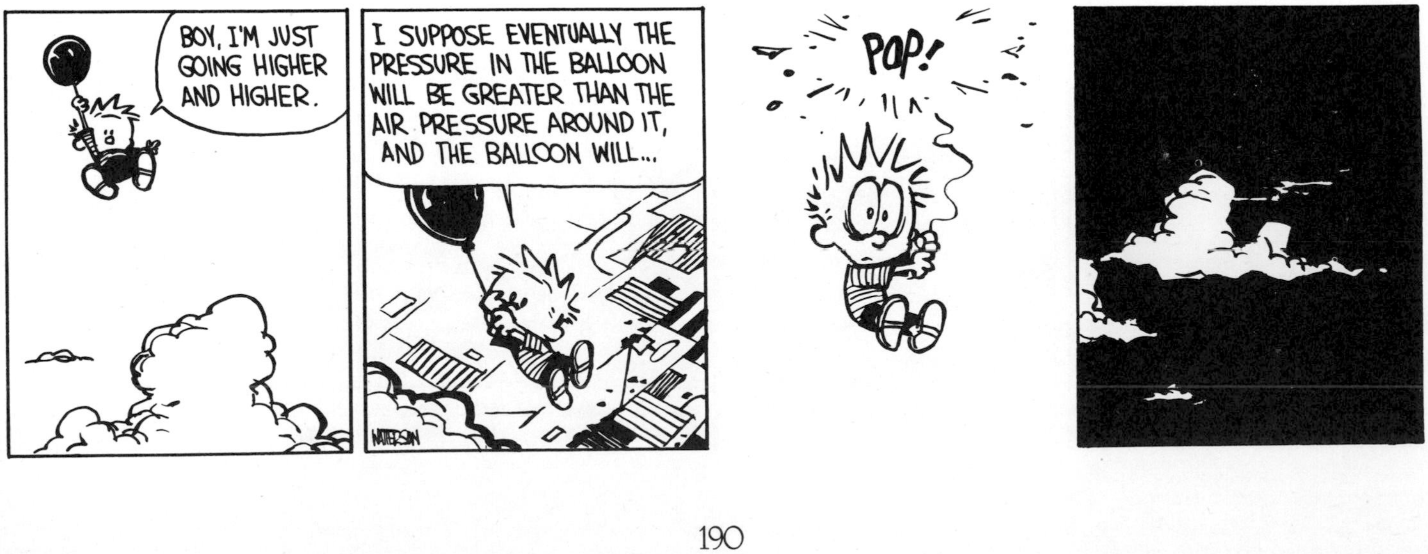
BOY, I'M JUST GOING HIGHER AND HIGHER.
I SUPPOSE EVENTUALLY THE PRESSURE IN THE BALLOON WILL BE GREATER THAN THE AIR PRESSURE AROUND IT, AND THE BALLOON WILL...
WATTERSON
POP!

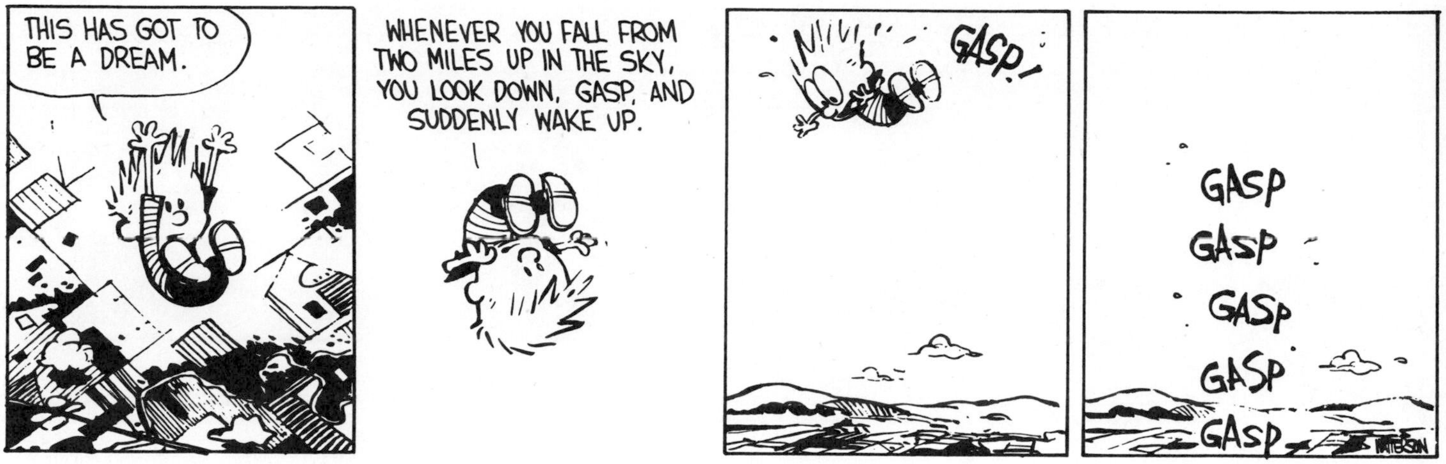
THIS HAS GOT TO BE A DREAM.
WHENEVER YOU FALL FROM TWO MILES UP IN THE SKY, YOU LOOK DOWN, GASP, AND SUDDENLY WAKE UP.
GASP!
GASP
GASP
GASP
GASP
GASP

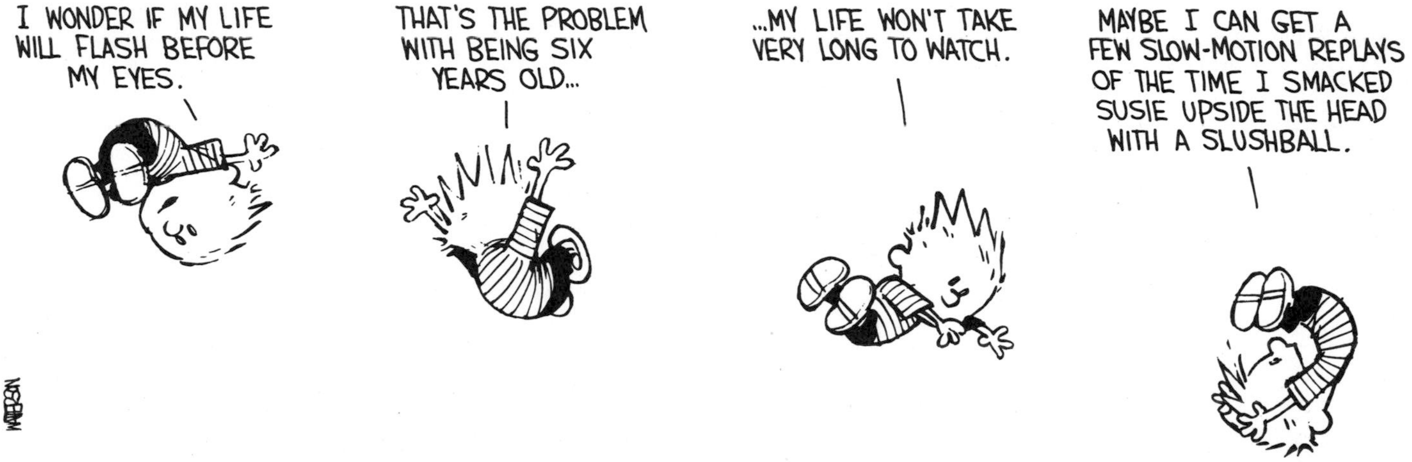
I WONDER IF MY LIFE WILL FLASH BEFORE MY EYES.
THAT'S THE PROBLEM WITH BEING SIX YEARS OLD...
...MY LIFE WON'T TAKE VERY LONG TO WATCH.
MAYBE I CAN GET A FEW SLOW-MOTION REPLAYS OF THE TIME I SMACKED SUSIE UPSIDE THE HEAD WITH A SLUSHBALL.

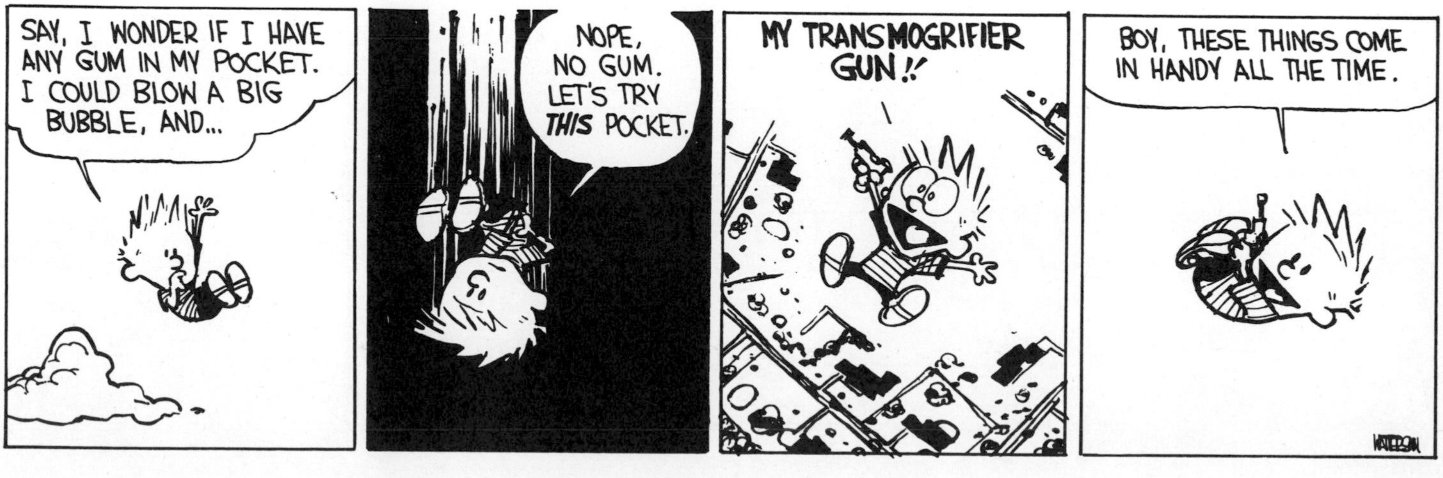
SAY, I WONDER IF I HAVE ANY GUM IN MY POCKET. I COULD BLOW A BIG BUBBLE, AND...
NOPE, NO GUM. LET'S TRY THIS POCKET.
MY TRANSMOGRIFIER GUN!!
BOY, THESE THINGS COME IN HANDY ALL THE TIME.

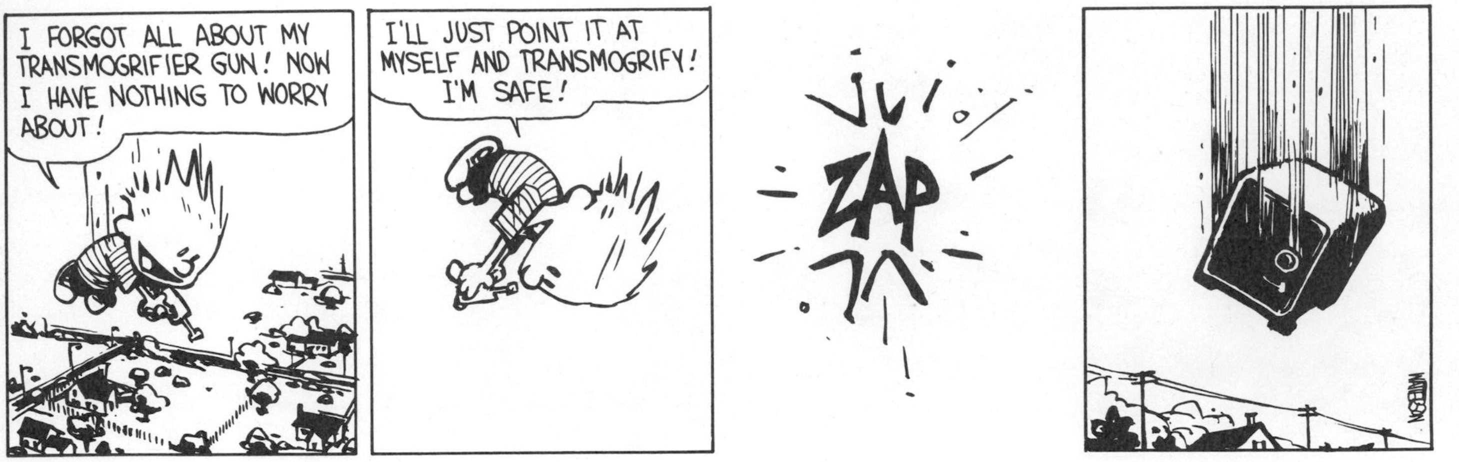

I FORGOT ALL ABOUT MY TRANSMOGRIFIER GUN! NOW I HAVE NOTHING TO WORRY ABOUT!
I'LL JUST POINT IT AT MYSELF AND TRANSMOGRIFY! I'M SAFE!
ZAP


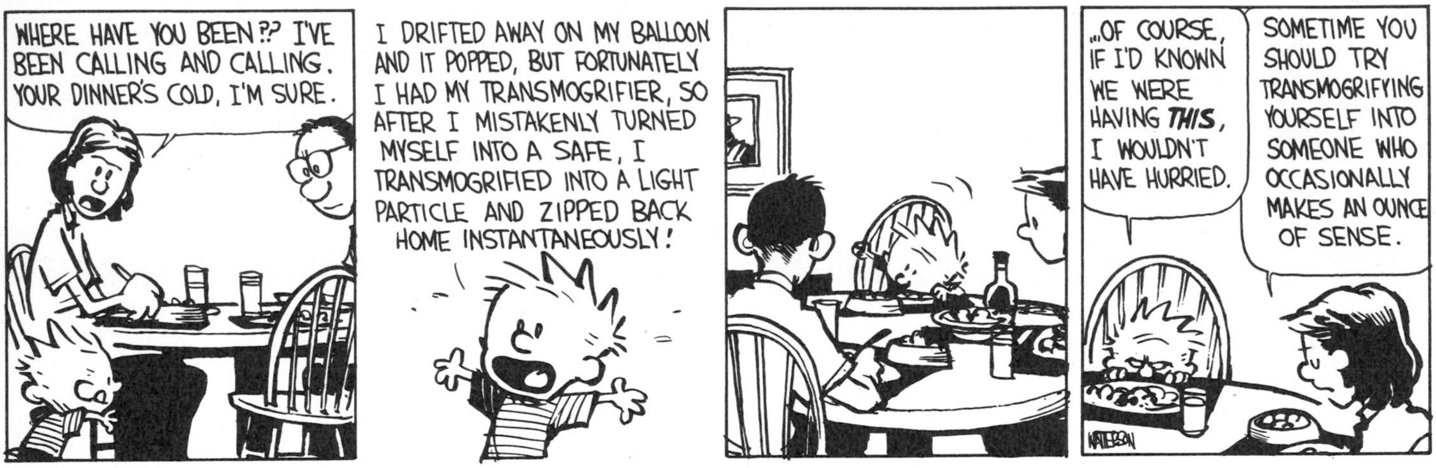

WHERE HAVE YOU BEEN?? I'VE BEEN CALLING AND CALLING. YOUR DINNER'S COLD, I'M SURE.
I DRIFTED AWAY ON MY BALLOON AND IT POPPED, BUT FORTUNATELY I HAD MY TRANSMOGRIFIER, SO AFTER I MISTAKENLY TURNED MYSELF INTO A SAFE, I TRANSMOGRIFIED INTO A LIGHT PARTICLE AND ZIPPED BACK HOME INSTANTANEOUSLY!
...OF COURSE, IF I'D KNOWN WE WERE HAVING **THIS**, I WOULDN'T HAVE HURRIED.
SOMETIME YOU SHOULD TRY TRANSMOGRIFYING YOURSELF INTO SOMEONE WHO OCCASIONALLY MAKES AN OUNCE OF SENSE.


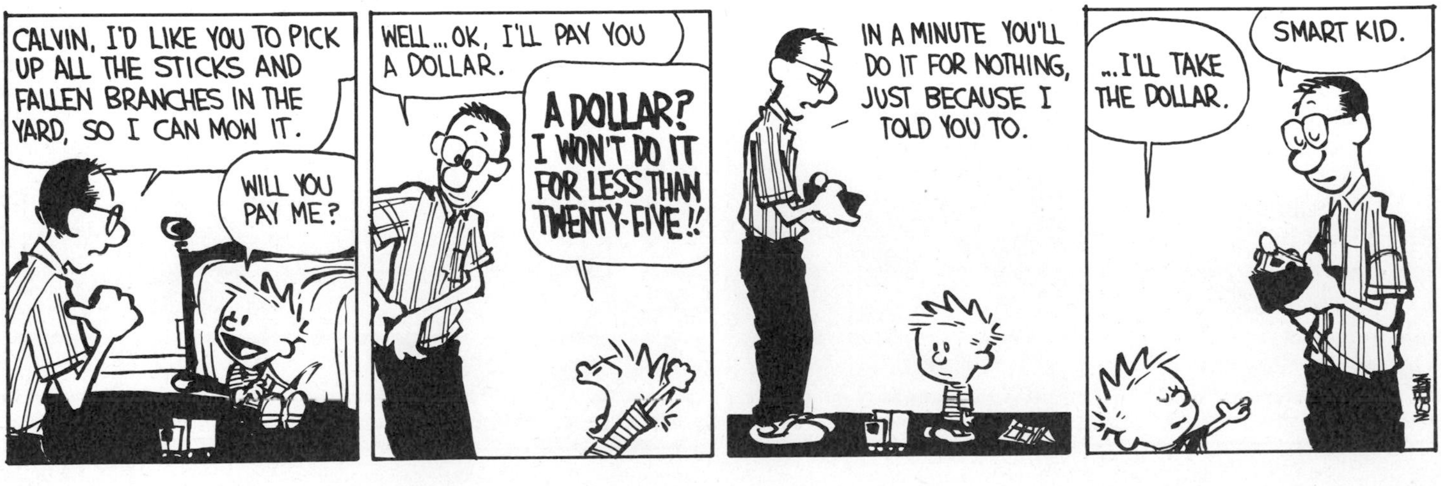

CALVIN, I'D LIKE YOU TO PICK UP ALL THE STICKS AND FALLEN BRANCHES IN THE YARD, SO I CAN MOW IT.
WILL YOU PAY ME?
WELL... OK, I'LL PAY YOU A DOLLAR.
A DOLLAR? I WON'T DO IT FOR LESS THAN TWENTY-FIVE!!
IN A MINUTE YOU'LL DO IT FOR NOTHING, JUST BECAUSE I TOLD YOU TO.
...I'LL TAKE THE DOLLAR.
SMART KID.

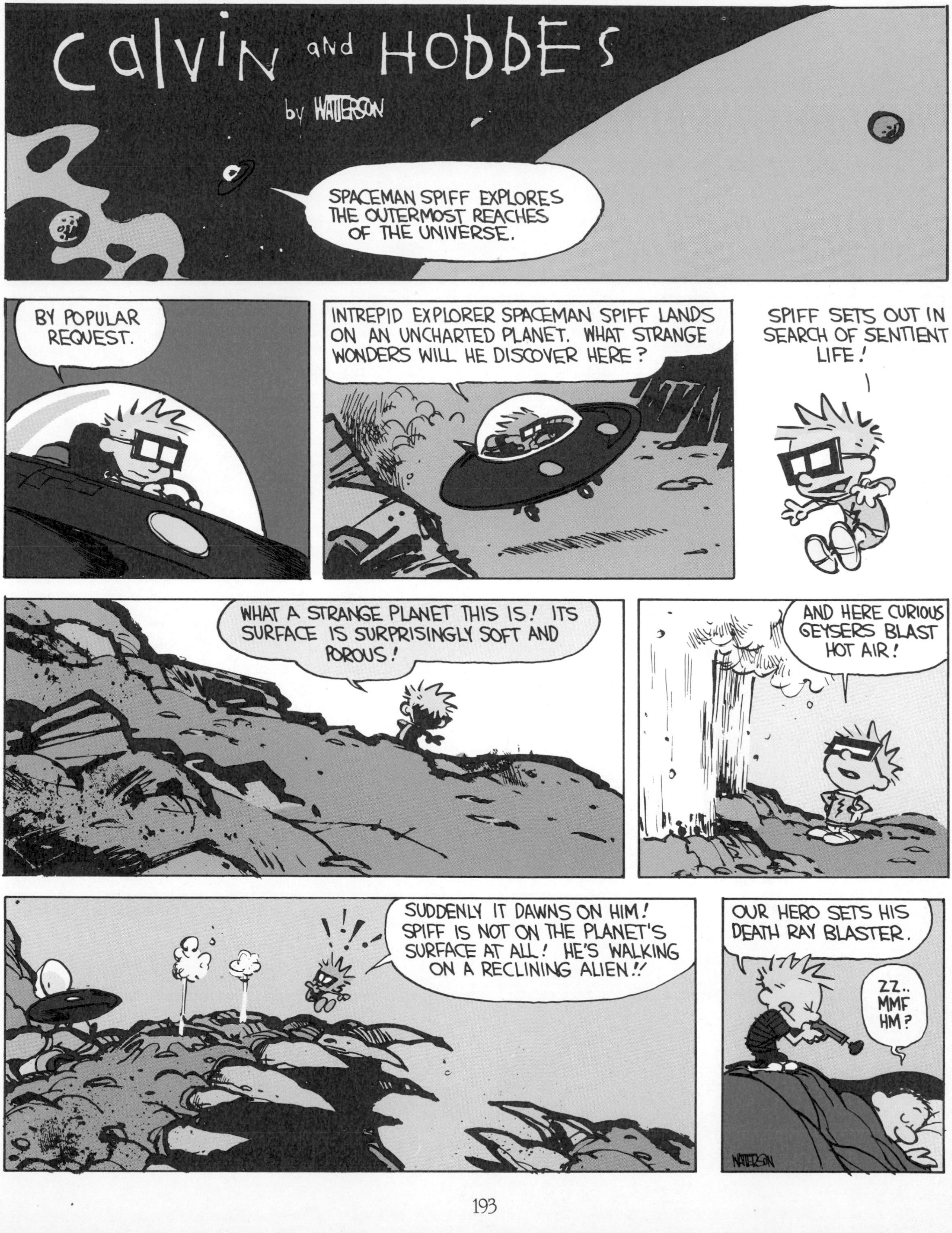
Calvin and HOBBES
by WATTERSON
SPACEMAN SPIFF EXPLORES THE OUTERMOST REACHES OF THE UNIVERSE.
BY POPULAR REQUEST.
INTREPID EXPLORER SPACEMAN SPIFF LANDS ON AN UNCHARTED PLANET. WHAT STRANGE WONDERS WILL HE DISCOVER HERE?
SPIFF SETS OUT IN SEARCH OF SENTIENT LIFE!
WHAT A STRANGE PLANET THIS IS! ITS SURFACE IS SURPRISINGLY SOFT AND POROUS!
AND HERE CURIOUS GEYSERS BLAST HOT AIR!
SUDDENLY IT DAWNS ON HIM! SPIFF IS NOT ON THE PLANET'S SURFACE AT ALL! HE'S WALKING ON A RECLINING ALIEN!!
OUR HERO SETS HIS DEATH RAY BLASTER.
ZZ.. MMF HM?
WATTERSON

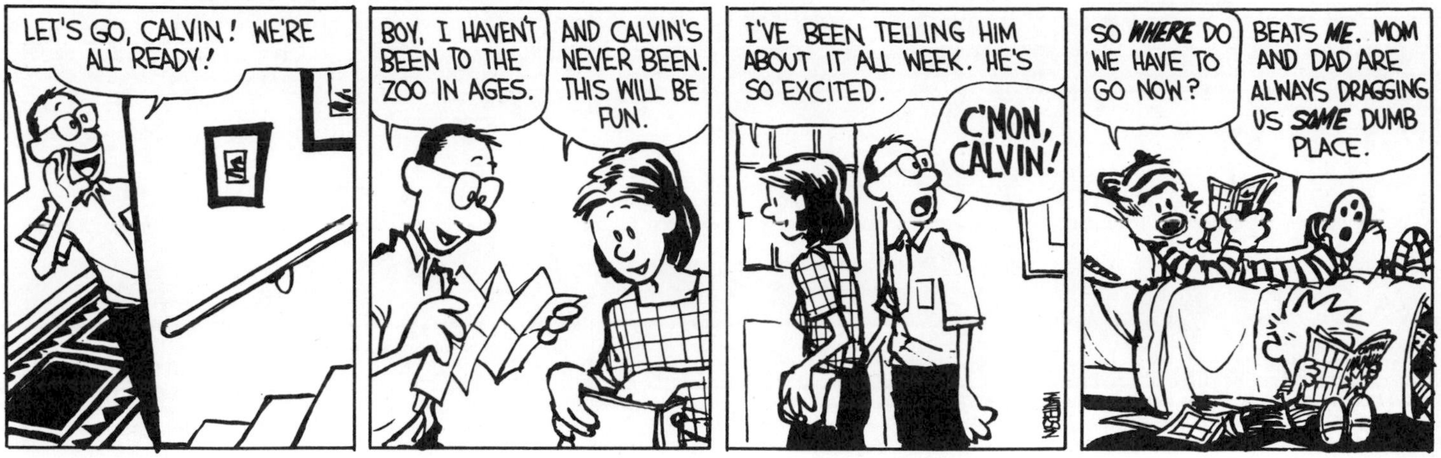
LET'S GO, CALVIN! WE'RE ALL READY!
BOY, I HAVEN'T BEEN TO THE ZOO IN AGES.
AND CALVIN'S NEVER BEEN. THIS WILL BE FUN.
I'VE BEEN TELLING HIM ABOUT IT ALL WEEK. HE'S SO EXCITED.
C'MON, CALVIN!
SO WHERE DO WE HAVE TO GO NOW?
BEATS ME. MOM AND DAD ARE ALWAYS DRAGGING US SOME DUMB PLACE.

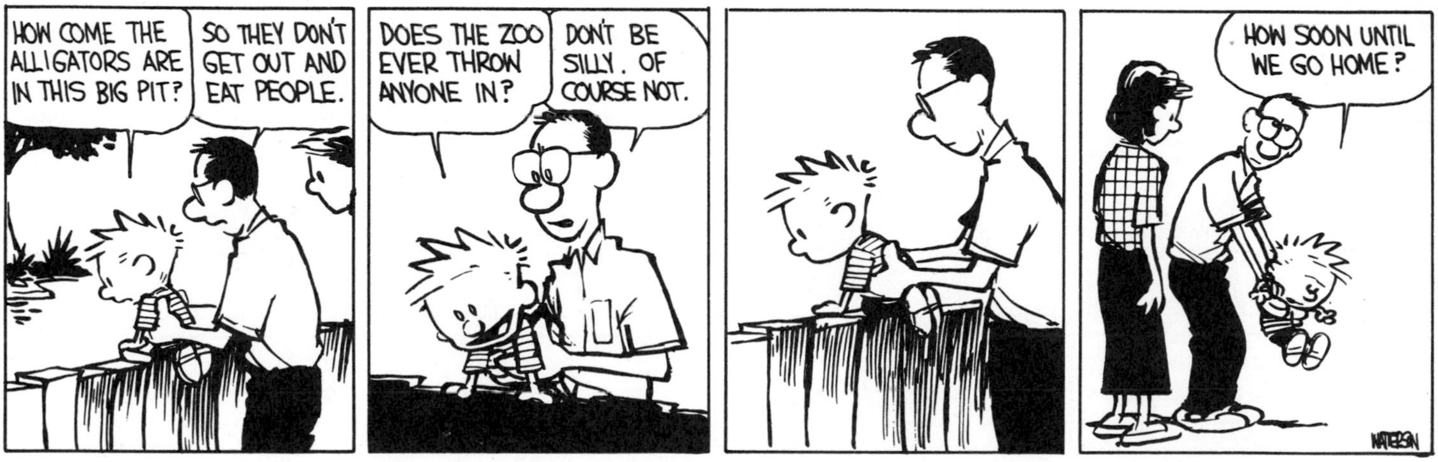
HOW COME THE ALLIGATORS ARE IN THIS BIG PIT?
SO THEY DON'T GET OUT AND EAT PEOPLE.
DOES THE ZOO EVER THROW ANYONE IN?
DON'T BE SILLY. OF COURSE NOT.
HOW SOON UNTIL WE GO HOME?

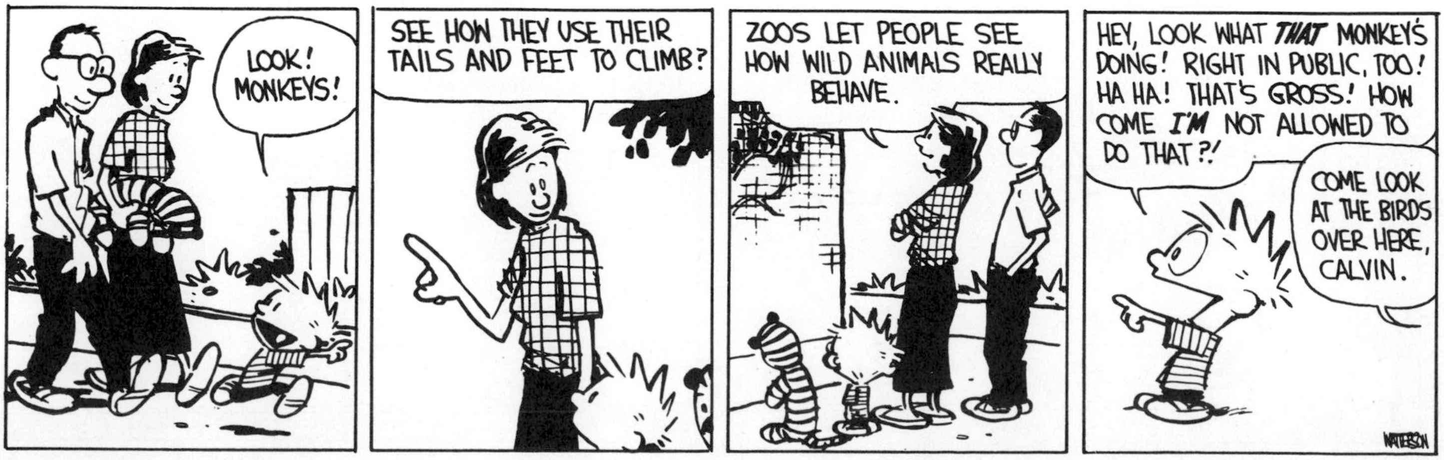
LOOK! MONKEYS!
SEE HOW THEY USE THEIR TAILS AND FEET TO CLIMB?
ZOOS LET PEOPLE SEE HOW WILD ANIMALS REALLY BEHAVE.
HEY, LOOK WHAT THAT MONKEY'S DOING! RIGHT IN PUBLIC, TOO! HA HA! THAT'S GROSS! HOW COME I'M NOT ALLOWED TO DO THAT?!
COME LOOK AT THE BIRDS OVER HERE, CALVIN.

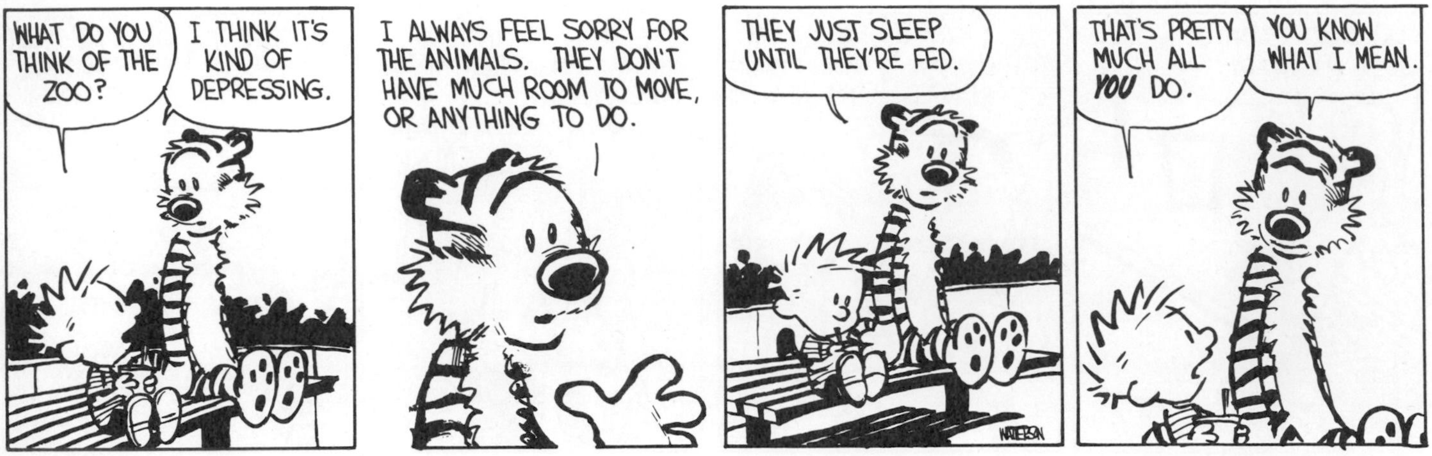
WHAT DO YOU THINK OF THE ZOO?
I THINK IT'S KIND OF DEPRESSING.
I ALWAYS FEEL SORRY FOR THE ANIMALS. THEY DON'T HAVE MUCH ROOM TO MOVE, OR ANYTHING TO DO.
THEY JUST SLEEP UNTIL THEY'RE FED.
THAT'S PRETTY MUCH ALL **YOU** DO.
YOU KNOW WHAT I MEAN.
WATTERSON

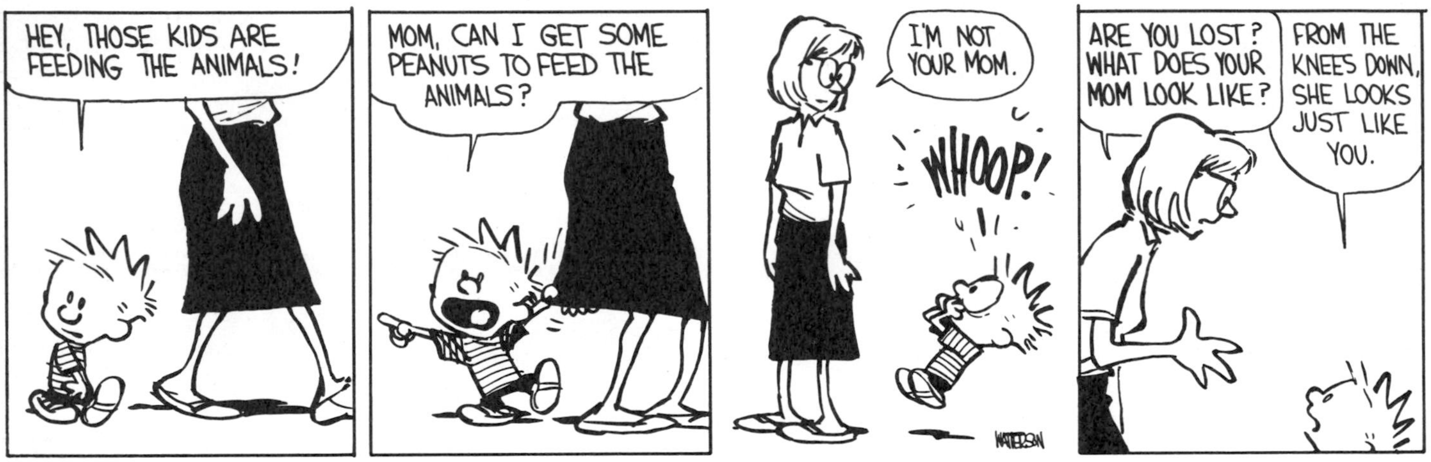
HEY, THOSE KIDS ARE FEEDING THE ANIMALS!
MOM, CAN I GET SOME PEANUTS TO FEED THE ANIMALS?
I'M NOT YOUR MOM.
WHOOP!
WATTERSON
ARE YOU LOST? WHAT DOES YOUR MOM LOOK LIKE?
FROM THE KNEES DOWN, SHE LOOKS JUST LIKE YOU.

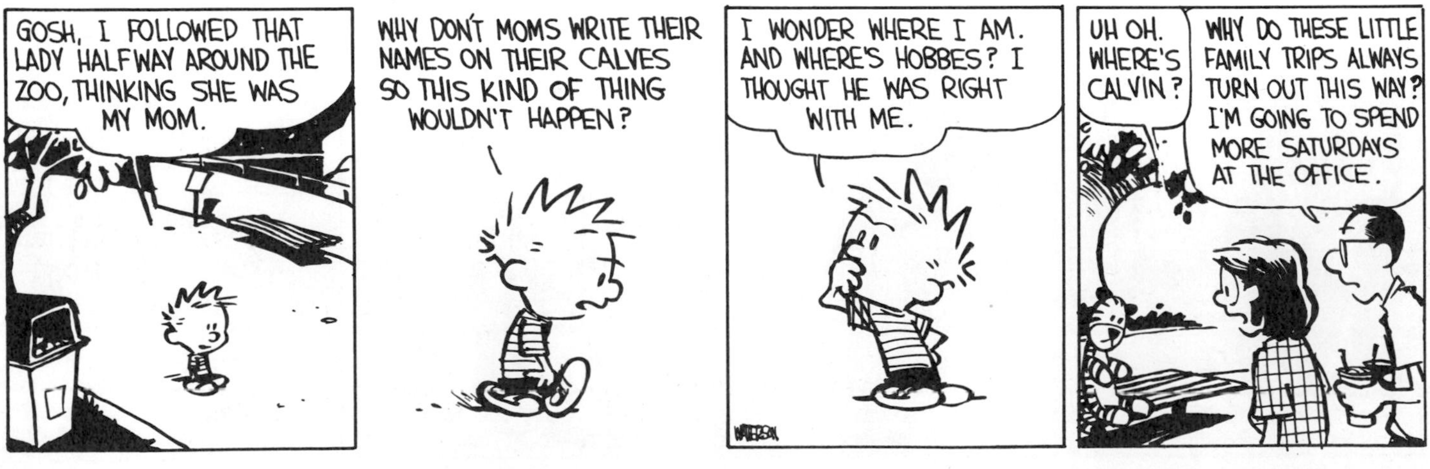
GOSH, I FOLLOWED THAT LADY HALFWAY AROUND THE ZOO, THINKING SHE WAS MY MOM.
WHY DON'T MOMS WRITE THEIR NAMES ON THEIR CALVES SO THIS KIND OF THING WOULDN'T HAPPEN?
I WONDER WHERE I AM. AND WHERE'S HOBBES? I THOUGHT HE WAS RIGHT WITH ME.
WATTERSON
UH OH. WHERE'S CALVIN?
WHY DO THESE LITTLE FAMILY TRIPS ALWAYS TURN OUT THIS WAY? I'M GOING TO SPEND MORE SATURDAYS AT THE OFFICE.

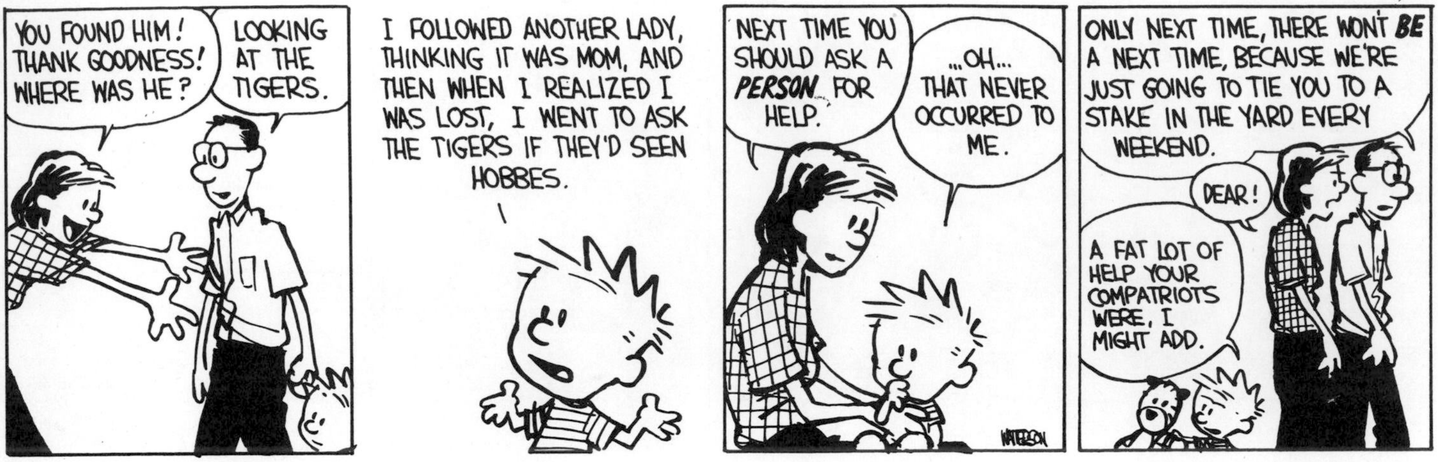
YOU FOUND HIM! THANK GOODNESS! WHERE WAS HE?
LOOKING AT THE TIGERS.
I FOLLOWED ANOTHER LADY, THINKING IT WAS MOM, AND THEN WHEN I REALIZED I WAS LOST, I WENT TO ASK THE TIGERS IF THEY'D SEEN HOBBES.
NEXT TIME YOU SHOULD ASK A PERSON FOR HELP.
...OH... THAT NEVER OCCURRED TO ME.
ONLY NEXT TIME, THERE WON'T BE A NEXT TIME, BECAUSE WE'RE JUST GOING TO TIE YOU TO A STAKE IN THE YARD EVERY WEEKEND.
DEAR!
A FAT LOT OF HELP YOUR COMPATRIOTS WERE, I MIGHT ADD.

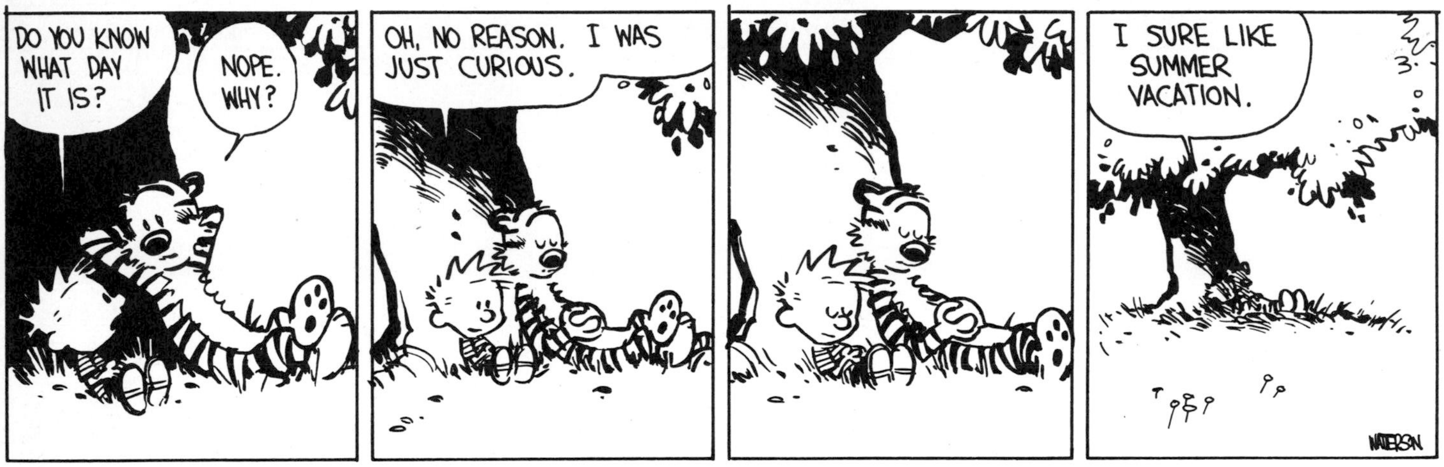
DO YOU KNOW WHAT DAY IT IS?
NOPE. WHY?
OH, NO REASON. I WAS JUST CURIOUS.
I SURE LIKE SUMMER VACATION.

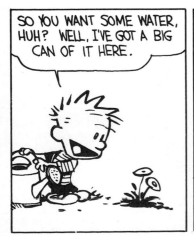

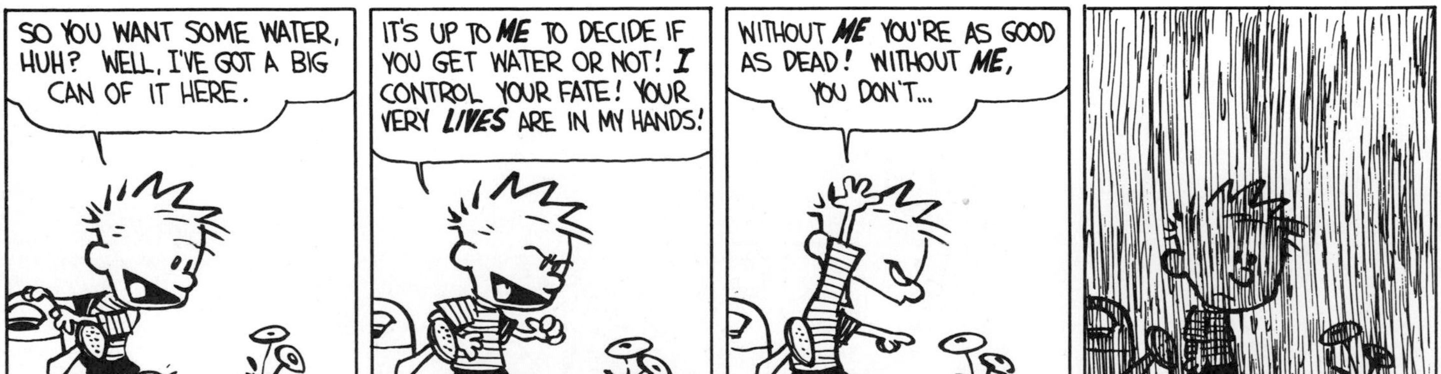
SO YOU WANT SOME WATER, HUH? WELL, I'VE GOT A BIG CAN OF IT HERE.
IT'S UP TO ME TO DECIDE IF YOU GET WATER OR NOT! I CONTROL YOUR FATE! YOUR VERY LIVES ARE IN MY HANDS!
WITHOUT ME YOU'RE AS GOOD AS DEAD! WITHOUT ME, YOU DON'T...

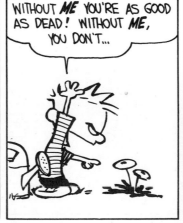

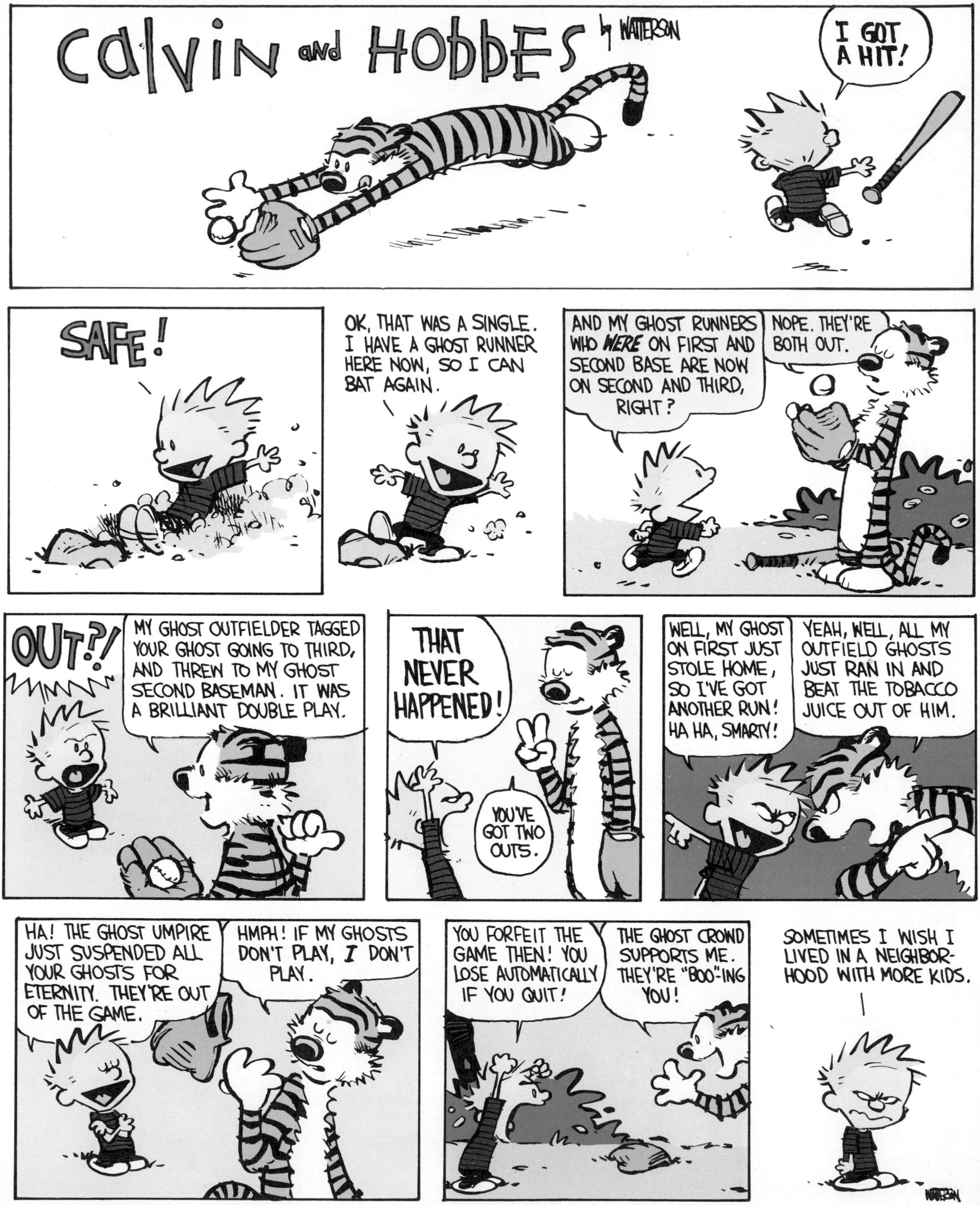
Calvin and HOBBES
by WATTERSON
I GOT A HIT!
SAFE!
OK, THAT WAS A SINGLE. I HAVE A GHOST RUNNER HERE NOW, SO I CAN BAT AGAIN.
AND MY GHOST RUNNERS WHO WERE ON FIRST AND SECOND BASE ARE NOW ON SECOND AND THIRD, RIGHT?
NOPE. THEY'RE BOTH OUT.
OUT?!
MY GHOST OUTFIELDER TAGGED YOUR GHOST GOING TO THIRD, AND THREW TO MY GHOST SECOND BASEMAN. IT WAS A BRILLIANT DOUBLE PLAY.
THAT NEVER HAPPENED!
YOU'VE GOT TWO OUTS.
WELL, MY GHOST ON FIRST JUST STOLE HOME, SO I'VE GOT ANOTHER RUN! HA HA, SMARTY!
YEAH, WELL, ALL MY OUTFIELD GHOSTS JUST RAN IN AND BEAT THE TOBACCO JUICE OUT OF HIM.
HA! THE GHOST UMPIRE JUST SUSPENDED ALL YOUR GHOSTS FOR ETERNITY. THEY'RE OUT OF THE GAME.
HMPH! IF MY GHOSTS DON'T PLAY, I DON'T PLAY.
YOU FORFEIT THE GAME THEN! YOU LOSE AUTOMATICALLY IF YOU QUIT!
THE GHOST CROWD SUPPORTS ME. THEY'RE "BOO"-ING YOU!
SOMETIMES I WISH I LIVED IN A NEIGHBORHOOD WITH MORE KIDS.
WATTERSON

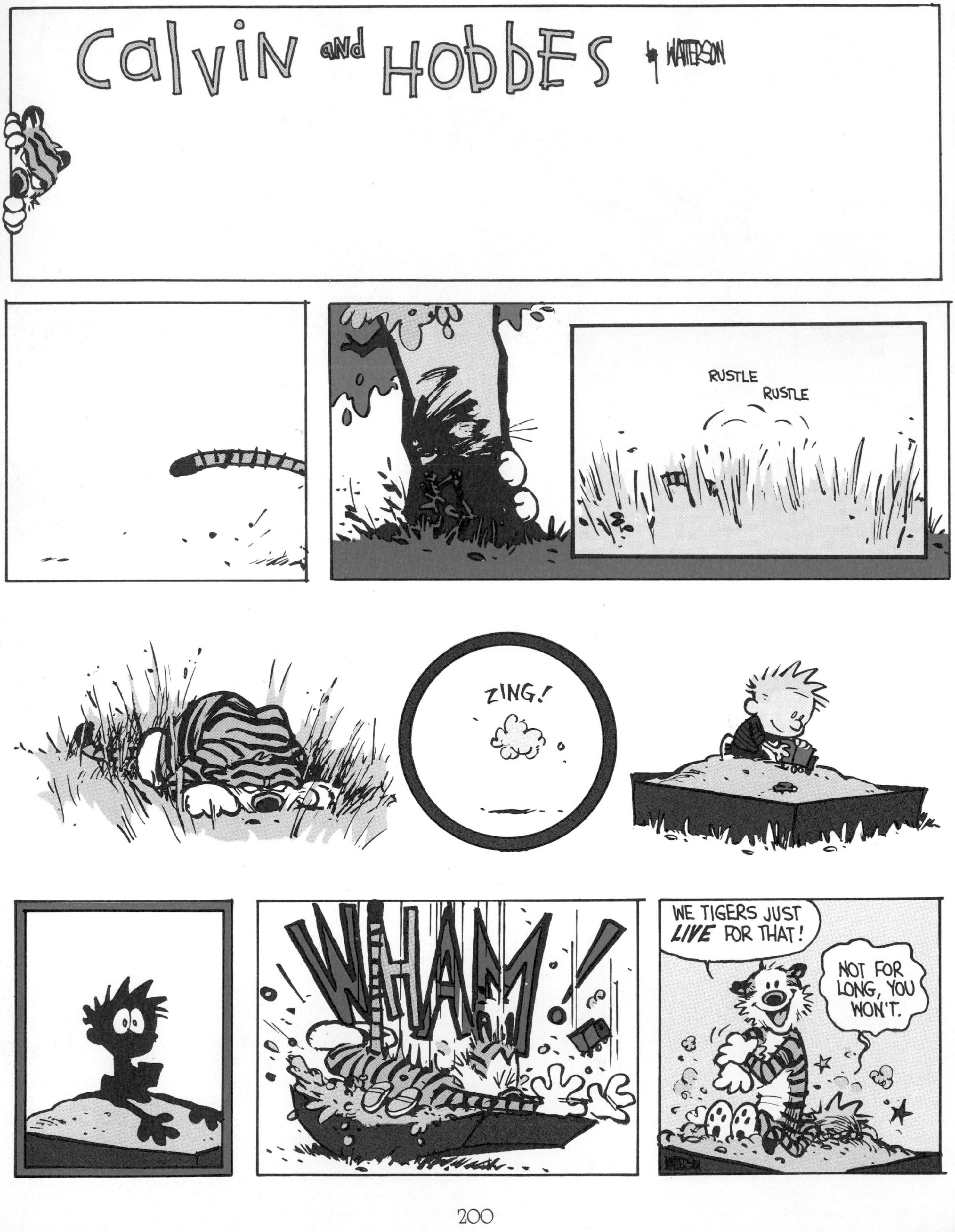
Calvin and HOBBES by WATTERSON
RUSTLE RUSTLE
ZING!
WHAM!
WE TIGERS JUST *LIVE* FOR THAT!
NOT FOR LONG, YOU WON'T.

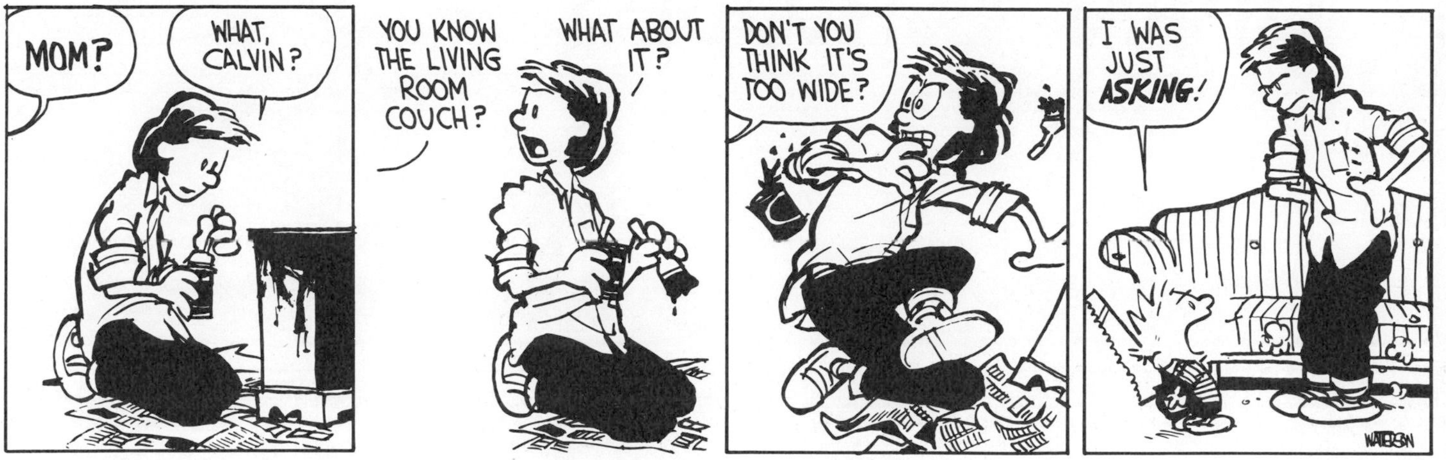
MOM?
WHAT, CALVIN?
YOU KNOW THE LIVING ROOM COUCH?
WHAT ABOUT IT?
DON'T YOU THINK IT'S TOO WIDE?
I WAS JUST ASKING!
WATTERSON

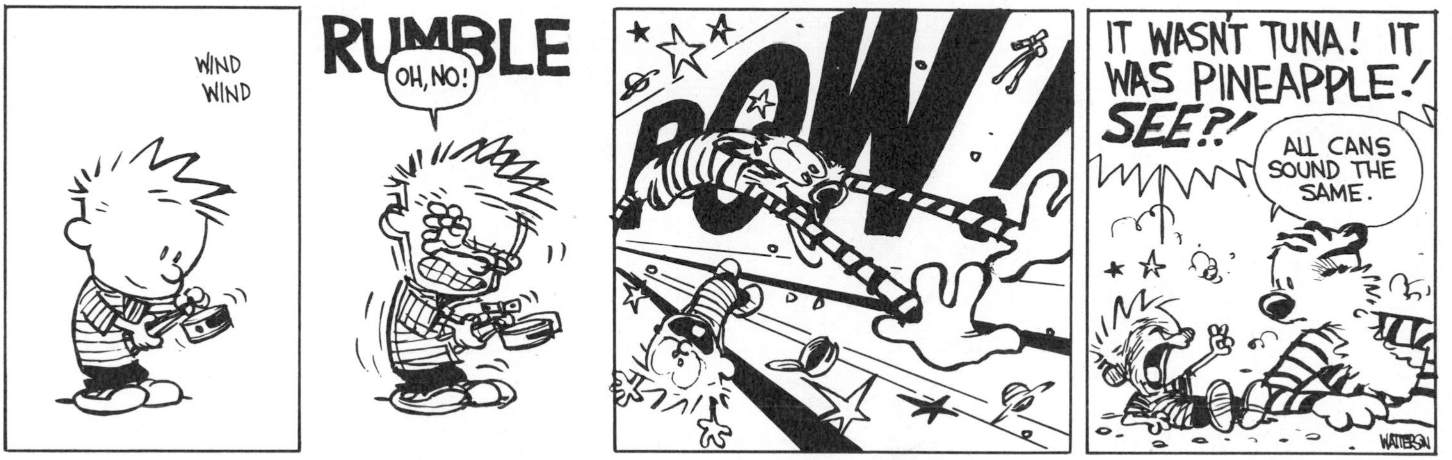
WIND WIND
RUMBLE
OH, NO!
POW!
IT WASN'T TUNA! IT WAS PINEAPPLE! SEE?!
ALL CANS SOUND THE SAME.
WATTERSON

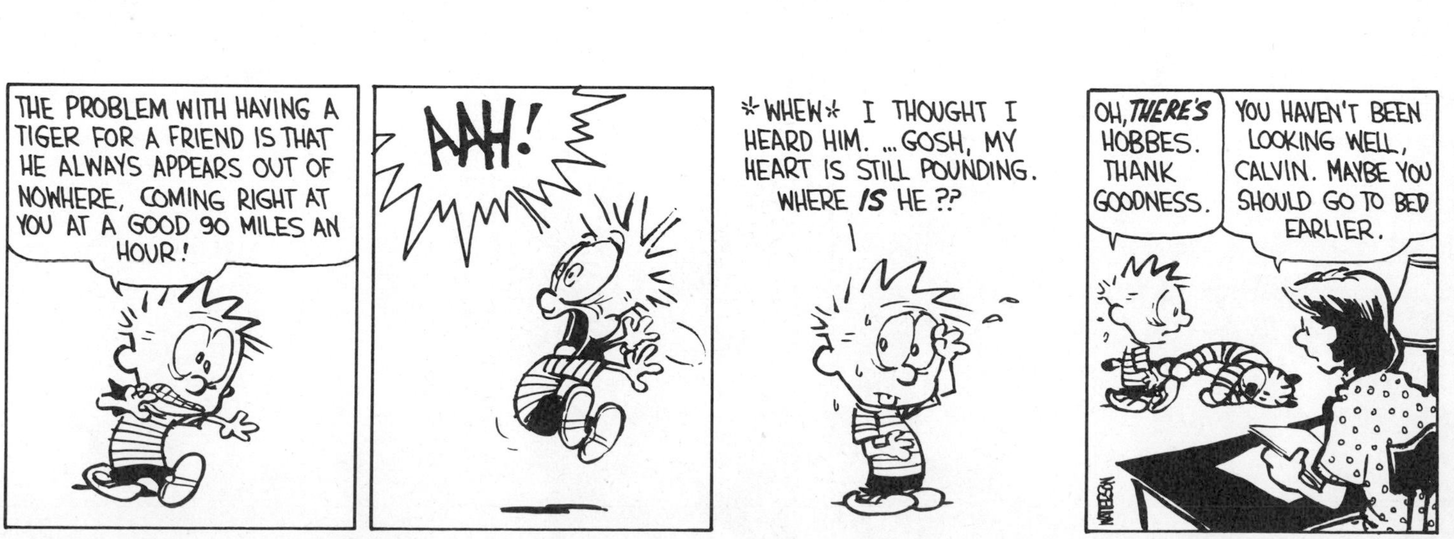
THE PROBLEM WITH HAVING A TIGER FOR A FRIEND IS THAT HE ALWAYS APPEARS OUT OF NOWHERE, COMING RIGHT AT YOU AT A GOOD 90 MILES AN HOUR!
AAH!
*WHEW* I THOUGHT I HEARD HIM. ...GOSH, MY HEART IS STILL POUNDING. WHERE IS HE??
OH, THERE'S HOBBES. THANK GOODNESS.
YOU HAVEN'T BEEN LOOKING WELL, CALVIN. MAYBE YOU SHOULD GO TO BED EARLIER.
WATTERSON

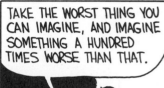

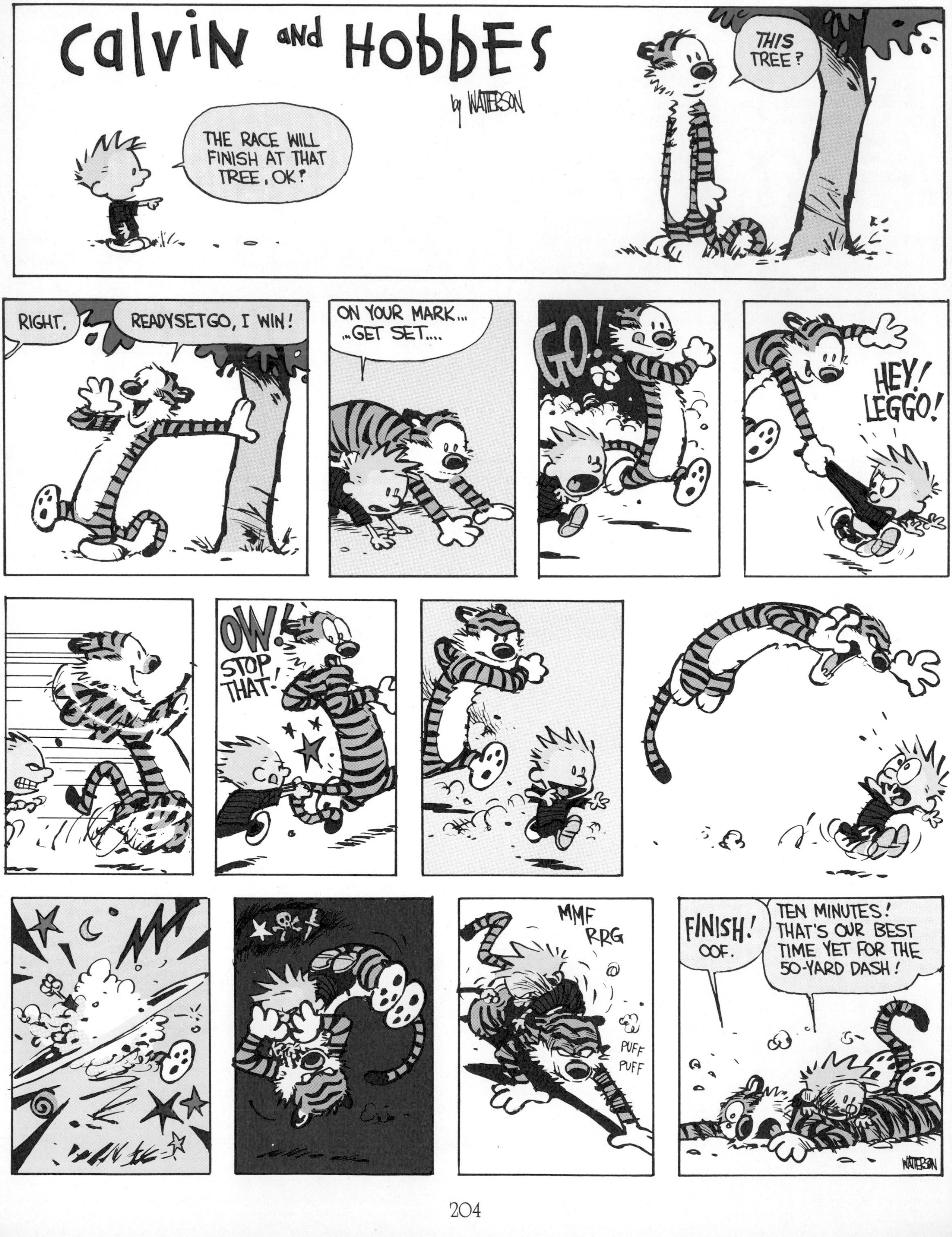
Calvin and HOBBES
by WATTERSON
THE RACE WILL FINISH AT THAT TREE, OK?
THIS TREE?
RIGHT.
READYSETGO, I WIN!
ON YOUR MARK... ...GET SET....
GO!
HEY! LEGGO!
OW! STOP THAT!
MMF
RRG
PUFF
PUFF
FINISH! OOF.
TEN MINUTES! THAT'S OUR BEST TIME YET FOR THE 50-YARD DASH!
WATTERSON

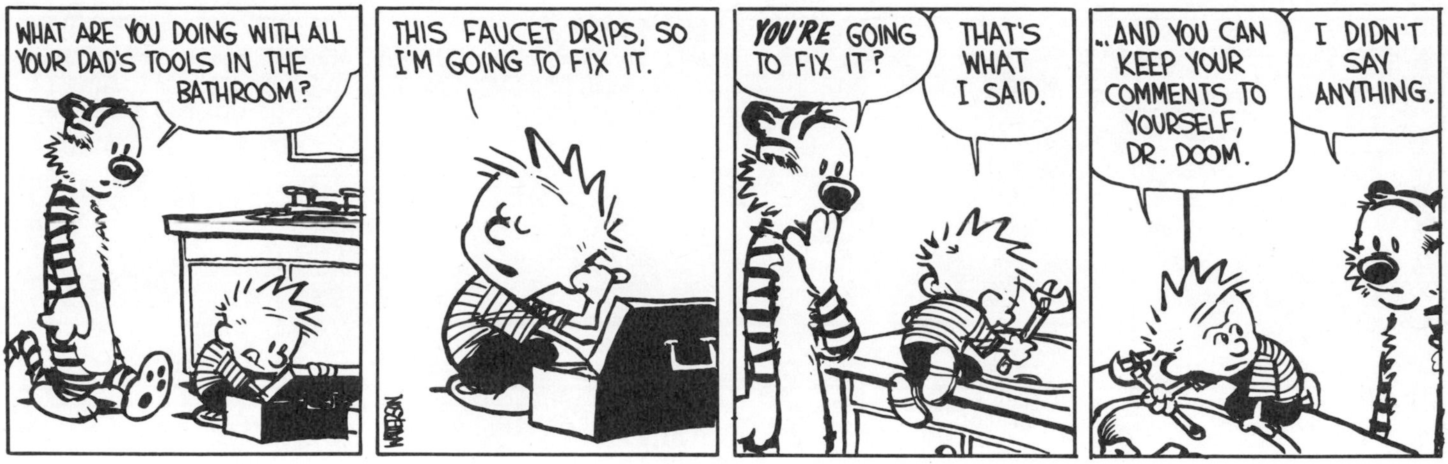
WHAT ARE YOU DOING WITH ALL YOUR DAD'S TOOLS IN THE BATHROOM?
THIS FAUCET DRIPS, SO I'M GOING TO FIX IT.
YOU'RE GOING TO FIX IT?
THAT'S WHAT I SAID.
...AND YOU CAN KEEP YOUR COMMENTS TO YOURSELF, DR. DOOM.
I DIDN'T SAY ANYTHING.

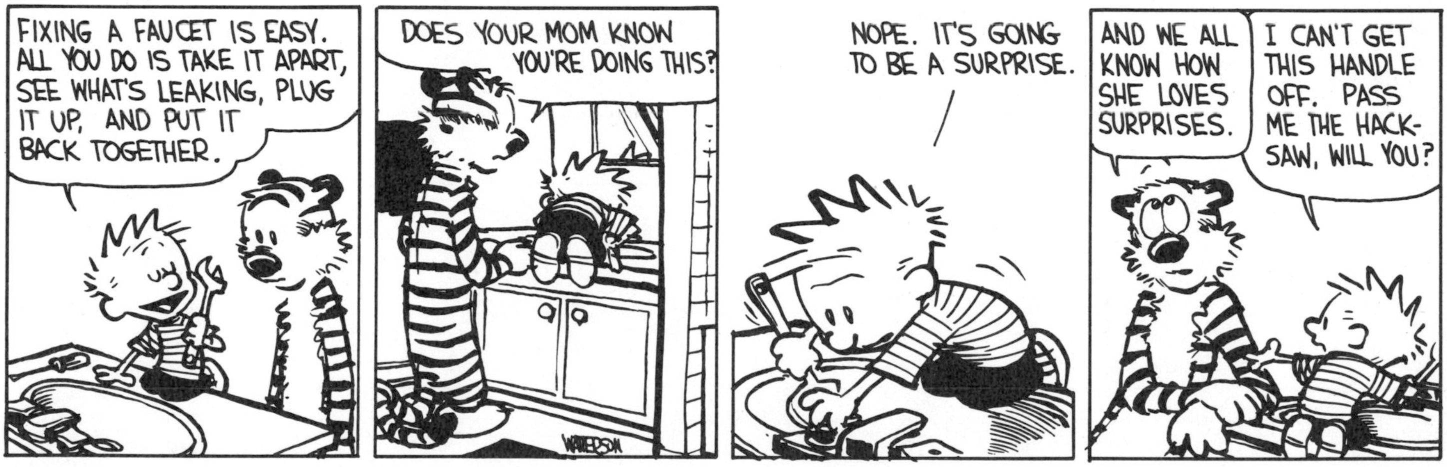
FIXING A FAUCET IS EASY. ALL YOU DO IS TAKE IT APART, SEE WHAT'S LEAKING, PLUG IT UP, AND PUT IT BACK TOGETHER.
DOES YOUR MOM KNOW YOU'RE DOING THIS?
NOPE. IT'S GOING TO BE A SURPRISE.
AND WE ALL KNOW HOW SHE LOVES SURPRISES.
I CAN'T GET THIS HANDLE OFF. PASS ME THE HACK-SAW, WILL YOU?

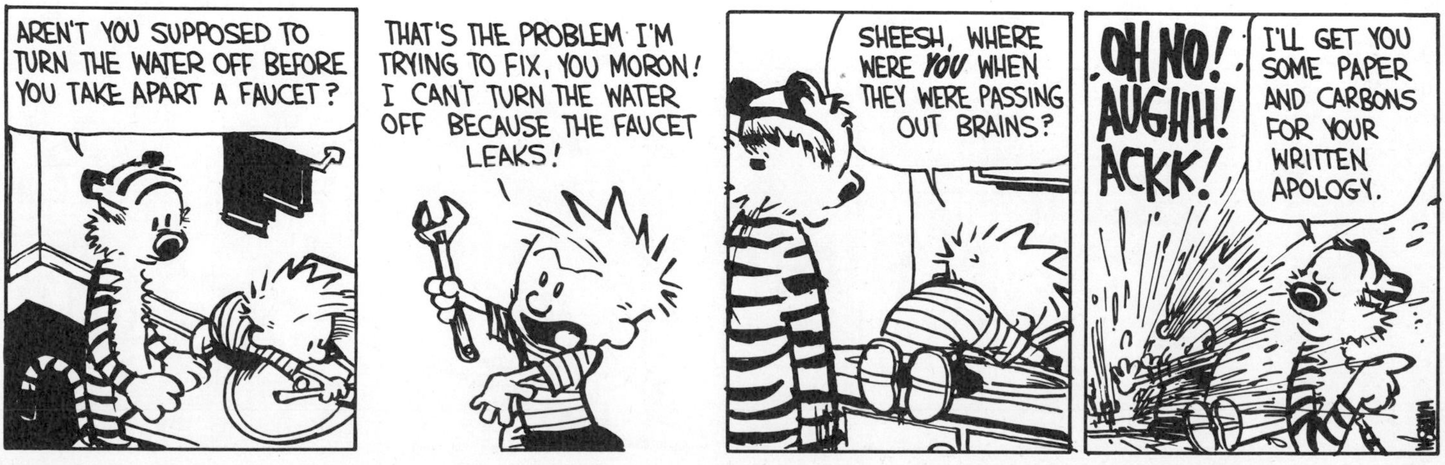
AREN'T YOU SUPPOSED TO TURN THE WATER OFF BEFORE YOU TAKE APART A FAUCET?
THAT'S THE PROBLEM I'M TRYING TO FIX, YOU MORON! I CAN'T TURN THE WATER OFF BECAUSE THE FAUCET LEAKS!
SHEESH, WHERE WERE YOU WHEN THEY WERE PASSING OUT BRAINS?
OH NO! AUGHH! ACKK!
I'LL GET YOU SOME PAPER AND CARBONS FOR YOUR WRITTEN APOLOGY.

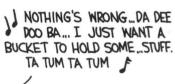

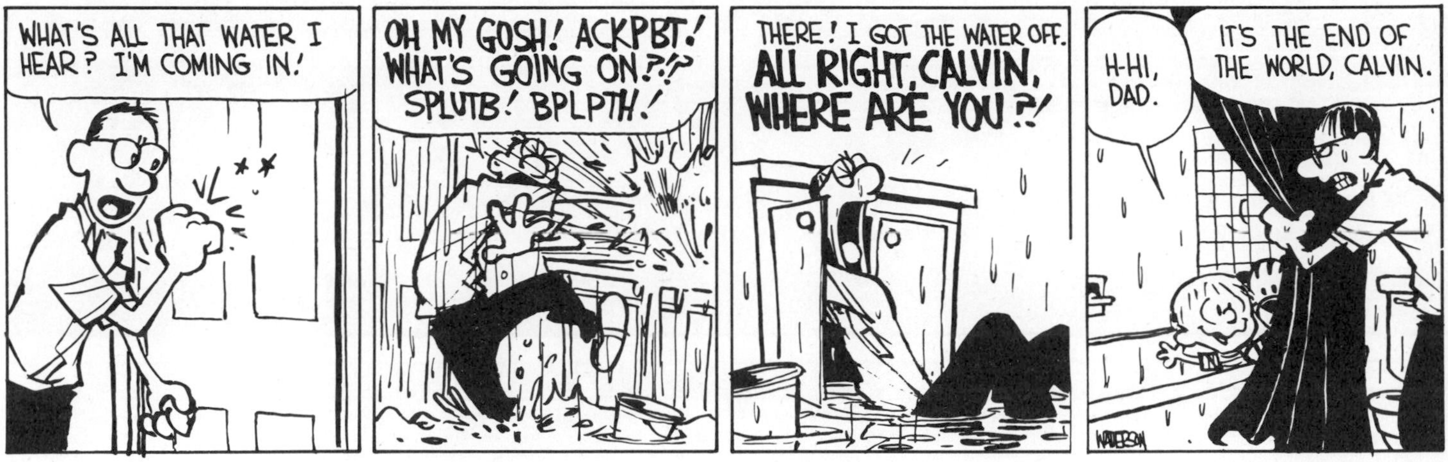

WHAT'S ALL THAT WATER I HEAR? I'M COMING IN!
OH MY GOSH! ACKPBT! WHAT'S GOING ON?!? SPLUTB! BPLPTH!
THERE! I GOT THE WATER OFF. ALL RIGHT, CALVIN, WHERE ARE YOU?!
H-HI, DAD.
IT'S THE END OF THE WORLD, CALVIN.
WATTERSON


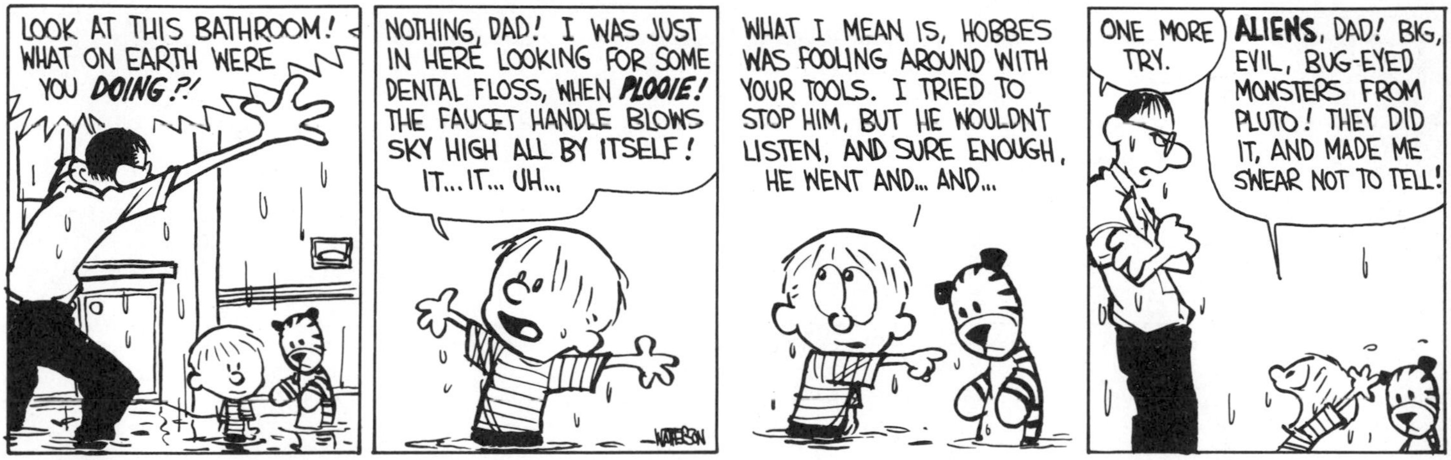

LOOK AT THIS BATHROOM! WHAT ON EARTH WERE YOU DOING?!
NOTHING, DAD! I WAS JUST IN HERE LOOKING FOR SOME DENTAL FLOSS, WHEN PLOOIE! THE FAUCET HANDLE BLOWS SKY HIGH ALL BY ITSELF! IT... IT... UH...
WATTERSON
WHAT I MEAN IS, HOBBES WAS FOOLING AROUND WITH YOUR TOOLS. I TRIED TO STOP HIM, BUT HE WOULDN'T LISTEN, AND SURE ENOUGH, HE WENT AND... AND...
ONE MORE TRY.
ALIENS, DAD! BIG, EVIL, BUG-EYED MONSTERS FROM PLUTO! THEY DID IT, AND MADE ME SWEAR NOT TO TELL!


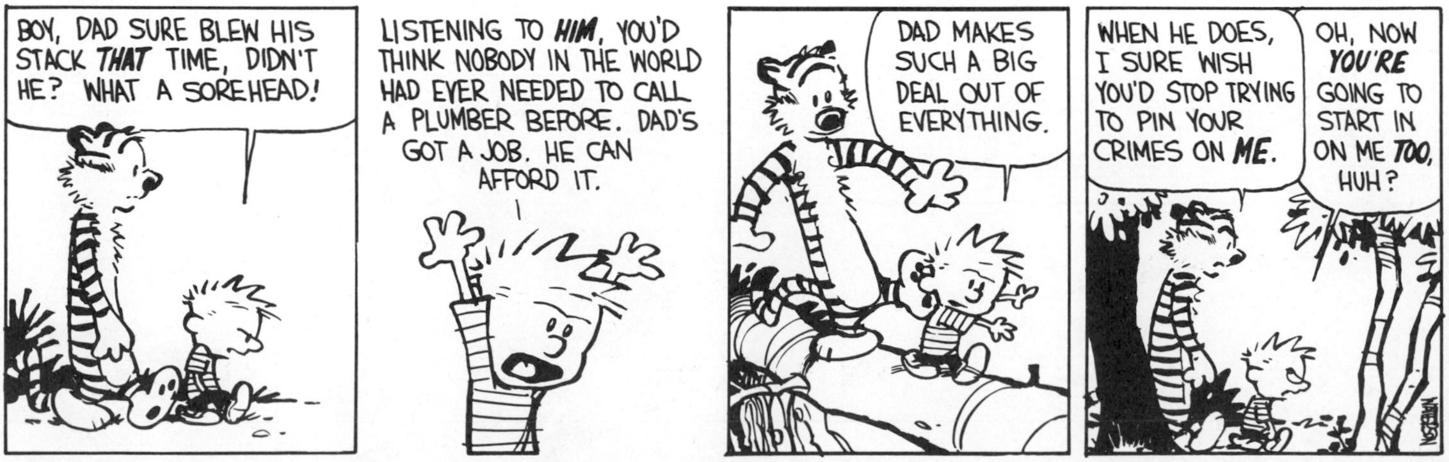

BOY, DAD SURE BLEW HIS STACK THAT TIME, DIDN'T HE? WHAT A SOREHEAD!
LISTENING TO HIM, YOU'D THINK NOBODY IN THE WORLD HAD EVER NEEDED TO CALL A PLUMBER BEFORE. DAD'S GOT A JOB. HE CAN AFFORD IT.
DAD MAKES SUCH A BIG DEAL OUT OF EVERYTHING.
WHEN HE DOES, I SURE WISH YOU'D STOP TRYING TO PIN YOUR CRIMES ON ME.
OH, NOW YOU'RE GOING TO START IN ON ME TOO, HUH?
WATTERSON

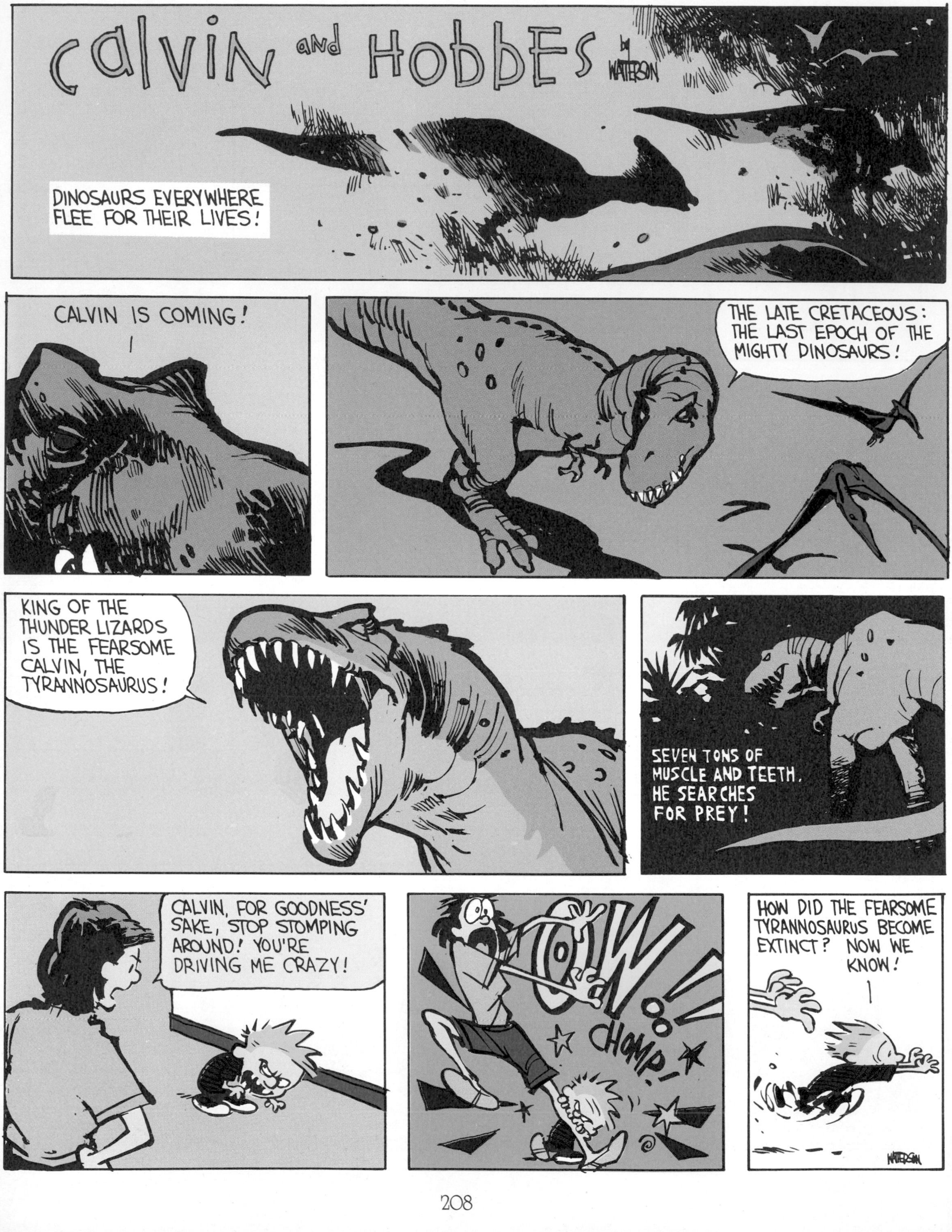
Calvin and Hobbes by WATTERSON
DINOSAURS EVERYWHERE FLEE FOR THEIR LIVES!
CALVIN IS COMING!
THE LATE CRETACEOUS: THE LAST EPOCH OF THE MIGHTY DINOSAURS!
KING OF THE THUNDER LIZARDS IS THE FEARSOME CALVIN, THE TYRANNOSAURUS!
SEVEN TONS OF MUSCLE AND TEETH. HE SEARCHES FOR PREY!
CALVIN, FOR GOODNESS' SAKE, STOP STOMPING AROUND! YOU'RE DRIVING ME CRAZY!
OW!!
CHOMP!
OOO!!
HOW DID THE FEARSOME TYRANNOSAURUS BECOME EXTINCT? NOW WE KNOW!
WATTERSON

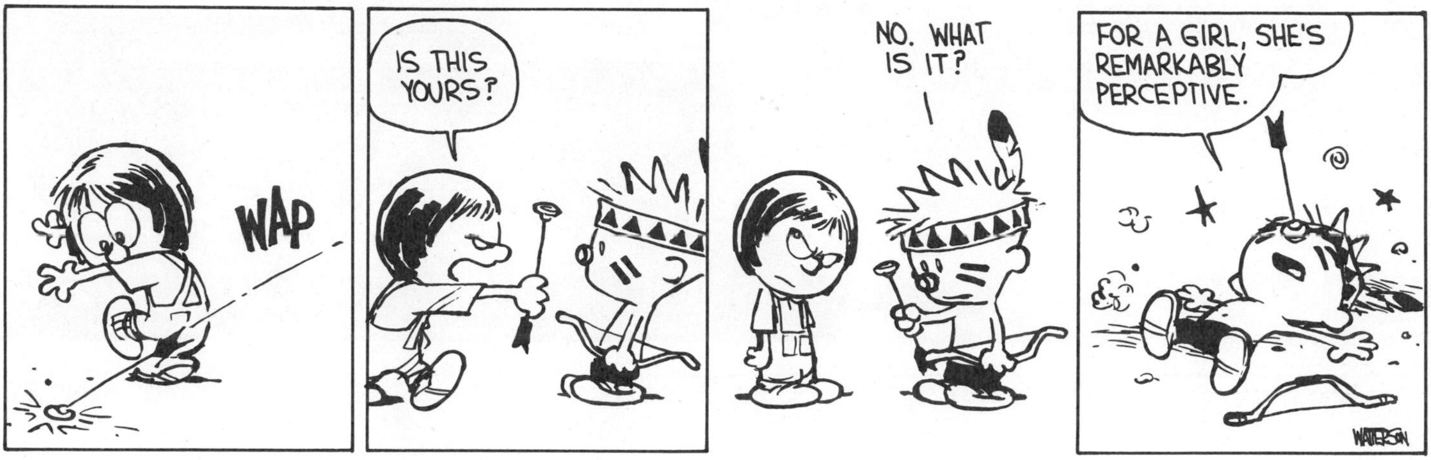
WAP
IS THIS YOURS?
NO. WHAT IS IT?
FOR A GIRL, SHE'S REMARKABLY PERCEPTIVE.

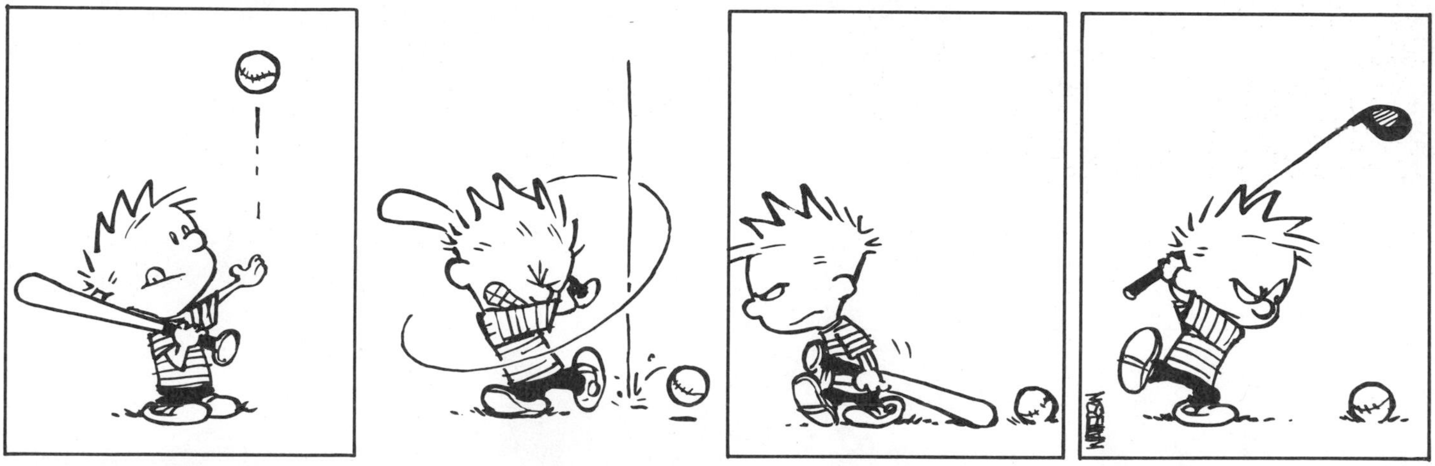

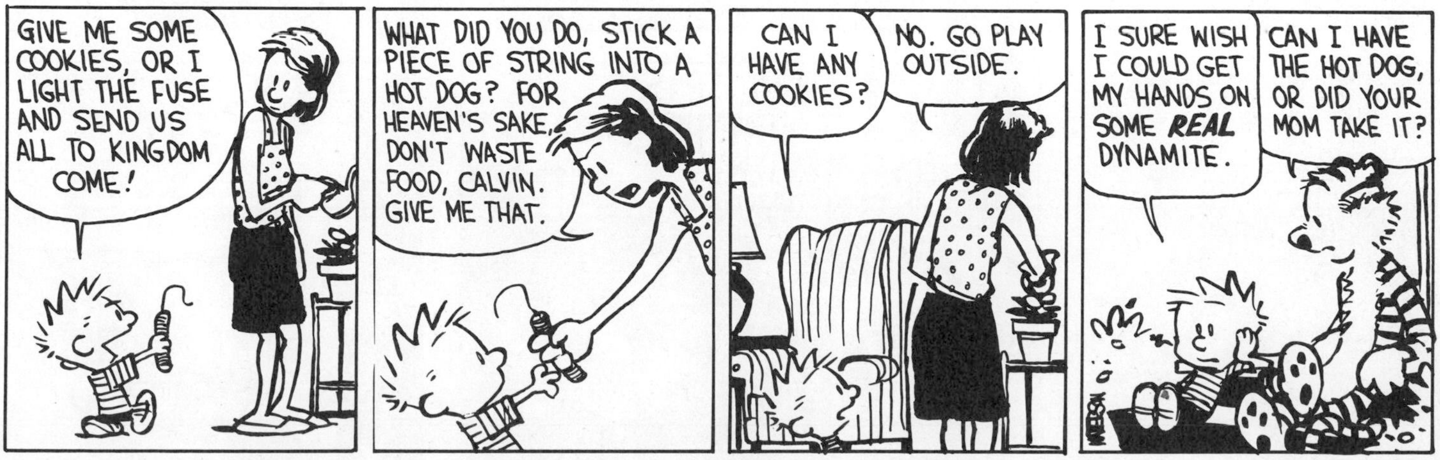
GIVE ME SOME COOKIES, OR I LIGHT THE FUSE AND SEND US ALL TO KINGDOM COME!
WHAT DID YOU DO, STICK A PIECE OF STRING INTO A HOT DOG? FOR HEAVEN'S SAKE, DON'T WASTE FOOD, CALVIN. GIVE ME THAT.
CAN I HAVE ANY COOKIES?
NO. GO PLAY OUTSIDE.
I SURE WISH I COULD GET MY HANDS ON SOME *REAL* DYNAMITE.
CAN I HAVE THE HOT DOG, OR DID YOUR MOM TAKE IT?

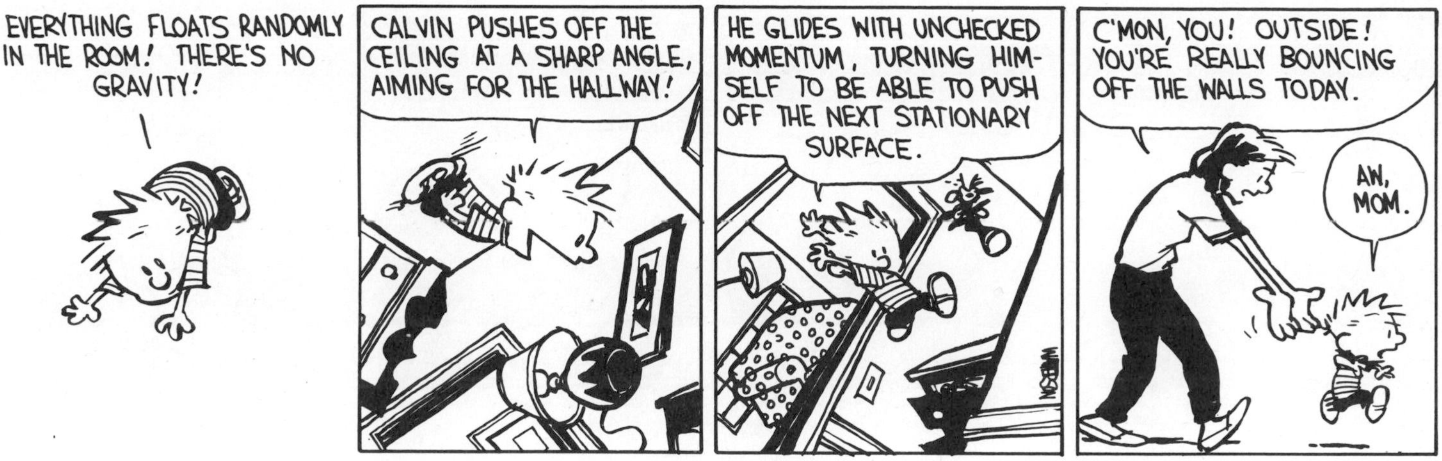
EVERYTHING FLOATS RANDOMLY IN THE ROOM! THERE'S NO GRAVITY!
CALVIN PUSHES OFF THE CEILING AT A SHARP ANGLE, AIMING FOR THE HALLWAY!
HE GLIDES WITH UNCHECKED MOMENTUM, TURNING HIMSELF TO BE ABLE TO PUSH OFF THE NEXT STATIONARY SURFACE.
C'MON, YOU! OUTSIDE! YOU'RE REALLY BOUNCING OFF THE WALLS TODAY.
AW, MOM.

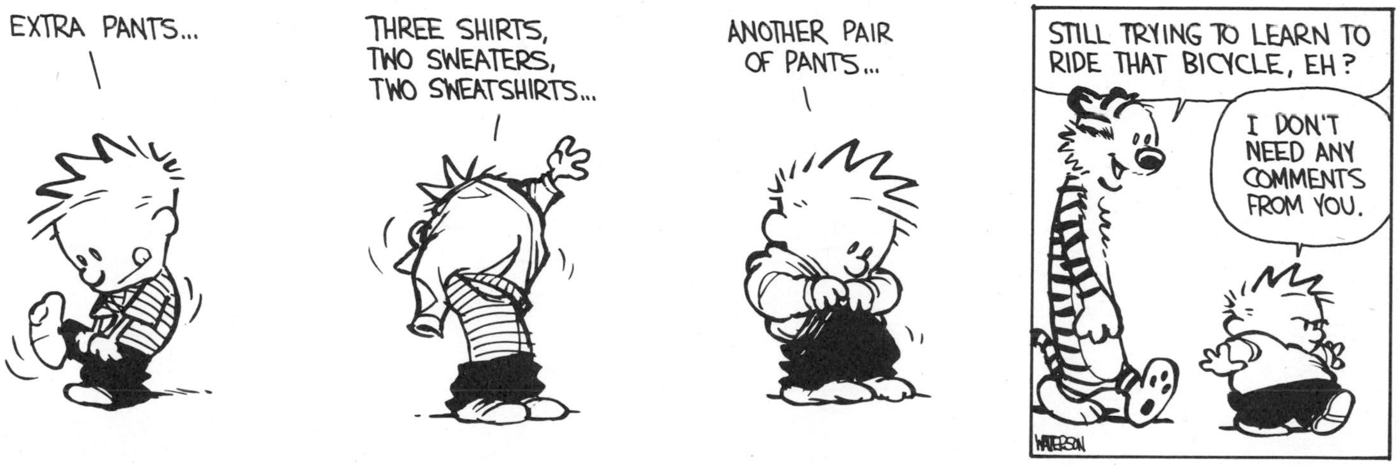
EXTRA PANTS...
THREE SHIRTS, TWO SWEATERS, TWO SWEATSHIRTS...
ANOTHER PAIR OF PANTS...
STILL TRYING TO LEARN TO RIDE THAT BICYCLE, EH?
I DON'T NEED ANY COMMENTS FROM YOU.

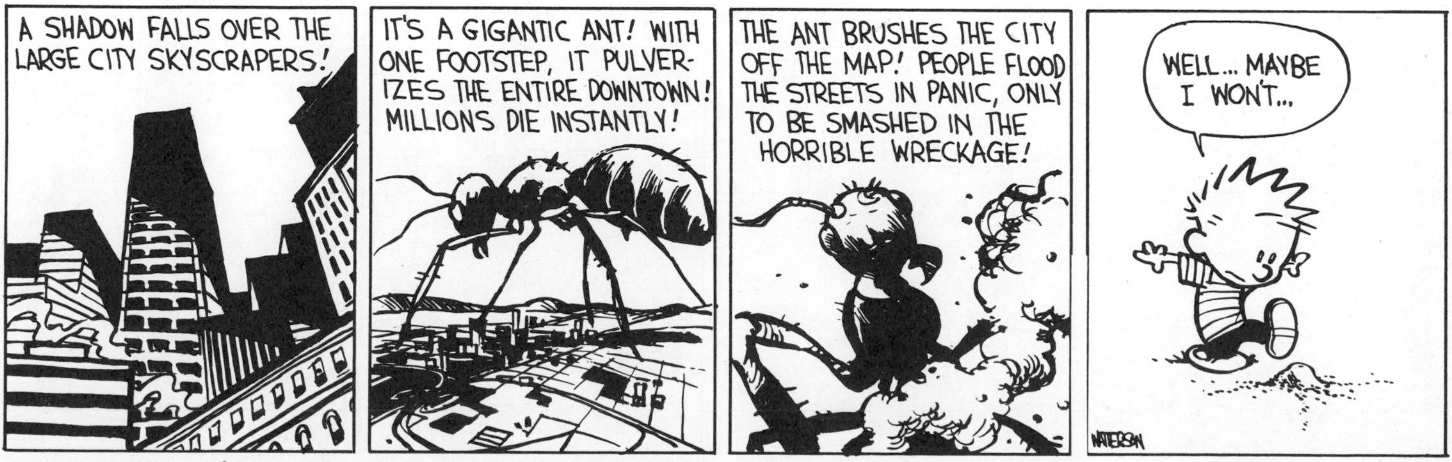
A SHADOW FALLS OVER THE LARGE CITY SKYSCRAPERS!
IT'S A GIGANTIC ANT! WITH ONE FOOTSTEP, IT PULVERIZES THE ENTIRE DOWNTOWN! MILLIONS DIE INSTANTLY!
THE ANT BRUSHES THE CITY OFF THE MAP! PEOPLE FLOOD THE STREETS IN PANIC, ONLY TO BE SMASHED IN THE HORRIBLE WRECKAGE!
WELL... MAYBE I WON'T...

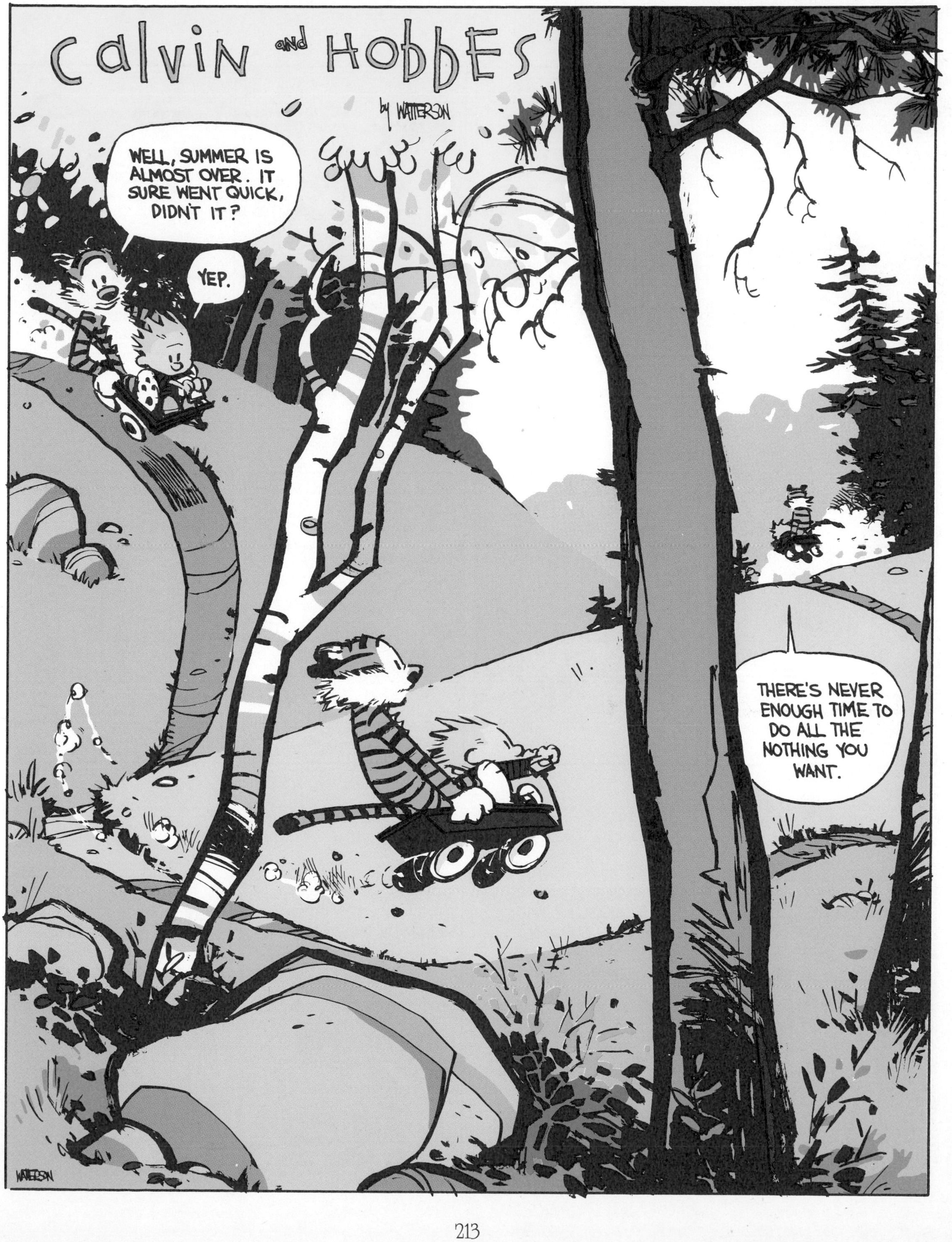
Calvin and HOBBES
by WATTERSON
WELL, SUMMER IS ALMOST OVER. IT SURE WENT QUICK, DIDN'T IT?
YEP.
THERE'S NEVER ENOUGH TIME TO DO ALL THE NOTHING YOU WANT.
WATTERSON

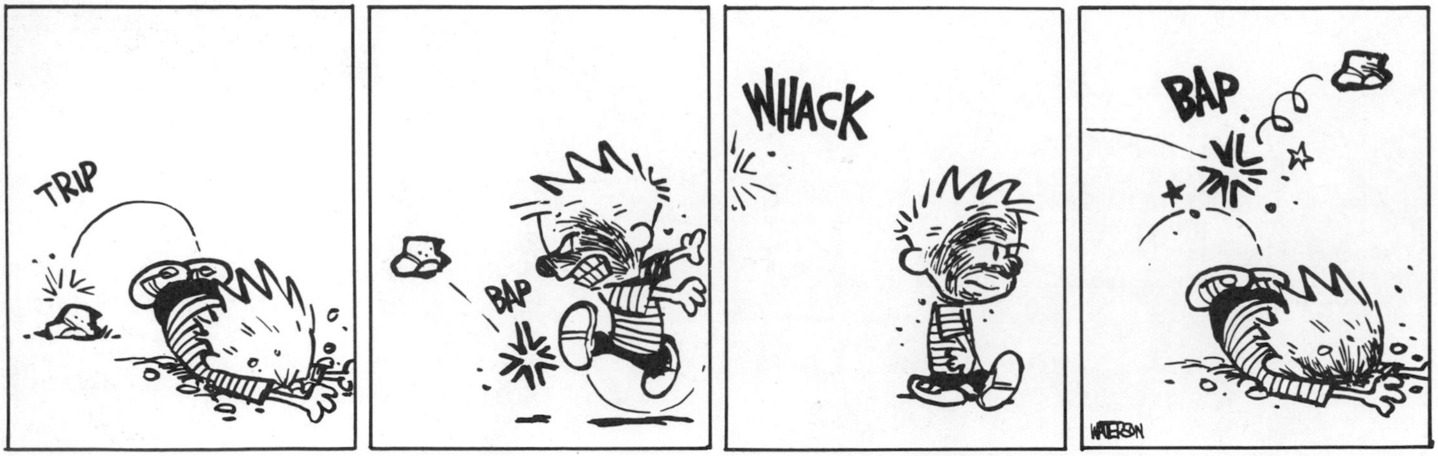
TRIP
BAP
WHACK
BAP
WATTERSON

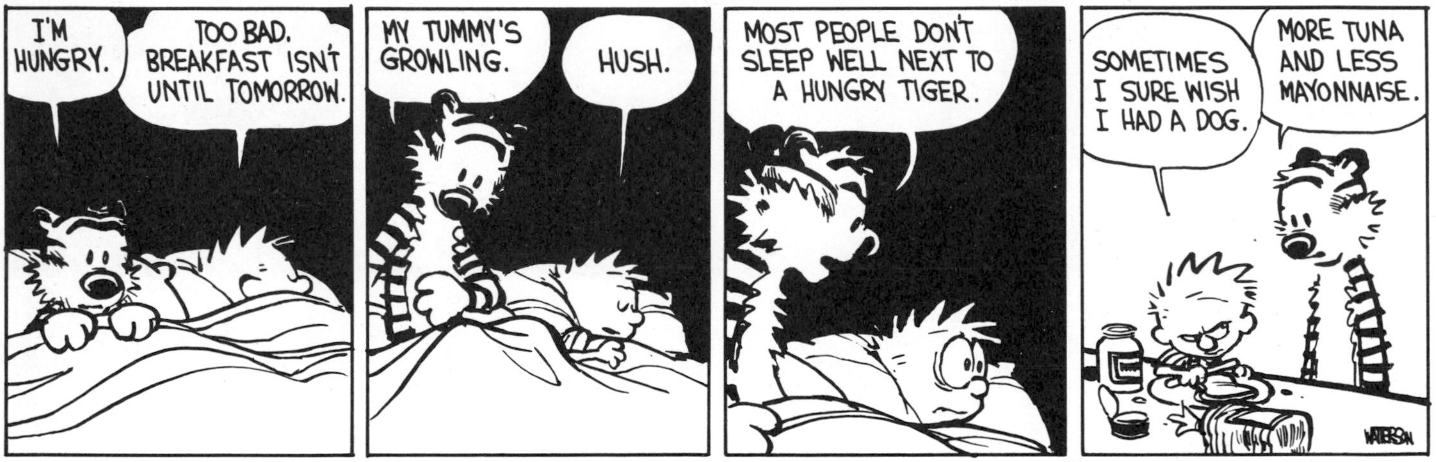
I'M HUNGRY.
TOO BAD. BREAKFAST ISN'T UNTIL TOMORROW.
MY TUMMY'S GROWLING.
HUSH.
MOST PEOPLE DON'T SLEEP WELL NEXT TO A HUNGRY TIGER.
SOMETIMES I SURE WISH I HAD A DOG.
MORE TUNA AND LESS MAYONNAISE.
WATTERSON

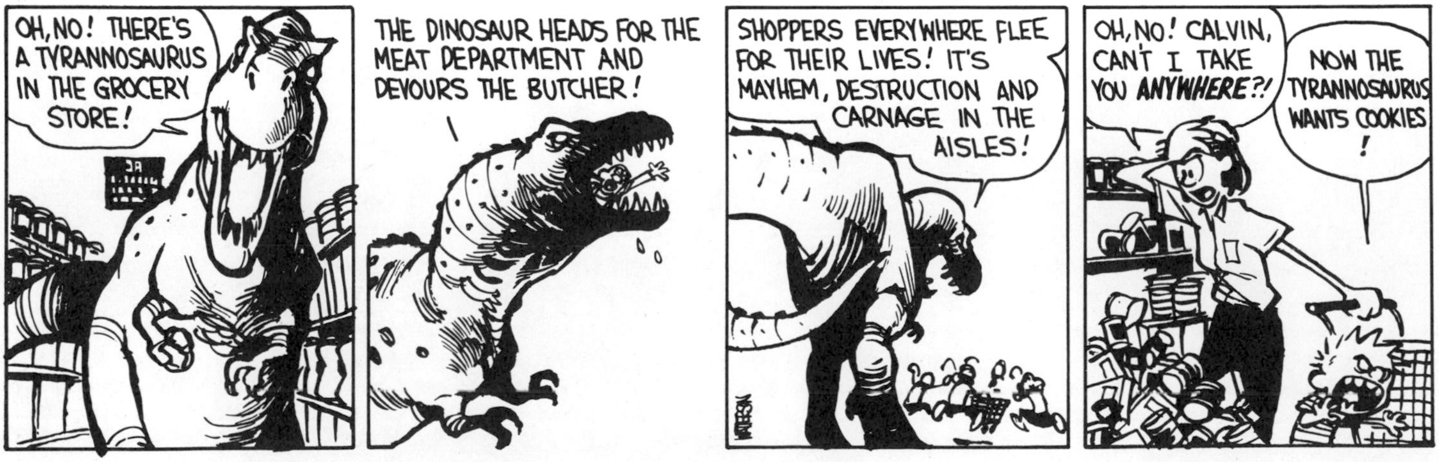
OH, NO! THERE'S A TYRANNOSAURUS IN THE GROCERY STORE!
THE DINOSAUR HEADS FOR THE MEAT DEPARTMENT AND DEVOURS THE BUTCHER!
SHOPPERS EVERYWHERE FLEE FOR THEIR LIVES! IT'S MAYHEM, DESTRUCTION AND CARNAGE IN THE AISLES!
WATTERSON
OH, NO! CALVIN, CAN'T I TAKE YOU ANYWHERE?!
NOW THE TYRANNOSAURUS WANTS COOKIES!

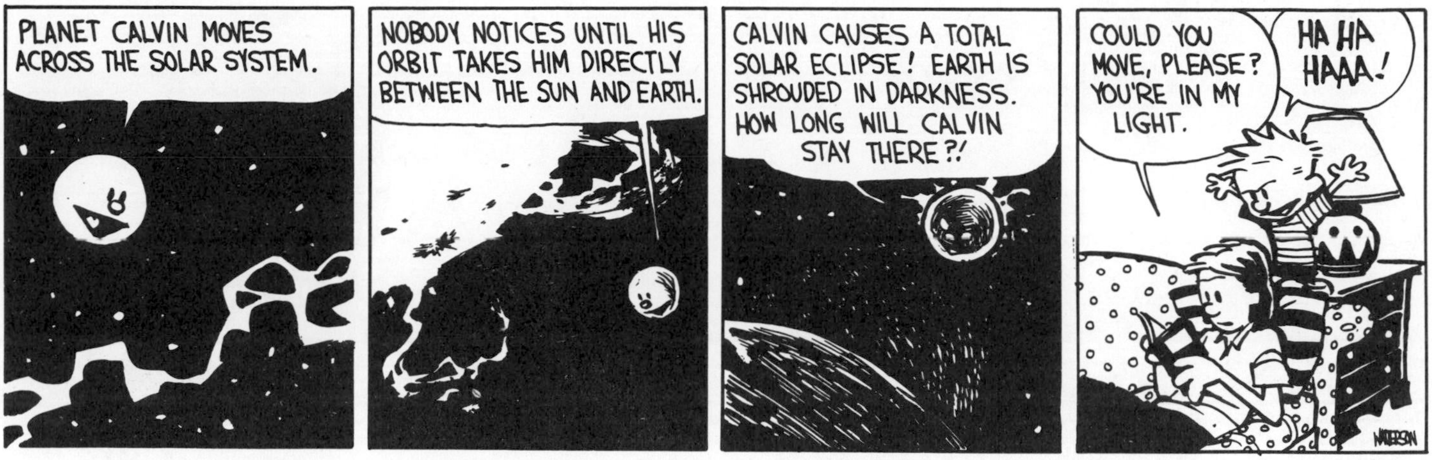
PLANET CALVIN MOVES ACROSS THE SOLAR SYSTEM.
NOBODY NOTICES UNTIL HIS ORBIT TAKES HIM DIRECTLY BETWEEN THE SUN AND EARTH.
CALVIN CAUSES A TOTAL SOLAR ECLIPSE! EARTH IS SHROUDED IN DARKNESS. HOW LONG WILL CALVIN STAY THERE?!
COULD YOU MOVE, PLEASE? YOU'RE IN MY LIGHT.
HA HA HAAA!
WATTERSON

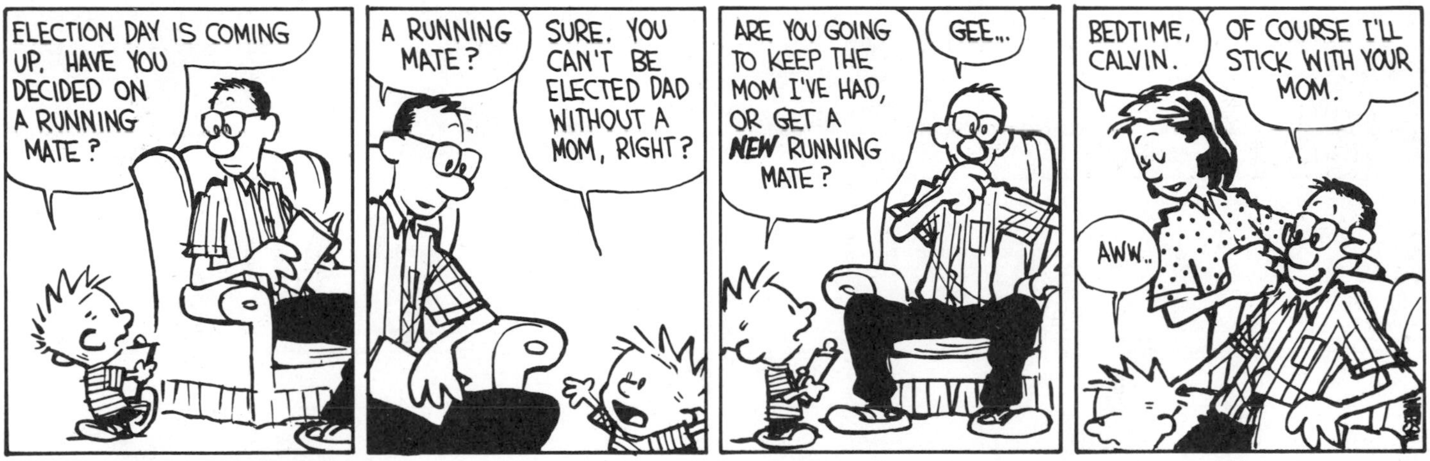
ELECTION DAY IS COMING UP. HAVE YOU DECIDED ON A RUNNING MATE?
A RUNNING MATE?
SURE. YOU CAN'T BE ELECTED DAD WITHOUT A MOM, RIGHT?
ARE YOU GOING TO KEEP THE MOM I'VE HAD, OR GET A NEW RUNNING MATE?
GEE...
BEDTIME, CALVIN.
OF COURSE I'LL STICK WITH YOUR MOM.
AWW..

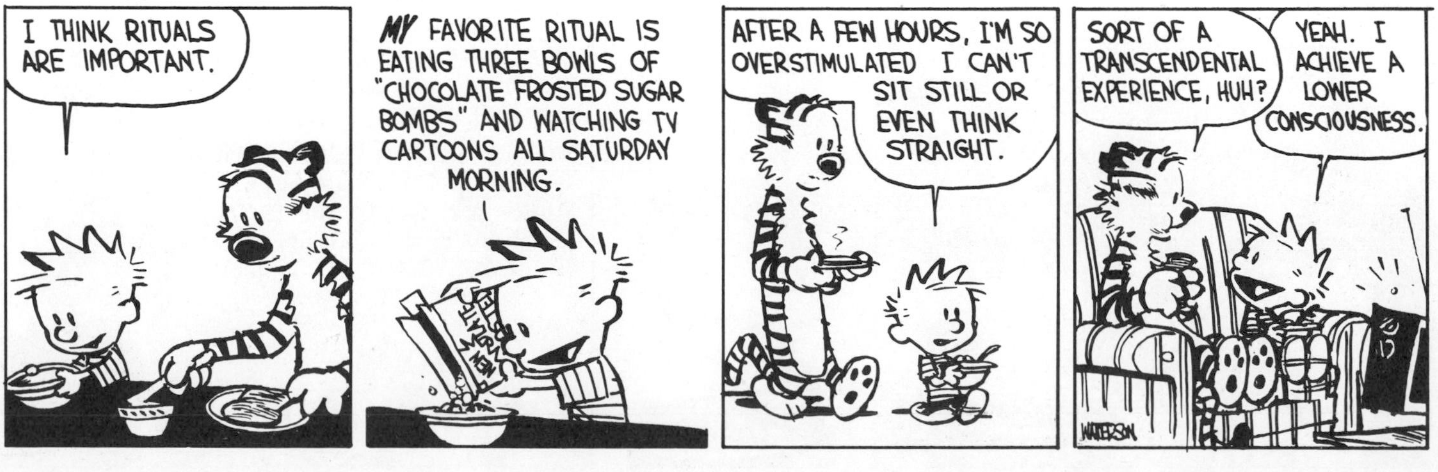
I THINK RITUALS ARE IMPORTANT.
MY FAVORITE RITUAL IS EATING THREE BOWLS OF "CHOCOLATE FROSTED SUGAR BOMBS" AND WATCHING TV CARTOONS ALL SATURDAY MORNING.
AFTER A FEW HOURS, I'M SO OVERSTIMULATED I CAN'T SIT STILL OR EVEN THINK STRAIGHT.
SORT OF A TRANSCENDENTAL EXPERIENCE, HUH?
YEAH. I ACHIEVE A LOWER CONSCIOUSNESS.
WATTERSON

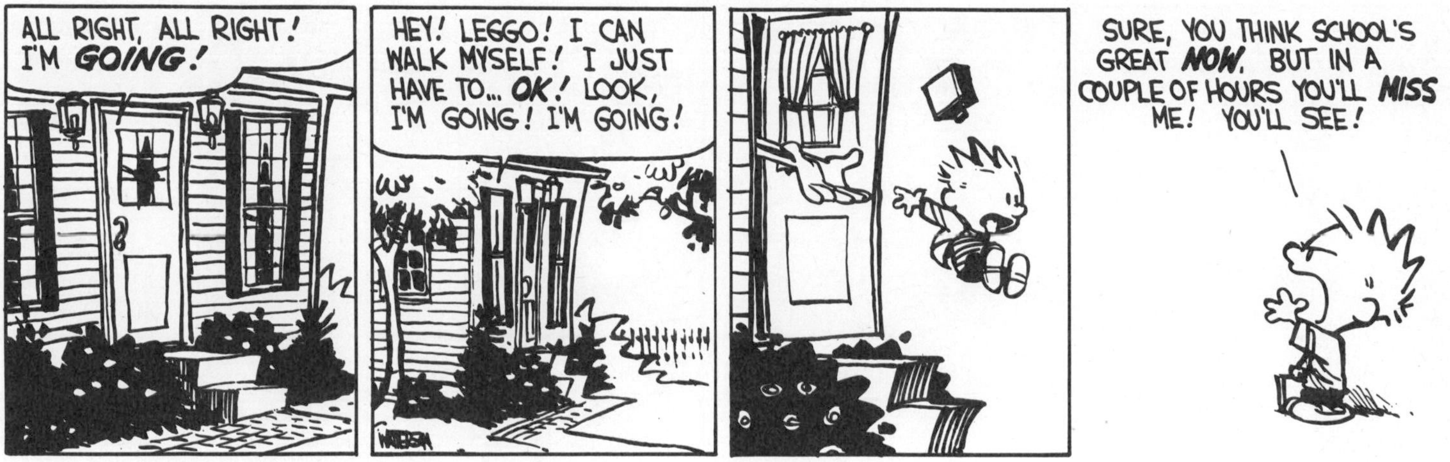
ALL RIGHT, ALL RIGHT! I'M GOING!
HEY! LEGGO! I CAN WALK MYSELF! I JUST HAVE TO... OK! LOOK, I'M GOING! I'M GOING!
SURE, YOU THINK SCHOOL'S GREAT NOW, BUT IN A COUPLE OF HOURS YOU'LL MISS ME! YOU'LL SEE!

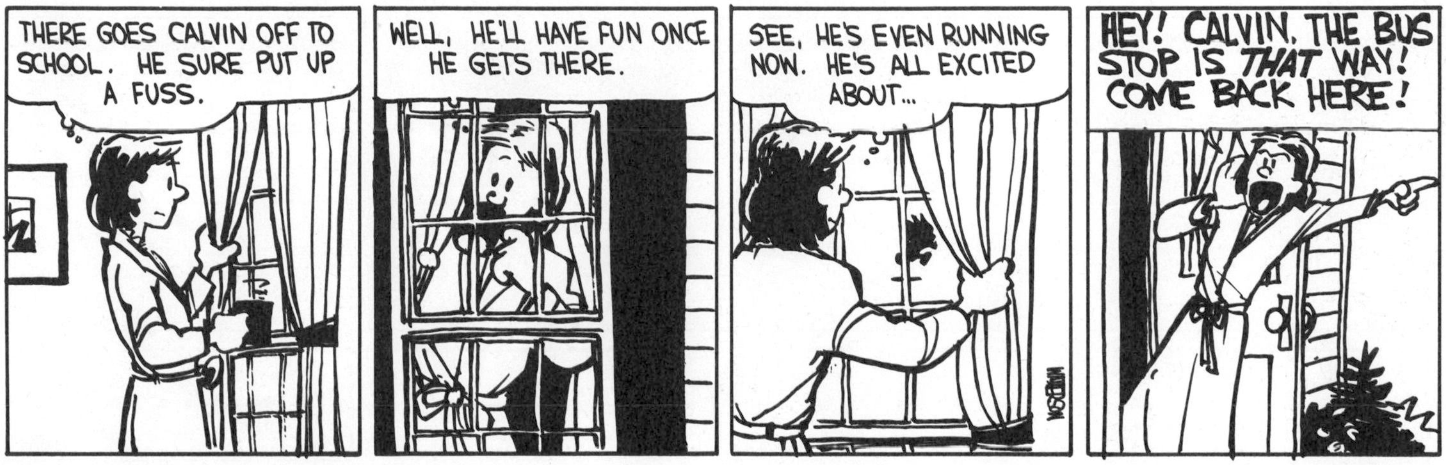
THERE GOES CALVIN OFF TO SCHOOL. HE SURE PUT UP A FUSS.
WELL, HE'LL HAVE FUN ONCE HE GETS THERE.
SEE, HE'S EVEN RUNNING NOW. HE'S ALL EXCITED ABOUT...
HEY! CALVIN, THE BUS STOP IS THAT WAY! COME BACK HERE!

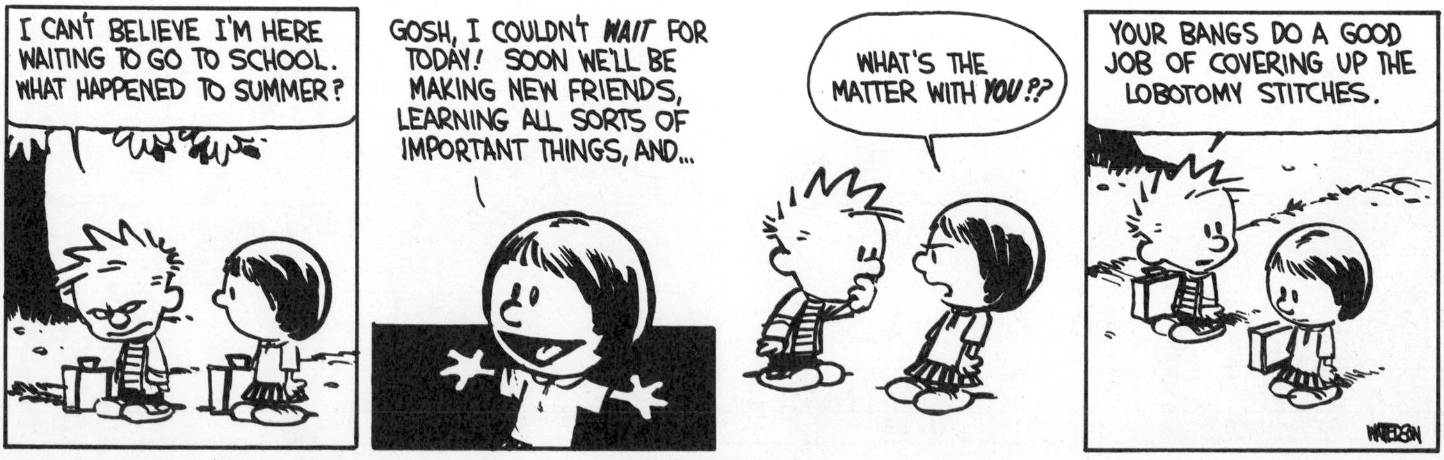
I CAN'T BELIEVE I'M HERE WAITING TO GO TO SCHOOL. WHAT HAPPENED TO SUMMER?
GOSH, I COULDN'T WAIT FOR TODAY! SOON WE'LL BE MAKING NEW FRIENDS, LEARNING ALL SORTS OF IMPORTANT THINGS, AND...
WHAT'S THE MATTER WITH YOU?!?
YOUR BANGS DO A GOOD JOB OF COVERING UP THE LOBOTOMY STITCHES.

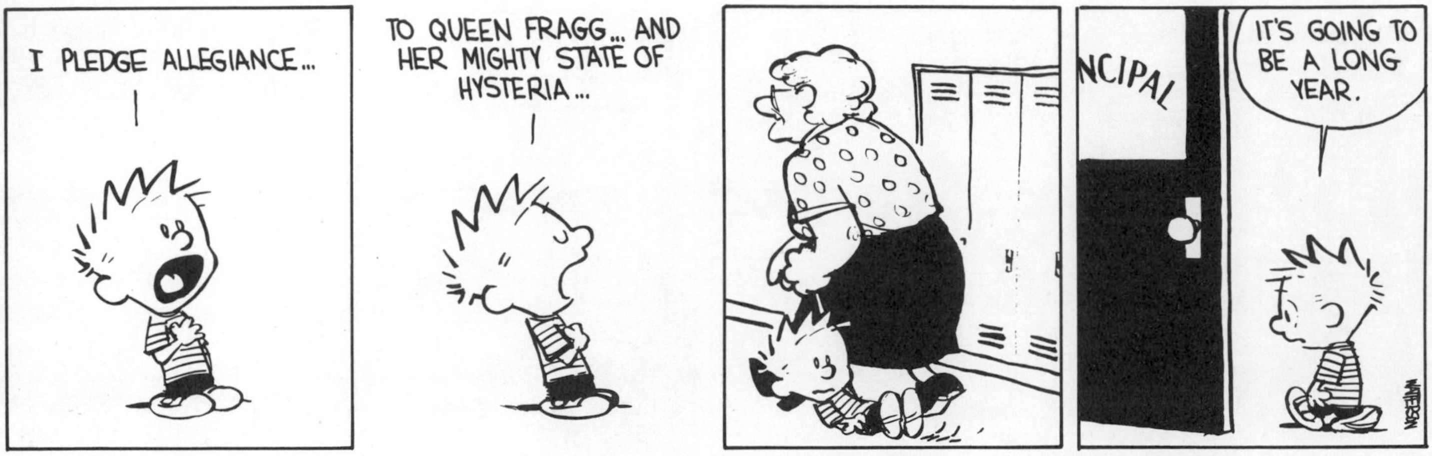
I PLEDGE ALLEGIANCE...
TO QUEEN FRAGG... AND HER MIGHTY STATE OF HYSTERIA...
NCIPAL
IT'S GOING TO BE A LONG YEAR.

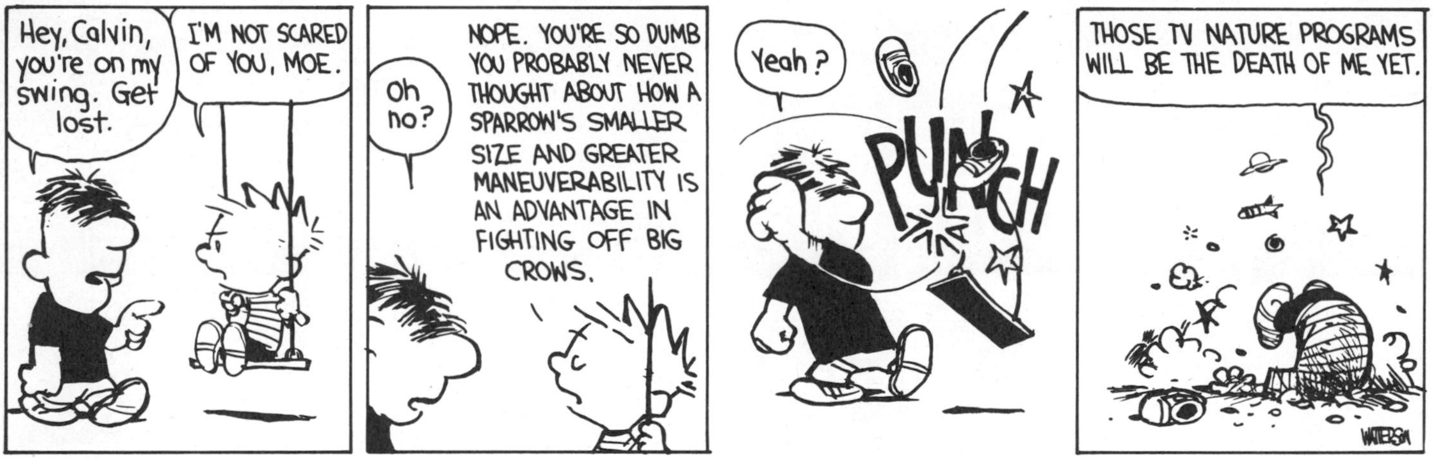
Hey, Calvin, you're on my swing. Get lost.
I'M NOT SCARED OF YOU, MOE.
Oh no?
NOPE. YOU'RE SO DUMB YOU PROBABLY NEVER THOUGHT ABOUT HOW A SPARROW'S SMALLER SIZE AND GREATER MANEUVERABILITY IS AN ADVANTAGE IN FIGHTING OFF BIG CROWS.
Yeah?
PUNCH
THOSE TV NATURE PROGRAMS WILL BE THE DEATH OF ME YET.

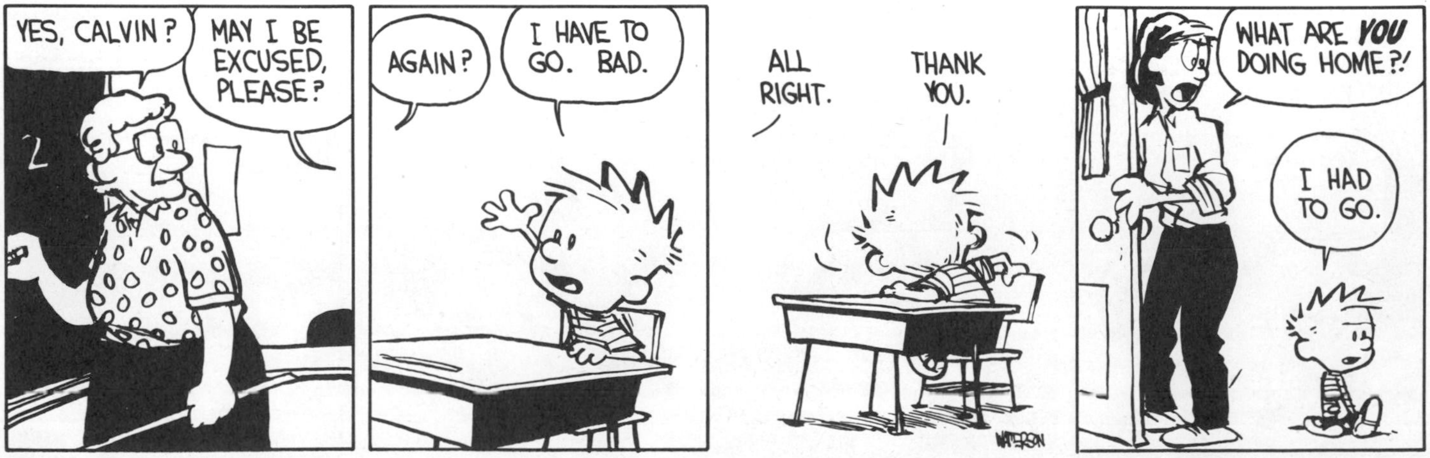
YES, CALVIN?
MAY I BE EXCUSED, PLEASE?
AGAIN?
I HAVE TO GO. BAD.
ALL RIGHT.
THANK YOU.
WHAT ARE YOU DOING HOME?!
I HAD TO GO.

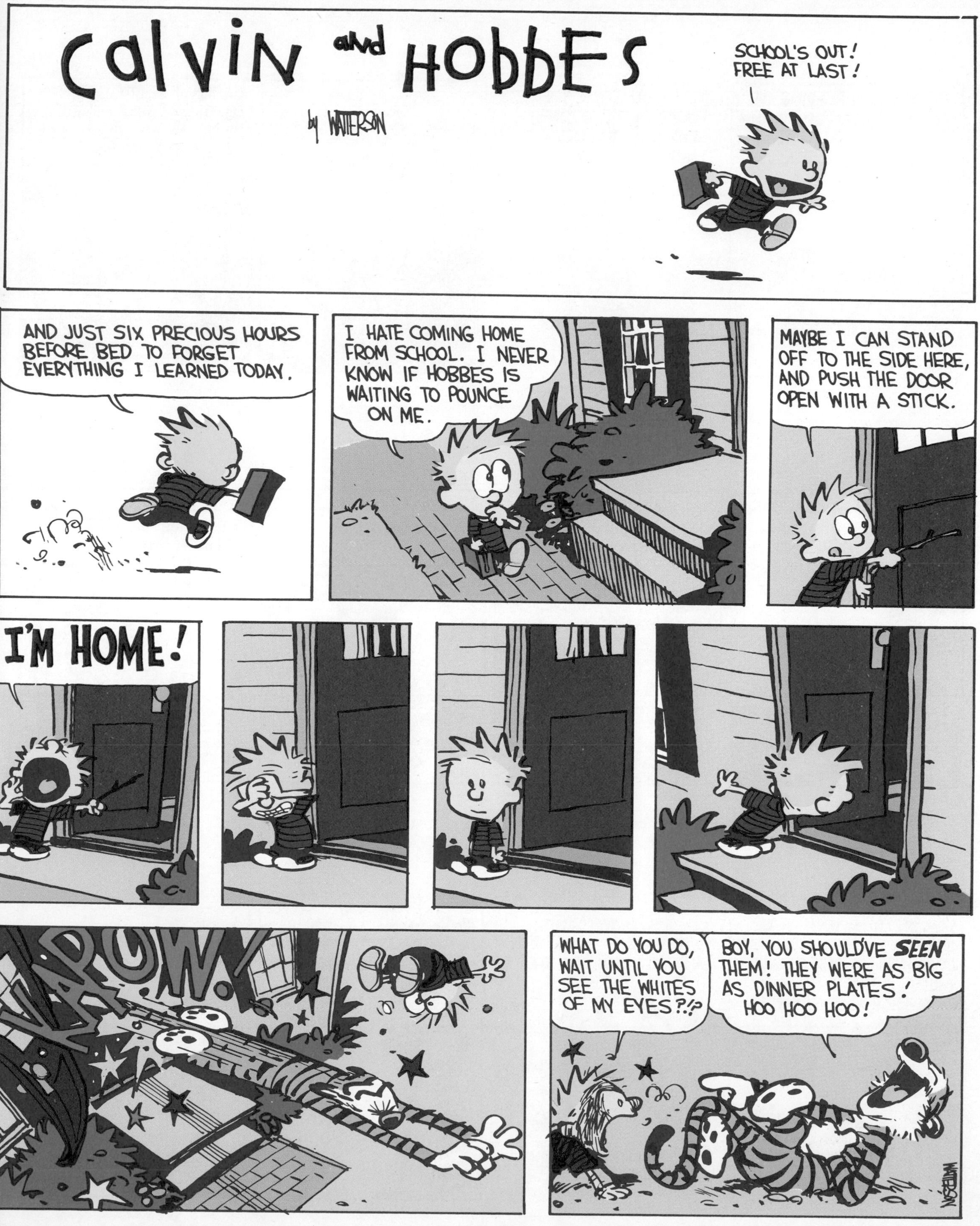
Calvin and HOBBES
by WATTERSON
SCHOOL'S OUT! FREE AT LAST!
AND JUST SIX PRECIOUS HOURS BEFORE BED TO FORGET EVERYTHING I LEARNED TODAY.
I HATE COMING HOME FROM SCHOOL. I NEVER KNOW IF HOBBES IS WAITING TO POUNCE ON ME.
MAYBE I CAN STAND OFF TO THE SIDE HERE, AND PUSH THE DOOR OPEN WITH A STICK.
I'M HOME!
WAPOW!
WHAT DO YOU DO, WAIT UNTIL YOU SEE THE WHITES OF MY EYES?!?
BOY, YOU SHOULD'VE SEEN THEM! THEY WERE AS BIG AS DINNER PLATES! HOO HOO HOO!
WATTERSON

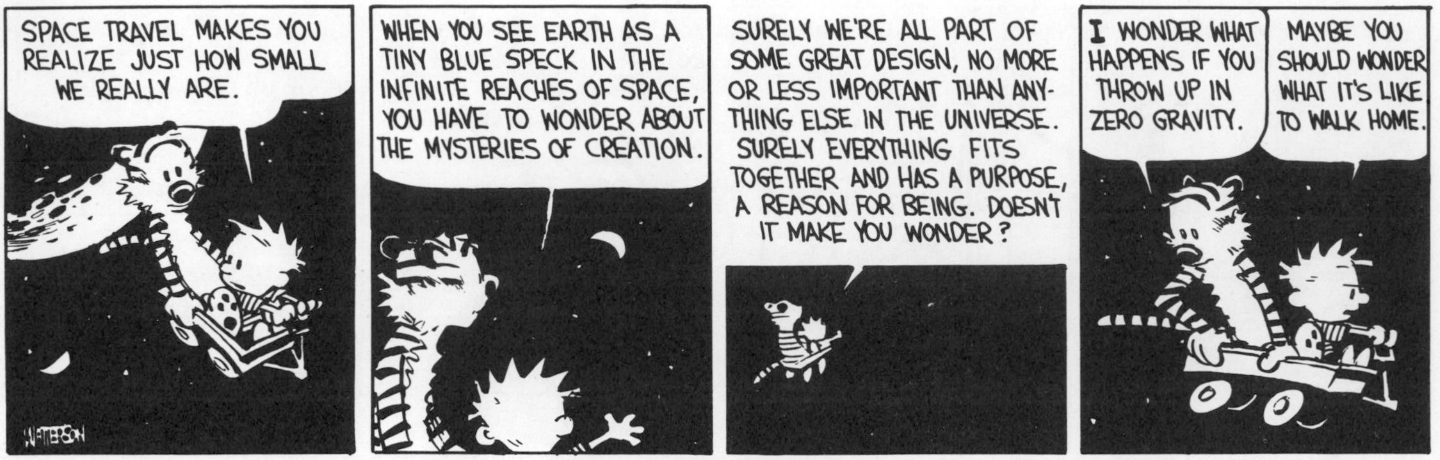

SPACE TRAVEL MAKES YOU REALIZE JUST HOW SMALL WE REALLY ARE.
WATTERSON
WHEN YOU SEE EARTH AS A TINY BLUE SPECK IN THE INFINITE REACHES OF SPACE, YOU HAVE TO WONDER ABOUT THE MYSTERIES OF CREATION.
SURELY WE'RE ALL PART OF SOME GREAT DESIGN, NO MORE OR LESS IMPORTANT THAN ANYTHING ELSE IN THE UNIVERSE. SURELY EVERYTHING FITS TOGETHER AND HAS A PURPOSE, A REASON FOR BEING. DOESN'T IT MAKE YOU WONDER?
I WONDER WHAT HAPPENS IF YOU THROW UP IN ZERO GRAVITY.
MAYBE YOU SHOULD WONDER WHAT IT'S LIKE TO WALK HOME.


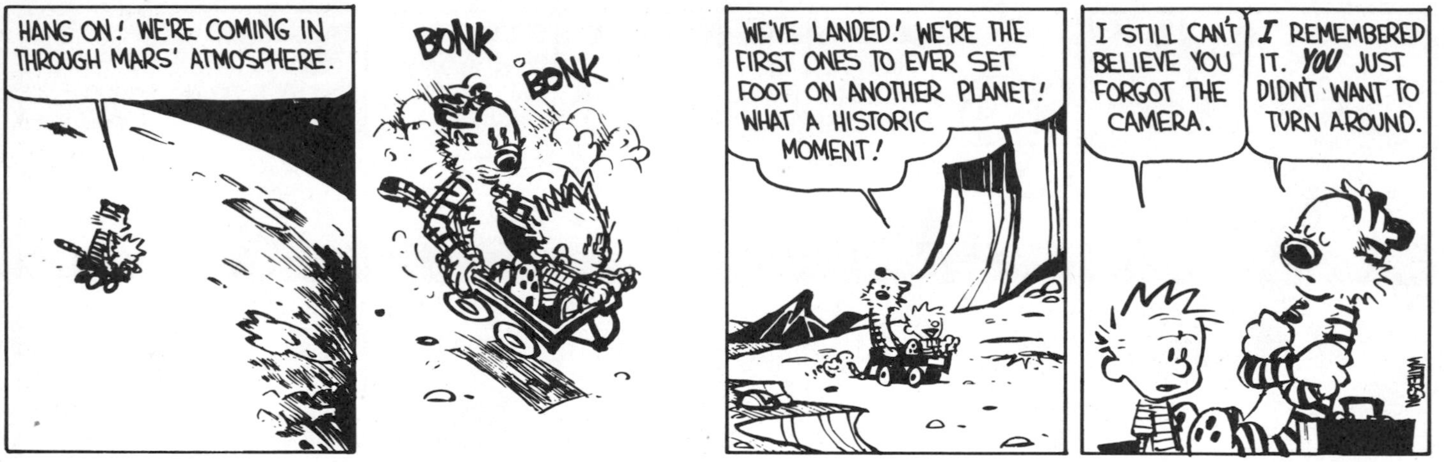

HANG ON! WE'RE COMING IN THROUGH MARS' ATMOSPHERE.
BONK
BONK
WE'VE LANDED! WE'RE THE FIRST ONES TO EVER SET FOOT ON ANOTHER PLANET! WHAT A HISTORIC MOMENT!
I STILL CAN'T BELIEVE YOU FORGOT THE CAMERA.
I REMEMBERED IT. YOU JUST DIDN'T WANT TO TURN AROUND.
WATTERSON


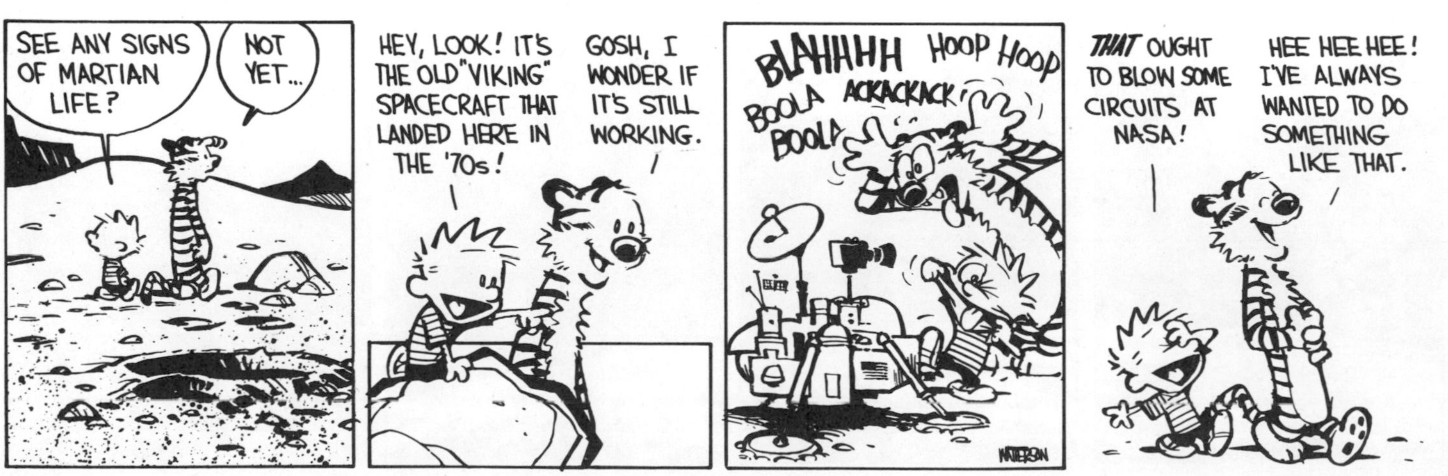

SEE ANY SIGNS OF MARTIAN LIFE?
NOT YET...
HEY, LOOK! IT'S THE OLD "VIKING" SPACECRAFT THAT LANDED HERE IN THE '70s!
GOSH, I WONDER IF IT'S STILL WORKING.
BLAHHHH HOOP HOOP
BOOLA ACKACKACK
BOOLA
WATTERSON
THAT OUGHT TO BLOW SOME CIRCUITS AT NASA!
HEE HEE HEE! I'VE ALWAYS WANTED TO DO SOMETHING LIKE THAT.

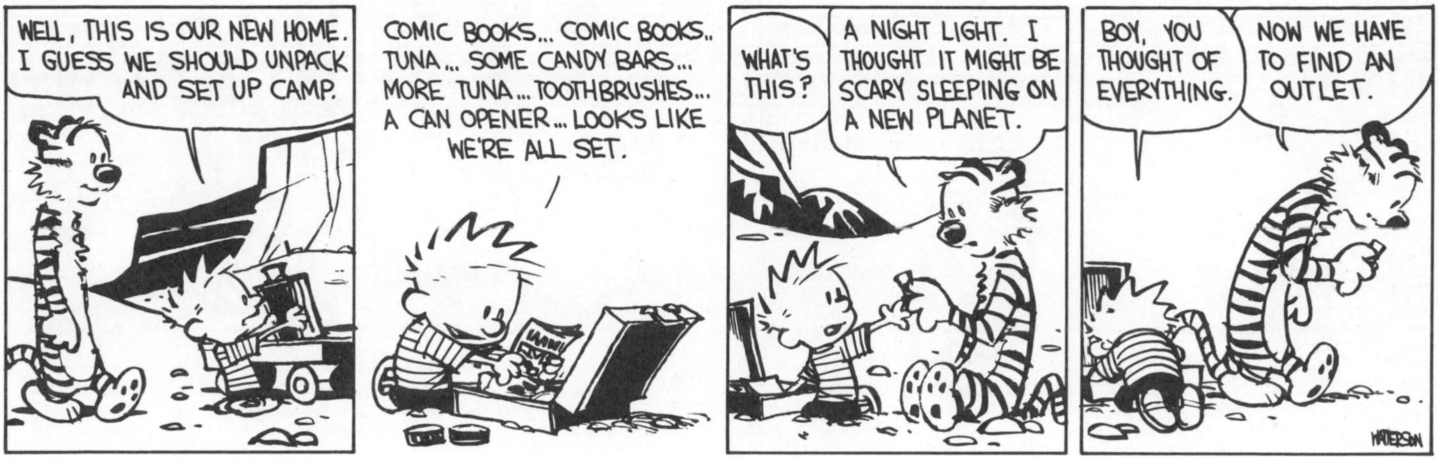
WELL, THIS IS OUR NEW HOME. I GUESS WE SHOULD UNPACK AND SET UP CAMP.
COMIC BOOKS... COMIC BOOKS.. TUNA... SOME CANDY BARS... MORE TUNA... TOOTHBRUSHES... A CAN OPENER... LOOKS LIKE WE'RE ALL SET.
WHAT'S THIS?
A NIGHT LIGHT. I THOUGHT IT MIGHT BE SCARY SLEEPING ON A NEW PLANET.
BOY, YOU THOUGHT OF EVERYTHING.
NOW WE HAVE TO FIND AN OUTLET.
WATTERSON

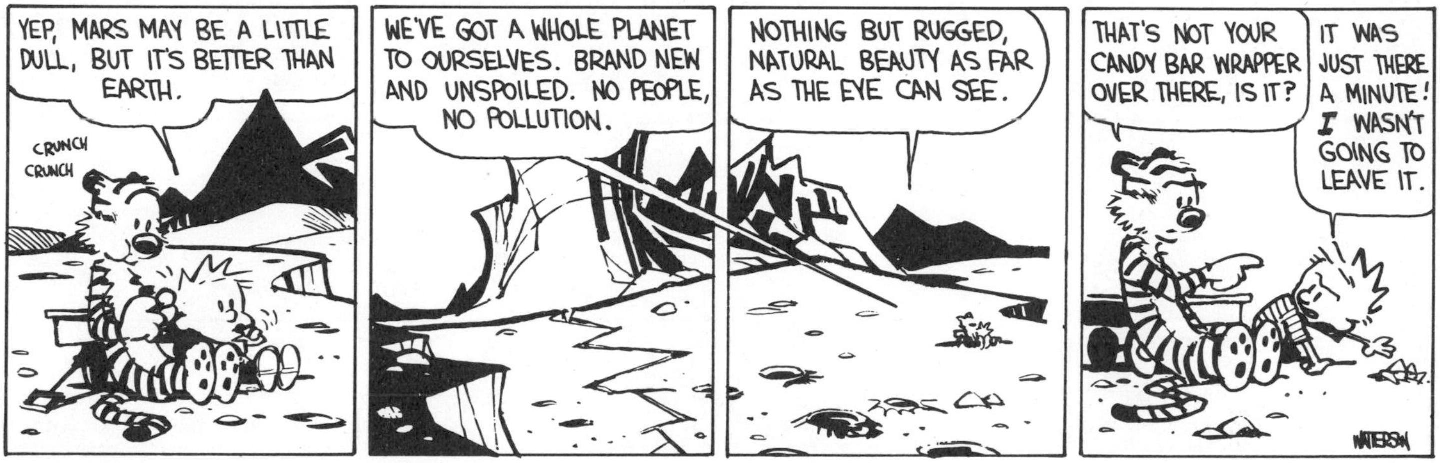
YEP, MARS MAY BE A LITTLE DULL, BUT IT'S BETTER THAN EARTH.
CRUNCH CRUNCH
WE'VE GOT A WHOLE PLANET TO OURSELVES. BRAND NEW AND UNSPOILED. NO PEOPLE, NO POLLUTION.
NOTHING BUT RUGGED, NATURAL BEAUTY AS FAR AS THE EYE CAN SEE.
THAT'S NOT YOUR CANDY BAR WRAPPER OVER THERE, IS IT?
IT WAS JUST THERE A MINUTE! I WASN'T GOING TO LEAVE IT.
WATTERSON

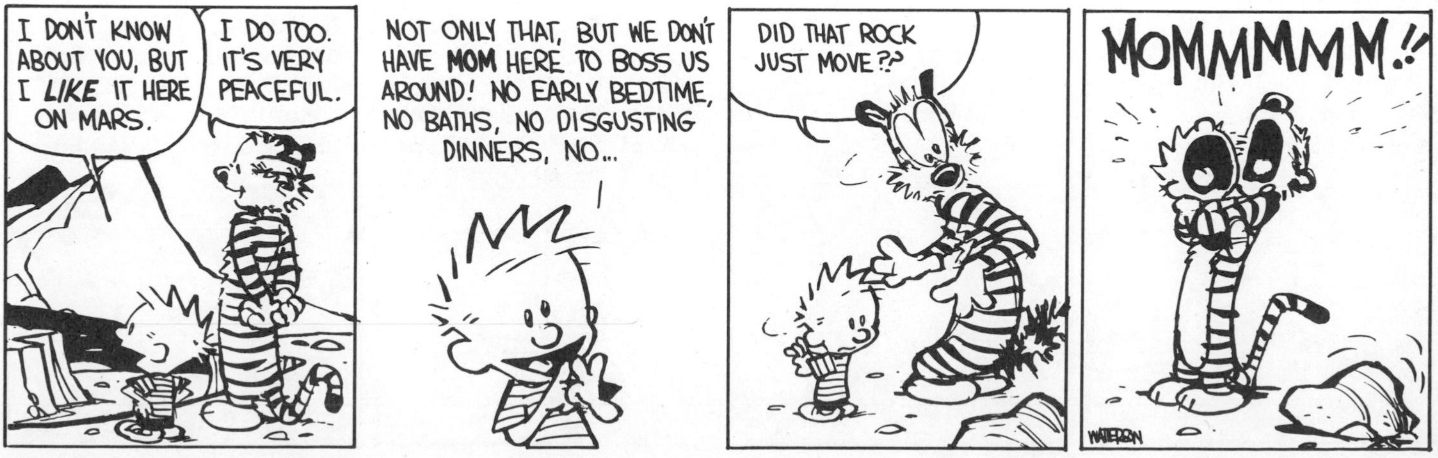
I DON'T KNOW ABOUT YOU, BUT I LIKE IT HERE ON MARS.
I DO TOO. IT'S VERY PEACEFUL.
NOT ONLY THAT, BUT WE DON'T HAVE MOM HERE TO BOSS US AROUND! NO EARLY BEDTIME, NO BATHS, NO DISGUSTING DINNERS, NO...
DID THAT ROCK JUST MOVE?!
MOMMMMM!!
WATTERSON

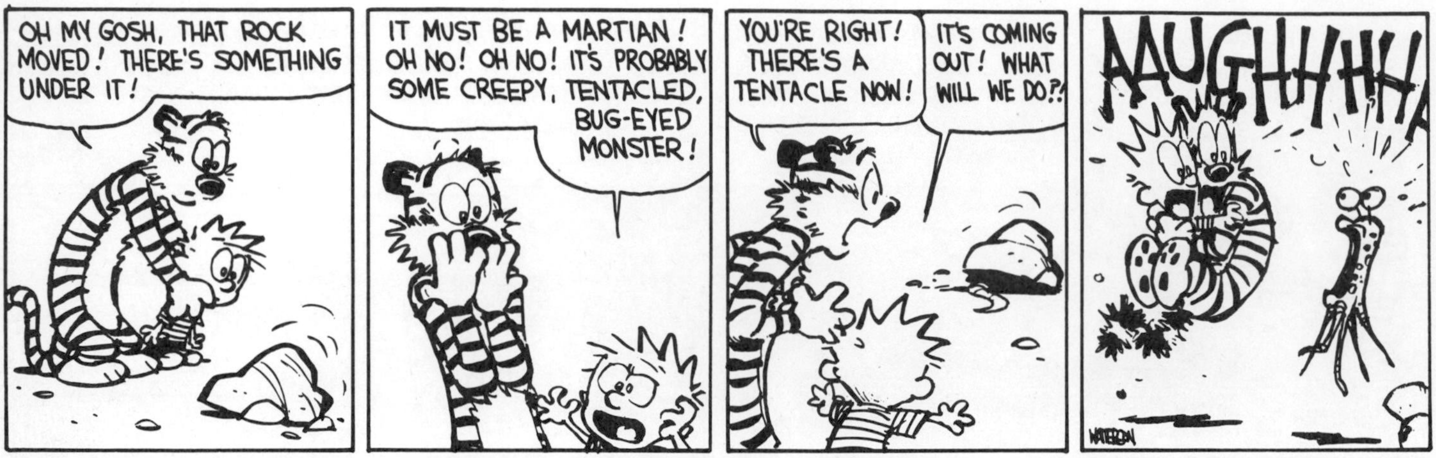
OH MY GOSH, THAT ROCK MOVED! THERE'S SOMETHING UNDER IT!
IT MUST BE A MARTIAN! OH NO! OH NO! IT'S PROBABLY SOME CREEPY, TENTACLED, BUG-EYED MONSTER!
YOU'RE RIGHT! THERE'S A TENTACLE NOW!
IT'S COMING OUT! WHAT WILL WE DO?!
AAUGHHHHHA
WATTERSON

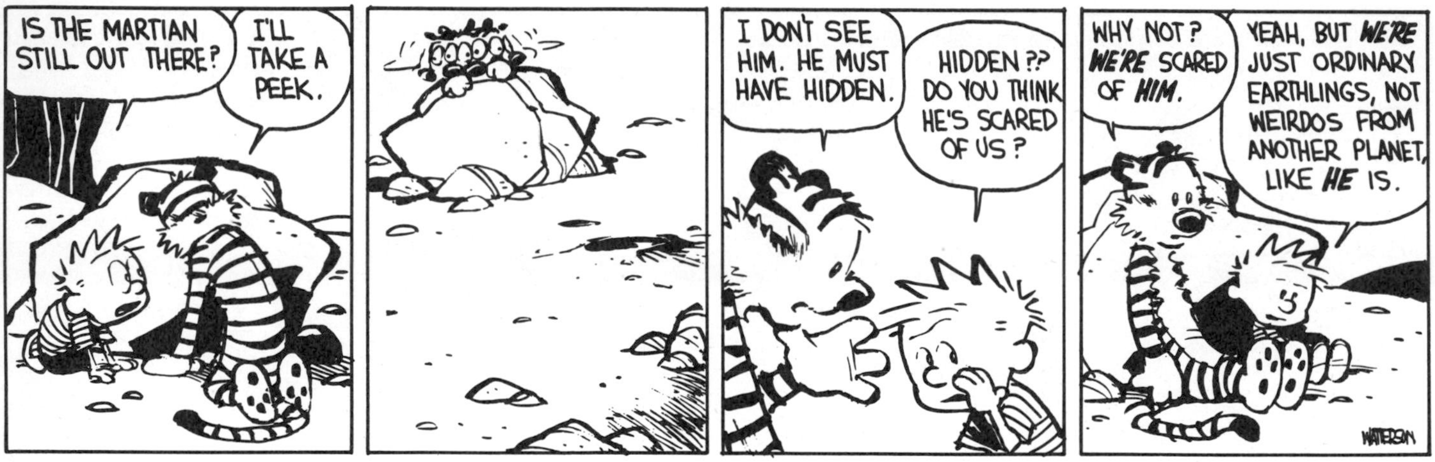
IS THE MARTIAN STILL OUT THERE?
I'LL TAKE A PEEK.
I DON'T SEE HIM. HE MUST HAVE HIDDEN.
HIDDEN ?? DO YOU THINK HE'S SCARED OF US?
WHY NOT? *WE'RE* SCARED OF *HIM*.
YEAH, BUT *WE'RE* JUST ORDINARY EARTHLINGS, NOT WEIRDOS FROM ANOTHER PLANET, LIKE *HE* IS.
WATTERSON

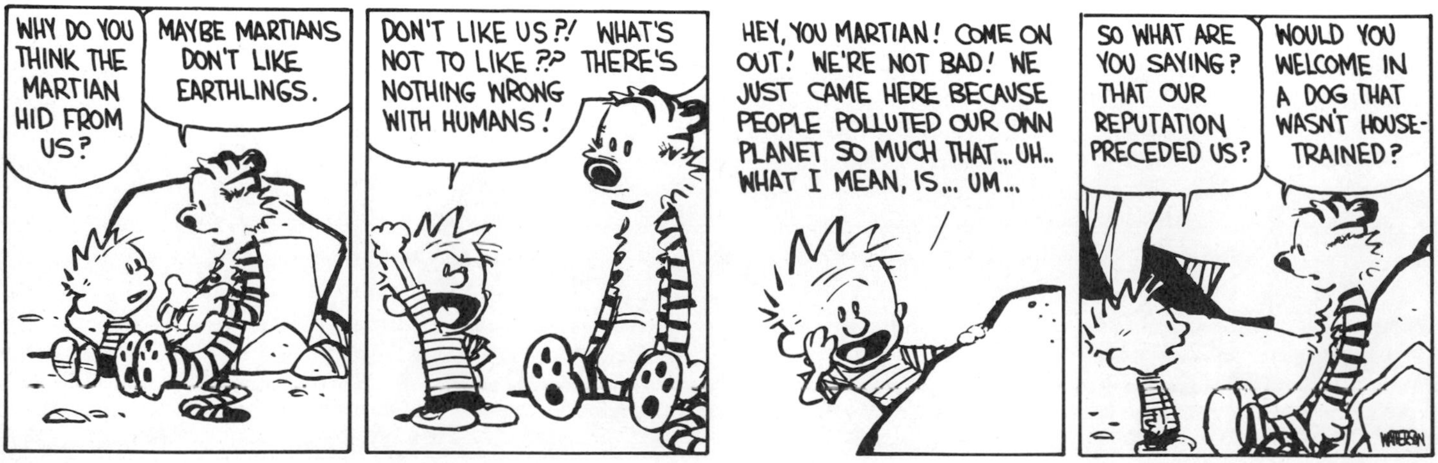
WHY DO YOU THINK THE MARTIAN HID FROM US?
MAYBE MARTIANS DON'T LIKE EARTHLINGS.
DON'T LIKE US?! WHAT'S NOT TO LIKE ?? THERE'S NOTHING WRONG WITH HUMANS!
HEY, YOU MARTIAN! COME ON OUT! WE'RE NOT BAD! WE JUST CAME HERE BECAUSE PEOPLE POLLUTED OUR OWN PLANET SO MUCH THAT... UH.. WHAT I MEAN, IS... UM...
SO WHAT ARE YOU SAYING? THAT OUR REPUTATION PRECEDED US?
WOULD YOU WELCOME IN A DOG THAT WASN'T HOUSE-TRAINED?
WATTERSON

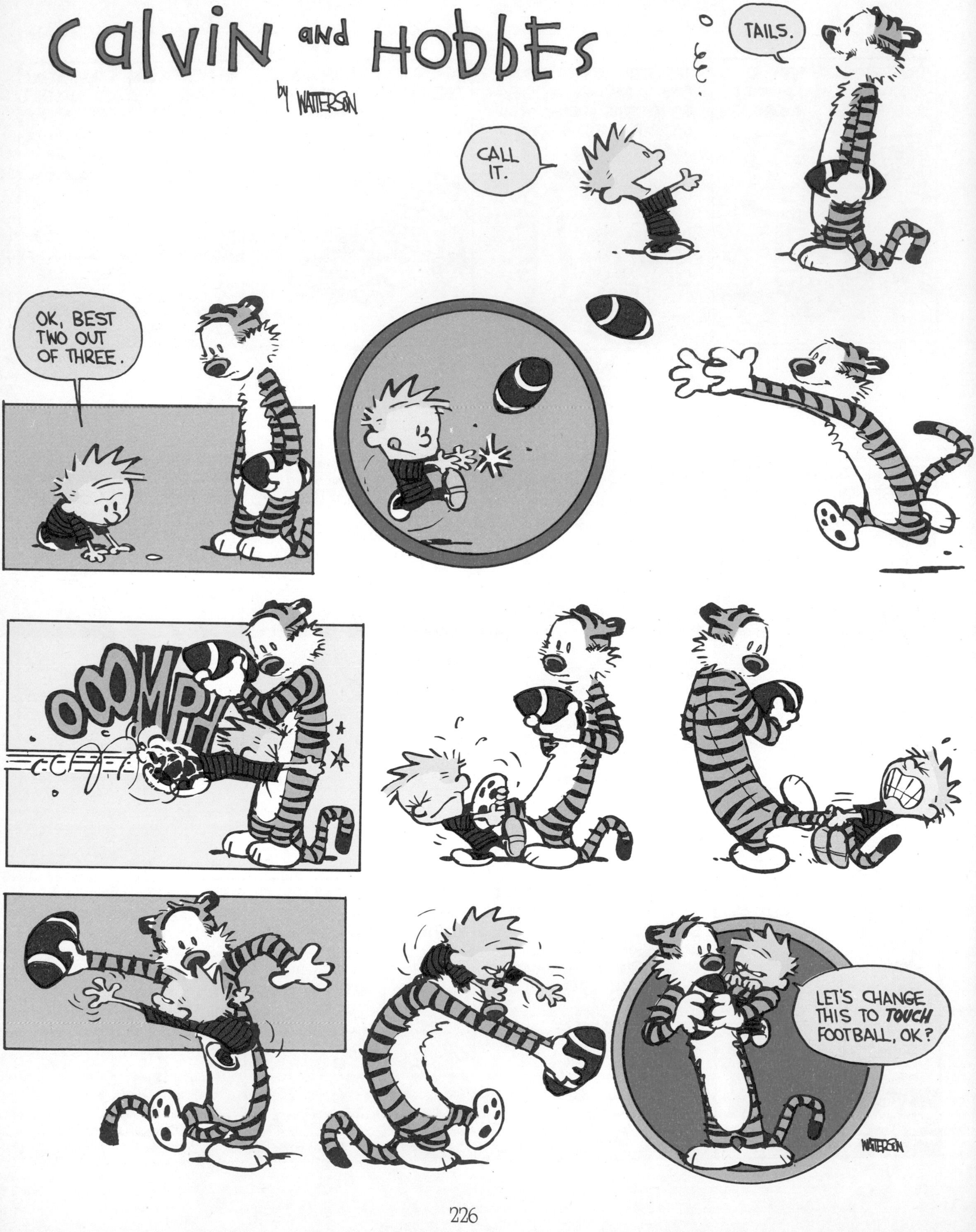
Calvin and HOBBES
by WATTERSON
CALL IT.
TAILS.
OK, BEST TWO OUT OF THREE.
OOOMPH
LET'S CHANGE THIS TO *TOUCH* FOOTBALL, OK?
WATTERSON

**Panel 1:** HI SUSIE! GUESS WHAT I BROUGHT FOR LUNCH.

**Panel 2:** NO! GO SIT BY SOMEONE ELSE, OK? YOU ALWAYS SAY YOUR LUNCH IS SOMETHING REVOLTING, AND I DON'T WANT TO HEAR IT!

**Panel 3:** GEE WHIZ, WHAT'S WRONG WITH YOU? MY LUNCH IS PEANUT BUTTER. WHAT'S SO DISGUSTING ABOUT THAT?!

**Panel 4:** HMPH. I'M GLAD THAT ONE DAY OUT OF THE YEAR YOU CAN BE CIVIL.

IT'S MY *DESSERT* THAT'S GROSS! LOOK, A THERMOS FULL OF PHLEGM!

**Panel 5:** CALVIN, WILL YOU RUN AND GET MY PURSE, PLEASE? I NEED THE CALCULATOR.

SURE.

**Panel 6:** HERE YOU ARE.

THANKS.

**Panel 7:** AHEM.

**Panel 8:** I'M NOT GOING TO TIP YOU!!

HUH! SEE IF I EVER FETCH ANYTHING AGAIN.

**Panel 9:** ELECTION DAY IS COMING UP, DAD. PEOPLE WANT TO KNOW WHERE YOU STAND ON THE ISSUES.

**Panel 10:** SUCH AS?

LATER BEDTIMES, EXPANDED TV PRIVILEGES, SHORTER SCHOOL WEEKS, AND LESS DISCIPLINE.

**Panel 11:** I'M AGAINST THEM ALL.

I SEE.

**Panel 12:** HOW'S YOUR IRA? PRETTY WELL FUNDED?

GO TO BED.

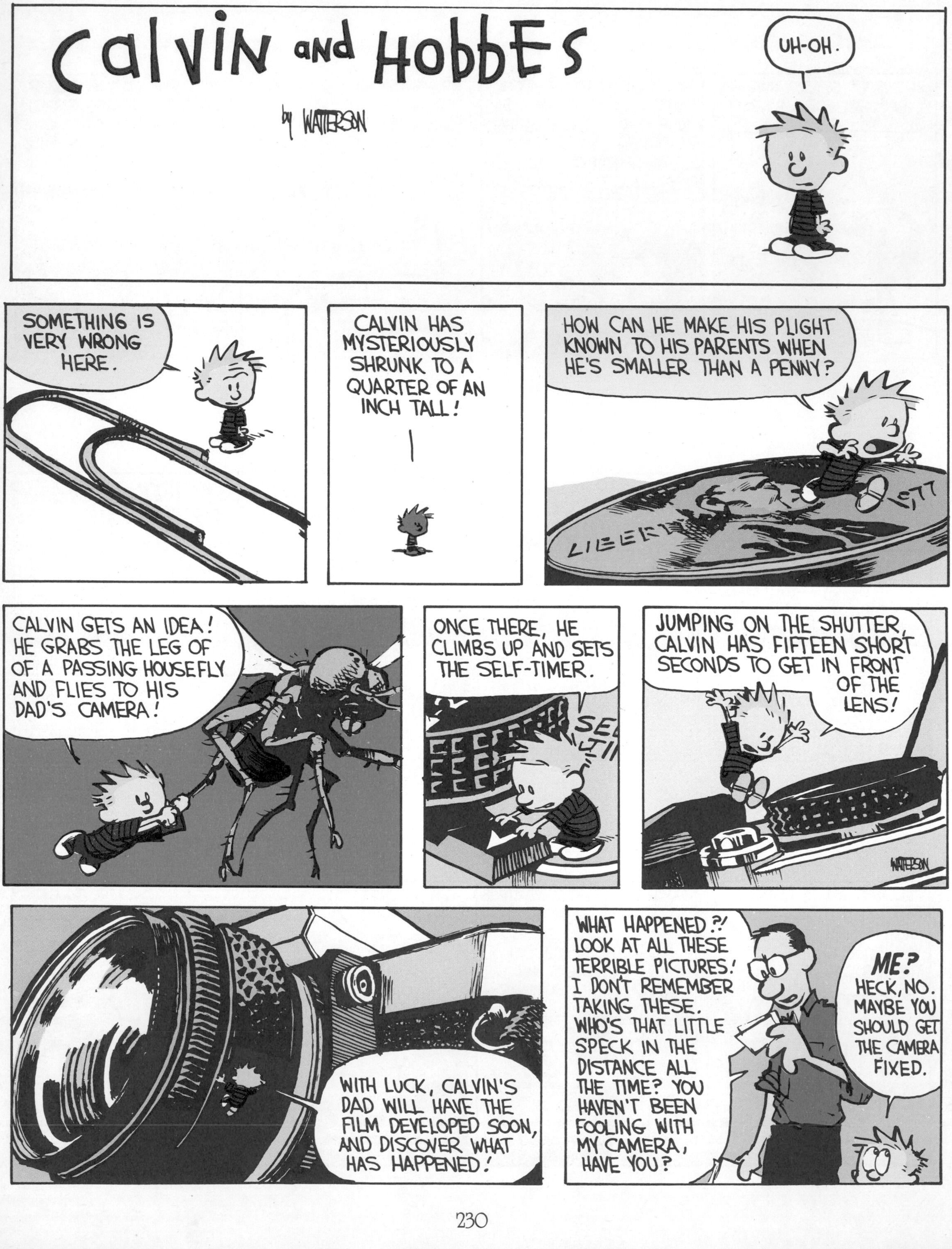
Calvin and Hobbes
by WATTERSON
UH-OH.
SOMETHING IS VERY WRONG HERE.
CALVIN HAS MYSTERIOUSLY SHRUNK TO A QUARTER OF AN INCH TALL!
HOW CAN HE MAKE HIS PLIGHT KNOWN TO HIS PARENTS WHEN HE'S SMALLER THAN A PENNY?
LIBERTY
CALVIN GETS AN IDEA! HE GRABS THE LEG OF OF A PASSING HOUSEFLY AND FLIES TO HIS DAD'S CAMERA!
ONCE THERE, HE CLIMBS UP AND SETS THE SELF-TIMER.
JUMPING ON THE SHUTTER, CALVIN HAS FIFTEEN SHORT SECONDS TO GET IN FRONT OF THE LENS!
WATTERSON
WITH LUCK, CALVIN'S DAD WILL HAVE THE FILM DEVELOPED SOON, AND DISCOVER WHAT HAS HAPPENED!
WHAT HAPPENED?! LOOK AT ALL THESE TERRIBLE PICTURES! I DON'T REMEMBER TAKING THESE. WHO'S THAT LITTLE SPECK IN THE DISTANCE ALL THE TIME? YOU HAVEN'T BEEN FOOLING WITH MY CAMERA, HAVE YOU?
ME? HECK, NO. MAYBE YOU SHOULD GET THE CAMERA FIXED.

I THINK THE WORST OF THIS IS OVER, SO JUST TRY TO GET SOME SLEEP.

I'M GOING BACK TO BED, BUT GIVE ME A CALL IF YOU FEEL SICK AGAIN, OK? NOW GET SOME REST.

MM HMM.

POOR LITTLE KID.

YECCHHH! THERE IS NOTHING WORSE THAN A SICK ROOMMATE! FACE *THAT* WAY!

IT'S SCARY BEING SICK... ESPECIALLY AT NIGHT.

WHAT IF SOMETHING IS *REALLY* WRONG WITH ME, AND I HAVE TO GO TO THE HOSPITAL??

WHAT IF THEY STICK ME FULL OF TUBES AND HOSES? WHAT IF THEY HAVE TO OPERATE? WHAT IF THE OPERATION FAILS? WHAT IF THIS IS MY... MY... LAST NIGHT... *ALIVE??*

THEN I CAN LOOK FORWARD TO HAVING THE BED TO MYSELF TOMORROW.

FEW THINGS ARE LESS COMFORTING THAN A TIGER WHO'S UP TOO LATE.

FEELING ANY BETTER THIS MORNING, CALVIN?

NO.

I GUESS I'D BETTER MAKE YOU AN APPOINTMENT WITH THE DOCTOR.

OK.

IT'S SATURDAY, BY THE WAY. YOU WON'T MISS SCHOOL.

I KNOW.

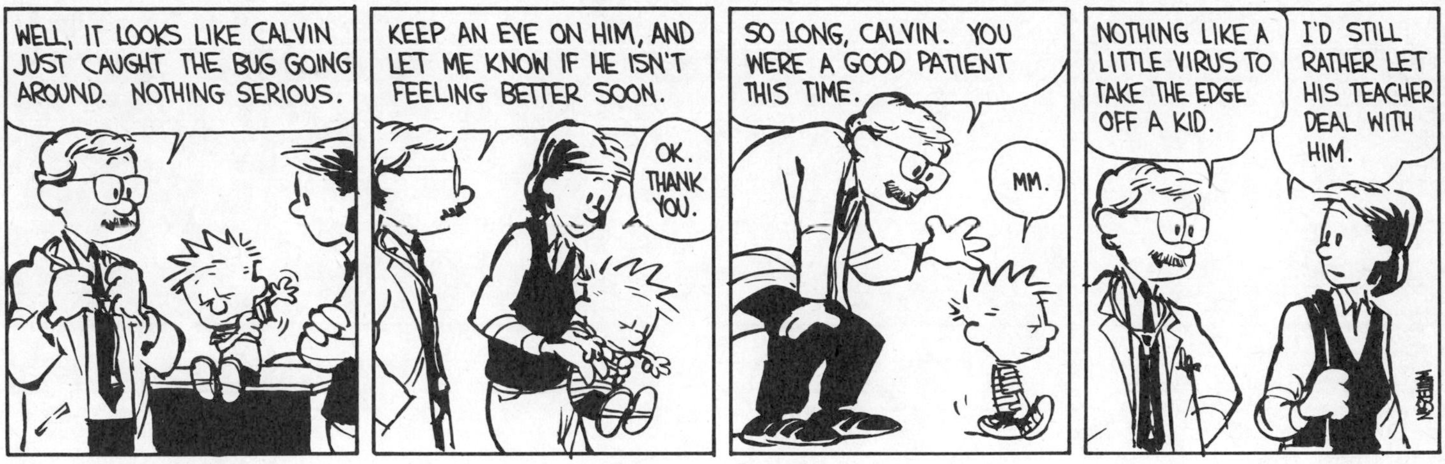
WELL, IT LOOKS LIKE CALVIN JUST CAUGHT THE BUG GOING AROUND. NOTHING SERIOUS.
KEEP AN EYE ON HIM, AND LET ME KNOW IF HE ISN'T FEELING BETTER SOON.
OK. THANK YOU.
SO LONG, CALVIN. YOU WERE A GOOD PATIENT THIS TIME.
MM.
NOTHING LIKE A LITTLE VIRUS TO TAKE THE EDGE OFF A KID.
I'D STILL RATHER LET HIS TEACHER DEAL WITH HIM.

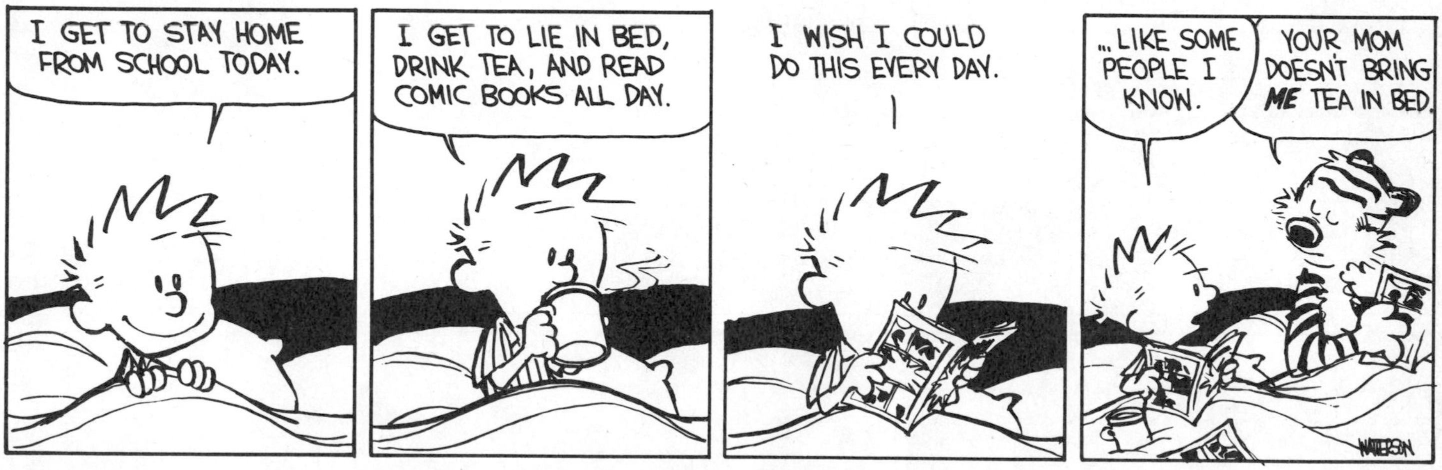
I GET TO STAY HOME FROM SCHOOL TODAY.
I GET TO LIE IN BED, DRINK TEA, AND READ COMIC BOOKS ALL DAY.
I WISH I COULD DO THIS EVERY DAY.
...LIKE SOME PEOPLE I KNOW.
YOUR MOM DOESN'T BRING ME TEA IN BED.

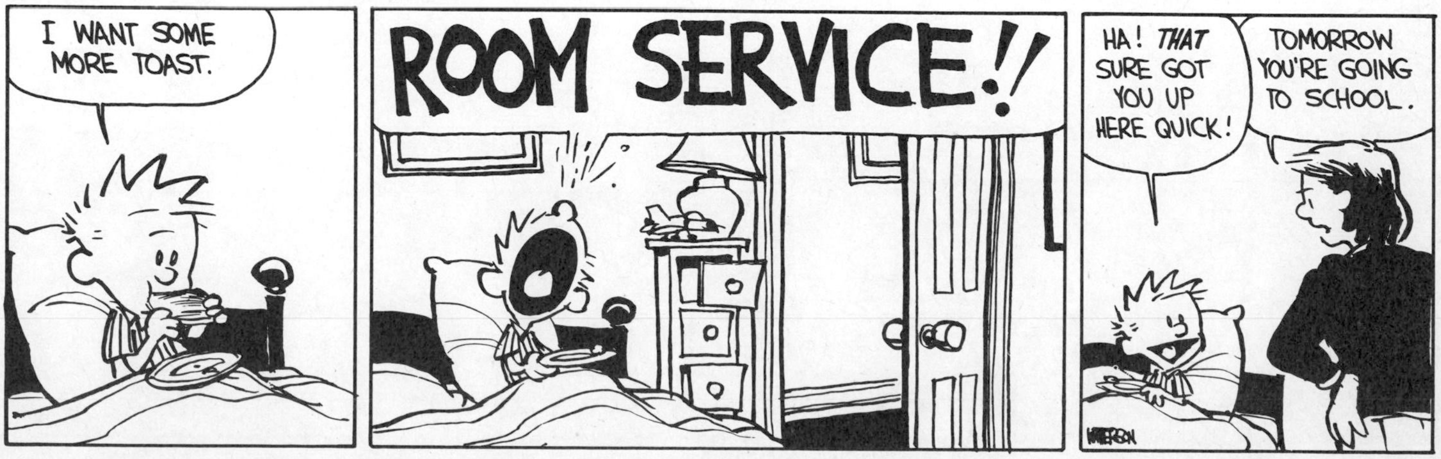
I WANT SOME MORE TOAST.
ROOM SERVICE!!
HA! THAT SURE GOT YOU UP HERE QUICK!
TOMORROW YOU'RE GOING TO SCHOOL.

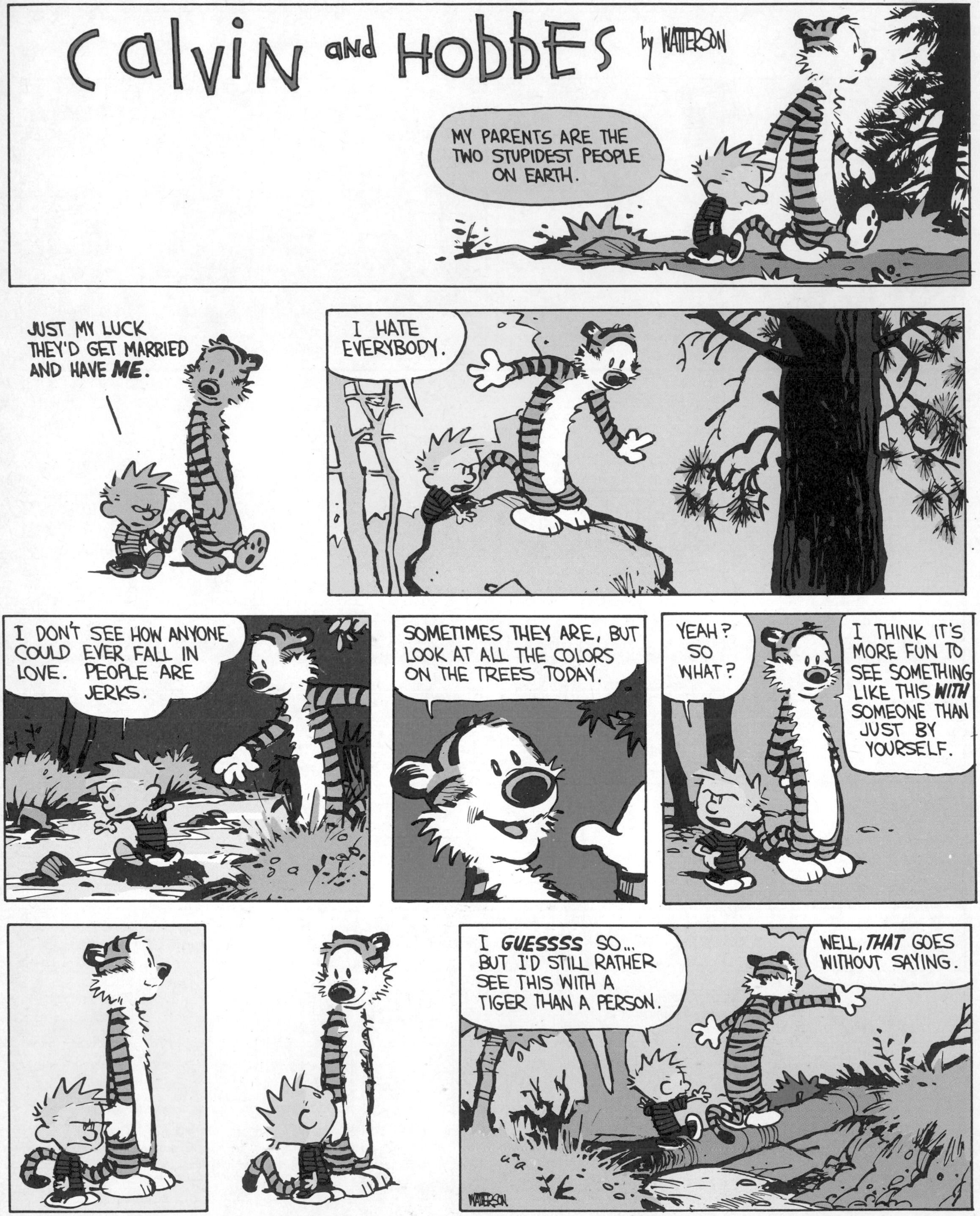
Calvin and HOBBES by WATTERSON
MY PARENTS ARE THE TWO STUPIDEST PEOPLE ON EARTH.
JUST MY LUCK THEY'D GET MARRIED AND HAVE ME.
I HATE EVERYBODY.
I DON'T SEE HOW ANYONE COULD EVER FALL IN LOVE. PEOPLE ARE JERKS.
SOMETIMES THEY ARE, BUT LOOK AT ALL THE COLORS ON THE TREES TODAY.
YEAH? SO WHAT?
I THINK IT'S MORE FUN TO SEE SOMETHING LIKE THIS WITH SOMEONE THAN JUST BY YOURSELF.
I GUESSSS SO... BUT I'D STILL RATHER SEE THIS WITH A TIGER THAN A PERSON.
WELL, THAT GOES WITHOUT SAYING.
WATTERSON

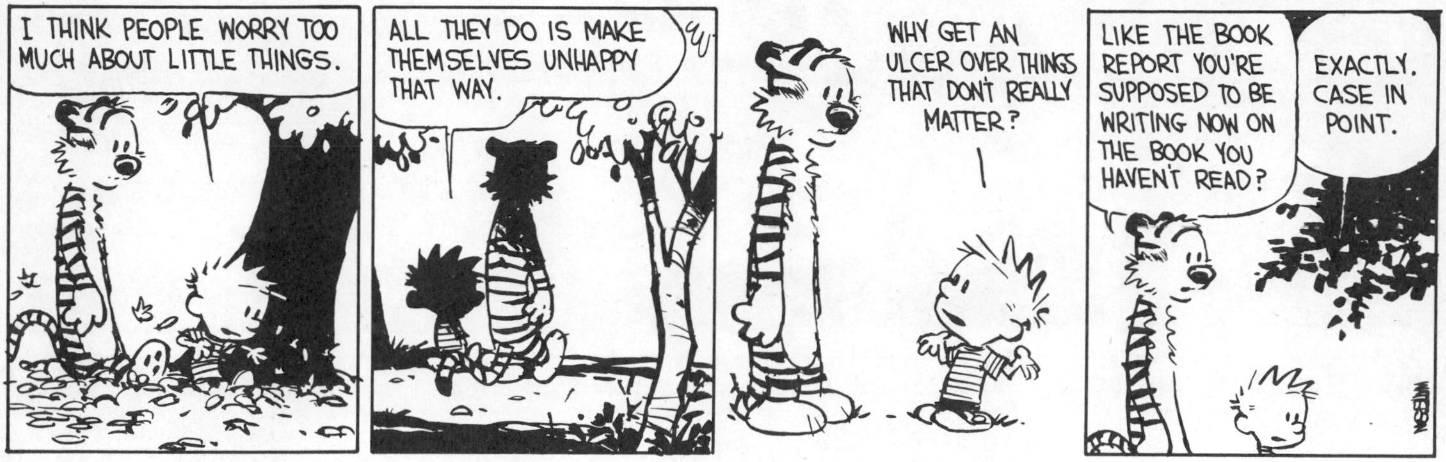
I THINK PEOPLE WORRY TOO MUCH ABOUT LITTLE THINGS.
ALL THEY DO IS MAKE THEMSELVES UNHAPPY THAT WAY.
WHY GET AN ULCER OVER THINGS THAT DON'T REALLY MATTER?
LIKE THE BOOK REPORT YOU'RE SUPPOSED TO BE WRITING NOW ON THE BOOK YOU HAVEN'T READ?
EXACTLY. CASE IN POINT.

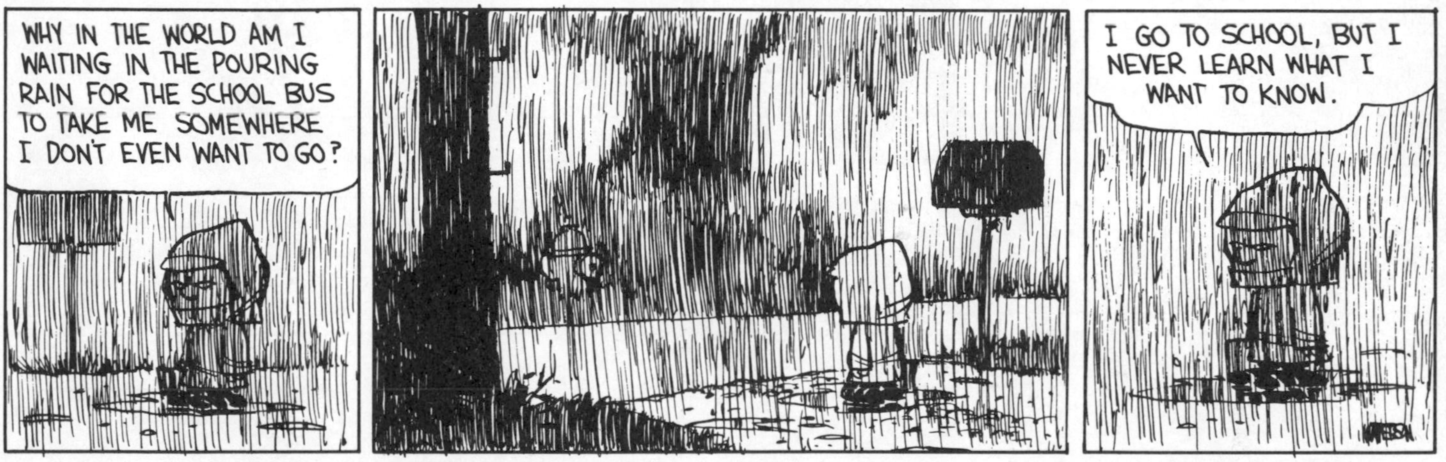
WHY IN THE WORLD AM I WAITING IN THE POURING RAIN FOR THE SCHOOL BUS TO TAKE ME SOMEWHERE I DON'T EVEN WANT TO GO?
I GO TO SCHOOL, BUT I NEVER LEARN WHAT I WANT TO KNOW.

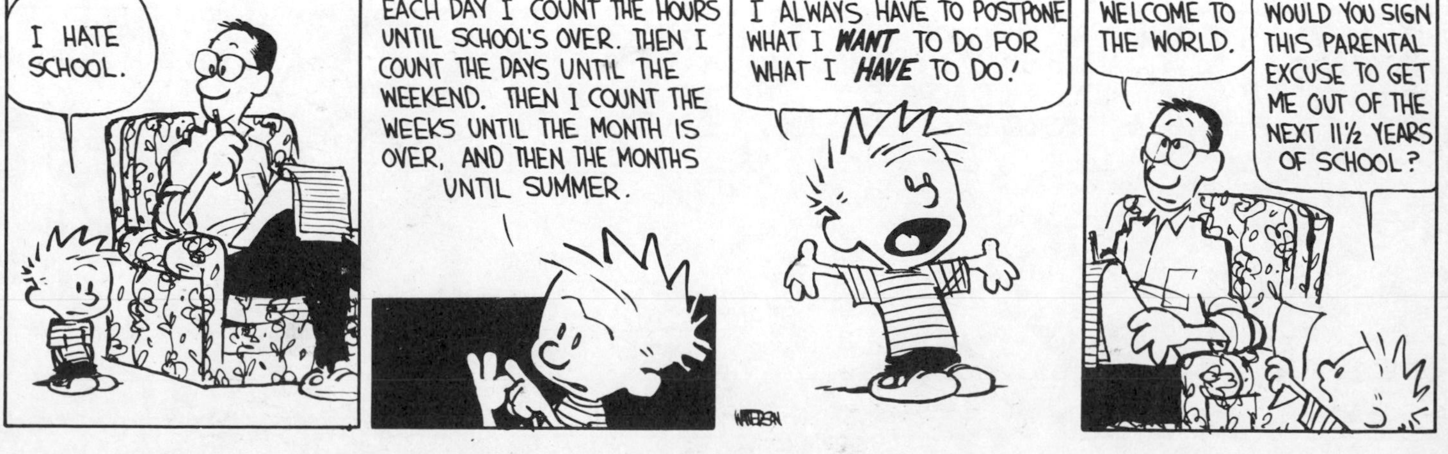
I HATE SCHOOL.
EACH DAY I COUNT THE HOURS UNTIL SCHOOL'S OVER. THEN I COUNT THE DAYS UNTIL THE WEEKEND. THEN I COUNT THE WEEKS UNTIL THE MONTH IS OVER, AND THEN THE MONTHS UNTIL SUMMER.
I ALWAYS HAVE TO POSTPONE WHAT I WANT TO DO FOR WHAT I HAVE TO DO!
WELCOME TO THE WORLD.
WOULD YOU SIGN THIS PARENTAL EXCUSE TO GET ME OUT OF THE NEXT 11½ YEARS OF SCHOOL?

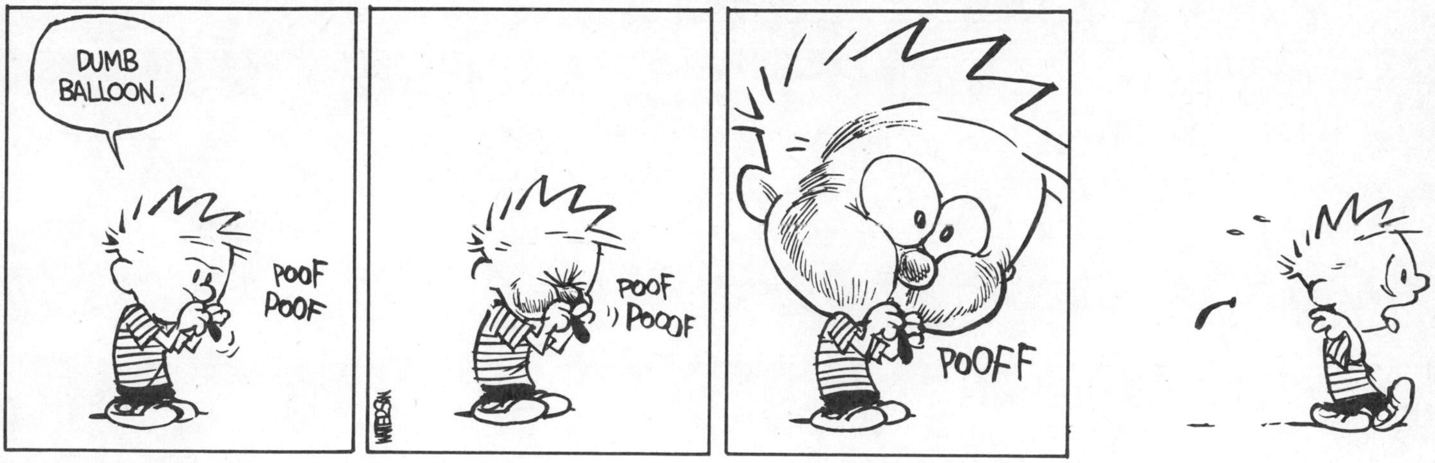
DUMB BALLOON.
POOF POOF
POOF POOOF
POOFF

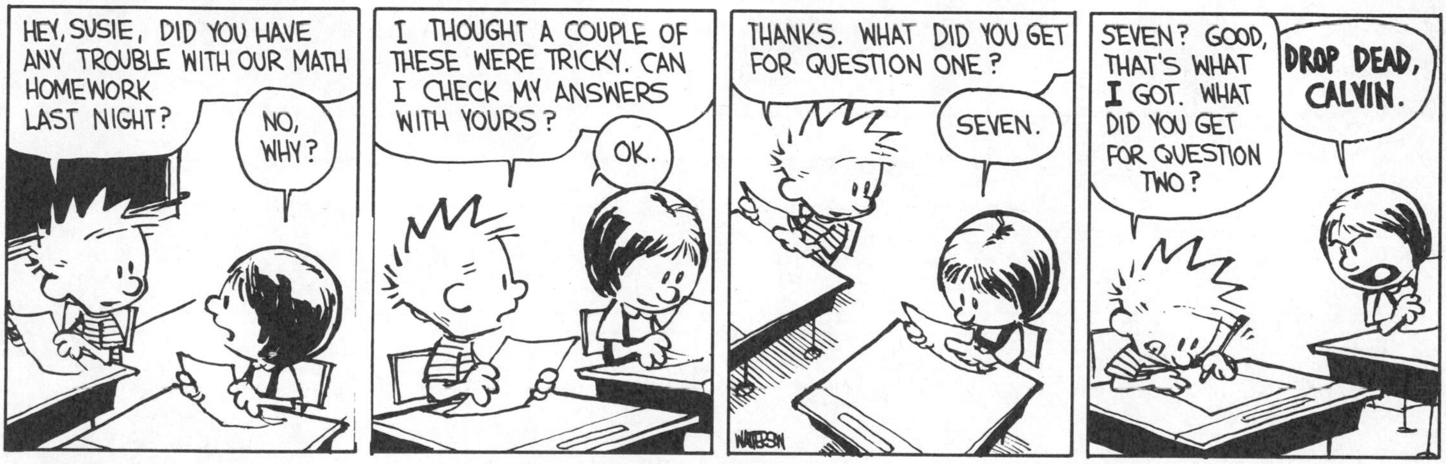
HEY, SUSIE, DID YOU HAVE ANY TROUBLE WITH OUR MATH HOMEWORK LAST NIGHT?
NO, WHY?
I THOUGHT A COUPLE OF THESE WERE TRICKY. CAN I CHECK MY ANSWERS WITH YOURS?
OK.
THANKS. WHAT DID YOU GET FOR QUESTION ONE?
SEVEN.
SEVEN? GOOD, THAT'S WHAT I GOT. WHAT DID YOU GET FOR QUESTION TWO?
DROP DEAD, CALVIN.

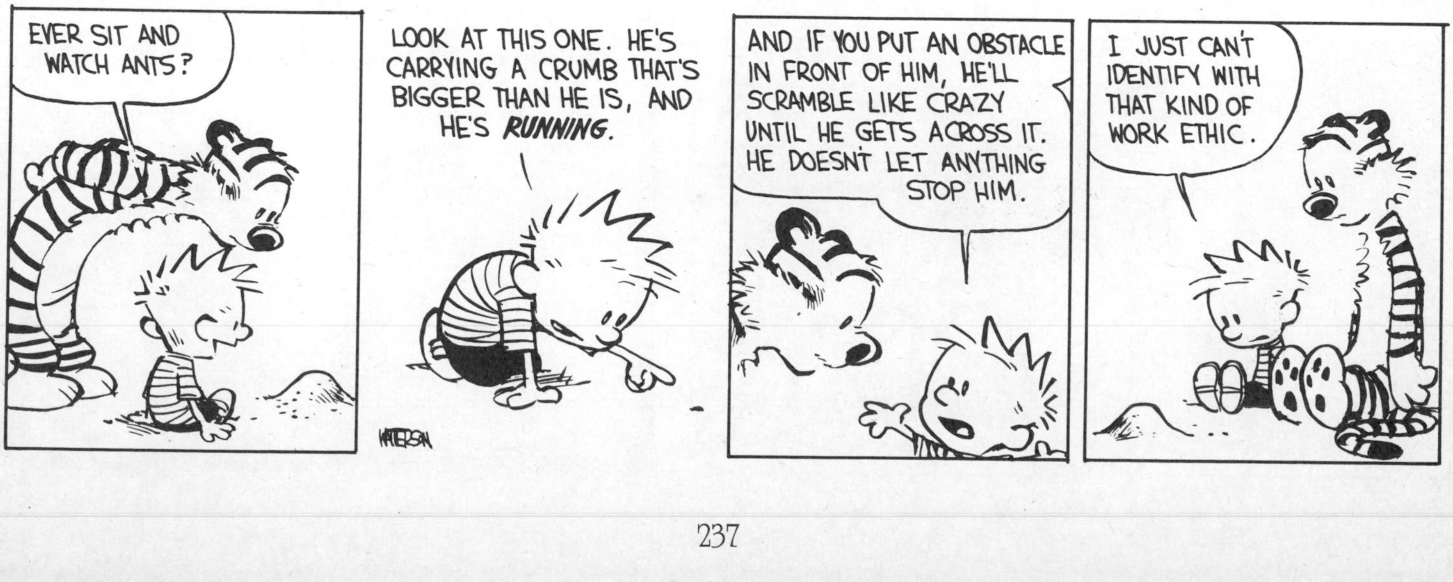
EVER SIT AND WATCH ANTS?
LOOK AT THIS ONE. HE'S CARRYING A CRUMB THAT'S BIGGER THAN HE IS, AND HE'S RUNNING.
AND IF YOU PUT AN OBSTACLE IN FRONT OF HIM, HE'LL SCRAMBLE LIKE CRAZY UNTIL HE GETS ACROSS IT. HE DOESN'T LET ANYTHING STOP HIM.
I JUST CAN'T IDENTIFY WITH THAT KIND OF WORK ETHIC.

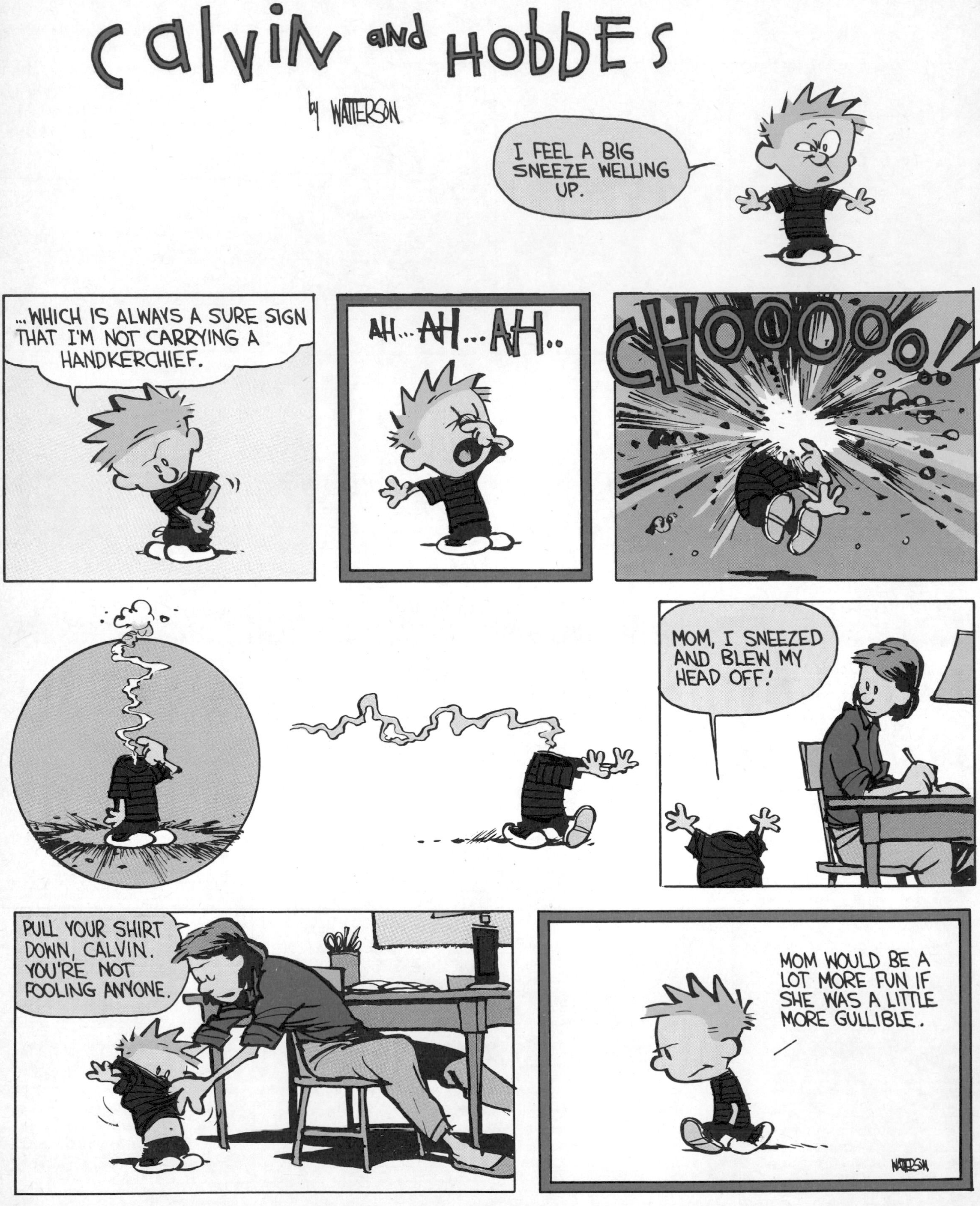
Calvin and HOBBES
by WATTERSON
I FEEL A BIG SNEEZE WELLING UP.
...WHICH IS ALWAYS A SURE SIGN THAT I'M NOT CARRYING A HANDKERCHIEF.
AH... AH... AH..
CHOOOOOO!!
MOM, I SNEEZED AND BLEW MY HEAD OFF!
PULL YOUR SHIRT DOWN, CALVIN. YOU'RE NOT FOOLING ANYONE.
MOM WOULD BE A LOT MORE FUN IF SHE WAS A LITTLE MORE GULLIBLE.
WATTERSON

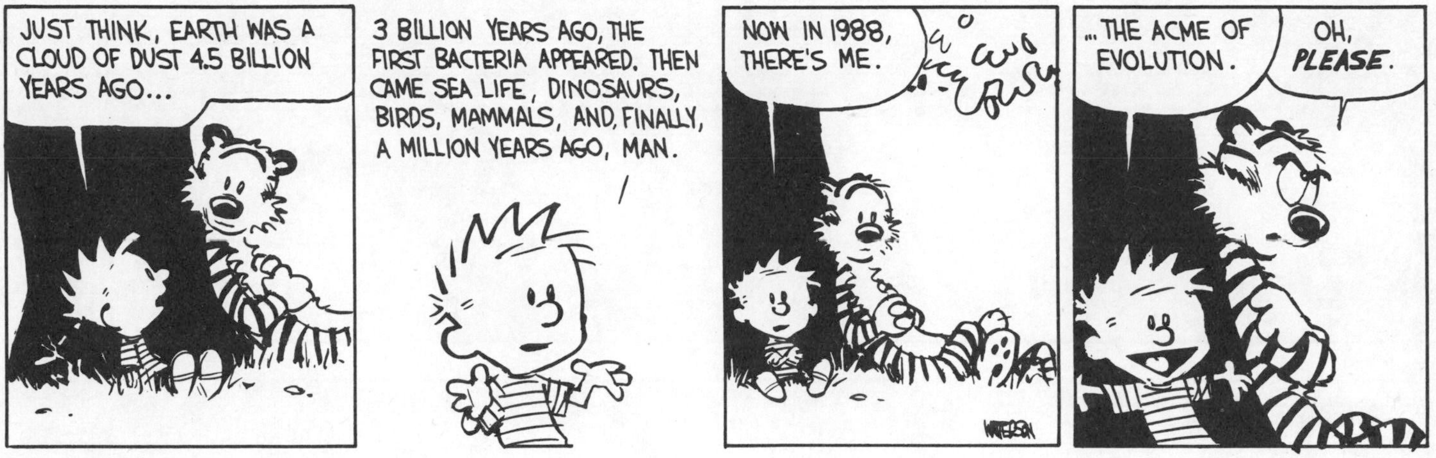
JUST THINK, EARTH WAS A CLOUD OF DUST 4.5 BILLION YEARS AGO...
3 BILLION YEARS AGO, THE FIRST BACTERIA APPEARED. THEN CAME SEA LIFE, DINOSAURS, BIRDS, MAMMALS, AND, FINALLY, A MILLION YEARS AGO, MAN.
NOW IN 1988, THERE'S ME.
...THE ACME OF EVOLUTION.
OH, *PLEASE*.
WATTERSON

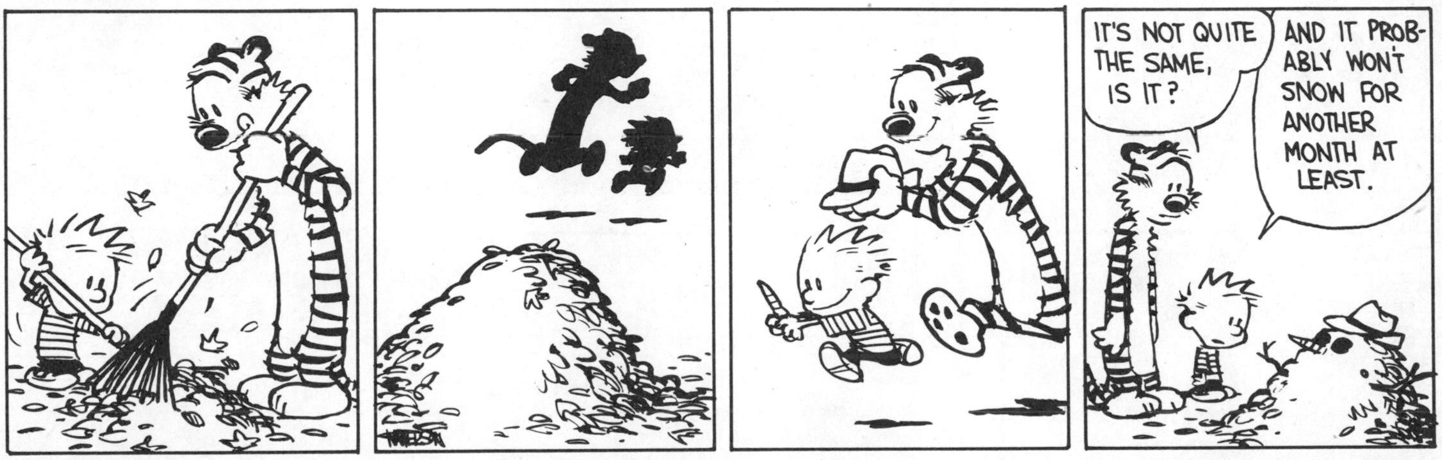
WATTERSON
IT'S NOT QUITE THE SAME, IS IT?
AND IT PROBABLY WON'T SNOW FOR ANOTHER MONTH AT LEAST.

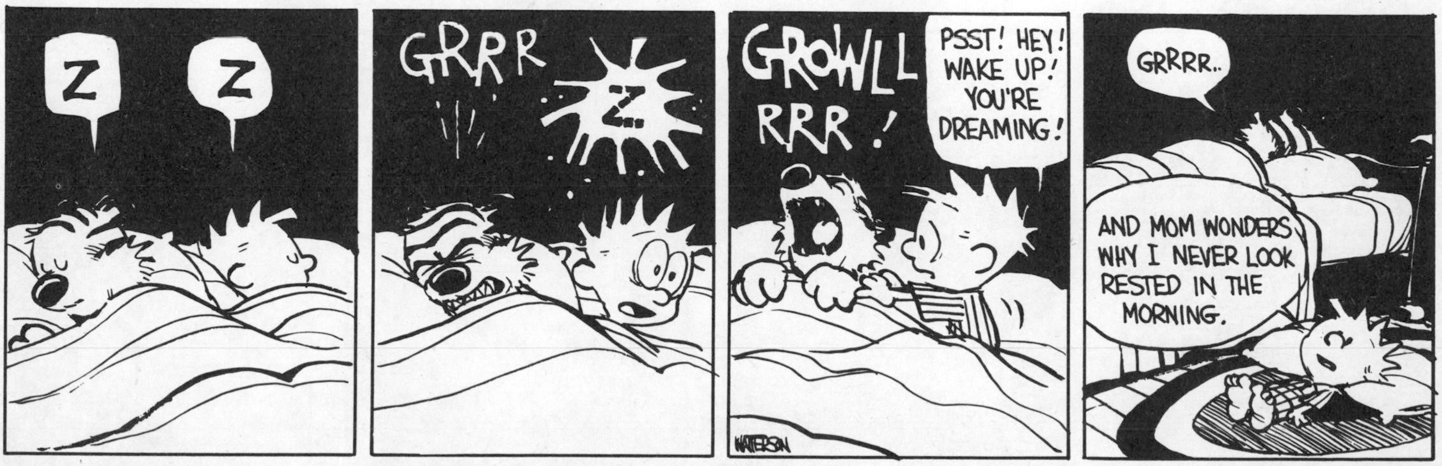
Z
Z
GRRR
Z
GROWLL RRR!
PSST! HEY! WAKE UP! YOU'RE DREAMING!
WATTERSON
GRRRR..
AND MOM WONDERS WHY I NEVER LOOK RESTED IN THE MORNING.

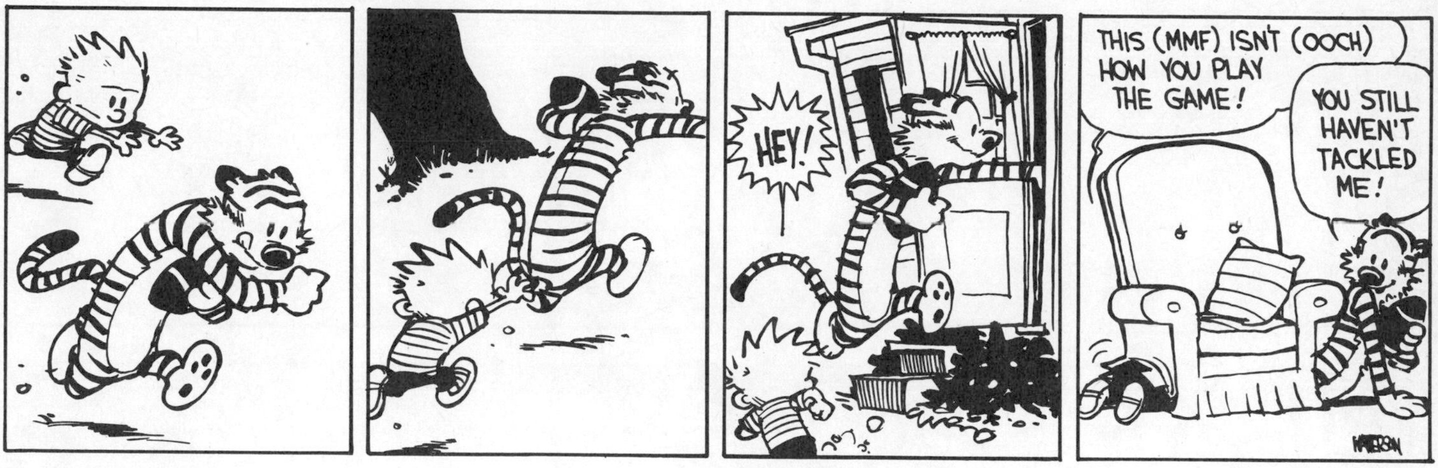
HEY!
THIS (MMF) ISN'T (OOCH) HOW YOU PLAY THE GAME!
YOU STILL HAVEN'T TACKLED ME!

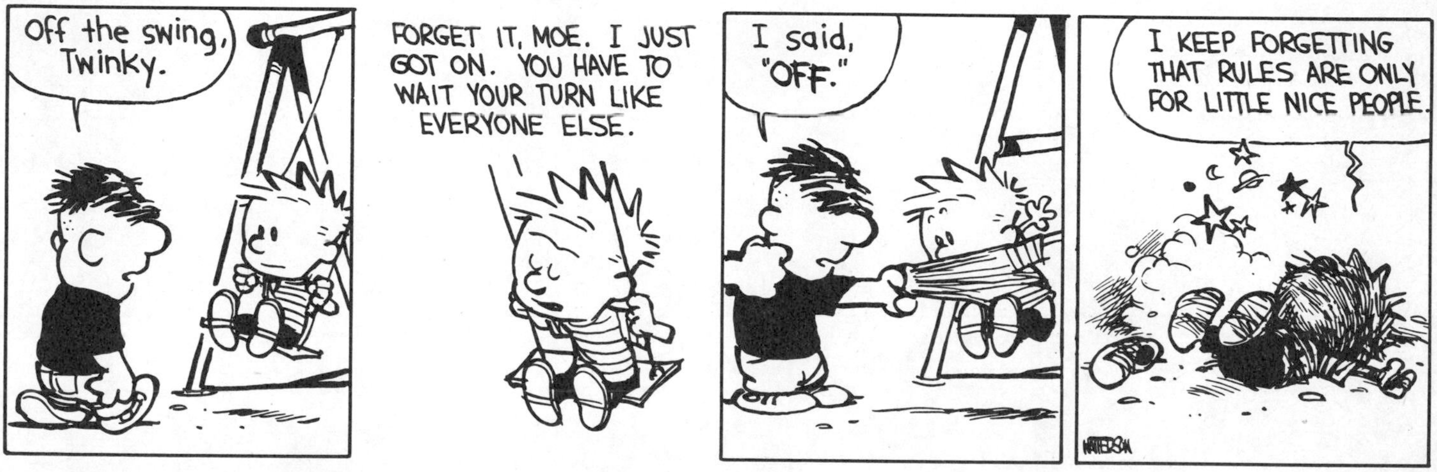
Off the swing, Twinky.
FORGET IT, MOE. I JUST GOT ON. YOU HAVE TO WAIT YOUR TURN LIKE EVERYONE ELSE.
I said, "OFF."
I KEEP FORGETTING THAT RULES ARE ONLY FOR LITTLE NICE PEOPLE.

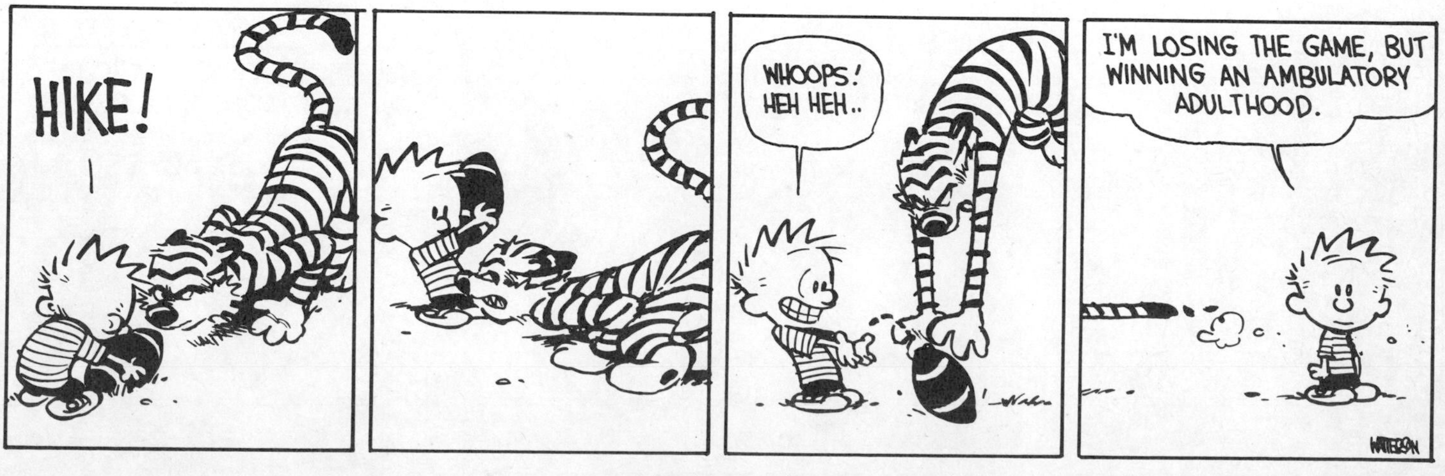
HIKE!
WHOOPS! HEH HEH..
I'M LOSING THE GAME, BUT WINNING AN AMBULATORY ADULTHOOD.

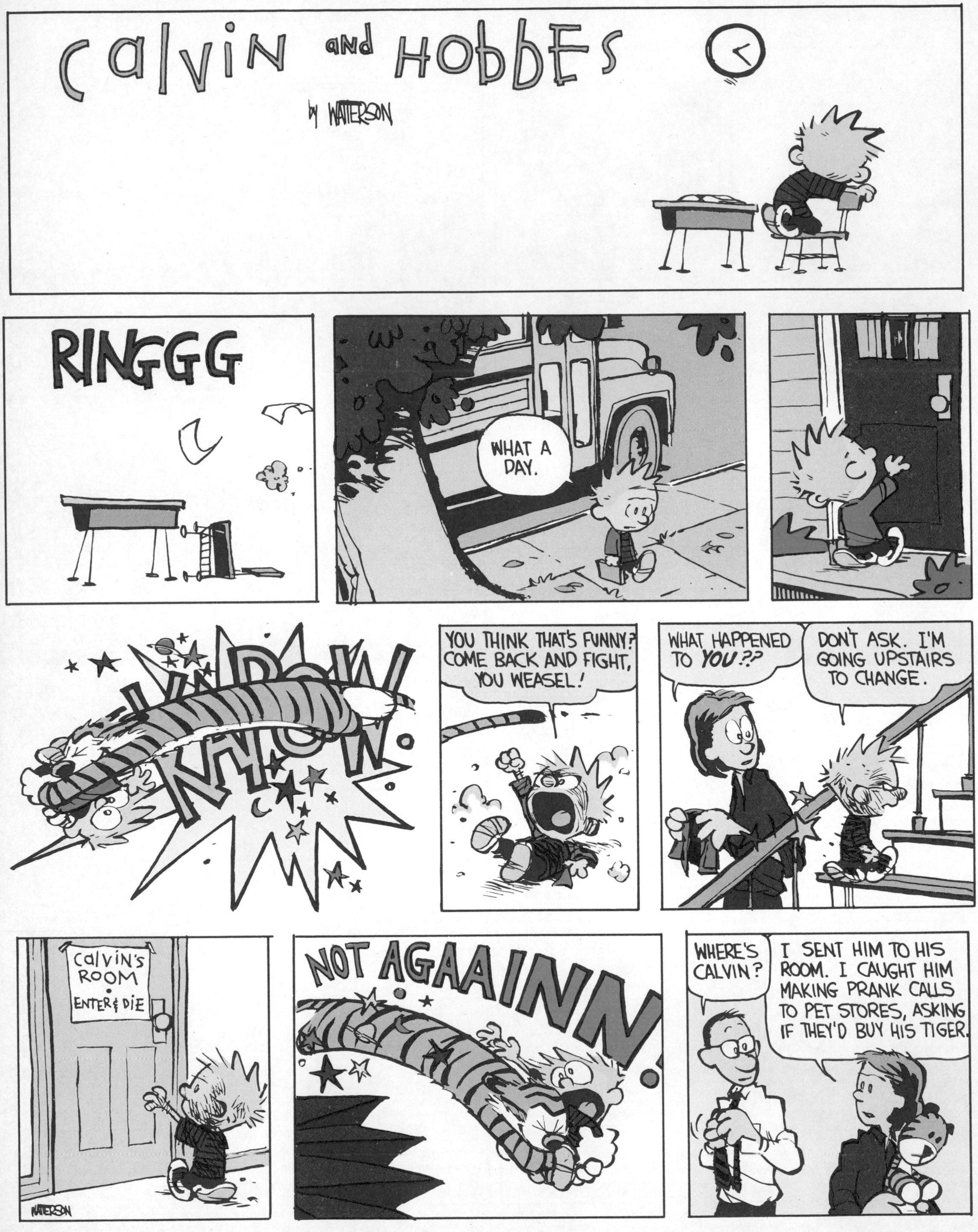
Calvin and HOBBES
by WATTERSON
RINGGG
WHAT A DAY.
KABOOM
YOU THINK THAT'S FUNNY? COME BACK AND FIGHT, YOU WEASEL!
WHAT HAPPENED TO YOU??
DON'T ASK. I'M GOING UPSTAIRS TO CHANGE.
Calvin's ROOM • ENTER & DIE
WATTERSON
NOT AGAAINNN!
WHERE'S CALVIN?
I SENT HIM TO HIS ROOM. I CAUGHT HIM MAKING PRANK CALLS TO PET STORES, ASKING IF THEY'D BUY HIS TIGER.

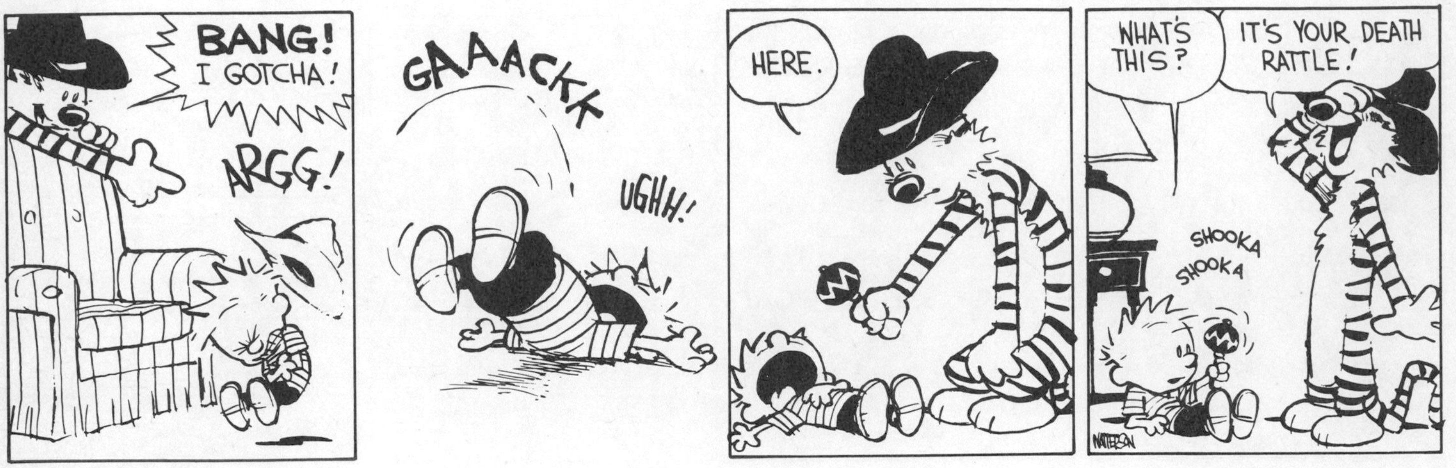
BANG! I GOTCHA!
ARGG!
GAAACKK
UGHH!
HERE.
WHAT'S THIS?
IT'S YOUR DEATH RATTLE!
SHOOKA SHOOKA
WATTERSON

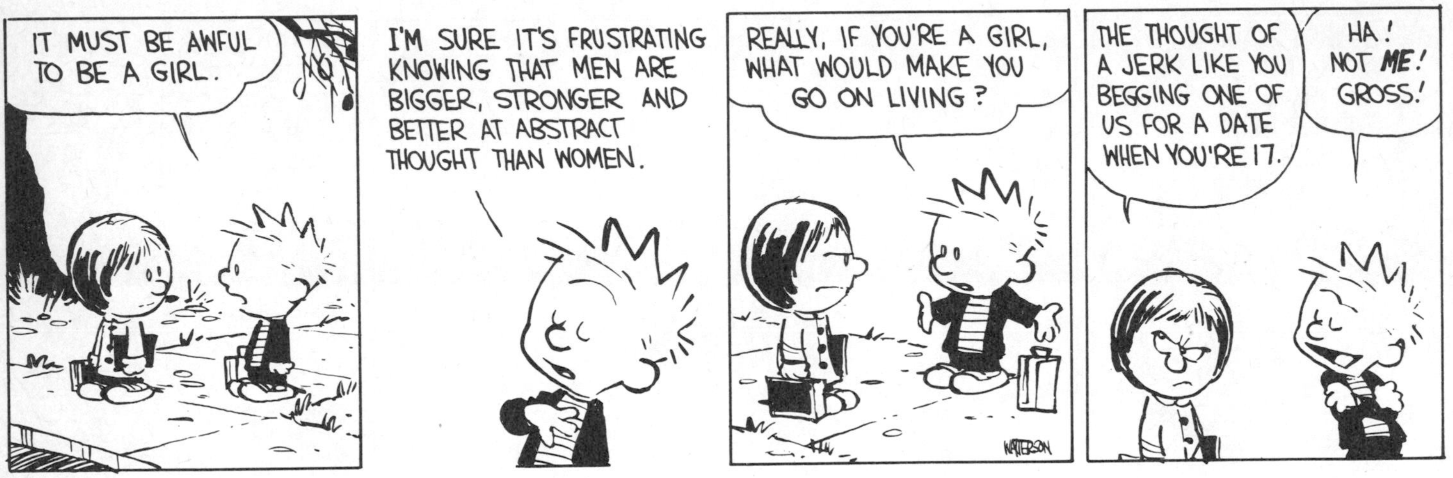
IT MUST BE AWFUL TO BE A GIRL.
I'M SURE IT'S FRUSTRATING KNOWING THAT MEN ARE BIGGER, STRONGER AND BETTER AT ABSTRACT THOUGHT THAN WOMEN.
REALLY, IF YOU'RE A GIRL, WHAT WOULD MAKE YOU GO ON LIVING?
WATTERSON
THE THOUGHT OF A JERK LIKE YOU BEGGING ONE OF US FOR A DATE WHEN YOU'RE 17.
HA! NOT ME! GROSS!

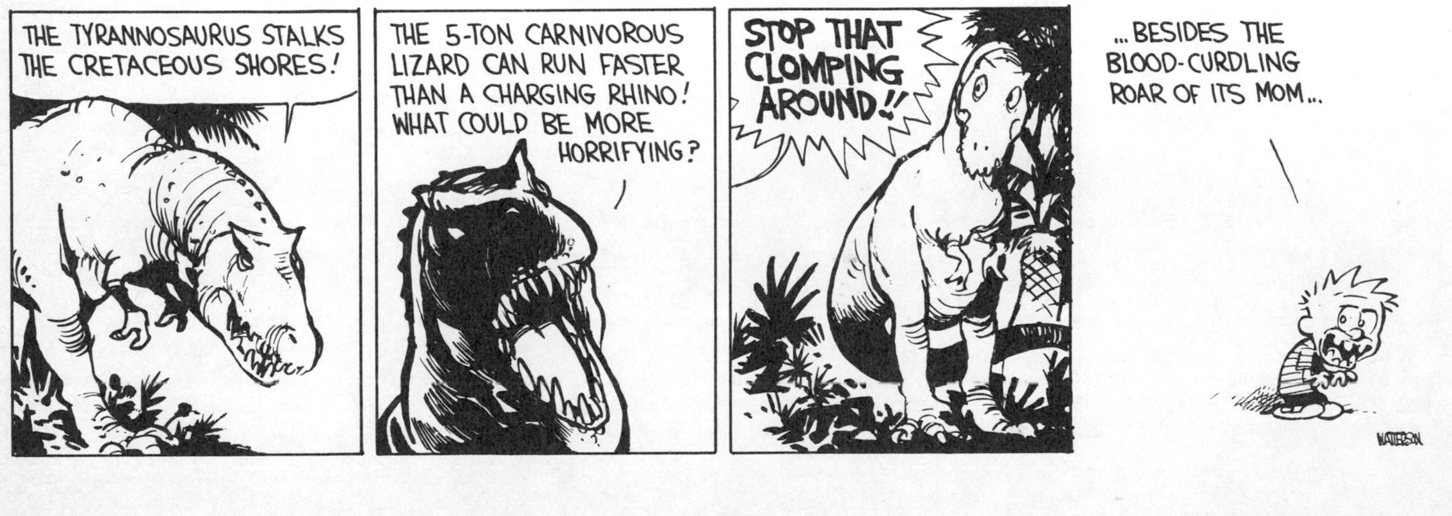
THE TYRANNOSAURUS STALKS THE CRETACEOUS SHORES!
THE 5-TON CARNIVOROUS LIZARD CAN RUN FASTER THAN A CHARGING RHINO! WHAT COULD BE MORE HORRIFYING?
STOP THAT CLOMPING AROUND!!
...BESIDES THE BLOOD-CURDLING ROAR OF ITS MOM...
WATTERSON

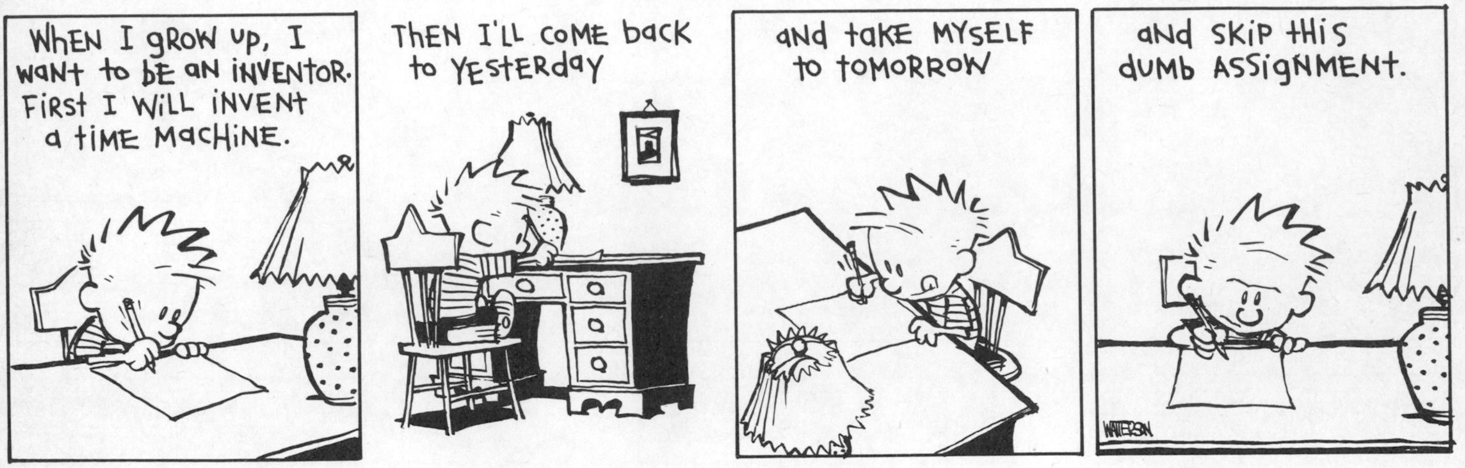
WHEN I GROW UP, I WANT TO BE AN INVENTOR. FIRST I WILL INVENT A TIME MACHINE.
THEN I'LL COME BACK TO YESTERDAY
AND TAKE MYSELF TO TOMORROW
AND SKIP THIS DUMB ASSIGNMENT.
WATTERSON

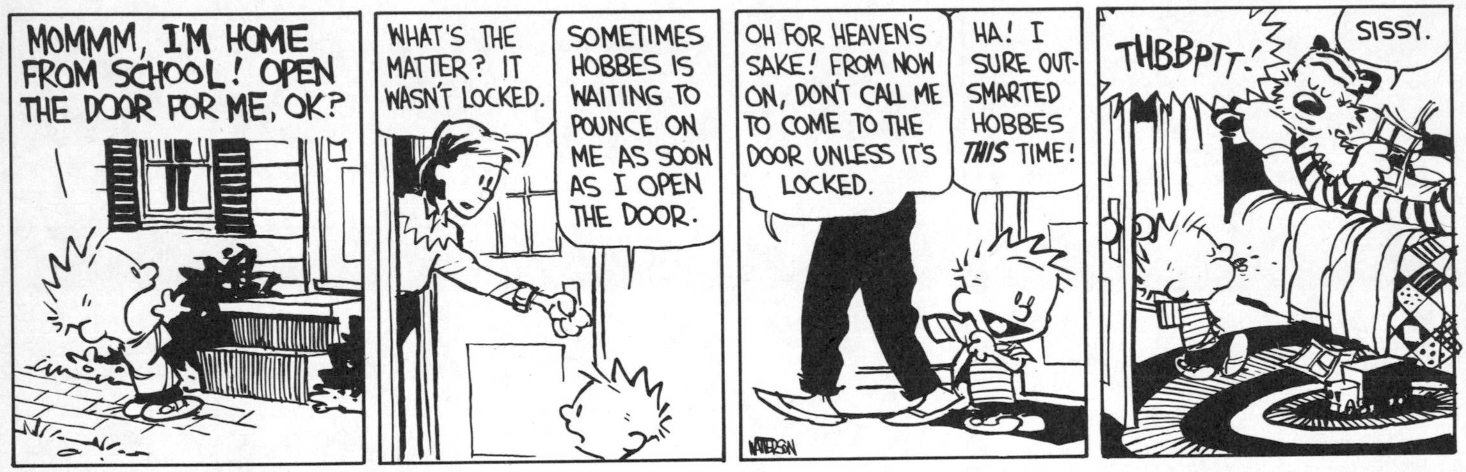
MOMMM, I'M HOME FROM SCHOOL! OPEN THE DOOR FOR ME, OK?
WHAT'S THE MATTER? IT WASN'T LOCKED.
SOMETIMES HOBBES IS WAITING TO POUNCE ON ME AS SOON AS I OPEN THE DOOR.
OH FOR HEAVEN'S SAKE! FROM NOW ON, DON'T CALL ME TO COME TO THE DOOR UNLESS IT'S LOCKED.
HA! I SURE OUT-SMARTED HOBBES THIS TIME!
WATTERSON
THBBPTT!
SISSY.

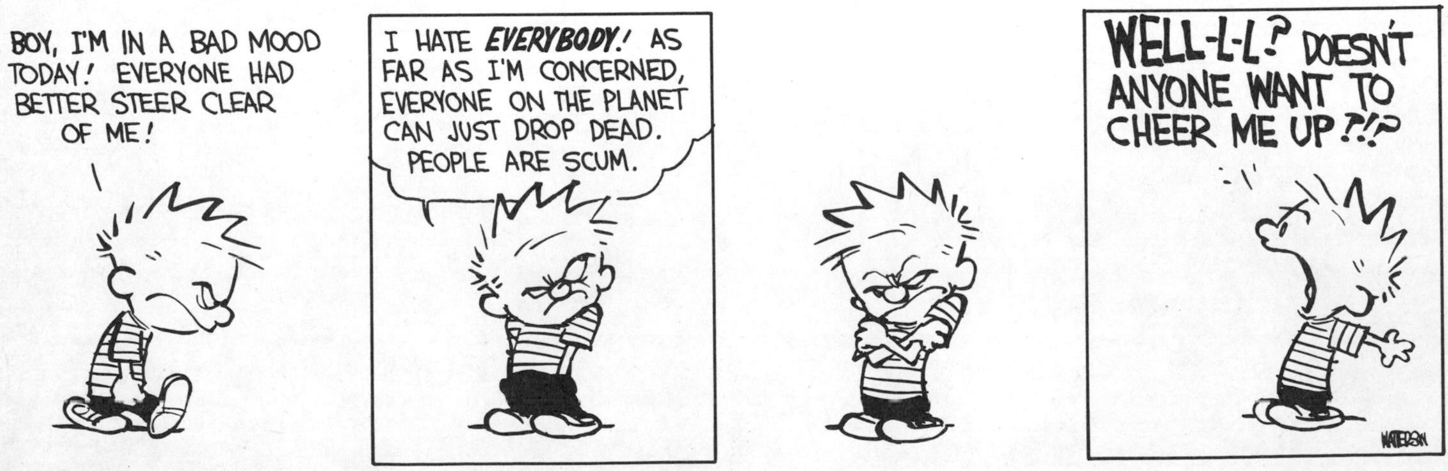
BOY, I'M IN A BAD MOOD TODAY! EVERYONE HAD BETTER STEER CLEAR OF ME!
I HATE EVERYBODY! AS FAR AS I'M CONCERNED, EVERYONE ON THE PLANET CAN JUST DROP DEAD. PEOPLE ARE SCUM.
WELL-L-L? DOESN'T ANYONE WANT TO CHEER ME UP?!?
WATTERSON

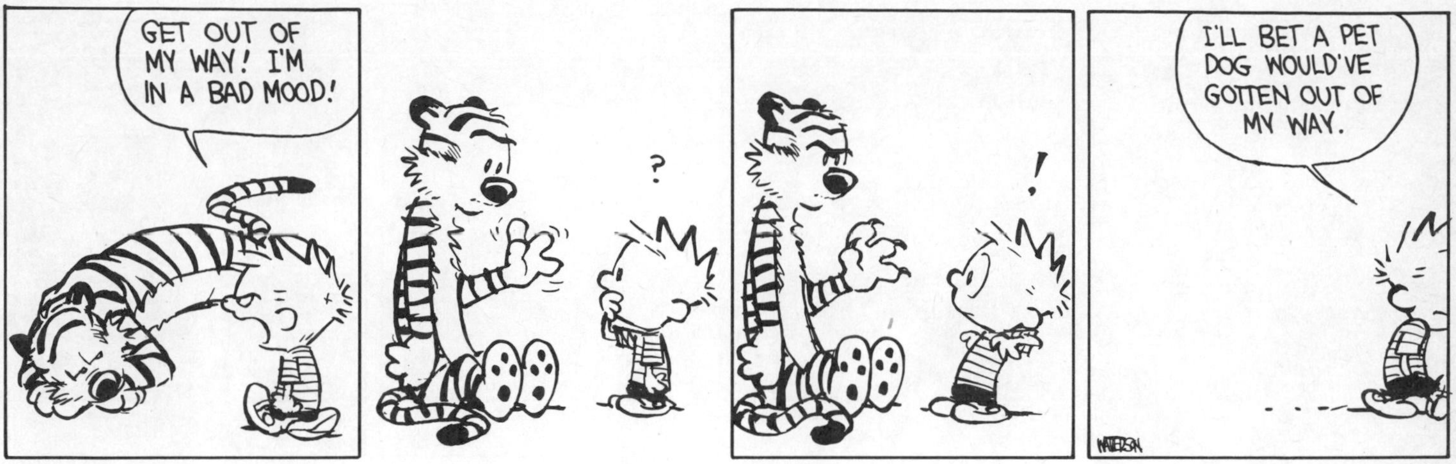
GET OUT OF MY WAY! I'M IN A BAD MOOD!
?
!
I'LL BET A PET DOG WOULD'VE GOTTEN OUT OF MY WAY.

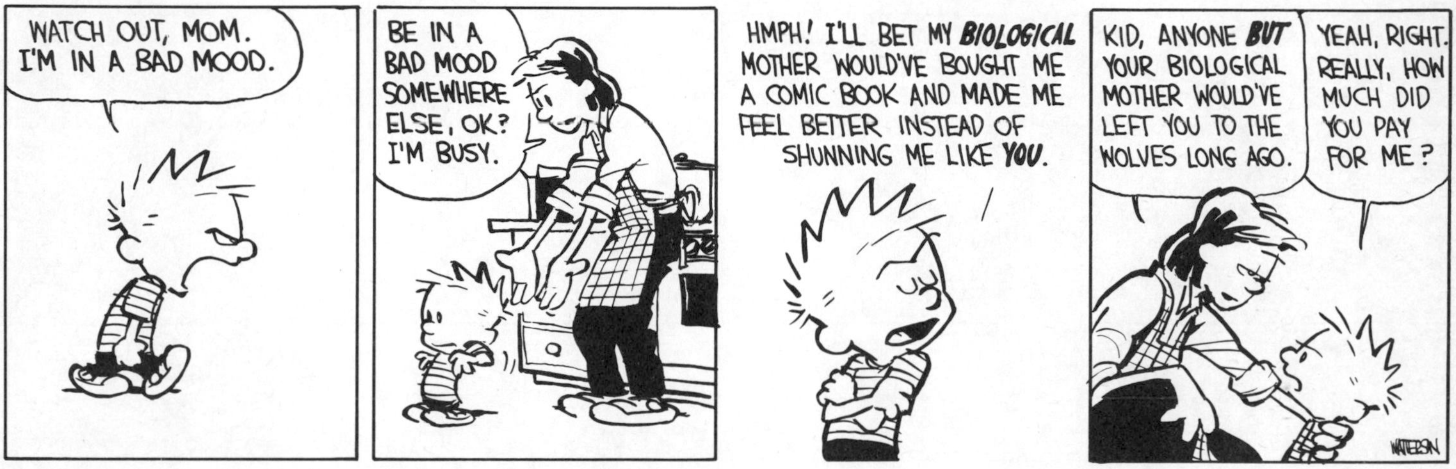
WATCH OUT, MOM. I'M IN A BAD MOOD.
BE IN A BAD MOOD SOMEWHERE ELSE, OK? I'M BUSY.
HMPH! I'LL BET MY BIOLOGICAL MOTHER WOULD'VE BOUGHT ME A COMIC BOOK AND MADE ME FEEL BETTER INSTEAD OF SHUNNING ME LIKE YOU.
KID, ANYONE BUT YOUR BIOLOGICAL MOTHER WOULD'VE LEFT YOU TO THE WOLVES LONG AGO.
YEAH, RIGHT. REALLY, HOW MUCH DID YOU PAY FOR ME?

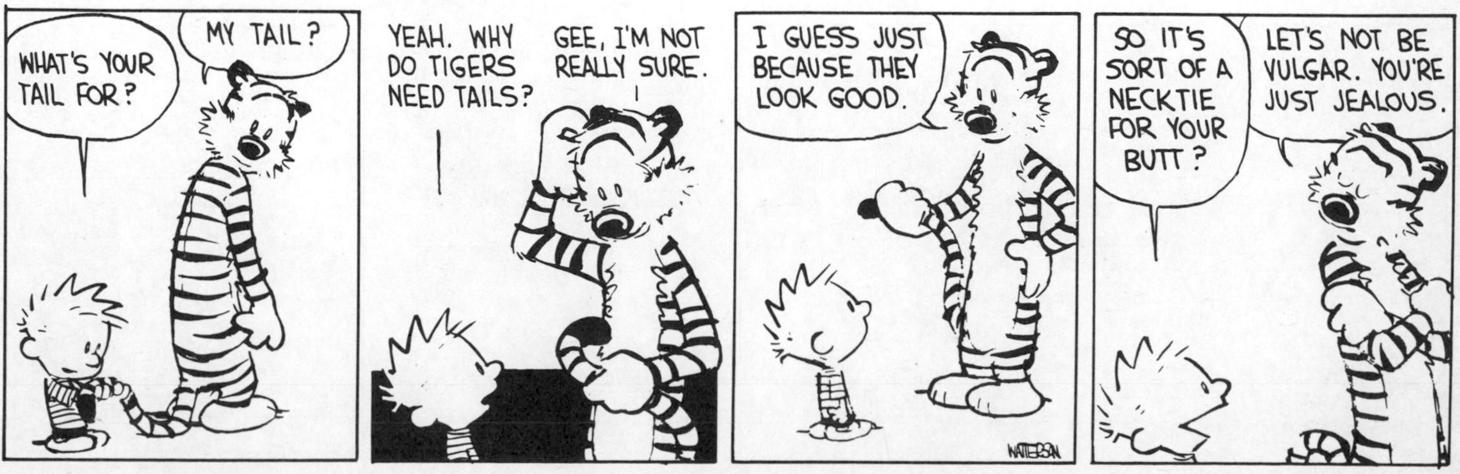
WHAT'S YOUR TAIL FOR?
MY TAIL?
YEAH. WHY DO TIGERS NEED TAILS?
GEE, I'M NOT REALLY SURE.
I GUESS JUST BECAUSE THEY LOOK GOOD.
SO IT'S SORT OF A NECKTIE FOR YOUR BUTT?
LET'S NOT BE VULGAR. YOU'RE JUST JEALOUS.

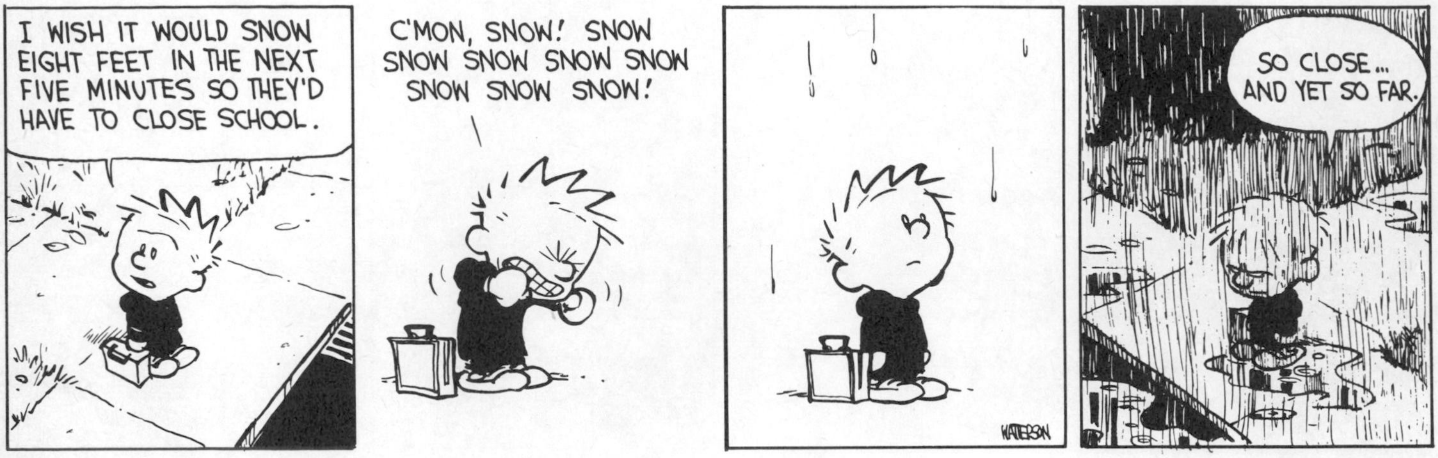
I WISH IT WOULD SNOW EIGHT FEET IN THE NEXT FIVE MINUTES SO THEY'D HAVE TO CLOSE SCHOOL.
C'MON, SNOW! SNOW SNOW SNOW SNOW SNOW SNOW SNOW SNOW!
SO CLOSE... AND YET SO FAR.

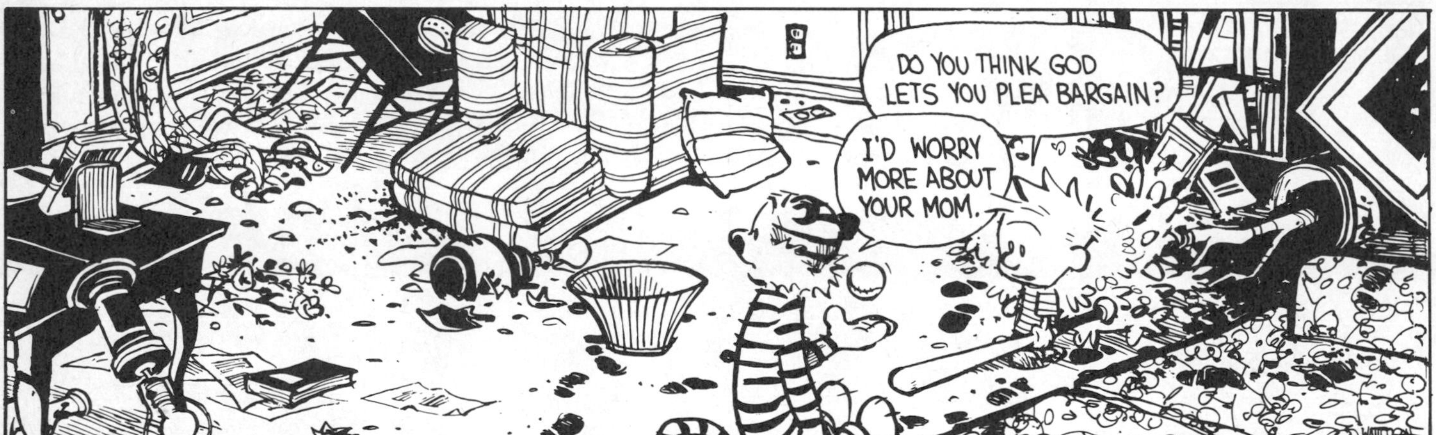
DO YOU THINK GOD LETS YOU PLEA BARGAIN?
I'D WORRY MORE ABOUT YOUR MOM.

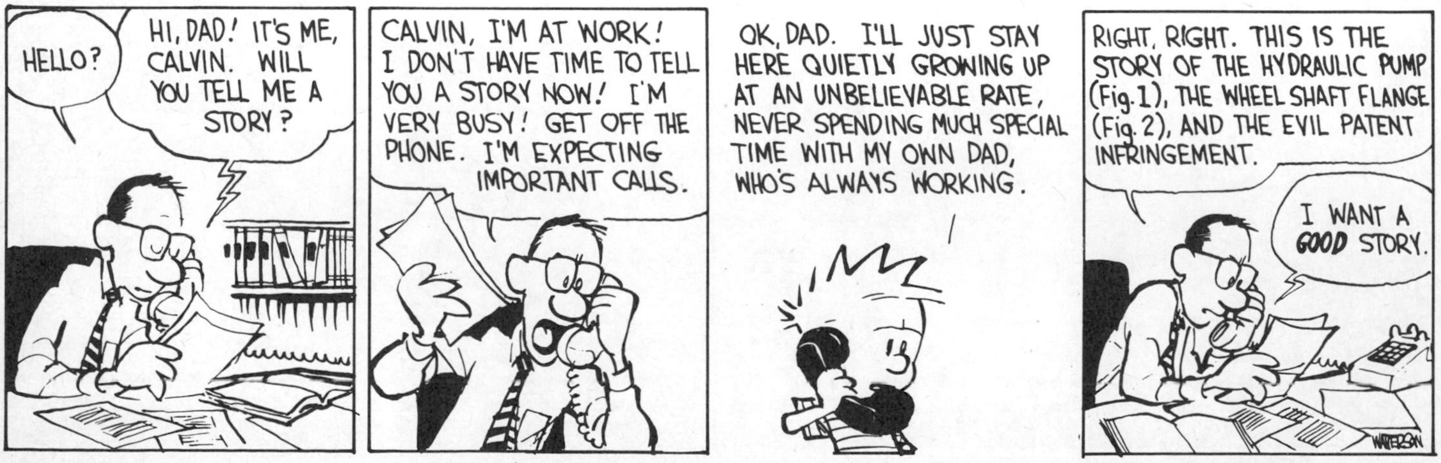
HELLO?
HI, DAD! IT'S ME, CALVIN. WILL YOU TELL ME A STORY?
CALVIN, I'M AT WORK! I DON'T HAVE TIME TO TELL YOU A STORY NOW! I'M VERY BUSY! GET OFF THE PHONE. I'M EXPECTING IMPORTANT CALLS.
OK, DAD. I'LL JUST STAY HERE QUIETLY GROWING UP AT AN UNBELIEVABLE RATE, NEVER SPENDING MUCH SPECIAL TIME WITH MY OWN DAD, WHO'S ALWAYS WORKING.
RIGHT, RIGHT. THIS IS THE STORY OF THE HYDRAULIC PUMP (Fig. 1), THE WHEEL SHAFT FLANGE (Fig. 2), AND THE EVIL PATENT INFRINGEMENT.
I WANT A GOOD STORY.

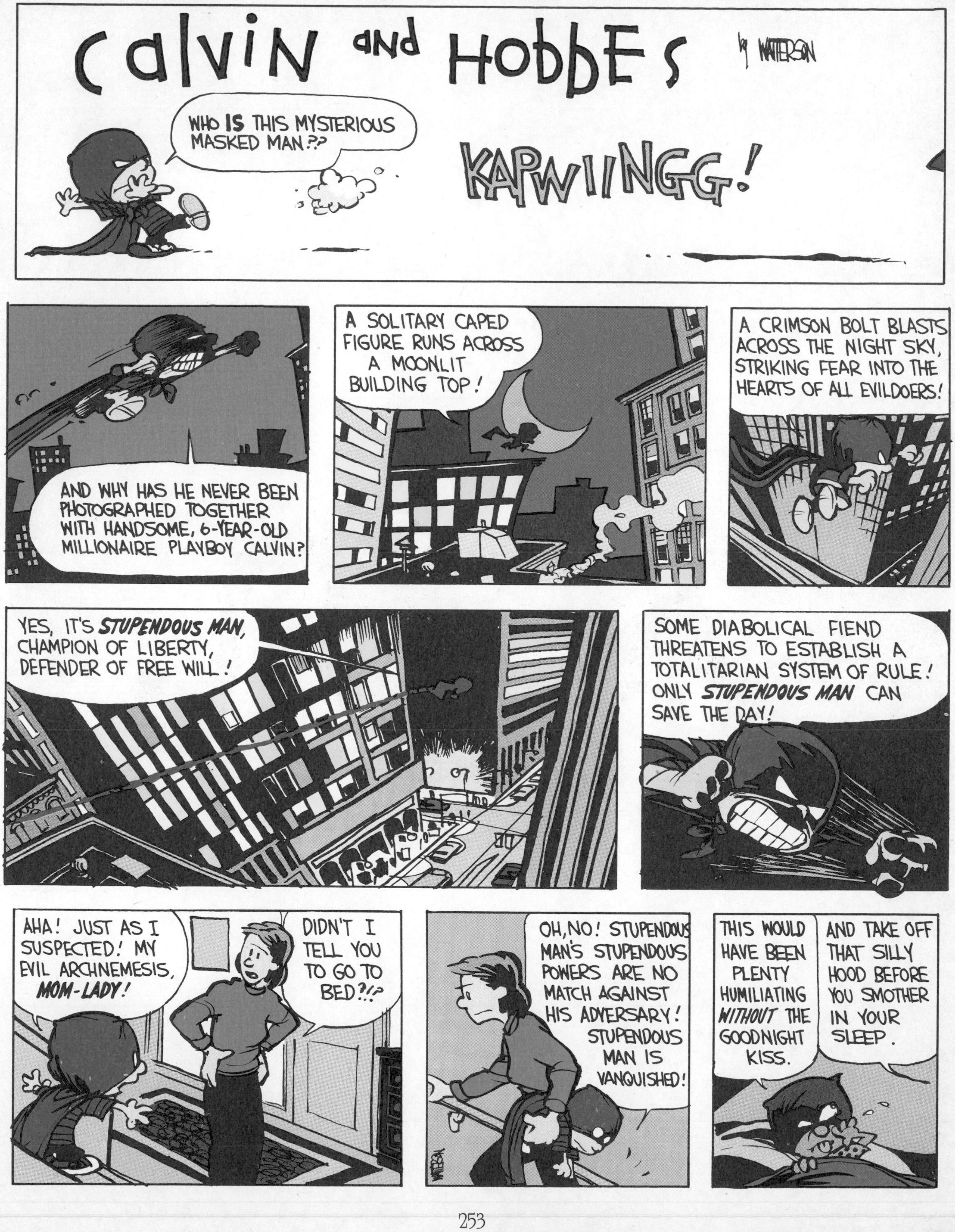
Calvin and HobbEs
by WATTERSON
WHO IS THIS MYSTERIOUS MASKED MAN?!?
KAPWIINGG!
AND WHY HAS HE NEVER BEEN PHOTOGRAPHED TOGETHER WITH HANDSOME, 6-YEAR-OLD MILLIONAIRE PLAYBOY CALVIN?
A SOLITARY CAPED FIGURE RUNS ACROSS A MOONLIT BUILDING TOP!
A CRIMSON BOLT BLASTS ACROSS THE NIGHT SKY, STRIKING FEAR INTO THE HEARTS OF ALL EVILDOERS!
YES, IT'S STUPENDOUS MAN, CHAMPION OF LIBERTY, DEFENDER OF FREE WILL!
SOME DIABOLICAL FIEND THREATENS TO ESTABLISH A TOTALITARIAN SYSTEM OF RULE! ONLY STUPENDOUS MAN CAN SAVE THE DAY!
AHA! JUST AS I SUSPECTED! MY EVIL ARCHNEMESIS, MOM-LADY!
DIDN'T I TELL YOU TO GO TO BED?!?
OH, NO! STUPENDOUS MAN'S STUPENDOUS POWERS ARE NO MATCH AGAINST HIS ADVERSARY! STUPENDOUS MAN IS VANQUISHED!
THIS WOULD HAVE BEEN PLENTY HUMILIATING WITHOUT THE GOODNIGHT KISS.
AND TAKE OFF THAT SILLY HOOD BEFORE YOU SMOTHER IN YOUR SLEEP.

# The End